D1104358

MIKE MEYERS' CERTIFICATION
Passport ☆

Server+ ™

STEPHEN J. BIGELOW

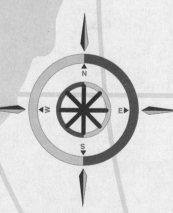

OSBORNE McGraw Hill

New York • Chicago • San Francisco
Lisbon • London • Madrid • Mexico City
Milan • New Delhi • San Juan
Seoul • Singapore • Sydney • Toronto

Osborne/**McGraw-Hill**
2600 Tenth Street
Berkeley, California 94710
U.S.A.

To arrange bulk purchase discounts for sales promotions, premiums, or fund-raisers, please contact Osborne/**McGraw-Hill** at the above address. For information on translations or book distributors outside the U.S.A., please see the International Contact Information on page xviii.

Mike Meyers' Server+ Certification Passport

Copyright © 2001 by The McGraw-Hill Companies. All rights reserved. Printed in the United States of America. Except as permitted under the Copyright Act of 1976, no part of this publication may be reproduced or distributed in any form or by any means, or stored in a database or retrieval system, without the prior written permission of the publisher, with the exception that the program listings may be entered, stored, and executed in a computer system, but they may not be reproduced for publication.

1234567890   2DOC 2DOC   01987654321

Book p/n 0-07-219587-8 and CD p/n 0-07-219586-X
parts of
ISBN 0-07-219364-6

Publisher Brandon A. Nordin	**Acquisitions Coordinator** Paulina Pobocha	**Indexer** Irv Hershman
Vice President & **Associate Publisher** Scott Rogers	**Technical Editor** Kevin Vaccaro	**Computer Designers** epic/Andrea Reider
	Copy Editor Dennis Weaver	**Illustrators** Michael Mueller
Acquisitions Editor Michael Sprague		Lyssa Sieben-Wald
	Proofreader Sossity Smith	
Senior Project Editor Pamela Woolf		**Cover Series Design** Ted Holladay

This book was composed with Quark XPress™.

Information has been obtained by Osborne/**McGraw-Hill** from sources believed to be reliable. However, because of the possibility of human or mechanical error by our sources, Osborne/**McGraw-Hill**, or others, Osborne/**McGraw-Hill** does not guarantee the accuracy, adequacy, or completeness of any information and is not responsible for any errors or omissions or the results obtained from use of such information.

Contents

1O NIC Adapters and Troubleshooting 365

About the Author

Stephen J. Bigelow is the founder and president of Dynamic Learning Systems—a technical writing, research, and small publishing company specializing in electronic and PC service topics. Bigelow is the author of 15 feature-length books for TAB/McGraw-Hill, and more than 100 major articles for mainstream electronics magazines such as *Popular Electronics*, *Electronics NOW*, *Circuit Cellar INK*, and *Electronic Service & Technology*. Bigelow is a contributing editor at *CNET* (the "PC Mechanic" column and feature articles) and a regular contributor with *SmartComputing*. Bigelow is also the editor and publisher of *The PC Toolbox™*—a premier PC service newsletter for computer enthusiasts and technicians. He is an Electrical Engineer with a BS EE from Central New England College in Worcester, MA. You may contact the author at www.dlspubs.com.

Check-In

May I See Your Passport?

What do you mean you don't have a passport? Why, it's sitting right in your hands, even as you read! This book is your passport to a very special place. You're about to begin a journey, my friend, a journey toward that magical place called *certification*! You don't need a ticket, you don't need a suitcase—just snuggle up and read this passport—it's all you need to get there. Are you ready? Let's go!

Your Travel Agent—Mike Meyers

Hello! My name's Mike Meyers. I've written a number of popular certification books and I'm the president of Total Seminars, LLC. On any given day, you'll find me replacing a hard drive, setting up a Web site, or writing code. I love every aspect of this book you hold in your hands. It's part of a powerful new book series called the *Mike Meyers' Certification Passports*. Every book in this series combines easy readability with a condensed format. In other words, the kind of book I always wanted when I went for my certifications. Putting this much information in an accessible format is an enormous challenge but I think we have achieved our goal and I am confident you'll agree.

I designed this series to do one thing and only one thing: to get you the only the information you need to achieve your certification. You won't find any fluff in here—the author, Stephen Bigelow, packed every page with nothing but the real nitty-gritty of the certification exam. Every page is packed with 100% pure concentrate of certification knowledge! But we didn't forget to make the book readable. I hope you enjoy the casual, friendly style—I want you to feel as though the author is speaking to you, discussing the certification, not just spewing facts at you.

My personal email address is mikem@totalsem.com. Please feel free to contact me directly if you have any questions, complaints, or compliments.

Your Destination—Server+

This book is your passport to the CompTIA Server+ exam. Server+ is one of the fastest growing certifications available today. Server+ tests your skills in advanced PC hardware issues—issues that we see in most server systems. You'll learn about SCSI, RAID, redundant hardware, and advanced memory, just to name a few of the major points. You will understand these technologies and appreciate how and when to use them. Last, you will gain a basic understanding of what happens when these technologies fail and what to look for. Server+ is a must-have certification for anyone who would ever consider approaching a server system with a screwdriver in his or her hand.

Server+ enjoys tremendous industry support with companies like 3Com, Adaptec, Intel, IBM, and Compaq providing support for this certification. Intel even dropped its own in-house certifications to support Server+! Server+ is recognized; Server+ is growing; Server+ is now!

Your Guide—Stephen J. Bigelow

Oh boy, are you in for a treat! Your guide, the author of this book, is none other than the great Stephen J. Bigelow! The man himself! If by some chance you don't know Stephen, let me tell you that he's the author of the famous *Troubleshooting, Maintaining and Repairing PCs*—just about the most important PC book ever written! Most techs consider this book "standard issue" for our shelf—if you don't already own *Troubleshooting, Maintaining and Repairing PCs*, well, get it! Plus, you may know Stephen from his popular CNet articles as well as more than 30 other wonderful books. Stephen has adopted Server+ as an area of great personal interest and it won't take you very many pages into this book to see that when it comes to Server+, Steve is your one-stop source!

Steve wants you to know that your input is very important. You can contact Steve at steve@totalsem.com to discuss any issues or questions relating to the book.

Why the Travel Theme?

One of my favorite topics is the parallel of gaining a certification to a taking a trip. All the elements are the same: preparation, an itinerary, a route—even mishaps along the way. Let me show you how it all works.

This book is divided into 10 chapters. Each chapter begins with an Itinerary, which provides objectives covered in each chapter and an ETA to give you an idea of the time involved learning the skills in that chapter. Each chapter is broken down by real exam objectives, either those officially stated by the certifying body or if the vendor doesn't provide these, our experts take on the best way to approach the topics. Also, each chapter contains a number of helpful items to bring out points of interest:

Exam Tip
Points out critical topics you're likely to see on the actual exam.

Travel Assistance

Provides you with additional sources such as books and Web sites to give you more information.

Local Lingo

Describes special terms in detail in a way you can easily understand.

Travel Advisory

Warns you of common pitfalls, misconceptions. and downright physical peril.

The end of the chapter gives you two handy tools: The Checkpoint reviews each objective covered in the chapter with a handy synopsis—a great way to quickly review. Plus, you'll find end of chapter questions (and answers) to test your newly acquired skills.

But the fun doesn't stop there! After you've read the book, pull out the CD and take advantage of the free practice questions! Use the full practice exam to hone your skills and keep the book handy to check answers. If you want even more practice, log on to http://www.osborne.com/passport. For a nominal fee you'll get additional high-quality practice questions. When you're passing the practice questions, you're ready to take the exam—go get certified!

The End of the Trail

The IT industry changes and grows constantly—and so should you. Finishing one certification is just a step in an ongoing process of gaining more and more certifications to match your constantly changing and growing skills. Read the Career Flight Path at the end of the book to see where this certification fits into your personal certification goals. Remember, in the IT business, if you're not moving forward, you are way behind!

Good luck on your certification! Stay in touch.

Mike Meyers
Series Editor
Mike Meyers' Sever+Certification Passport

INTERNATIONAL CONTACT INFORMATION

AUSTRALIA
McGraw-Hill Book Company Australia Pty. Ltd.
TEL +61-2-9417-9899
FAX +61-2-9417-5687
http://www.mcgraw-hill.com.au
books-it_sydney@mcgraw-hill.com

CANADA
McGraw-Hill Ryerson Ltd.
TEL +905-430-5000
FAX +905-430-5020
http://www.mcgrawhill.ca

GREECE, MIDDLE EAST,
NORTHERN AFRICA
McGraw-Hill Hellas
TEL +30-1-656-0990-3-4
FAX +30-1-654-5525

MEXICO (Also serving Latin America)
McGraw-Hill Interamericana Editores S.A. de C.V.
TEL +525-117-1583
FAX +525-117-1589
http://www.mcgraw-hill.com.mx
fernando_castellanos@mcgraw-hill.com

SINGAPORE (Serving Asia)
McGraw-Hill Book Company
TEL +65-863-1580
FAX +65-862-3354
http://www.mcgraw-hill.com.sg
mghasia@mcgraw-hill.com

SOUTH AFRICA
McGraw-Hill South Africa
TEL +27-11-622-7512
FAX +27-11-622-9045
robyn_swanepoel@mcgraw-hill.com

UNITED KINGDOM & EUROPE
(Excluding Southern Europe)
McGraw-Hill Education Europe
TEL +44-1-628-502500
FAX +44-1-628-770224
http://www.mcgraw-hill.co.uk
computing_neurope@mcgraw-hill.com

ALL OTHER INQUIRIES Contact:
Osborne/McGraw-Hill
TEL +1-510-549-6600
FAX +1-510-883-7600
http://www.osborne.com
omg_international@mcgraw-hill.com

Network
Hardware
Concepts

	NEWBIE	SOME EXPERIENCE	EXPERT
ETA	6 hours	4 hours	2 hours

1

Although individual computers can be quite powerful, they are still "individual." Sharing files and resources among individual computers typically means copying a file to a diskette, then manually walking that diskette to other systems—for example, working on a document after work, then returning that updated document to work the next day in order to print it. Obviously, this is a cumbersome and time-consuming process. If there were a means of "connecting" two or more computers, you could access your work from another location (such as access a work computer from another computer in your home), finish the work that night, and immediately send the work to a printer located back at the office. This is the underlying premise behind a *network*—two or more computers connected together in order to share files, resources, and even applications. This chapter introduces you to the basic concepts and terminology needed to understand the tangible elements of common networks and servers.

Objective 1.01   Network Basics

A networked computer that provides resources is called a *server*. The computer accessing those resources is referred to as a *workstation* or *client*. Servers are usually the most powerful computers on the network because they require the added processing power to service the many requests of other computers sharing their resources. By comparison, workstations or clients are usually PCs that are cheaper and less powerful. As a rule, a computer may be a server *or* a workstation, but rarely both (this separation greatly simplifies the management and administration of the network). Of course, all of the computers on a network must be physically connected, and such connections are typically established with network interface card (NIC) adapters, and copper (or fiber-optic) cabling. The very latest network installations are even including wireless connections.

Local Lingo

Workstation or client   The computer that accesses network resources.

Server   The computer that provides the resources.

Advantages of a Network

With individual computers, applications and resources (such as printers or scanners) must be duplicated between PCs. For example, if two data analysts want to work on an Excel spreadsheet and print their results each day, both computers will need a copy of Excel and a printer. If the users needed to share data, it would have to be shuttled between the PCs on diskette or CD-RW. And if users needed to share computers, they would have to wade through the other user's system—each with its own desktop setup, applications, folder arrangement, and so on. In short, it would be a wasteful, frustrating, and error-prone process. As more users become involved, it wouldn't take long before the whole process would be impossible to handle. However, if those two computers in our example were networked together, both users could use Excel across the network, access the same raw data, and then output their results to a single "common" printer attached to the network. If more users were then added to the network, all users could share the application, data, and resources in a uniform fashion. As a rule, computers that are part of a network can share the following:

- Documents (memos, spreadsheets, invoices, and so on)
- E-mail messages
- Word-processing software
- Project-tracking software
- Illustrations, photographs, videos, and audio files
- Live audio and video broadcasts
- Printers
- Fax machines
- Modems
- CD-ROM drives and other removable media drives (such as Zip and Jaz drives)
- Hard drives

> ### Exam Tip
>
> The network administrator can configure the network, control user accounts, and manage network security.

Because many computers can operate on one network, the entire network can be efficiently managed from a central point (a *network administrator*). Consider the previous example and suppose that a new version of Excel became available to the data analysts. With individual computers, each system would have to be upgraded and checked separately. That's not such a big deal with only two systems, but when there are dozens (or hundreds) of PCs in the company, individual upgrades can quickly become costly and impractical. With a network, an application only needs to be updated on its server once—then all the network's workstations can use the updated software immediately. Centralized administration also allows security and system monitoring to take place from one location.

Network Sizes

Computer networks typically fit into one of three groups depending on their size and function. A *local area network* (LAN) is the basic classification of any computer network. LAN architecture can range from simple (two computers connected by a cable) to complex (hundreds of connected computers and peripherals throughout a major corporation). The distinguishing feature of a LAN is that it is confined to a limited geographic area such as a single building or department. If the computers are connected over several buildings across a large metropolitan area, the network is sometimes termed a *metropolitan area network* (MAN). By comparison, a *wide area network* (WAN) has no geographical limit. It can connect computers and peripheral devices on opposite sides of the world. In most cases, a WAN is made up of a number of interconnected LANs—perhaps the ultimate WAN is the Internet.

> **Local Lingo**
>
> **Wide area network (WAN)** A network intended to cover a wide geographical area. An example of the ultimate WAN is the Internet with its global reach.

Objective 1.02 **Network Types**

Networks are generally divided into two distinct categories: *peer to peer* and *server-based*. This is an important distinction because these two categories are vastly different and offer different capabilities to the users. Peer-to-peer networks are simpler and less expensive network arrangements that appear in small organizations (such as home office or small workgroup applications). Server-based networks are found in mid-sized and larger organizations where security, centralized administration, and high traffic capacity are important. Let's look a bit closer at server-based networks.

Server-Based Networks

In most network situations, the duality of peer-to-peer networks is simply not adequate. Limited traffic capability and security/management issues often mean that networks need to use dedicated servers. A *dedicated* server is a computer that functions only as a server to provide files and manage resources—it is *not* used as a client or workstation. Servers are optimized to handle requests from numerous network clients quickly, and ensure the security of files and directories. Consequently, server-based networks have become the standard models for modern business networking. Server-based networks are also known as *client/server* networks (sometimes denoted as *two-tier* architectures).

Travel Advisory

Servers provide specific resources and services to the network, and there may be several (perhaps many) servers available in any given network depending on the network's size and complexity.

As networks increase in size (i.e., as the number of connected computers increases, and the physical distance and traffic between them grows), more than one server is usually needed. Spreading the networking tasks among several servers ensures that each task will be performed as efficiently as possible. Servers must perform varied and complex tasks, and servers for large networks have become specialized to accommodate the expanding needs of users. Some examples of different server types include

- File and Print Servers
- Database Servers
- Application Servers

- Mail Servers
- Fax and Communication Servers
- Audio/Video Servers
- Chat Servers
- FTP Servers
- News Servers
- Gateway Servers
- Firewalls and Proxy Servers
- Web Servers

Server Software

One major issue that separates servers from peer computers is the use of software. No matter how powerful a server may be, it requires an operating system (i.e., Windows NT/2000 or Novell NetWare) that can take advantage of the server's resources. Servers also require their specific server applications in order to provide their services to the network. For example, a Web server may use Windows NT and Microsoft PWS. It's not important for you to fully understand software issues at this point. Chapter 2 covers network protocols and operating systems in more detail.

Exam Tip

Modern networks use Windows NT or 2000 as the operating system, and a growing number of networks are using Linux. A declining number of networks use Novell NetWare.

Client/Server Advantages

There is little doubt that server-based networks are more complicated to install and configure, but there are some compelling advantages over peer-to-peer networks:

- **Sharing** Servers allow for better resource organization and sharing. A server is intended to provide access to many files and printers while maintaining performance and security for the user. A server's data and resources can be centrally administered and controlled. This centralized approach makes it easier to find files and support resources than would otherwise be possible on individual computers.

- **Security**   In a server-based environment, one administrator can manage network security by setting network policies and applying them to every user.
- **Backups**   Backup routines are also simplified because only servers need to be backed up (client/workstation PCs do not). Server backups can be scheduled to occur automatically (according to a predetermined schedule) even if the servers are located on different parts of the physical network.
- **Fault Tolerance**   Because data is mainly held on servers, fault-tolerant data storage (such as RAID) can be added to the servers to prevent data loss due to drive failures or system crashes. This creates a more reliable server subject to less downtime.
- **Users**   A server-based network can support thousands of users. Such a large network would be impossible to manage as a peer-to-peer network, but current monitoring and network-management utilities make it possible to operate a server-based network for large numbers of users.

Server Reliability

Reliability is basically the notion of dependable and consistent operation—the probability that a component or system will perform a task for a specified period of time. This includes the server as well as the network, and is often measured as a function of the time between system failures using the term *MTBF* (mean time between failure). Data integrity and the ability to warn of impending hardware failures before they happen are two other aspects of reliability. Servers frequently include reliability features such as redundant power supplies and fans, predictive failure analysis for hard drives (SMART), and RAID (redundant array of independent disks) systems to ensure that a server continues to function and protect its data even when trouble occurs. Other reliability features include the memory self-test at boot time where the system detects and isolates bad memory blocks, as well as ECC (error checking and correcting) memory to improve data integrity.

Server High Availability

A server must constantly be "up" and ready for immediate use, allowing a user to access the resources they need in real time. This is the issue of *high availability*. Another aspect of highly available servers is the capability to quickly recover from a system failure (i.e., use a "hot spare" RAID disk to recover data from a failed drive). Highly available systems may or may not use redundant components (such as redundant power supplies), but they should support the hot swapping of key components. *Hot swapping* is the ability to pull out a failed component and plug in a new one while the power is still on and the system is operating. A highly available system has the ability to detect a potential failure and transparently redirect or *failover* the questionable processes to other devices or subsystems. For example, some SCSI drives can automatically move data from marginal sectors (i.e., sectors that produce occasional read errors) to spare sectors without the operating system or the user being aware of the change.

Local Lingo

Hot swapping   A critical feature of modern servers that allows devices to be exchanged without powering down the server. This minimizes interruptions in the server's operation.

In general, availability is measured as the percentage of time that a system is functioning and usable. For instance, a system that provides 99-percent availability on a 24 hours/day, 7 days/week basis would actually experience the loss of 88 processing hours a year (unacceptable to many users). However, a 99.999 percent level of availability translates to about 5.25 minutes of unscheduled downtime per year (though this level of availability may be quite costly to achieve).

Server Scalability

Computer customers of the past often bought mainframes twice the size they needed in anticipation of future growth, knowing that they would eventually "grow into" the machine. Today it's possible to select computers to fit the task now, then add more equipment as needs demand—this is known as *scalability*. A scalable PC has the ability to grow in size (capacity) and speed. Some machines offer limited scalability by design, while some can grow to virtually any size needed. Scalability includes the ability to add memory (RAM), add additional processors (i.e., for multiprocessing platforms), and add storage (hard drives), and still work within the limitations of the network operating system.

SMP

Because processors are a key element of server performance and scalability, it is a good time to cover multiprocessing in a little more detail. A *symmetric multiprocessing*

(SMP) machine is a computer that utilizes two or more processors. Each processor shares memory and uses only one copy of the operating system. SMP machines can scale by starting small (with only two processors), then adding more processors as business needs and applications grow. Beyond CPUs, such computers typically have the ability to scale memory, cache, and disks. Currently, SMP machines are designed to scale from 2–32 processors. Most SMP systems will show worthwhile improvements until they scale above eight processors (the diminishing return also varies based on the operating system and the applications in use). While UNIX systems with 16 or more processors are not uncommon today, Windows NT scalability is commonly thought to be limited to about four CPUs. In addition, many operating systems or database applications can only utilize the first 2GB of memory.

Server Clustering

Today, many high-end networks employ *server clusters*, where two or more server PCs act like a single server—providing higher availability and performance than a single server could handle. Applications can move from one server to another, or run on several servers at once, and all transactions are transparent to the users. Clustering provides higher availability and scalability than would be possible if the computers worked separately. Each node in the cluster typically has its own resources (processors, I/O, memory, OS, storage, and so on), and is responsible for its own set of users. The high availability of a server cluster is provided by *failover* capability. When one node fails, its resources can be reallocated to one or more other nodes in the cluster. Once the original node is restored to normal operation, its resources can be manually (or automatically) switched back. Server clusters are also easily scalable without an interruption of service. Upgrades can be performed by proactively failing over the functions of a server to others in the cluster, bringing that server down to add components, then bringing the server back up into the cluster and switching back its functions from the other servers.

Objective 1.03   ## Network Topology

In order to create a network, two or more PCs (and other peripheral devices) must be connected together. However, there are several ways to arrange these connections, and each connection scheme is known as a network *topology*. Each topology offers its own unique capabilities and limitations. Unfortunately, topologies aren't as simple as plugging one computer into another—each topology will require certain cabling, NIC adapters, network operating systems, and other devices. For example, a particular topology can dictate the type of cable that is used, and also how the cabling runs through floors, ceilings, and walls. While most network topologies use physical cables to connect one computer to another, a growing number of networks use wireless transceivers for at least some connections. Topology can also determine how computers communicate on the network. There are three traditional network topologies: bus, star, and ring.

Exam Tip

The three popular network topologies are bus, star, and ring, though many actual network implementations may mix topologies in one area or another.

Bus Topology

The *bus* is the simplest and most straightforward type of network topology, and is commonly used with Ethernet networks. With a bus (see Figure 1-1), computers are connected to each other in a straight line along a single main cable called a *trunk* (a backbone or segment). Bus networks are easy to connect and inexpensive to implement, and a computer failure won't impair the entire network. However, overall bus performance is limited, and cable breaks can shut down the entire network.

Bus Operation

Computers on a bus network communicate by addressing data to a particular computer and sending out that data to all computers on the cable. Only the computer whose address matches the address encoded in the original signal will accept the information—all other computers simply ignore the data. Because data goes out to all computers simultaneously, only one computer at a time can send messages. As you might expect, this also means the number of computers attached to the bus will affect network performance. The more computers there are on a bus, the more computers will be waiting to put data on the bus, and the slower the network will be.

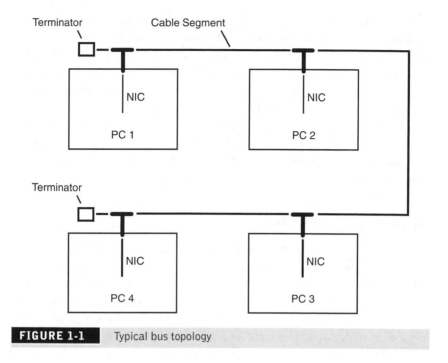

FIGURE 1-1   Typical bus topology

The electronic signals that represent data are sent to the entire network, and travel from one end of the cable to the other. If the signal is allowed to continue uninterrupted, it will keep bouncing back and forth along the cable, and this *signal bounce* can prevent other computers from sending data. The signal must be stopped after it has reached the proper destination address. To stop a signal from bouncing, a simple device called a *terminator* is placed at each end of the network cable to absorb the signals. This clears the cable so that other computers can send data. When using a bus topology, both ends of each cable segment *must* be plugged into something. For example, a cable end can be plugged into a computer or a connector to extend the cable's length. Any open cable ends not plugged into something *must* be terminated to prevent signal bounce.

Bus Disruptions

Computers on a bus topology will either transmit data to other computers or listen for data from other computers on the network—they are not responsible for moving data from one computer to the next. As a result, if one computer fails, it does not affect the rest of the network. This is a main advantage of the bus topology. Unfortunately, bus-type networks are extremely sensitive to cable breaks. A break in the cable will occur if the cable is physically separated into two pieces (i.e., accidentally cut), or if at least one end of the cable becomes disconnected (i.e., someone fiddles with a cable connection behind the PC). In either case, one or both ends of the cable will not have a terminator, the signal will bounce, and all network activity will stop, causing the network to go down. The individual computers on the network will still be able to function as stand-alone PCs, but they will not be able to communicate with each other or access shared resources as long as the cable remains broken. The computers on the down segment will continually attempt to establish a connection, and this will slow the workstations' performance until the problem is resolved.

Expanding the Bus

It is fairly easy to expand the bus topology to accommodate more users and peripheral devices. Simply remove a terminator from one end of the network trunk, add a cable to another PC's T connector, then replace the terminator at that last T connector (see Figure 1-1). If you need to extend a given cable length to make it longer, you can fasten two cable lengths together using a *barrel connector*. However, connections tend to degrade signal strength, so should be used only when absolutely necessary. Too many connectors can prevent the signal from being received correctly. One continuous cable is preferable to connecting several smaller ones with connectors. As an alternative, a *repeater* can be used to connect two cable lengths. A repeater actually boosts the signal strength, so the signal remains stronger across multiple connectors or a longer piece of cable.

Star Topology

The *star* topology is slightly more sophisticated than a bus approach because all PCs on the network are tied to a central connection point called a *hub* (see Figure 1-2). A star network is a bit more robust than the bus approach because connections are direct from the PC to the hub. It's an easy matter to add clients to the network simply by connecting them to an available port in the hub (multiple hubs can be ganged together for larger networks with additional users). Since each connection is independent, you don't need to worry about terminators, and a cable problem or PC fault will only affect that particular workstation—it won't disable the entire network. However, more cabling is often required because each PC needs its own cable to the hub. Also, a hub failure can disable all of the PCs attached to it (though this is a fairly easy issue to troubleshoot).

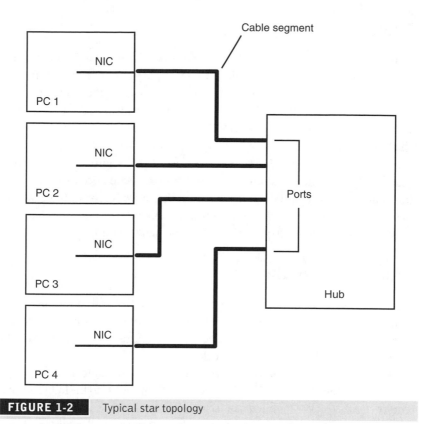

FIGURE 1-2   Typical star topology

Star Operation

Computers on a star network communicate by addressing data to a particular computer and sending out that data through the hub to all computers on the network. Only the computer whose address matches the address encoded in the original signal will accept the information—all other computers simply ignore the data. Because data goes out to all computers simultaneously, only one computer at a time can send messages. This means the number of computers attached to the star will affect network performance. The more computers there are on a star network, the more computers will be waiting to send data to the hub and the slower the network will be. Unlike the bus topology, star network connections are not bothered by signal bounce, so no special termination is needed. You simply connect the PC's NIC adapter port to the corresponding hub port.

Star Disruptions

Computers on a star topology will either transmit data through the hub to other computers or listen for data from the hub—they are not responsible for moving data from one computer to another. As a result, if one computer fails, it does not affect the rest of the network. This is an important advantage of the star topology. Also, the fact that all of the network's PCs must come together to a single point (the hub) means that the hub(s), server(s), and other key network devices can all be conveniently located and serviced in one place. This improves network troubleshooting and administration. If a break or disconnection occurs with a cable, only that PC is affected, and the remainder of the network can continue on normally. However, since the hub serves as a central communication point in the star topology, a hub failure will quickly disable all of the PCs attached to it.

Expanding the Star

It is fairly easy to expand the star topology to accommodate more users and peripheral devices. Additional users can simply be connected to an available port on an existing hub. However, the added wiring becomes problematic. When a nearby PC is added to a bus-type network, you only need to attach the new PC in-line with the existing trunk wiring. When a new PC is added to a star-type network, you may need to run an entirely new cable from the PC to the hub. This may require dozens (maybe hundreds) of feet of additional wiring, which may need to be routed through floors, walls, and ceilings depending on what's between the user and the hub.

Ring Topology

The *ring* topology (usually called *token ring*) is a bit more sophisticated than a bus approach because the trunk cable that connects all PCs on the network basically forms a loop (see Figure 1-3). Computers are connected in a continuous network loop in which a key piece of data (called a *token*) is passed from one computer to the next. The token is a data frame (or packet) that is continuously passed around the ring. In actual practice, token ring networks are physically implemented in a star configuration but managed logically as a loop. Workstations on a token ring network are attached to a specialized hub called a *multistation access unit* (MAU). It's an easy matter to add clients to the network simply by connecting them to an available port in the MAU (several MAUs can be ganged together for larger networks with additional users). Since the overall effect is that of a loop, you don't

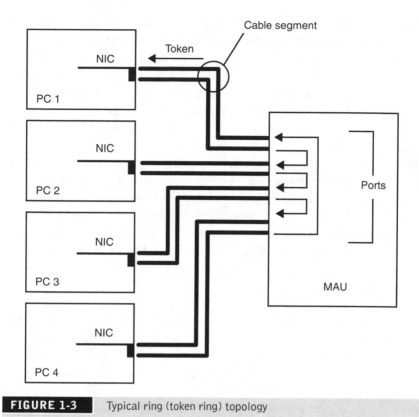

| FIGURE 1-3 | Typical ring (token ring) topology |

need to worry about terminators. The token-passing approach ensures that all PCs have equal access to the network, even when there are many users. On the negative side, more cabling is often required because each PC needs its own cabling to the MAU. Also, each computer must pass a token to the next, so a PC failure (or a MAU fault) can impair the entire network. This can easily complicate the troubleshooting process.

Ring Operation

The most popular method of transmitting data around a ring is called *token passing*. The token itself is little more than a short sequence of data bits that travel around a token ring network, and each network has only one token. The token is passed (received and retransmitted) from computer to computer. An advantage of this retransmission is that each PC in the loop acts as a *repeater*—boosting the data signal to the next workstation. This process of token passing continues until the token reaches a computer that has data to send. The sending computer modifies the token, puts an electronic address on the data, and reinserts this new data package into the ring.

This data package passes by each computer until it finds the one with an address that matches the address on the data. The receiving computer takes the data and attaches a verification message to the token, which is readdressed to the sender and returned to the ring. The sending computer eventually receives the verification message, indicating that the data has been received. After verification, the sending computer creates a new token and inserts it on the network. The token continues to circulate within the ring until another workstation needs it to send data. Unlike the bus topology, ring network connections are not bothered by signal bounce, so no special termination is needed. You simply connect the PC's NIC adapter port to the corresponding MAU port to add that PC to the loop.

Ring Disruptions

Computers in a token ring topology are constantly receiving and retransmitting tokens from one computer to the next. As a result, if one computer fails or a cable breaks, it interrupts the rest of the network. Since token rings also use MAUs to pass data from one PC to the next (see Figure 1-3), a MAU failure can also disable the network. These are important disadvantages of token ring topology, and can present a technician with serious troubleshooting problems when faced with locating the break in a token ring. On the plus side, a MAU provides a centralized communication point for network administration and maintenance.

Expanding the Ring

Because a token ring is physically structured very similarly to a star network, it's fairly easy to expand the ring topology in order to accommodate more users and peripheral devices. Additional users can simply be connected to an available port

---

Travel Advisory

The idea of a "ring" is only from a logical perspective. From a practical standpoint, the network is wired as a "star"—a MAU is used to provide the ring feature.

on an existing MAU. As with star clients, however, the added wiring can be problematic. When a nearby PC is added to a bus-type network, you only need to attach the new PC inline with the existing trunk wiring. When a new PC is added to a token ring network, you may need to run an entirely new cable from the PC to the MAU. This may require dozens (maybe hundreds) of feet of additional wiring, which may need to be routed through floors, walls, and ceilings depending on what's between the user and network's MAU.

Objective 1.04   Network Hardware

Now that you've had a chance to learn about server types and network topologies, it's time to learn a bit more about the various hardware elements involved with the implementation of a network. Network hardware has a profound impact on the speed, quality, and overall performance of the network. For the purposes of this book, network hardware includes hubs, repeaters, bridges, routers, gateways, network interface cards, and cabling.

Travel Advisory

Be careful when connecting hubs. Crossover cables are wired differently than standard patch cables, and one will not work correctly in place of the other. Check with the hub manufacturer to determine whether you need a standard patch cable or a crossover cable.

Hubs

A hub is a central connection device that joins computers in a star topography. A variation of the hub is a multistation access unit (or MAU, sometimes called a token ring hub) used to connect PCs in a token ring topology. Hubs are now standard equipment in modern networks, and are typically classified as *passive* or *active*. A passive hub does not process data at all—it's basically just a connection panel. By comparison, active hubs (sometimes called repeaters) regenerate the data in order to maintain adequate signal strength. Some hubs also have the ability to handle additional tasks such as bridging, routing, and switching. Hub-based systems are versatile, and offer several advantages over systems that do not use hubs. For example, with an ordinary bus topology, a break in the cable will take the network down. But with hubs, a break in any of the cables attached to the hub affects only that limited segment of the network. An emerging generation of hubs will accommodate several different types of cables. These are called *hybrid hubs*.

Repeaters

As electrical signals travel along a cable, they degrade and become distorted. This effect is called *attenuation*. As cable lengths increase, the effects of attenuation worsen. If a cable is long enough, attenuation will finally make a signal unrecognizable, and this will cause data errors in the network. Installing a repeater enables signals to travel farther by regenerating the network's signals and sending them out again on other cable lengths. The *repeater* takes a weak signal from one cable, regenerates it, and passes it to the next cable. As you saw above, active hubs frequently act as repeaters, but stand-alone repeaters may be needed to support very long cable lengths.

Exam Tip
A *repeater* is used for baseband systems, while an *amplifier* is used for broadband systems.

It is important to realize that repeaters are simply signal amplifiers. They do not translate or filter the network signals from one cable to another. For a repeater to work properly, both cables joined by the repeater must use the same packets, logical protocols, and access method. The two most common access methods are carrier sense multiple access with collision detection (CSMA/CD) and token passing. A repeater cannot connect a segment using CSMA/CD to a segment using the token-passing access method. It will not allow an Ethernet network to talk to a token ring network—there are other more sophisticated devices used for that type of translation. However, repeaters *can* move packets from one kind of physical media to another. For example, a repeater can take an Ethernet packet coming from a thin coaxial cable and pass it on to a fiber-optic cable (provided that the repeater is capable of accepting the physical connections).

Bridges

A *bridge* offers more features for a busy network. A bridge can act like a repeater to extend the effective length of a network cable. However, a bridge has more "intelligence," and can also divide a network to isolate excessive traffic or problem data. For example, if the volume of traffic from one or two computers (or a single department) is flooding the network with data and slowing down the entire operation, a bridge could isolate those computers (or department). Rather than distinguish between one protocol and another, bridges simply pass all protocols along the network. Since all protocols pass across bridges, it is up to the individual computers to determine which protocols they can recognize. Bridges can also link different physical media such as twisted-pair cable and thin coaxial cable.

Routing Data

A bridge also offers superior data-handling capabilities not provided by hubs and repeaters. Bridges "listen" to all traffic, check the source and destination address of each packet, and build a routing table (as information becomes available) so that they can sort data to different parts of the network efficiently. Bridges actually have the ability to learn how to forward data. As traffic passes through the bridge, information about the computer addresses is stored in the bridge's memory. The bridge uses this information to build a routing table based on source addresses. Initially, the bridge's memory is empty, and so is the routing table. As packets are transmitted, the source address is copied to the routing table. With this address information, the bridge eventually learns which computers are on which segment of the network.

When the bridge receives a packet, the source address is compared to the routing table. If the source address is not there, it is added to the table. The bridge then compares the destination address with the routing table database. If the destination address is in the routing table and is on the same network segment as the source address, the packet is discarded (because it's assumed that another PC on the same part of the network has received the data). This filtering helps to reduce network traffic and isolate different parts of the network. If the destination address is in the routing table and not in the same segment as the source address, the bridge forwards the packet out of the appropriate port to reach the destination address. If the destination address is not in the routing table, the bridge forwards the packet to all its ports except the one on which it originated.

Reducing Traffic

Remember that many PCs on a network may need to send data, but not all PCs may need to receive that data. Often, all PCs must receive data to see whether the information is intended for that workstation, then each must wait for an opportunity to send data itself. In a large network, this can significantly reduce network performance. However, large networks often group PCs into departments, and the data sent between departments is often far less than the traffic sent between PCs within the same department. By using bridges to separate the overall company network into several smaller departmental groups, it is possible to reduce the traffic going out to the entire network, and thus improve the overall network's performance.

Routers and Brouters

When you're working in more complex network environments that use several different network segments—each with different protocols and architectures—a bridge is often inadequate to handle fast and efficient communication between diverse segments. Such a complex network demands a sophisticated device that knows the address of each segment, determines the best path for sending data, and filters broadcast traffic to the local segment. This type of device is called a *router*. As with a bridge, routers can filter and isolate network traffic, and also connect network segments. Further, routers can switch and route packets across multiple networks. They do this by exchanging specific protocol information between separate networks. Routers have access to more packet information than bridges, and routers use this additional information to improve packet deliveries. Routers are used in complex networks because they provide better traffic management. For example, routers can share status and routing information with one another, and use this information to bypass slow or malfunctioning connections.

There are two principle router types: static and dynamic. A "static router" is sometimes called a "manual router" because all routes must be configured manually by the network administrator. Routing tables are fixed, so the static router always uses the same route (even if network activity changes). This means there's no guarantee that the router is using the shortest routes. By comparison, "dynamic routers" must be configured initially, but they will adapt to changing network conditions automatically—using lower cost or lower traffic routes as needed.

Routing Data

Routers maintain their own routing tables, which usually consist of network addresses (though host addresses can also be kept if the network needs it). To determine the destination address for incoming data, the routing table includes all known network addresses, logical instructions for connection to other networks, knowledge of the possible paths between routers, and even the costs of sending data over each path. Thus, a router uses its routing table to select the *best* route for data transmission based on costs and available paths. You should understand that the "routing tables" used for bridges and routers are *not* the same thing. Routers require specific addresses. They understand only the network numbers that allow them to communicate with other routers and local NIC addresses, so routers don't talk to remote computers.

When routers receive packets destined for a remote network, they send them to the router that manages the destination network. The use of routers allows designers to separate large networks into smaller ones, and routers offer an element of security between the segments. Unfortunately, routers must perform complex functions on each packet, so they are slower than most bridges. For example, as packets are passed from router to router, source and destination addresses are stripped off and then re-created. This enables a router to route a packet from a TCP/IP Ethernet network to a server on a TCP/IP token ring network—a feature unattainable with a bridge.

Reducing Traffic

Routers do not look at the destination node address. Instead, they look only at the network address, and will pass information only if the network address is known. Routers will not allow corrupted data to be passed onto the network. This ability to control the data passing through the router reduces the amount of traffic between networks, and allows routers to use these links more efficiently than bridges. Consequently, routers can greatly reduce the amount of traffic on the network and the wait time experienced by users.

> **Local Lingo**
>
> **Brouter**   An advanced router that includes the features of a bridge. As router technology continues to advance, you may see the term "brouter" fall into disuse.

Switches

Many network equipment companies incorporate a technology called switching into their router designs. Switches use basic logic to detect a packet's destination address (typically an IP address), then send the packet to the corresponding portion of the network. This behavior makes the network more efficient. If the switch doesn't know the destination, the router can query other routers in the network in an attempt to determine the correct path. Today, switching is an essential part of router design.

Gateways

A *gateway* acts as a powerful interpreter designed to connect radically different networks. Although slower than a bridge or router, a gateway can perform complex functions such as translating between networks that speak different languages (using techniques such as protocol and bandwidth conversion). For example, a gateway can convert a TCP/IP packet to a NetWare IPX packet (and vice versa). Gateways enable communication between entirely different architectures and environments. They effectively repackage and convert data going from one type of network to another so that each can understand the other's data. A gateway repackages information to match the requirements of the destination system, and changes the format of a message so that it conforms to the application running at the receiving end of the transfer. In most cases, gateways are task-specific, which means that they are dedicated to a particular type of transfer. They are often referred to by their task (i.e., "Windows NT Server-to-SNA Gateway").

Network Interface Cards

The network interface card (NIC) functions as an interface between the individual computer (server or client) and the network cabling (see Figure 1-4). Internally, the NIC must identify the PC on the network and buffer data between the computer and the cable. When sending data, the NIC must convert the data from parallel bytes into serial bits (then back again during reception). On the network side, a NIC must generate the electrical signals that travel over the network, manage access to the network, and make the physical connection to the cable. Every computer on the network must have at least one NIC port installed. Modern NICs increase their effective throughput using advanced techniques of *adapter teaming* such as *adapter fault tolerance* (AFT), which provides automatic

---

Local Lingo

Network interface card (NIC)   This is a PC hardware device that forms a critical interface between a computer (workstation or server) and the rest of the network.

FIGURE 1-4   The Symbios SYM22915 NIC (Courtesy of LSI Logic Corp.)

redundancy for your adapter. If the primary adapter fails, the secondary takes over. *Adaptive load balancing* (ALB) allows balancing the transmission data flow between two to four adapters.

Cabling

Finally, networks of all sizes and configurations depend on the physical cabling that connects all of the PCs and other hardware together. Cabling (also referred to as *network media*) comes in many different configurations, but common cabling used for everyday networking includes unshielded twisted pair (UTP), coaxial cable, shielded twisted pair (STP), and fiber-optic (FO) cable. As a technician, you should understand the three main considerations for cabling:

- Resistance to *crosstalk* (electrical currents between pairs of wires in the same cable)
- Resistance to interference from outside electrical fields (noise created by electric motors, power lines, relays, and transmitters)
- Ease of installation

These are important issues because cables resistant to crosstalk and interference can be run longer and support higher data transmission rates. For example, coaxial and shielded twisted-pair cable have a thin metal foil outer layer that offers good resistance to electrical noise, but the extra foil creates a larger, thicker cable that is more difficult to pull through conduit and walls during installation. Unshielded twisted pair is thinner and easier to install, but offers less resistance to electrical noise. By comparison, fiber-optic cable carries light signals instead of electrical pulses, so it is impervious to electrical interference. This allows fiber-optic cable to carry signals faster and farther than any other type of cable. Unfortunately, FO cable is often far more expensive than other cable types, and proper installation demands specialized tools and training.

Objective 1.05   Network Media

Every computer in any kind of network must ultimately be connected to one another. These connections are responsible for transmitting vast amounts of information between the computers and peripheral devices. Although wireless networking is growing in popularity, the vast majority of network connections are made physically, using a variety of cable types—each intended for a specific type of network architecture. We usually refer to this interconnecting wiring as *network media*. While there are well over 2,000 different types of cabling, most network applications use only three different cable types: coaxial, twisted pair, and fiber-optic cable.

Local Lingo

Network media   This term covers the wide variety of interconnections used to attach workstations to the server.

Coaxial Cable

Coaxial cable (or simply "coax") is an inexpensive, flexible, and rugged type of transmission cable. Coaxial cables use a single copper wire at the center of an internal insulating layer, then covered by a finely braided metal shield, and covered by a protective outer jacket (see Figure 1-5). Its light weight and flexibility make coaxial cable easy to install in a wide range of office environments. That wire in the middle of the coaxial cable is what actually carries the signal. It is often a

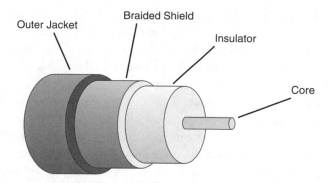

Outer Jacket

Braided Shield

Insulator

Core

FIGURE 1-5

solid copper wire, but might sometimes be stranded aluminum. A fairly thick dielectric insulating layer surrounds the core, and this separates the core from the metal shielding. A braided wire mesh acts as an electrical ground and protects the core from electrical noise and crosstalk. The shielding also protects transmitted data from electrical noise. For additional protection, a coaxial cable may incorporate one layer of foil insulation and one layer of braided metal shielding (*dual shielding*), or two layers of foil insulation and two layers of braided metal shielding (*quad shielded*). Additional shielding adds greatly to the cable's cost and weight. Finally, a protective outer cover of rubber, Teflon, or PVC plastic is used to jacket the cable. You'll generally find two types of coaxial cable used in networking: thin and thick.

All coaxial cables are attached using specialized quick-twist connectors called *BNC connectors*. A BNC T connector is an adapter used to attach two lengths of cable to your NIC. If you need to adapt two lengths of cable to make one longer run, use a BNC barrel connector. Finally, you'll need a BNC terminator to cap each end of the cable run (usually attached to the unused port of the last BNC T connectors).

Thinnet and Thicknet Cable

As the name implies, *thinnet* cable is thin—roughly 0.25 in (diameter)—and can carry electrical signals for over 600 ft. The cable industry refers to this common type of cable as RG-58. Thinnet cable presents a 50Ω impedance (signal resistance) to the data signals flowing through it. The cable's small diameter makes it flexible and easy to install just about anywhere.

Thicknet cable (sometimes called standard Ethernet cable because of its use with early Ethernet networks) offers a diameter of 0.5 in—twice the diameter of thinnet cable. The copper core wire is also thicker, and this allows thicknet cable to transfer signals well over 1,500 ft. This ability to carry signals a great distance makes thicknet an ideal choice for a backbone cable that's able to connect several smaller thinnet network segments. Unfortunately, thicknet cable does not bend easily, so it is considerably harder to install.

The transition from thicknet to thinnet cable is made with a transceiver device. The transceiver's sharp points pierce the thicknet cable (referred to as a *vampire tap*) in order to contact the cable's core and shielding. An output cable from the transceiver attaches to the computer's corresponding NIC port. In many cases, the NIC adapter requires an *attachment unit interface* (AUI) port connector (also known as a Digital Intel Xerox (DIX) connector) to accommodate the transceiver.

Cable Grades

Chances are that you'll be running coaxial cable through walls, in ceilings, under floors, and in or through other odd locations throughout your facility. It's important to remember that ordinary coaxial cable uses a jacket of PVC or other synthetic material that makes it easy to pull and route. However, building fire codes generally prohibit the use of everyday coaxial cable in a building's *plenum* (the shallow space in many buildings between the false ceiling and the floor above). During a fire, PVC jackets will burn and generate poisonous gases. Coaxial cable rated for plenum-grade use employs insulation and jacket materials that are certified to be fire resistant and produce a minimum amount of smoke. This reduces poisonous chemical fumes in the event of a fire. Plenum cable can also be used in the plenum area and in vertical runs (such as up a wall) without conduit. Be sure to review and understand the fire safety codes for your location when building, servicing, or expanding your network.

Twisted-Pair Cable

Another popular cable type that is commonly used with current networks is called *twisted pair*. As the name suggests, a twisted pair is little more than two insulated lengths of copper wire twisted around each other—though a typical twisted-pair cable carries two, three, or even four pairs of wire contained in a single plastic, PVC, or Teflon jacket (see Figure 1-6). The physical twisting of the wires works to cancel out electrical noise from adjacent pairs, as well as other noise sources such as motors, relays, and transformers. Twisted-pair cable is either shielded or unshielded, and the choice between these two may have a profound impact on the reliability of your data (especially if you must carry data over a distance).

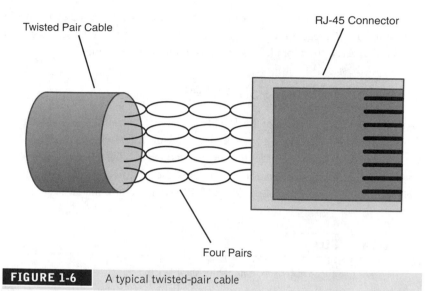

Twisted Pair Cable

RJ-45 Connector

Four Pairs

| FIGURE 1-6 | A typical twisted-pair cable |

Twisted-pair cabling uses RJ-45 telephone connectors. At first glance, these connectors look like the RJ-11 telephone connectors that attach your telephone cord to the wall. The RJ-45 connector is slightly larger, and will not fit into an RJ-11 telephone jack. The RJ-45 connector handles eight cable connections, while the RJ-11 supports only four. This means you can't accidentally exchange your telephone and network connectors.

Unshielded Twisted Pair (UTP)

When there are one or more pairs of twisted wire, but none of the pairs (nor the full cable) contains additional metal foil or braid for shielding, the twisted-pair cable is said to be *unshielded twisted pair* (UTP). UTP is an inexpensive and versatile cable that has been very popular with 10BaseT networks. The maximum cable length for a UTP network segment is about 328 ft. National standards organizations have specified the type of UTP cable that is to be used in a variety of building and wiring situations. These standards include five distinct categories for UTP denoted Category 1 through Category 5.

One reason why UTP is so popular is because many buildings are prewired for twisted-pair telephone systems using a type of UTP. In fact, extra UTP is often installed to meet future cabling needs as part of the facility's prewiring process. If preinstalled twisted-pair cable meets the category requirements to support data transmission, it can be used in a computer network directly. However, common telephone wire (Category 1 wire) might not have the twisting and other electrical characteristics required for clean, secure, computer data transmission.

Shielded Twisted Pair (STP)

In order to avoid degradation of the data because of crosstalk and noise, twisted pairs of wire are often shielded with a wrap of thin metal foil. A fine copper braid then surrounds all of the pairs, and a thick protective jacket of plastic, Teflon, or PVC is applied. These metal shields reduce signal errors and allow the cable to carry data faster over a greater distance. Other than the shielding, UTP and STP cable is identical.

> **Exam Tip**
>
> There are two types of twisted pair cable: shielded and unshielded.

IBM Cabling System

If you work with network cabling for any length of time, chances are that you'll encounter the IBM cabling system. IBM introduced its cabling system in 1984 to ensure that network cabling and connectors would meet the specifications of their own equipment. The IBM cabling system classifies cable into "types" rather than categories. For example, Category 3 cable (voice-grade UTP cable) is denoted as Type 3 cable in the IBM system.

One element unique to the IBM cabling system is the cable connector. These IBM Type A connectors (commonly known as *universal data connectors*) are different from standard BNC or other connectors. They are neither male nor female—you can connect one to another by flipping either one over. These IBM connectors require special faceplates and distribution panels to accommodate their unique shape.

Fiber-Optic Cable

Traditional wire cable handles data in the form of electrical signals (i.e., voltage and current). *Fiber-optic* (FO) cable is fundamentally different in that it uses specialized optical materials to carry data as pulses of light. This makes fiber-optic cable uniquely immune to electrical noise and crosstalk, and allows FO cable to carry a high data bandwidth over several miles with surprisingly effective security—that is, the FO cable cannot be tapped without interrupting the data. Fiber-optic cable transmissions are extremely fast, easily handling 100Mbps and with demonstrated data rates to 1Gbps.

An optical fiber consists of an extremely thin fiber of glass (called the *core*) surrounded by another layer of glass with slightly different optical characteristics (known as the *cladding*). The cladding effectively keeps light signals in the core material as it passes down the cable. Because each fiber only passes signals in one direction, a complete cable includes two strands in separate jackets: one strand transmits and the other receives. A coating of plastic surrounds each glass strand, and Kevlar fibers provide strength. Plastic (rather than glass) is sometimes used as the optical material because it is cheaper and easier to install, but plastic is not as optically clear as glass, and cannot carry light signals over the same long distance.

> **Travel Assistance**
>
> There is a tremendous amount of information regarding network cable types and standards. You can review the Data Communications Cabling **FAQ** at http://www.faqs.org/faqs/LANs/cabling-faq/ for more information.

Objective 1.06   Network Architectures

The *architecture* of a network is basically the way it is designed, and the way information is exchanged. There are two basic types of network architectures that you should be familiar with: Ethernet and token ring. This part of the chapter examines these architectures in more detail and explains the impact of cabling and access techniques.

Understanding the Packet

To the novice, it may seem that networks exchange information as a continuous stream of data between computers—this is not the case. Sending large amounts of data at one time causes other computers to wait idly while the data is being moved. This monopolizes the network and wastes the time of other users waiting to use the network—especially if a transmission error requires the data to be retransmitted. Rather than exchanging entire files at one time, data is broken down into much smaller chunks. Each chunk is wrapped with the essential details needed to get the data to its correct destination without errors. These organized chunks are called *packets* (or frames), and it may require many packets to transfer an entire file from one network computer to another.

By transferring data in small packets, wait times seen by other computers on the network are much smaller because numerous computers on the network take turns sending packets. Should a packet arrive at a destination computer in a damaged or unreadable state (because of signal attenuation), it is much easier and faster to retransmit that packet rather than the entire file. Packet data typically contains information (such as e-mail messages or files), but many other types of data can be exchanged in packets, such as command and control data or session control codes (i.e., feedback that indicates a packet was received properly, or requires retransmission).

Local Lingo

Packets   Network data that has been divided up and packaged with overhead information needed for transmission across the network. The format of a packet will vary depending on how the network is configured. Packets are reassembled at the destination to re-create the original data.

Packet Organization

A packet is basically made up of three parts: header, data, and trailer. Data is preceded by a *header*, which includes a signal that indicates a packet is being transmitted, a source address, a destination address, and clock information to synchronize the transmission. The actual data being sent is included after the header. The header of the packet may vary greatly in size depending on the particular network, but most networks include from 512 bytes to 4KB. Remember that most files are much larger than this, so it may take many packets to transmit a complete file. A *trailer* follows the data. The exact content of a trailer may vary, but a trailer usually contains error-checking information called a *cyclical redundancy check* (CRC). The CRC is a number produced by a mathematical calculation performed on the packet at its source. When the packet arrives at its destination, the calculation is made again. If the results of both calculations are the same, the data in the packet has remained intact. If the calculation at the destination differs from that at the source, the data has changed during the transmission, and a retransmission is requested.

Travel Advisory

The exact formation and length of a packet will depend on the network's communication protocol—the set of rules or standards that enable computers to connect with one another and exchange information with as little error as possible.

Access Methods

Of course, the computers on a network can't just start spewing packets at any point. While network traffic may seem to be moving simultaneously, a closer look will reveal that computers are actually taking turns placing their data on the network. If two computers place their data onto the network at the same time, both data packets would "collide" and be destroyed. The flow of network traffic must be carefully regulated. The rules that govern how data is sent onto (or taken from) a network are called the *access method*. An access method provides the traffic control needed to organize data transmissions on the network. It is also important to realize that all computers on the network must use the SAME access method. Otherwise, network problems would occur because some access methods would monopolize the cable. There are three major access methods: CSMA, token passing, and demand priority.

CSMA/CD

In the carrier sense multiple access with collision detection method (CSMA/CD), each computer on the network (clients and servers alike) checks to see that the cable is free before sending a packet. If data is currently on the cable, the computer will not send—it will wait and check the cable again. Once a computer has transmitted data on the cable, no other computer can transmit data until the original data has reached its destination and the cable is free again. This is often known as a *contention* method because two or more computers are contending for the network cable. If two or more computers happen to send data at exactly the same time, there will be a data collision. The two computers involved will stop transmitting for random periods of time, then attempt to retransmit. The CSMA/CD technique is only useful up to about 1.5 miles. Beyond that, it might not be possible for a computer at one end to sense that a computer at the other end is transmitting. CSMA/CD can be frustratingly slow when network traffic is heavy.

> **Exam Tip**
>
> CSMA/CD is the most common form of access method and is normally used with Ethernet networks.

CSMA/CA

The carrier sense multiple access with collision avoidance method (CSMA/CA) is similar to CSMA/CD, but allows each computer to signal its intention to transmit data before the packet is actually sent. This enables other computers to sense when a data collision might occur, and thus avoid transmissions that might result in collisions. The problem with this approach is that broadcasting the intent to transmit actually adds to the network traffic and can result in even slower network performance. This makes CSMA/CA the least popular access method.

Token Passing

With the token-passing method, a special type of packet (called a *token*) is circulated around a cable ring from computer to computer. In order for any computer on the ring to send data across the network, it must wait for a free token. When a free token is detected, the computer waiting for the token will take control of it. The sending computer then modifies the packet to include appropriate headers, data, and trailers, and sends the new packet on its way. The receiving computer accepts the packet and its data, then creates another token for the sending computer indicating that the packet had been received. When the sending computer receives this token, it creates a new free token and passes it back onto the ring. When a token is in use by a computer, other computers cannot transmit data. Because only one computer at a time can use the token, no contention (or collision) takes place, and no time is spent waiting for computers to resend tokens due to network traffic.

Demand Priority

The demand-priority method is a fairly new approach intended to service the 100Mbps Ethernet standard (IEEE 802.12 or 100VG-AnyLAN) based on the star (or star/bus) topology. Hubs manage network access by doing round-robin searches for requests to send from all nodes on the network. As with CSMA/CD, two computers using demand priority can cause contention by transmitting at exactly the same time. With demand priority, however, it is possible to decide which types of data will be given priority if contention occurs. If a hub receives two requests at the same time, the highest-priority request is serviced first. If the two requests are of the same priority, both requests are serviced by alternating between the two.

Demand priority offers several powerful advantages over CSMA/CD. First, communication only takes place between the sending computer, hub, and destination computer. This means transmissions are not broadcast to the entire network. Second, demand priority uses twisted-pair cabling (four pairs), which allows computers on the network to receive and transmit at the same.

Ethernet

Ethernet can trace its origins back to the late 1960s when the University of Hawaii developed a network that would connect computers across its large campus. This early network employed a bus topology, baseband transmission, and a CSMA/CD access method. Xerox built upon this scheme, and by 1975 introduced the first Ethernet networking products intended to operate over 2.5Mbps and connect more than 100 computers across a 1km trunk. This early implementation of Ethernet proved so popular that Xerox, Intel, and Digital (DEC) collaborated on the 10Mbps Ethernet standard (now one of several specifications allowing computers and data systems to connect and share cabling). Ethernet has become one of the most popular network architectures for the desktop computer, and is used in network environments of all sizes. Today, Ethernet is considered to be a nonproprietary industry standard that is widely supported by network hardware manufacturers.

Ethernet Packets

An Ethernet packet (commonly called a *frame* among Ethernet users) is between 64 and 1,518 bytes long (512–12,144 bits), and every packet includes control information. For example, the Ethernet II packet format used for Transmission

Control Protocol/Internet Protocol (TCP/IP) is the standard for data transmission over networks (including the Internet). This packet includes six distinct areas. The *preamble* marks the start of the packet (similar to the start bit used in serial communication). The *addresses* denote the destination and source addresses for the packet. A *type* entry is used to identify the network layer protocol—usually either IP (Internet Protocol) or IPX (Novell's Internetwork Packet Exchange). The packet's data then follows, and the packet is concluded by error checking (CRC) information.

Ethernet Performance Notes

Ethernet performance can be improved by dividing a crowded segment into two less-populated segments, then joining them with either a bridge or a router. This reduces the traffic on each segment—because fewer computers are attempting to transmit onto the segment, the apparent access time improves. You may consider dividing segments if new users are quickly joining the network or if new bandwidth-intensive applications (i.e., database or video software) are added to the network. Ethernet architecture is also quite versatile, and can use multiple communication protocols or connect mixed computing environments such as NetWare, UNIX, Windows, or Macintosh.

10BaseT (IEEE 802.3)

10BaseT is an Ethernet standard designed to support 10Mbps baseband data transmission over Category 3, 4, or 5 twisted-pair cable (UTP). UTP cable is more common, but STP can be substituted without difficulty. Cables are connected with RJ-45 connectors. Each computer uses two pairs of wire: one pair is used to receive and the other pair is used to transmit. While Ethernet LANs are traditionally configured in a bus topology, a growing number are set up as a star topology (using bus signaling and access methods). The hub of a 10BaseT network typically serves as a multiport repeater. The maximum length of a 10BaseT segment is 328 ft, though repeaters can be used to extend this maximum length. The minimum cable length between computers is 8 ft. A 10BaseT Ethernet LAN will serve up to 1,024 computers.

10Base2 (IEEE 802.3)

10Base2 is an Ethernet standard designed to support 10Mbps baseband data transmission over thin coaxial (thinnet) cable. Cables are connected with BNC connectors (including barrel connectors, T connectors, and terminators). 10Base2 Ethernet LANs are traditionally configured in a bus topology. The maximum length of a 10Base2 segment is 607 ft, though repeaters can join up to five segments to create an effective bus length of over 3,000 ft. The minimum cable length between computers is 2 ft. A 10Base2 Ethernet LAN will only serve up to 30 computers per segment, but this is often ideal for small department and workgroup situations.

10Base5 (IEEE 802.3)

10Base5 is an Ethernet scheme (called *standard Ethernet*) designed to support 10Mbps baseband data transmission over thick coaxial (thicknet) cable. 10Base5 Ethernet LANs are traditionally configured in a bus topology, and the maximum length of a 10Base5 segment is 1,640 ft, though repeaters can join up to five segments to create an effective bus length of over 8,200 ft. The backbone (or trunk) segment is the main cable from which transceiver cables are connected to stations and repeaters. The minimum cable length between transceivers is 8 ft. A 10Base5 Ethernet LAN will only serve up to 100 computers per segment, and this is often ideal for small to mid-sized network situations.

Travel Advisory

A thicknet network can combine as many as five cable segments connected by four repeaters, but only three segments can have computers attached. This means two segments are untapped, and are often known as "inter-repeater links." This is known as the 5-4-3 rule. Remember that the length of the transceiver cables is not used to measure the distance of the thicknet cable—only the end-to-end length of the thicknet cable segment itself is used.

Cabling a 10Base 5 network can be a bit more involved than other Ethernet configurations. The thicknet cabling includes *transceivers* that provide communications between the computer and the main LAN cable, and are attached to the main cable with vampire taps. Once a transceiver is placed on the main cable, a *transceiver cable* (a.k.a. a drop cable) connects the transceiver to the NIC. A transceiver cable attaches to a NIC through an AUI (or DIX) connector. Other cabling is attached with N-series connectors, including barrel connectors and terminators.

10BaseFL

It is also possible to run an Ethernet network over fiber-optic cable. 10BaseFL is designed to support 10Mbps baseband data transmission over fiber-optic cable between computers and repeaters. The main reason for using 10BaseFL is to accommodate long cable runs between repeaters, such as between buildings. The maximum distance for a 10BaseFL segment is about 6,500 ft.

100BaseVG

Originally developed by Hewlett-Packard, the 100BaseVG (voice grade) AnyLAN scheme is an emerging networking technology that combines elements of both Ethernet and token ring architectures. This type of architecture is known by several terms: 100VG, AnyLAN, 100BaseVG, or simply VG. 100BaseVG supports a minimum data rate of 100Mbps in a star (or cascaded star) topology across Category 3, 4, and 5 twisted-pair (as well as fiber-optic) cable. Because 100BaseVG is compatible with existing 10BaseT cabling systems, it is a simple matter to upgrade from existing 10BaseT installations (though new hubs and NIC adapters will be required). 100BaseVG uses the demand-priority access method that allows for two priority levels (low and high), and supports both Ethernet frames and token ring packets. While data transmission rates are higher, the cable distances of 100BaseVG are limited when compared to other implementations of Ethernet. A cable run from the 100BaseVG hub to a computer cannot exceed about 820 ft.

100Base"X"

There are several variations of the 100Base"X" family depending on the media being used. 100BaseT4 uses four-pair Category 3, 4, or 5 UTP cable, 100BaseTX uses two-pair Category 5 UTP or STP cable, and 100BaseFX uses two-strand fiber-optic cable. But all are referred to as Fast Ethernet because of their 100-Mbps transmission speeds. 100Base"X" also uses CSMA/CD in a star-wired bus topology (similar to 10BaseT where all cables are attached to a hub).

Token Ring

IBM introduced the token ring architecture in 1984 for personal, midrange, and mainframe computers. The main objective behind token ring was to establish a simple and reliable wiring method using twisted-pair cable, which could connect individual workstations to a central location. The architecture of a token ring network is technically a physical ring. However, rather than cabling the network PCs in an actual circle (which could make upgrades and workstation additions a real nightmare), the token ring approach uses a star topology where all PCs are connected to a central hub called a *multistation access unit* (MAU). In effect, the ring is provided by the MAU rather than by the physical cabling.

Cable segments can range from 148 ft–656 ft (depending whether the cable is shielded or unshielded), and requires a minimum of 8 ft between computers. A segment will support up to 72 computers using unshielded cable, though up to 260 computers can be supported on a segment with shielded cable. Rings can be connected through the use of bridges. Although Ethernet is more popular, many large companies are selecting token ring architecture to support mission-critical applications.

Token Ring Packets

The token ring packet is a bit more involved than an Ethernet packet, but contains the same essential information. A *start delimiter* indicates the start of a packet, and *access control* information describes the packet as a token (being passed around the network) or data (having a specific destination). *Packet control* information will carry details for all computers, or only for one computer. The packet is directed with a *destination address* and *source address*, and then the data to be transferred is included. Data may also include network commands or status information. A *packet check sequence* will provide CRC error-checking information, and an *end delimiter* marks the end of the packet. *Packet status* information is tagged onto the packet that tells whether the packet was recognized or copied, or if the destination address was even available. This information is passed back to the sending computer.

Token Ring Operation

Now is a good time to review token ring operation. When the network initializes, a token is generated that then travels around the ring and polls each computer until one of the computers wants to transmit data—that computer then takes control of the token. After a computer captures the token, it sends a data packet out to the network. The packet proceeds around the ring until it reaches the computer with the address that matches the destination in that packet. The destination computer copies the frame into a receive buffer, and updates the packet's Packet Status field to indicate that the information was received. The updated packet continues around the ring until it arrives back at the sending computer. The sending computer acknowledges the successful transmission, then removes the packet from the ring and transmits a new token back to the ring. It is important to remember that a computer cannot transmit unless it has possession of the token, and no other computer can transmit data while the token is in use by a computer. Only one token at a time can be active on the network, and the token can travel in only one direction around the ring.

System Monitoring and Fault Tolerance

One major advantage of the token ring architecture is its self-monitoring (or self-diagnosing) capability. Normally, the first computer to come online in a token ring network is assigned to monitor network activity. The monitoring computer verifies that packets are being delivered and received correctly by checking for packets that have circulated the ring more than once (and ensuring that only one token is on the network at a time). This monitoring process is called *beaconing*. A beacon announcement is produced every seven seconds. The beacon is passed from computer to computer throughout the entire ring. If a station does not receive an expected announcement from a PC upstream, it tries to notify the network. It sends a message of the neighbor that did not respond and attempts to diagnose the problem without disrupting the entire network. If a correction cannot be made automatically, service will be required.

In addition, MAUs incorporate a certain amount of fault tolerance. When one computer fails in a "true" token-passing network, the token cannot be passed and the network fails. MAUs are designed to detect a NIC failure and disconnect that computer from the network. This bypasses the failed PC so that the token can continue on to the next subsequent computer. This means a faulty computer or connection will not affect the rest of the token ring network.

CHECKPOINT

✔ **Objective 1.01: Network Basics**   Networks connect computers together in order to share files, resources, and even applications.

✔ **Objective 1.02: Network Types**   There are peer-to-peer and server-based networks. A networked computer that provides resources is called a *server*. The computer accessing those resources is referred to as a *workstation* or *client*. Server-based networks allow resources, security, and administration to all be handled from a single central location.

✔ **Objective 1.03: Network Topology** Bus, star, and ring are the three major topologies used in current networks. A *bus* topology connects all PCs in a single line (or "trunk"). Bus networks use terminators to prevent signal bounce across the cabling. A *star* topology connects all PCs to a single central hub without the use of terminators, but a hub failure can disable the entire network. The *ring* topology connects all PCs in a logical "loop," and uses a token to pass control of the network from system to system.

✔ **Objective 1.04: Network Hardware** A *bridge* can act like a repeater to extend the effective length of a network cable, but it can also divide a network to isolate excessive traffic or problem data. A *router* knows the address of each segment, determines the best path for sending data, and filters broadcast traffic to the local segment. A *gateway* can perform complex functions such as translating between networks that speak different languages (using techniques such as protocol and bandwidth conversion). The network interface card (or NIC, and also known as a LAN adapter) functions as an interface between the individual computer (server or client) and the network cabling.

✔ **Objective 1.05: Network Media** Cabling (or network media) comes in many different configurations, including unshielded twisted pair (UTP), coaxial cable, shielded twisted pair (STP), and fiber-optic (FO) cable. Coaxial cables are available in thinnet and thicknet versions. There are five categories of unshielded twisted-pair (UTP) cable. IBM cabling is separated into nine categories.

✔ **Objective 1.06: Network Architectures** Access methods regulate the flow of traffic on the network. There are three major access methods: CSMA, token passing, and demand priority. There are several types of Ethernet: 10BaseT, 10Base2, 10Base5, 10BaseFL, 100BaseVG, and 100BaseX. Token ring passes control from PC to PC through the use of special packets (called "tokens").

REVIEW QUESTIONS

1. A networked computer that provides resources is called a…

   A. Peer
   B. Node
   C. Server
   D. Client

2. A document that is loaded into your workstation's memory so that you can edit or use it locally is typically stored on a...

   A. Database server
   B. File and print server
   C. Web server
   D. Telnet server

3. The notion of dependable and consistent server operation is termed...

   A. Scalability
   B. Availability
   C. Reliability
   D. Redundancy

4. Grouping more than one server to perform the same job in the network is called...

   A. Clustering
   B. Failover
   C. Redundancy
   D. Scalability

5. Which topology connects computers to each other in a straight line along a single main cable called a trunk?

   A. Line
   B. Star
   C. Ring
   D. Bus

6. Which topology connects all PCs on the network to a central connection point called a hub?

   A. Line
   B. Star
   C. Ring
   D. Bus

7. Which topology/architecture will shut down if the MAU fails?

   A. Line
   B. Star
   C. Ring
   D. Bus

8. What kind of network hardware can also divide a network to isolate excessive traffic or problem data?

    A. Repeater

    B. Amplifier

    C. Bridge

    D. Patch panel

9. RG-58 is a type of…

    A. Coaxial cable

    B. Shielded twisted pair

    C. Unshielded twisted pair

    D. Fiber-optic cable

10. 10BaseT is a form of…

    A. Token ring

    B. ARCnet

    C. Gigabit Ethernet

    D. 10Mbps Ethernet

REVIEW ANSWERS

1. **C** Server: A server provides network resources which are requested by a workstation (or client). This is different than a peer-to-peer network where each member of the network can provide resources.

2. **B** File and print server: File and print servers manage the user's overall access and use of file and printer resources. The document stored on the file and print server is loaded into your workstation's memory so that you can edit or use it locally.

3. **C** Reliability: Reliability refers to dependable and consistent operation—the probability that a component or system will perform a task for a specified period of time—and is often measured as a function of the time between system failures using the term *MTBF* (mean time between failure).

4. **A** Clustering: Server clusters employ two or more server PCs that act like a single server to provide higher availability and performance than a single server could handle. Applications can move from one server to another, or run on several servers at once, and all transactions are transparent to end users.

5. **D** Bus: With a bus, computers are connected to each other in a straight line along a single main cable called a trunk (also called a backbone or segment). The bus is the simplest and most straightforward type of network topology, and is commonly used with Ethernet networks.

6. **B** Star: The star topology connects all PCs on the network to a central connection point called a hub. A star network is a bit more robust than the bus approach because connections are direct from the PC to the hub, so it's an easy matter to add clients to the network simply by connecting them to an available port in the hub.

7. **C** Ring: The computers in a token ring topology are constantly receiving and retransmitting tokens from one computer to the next. Since token rings also use MAUs to pass data from one PC to the next, a MAU failure can disable the network.

8. **C** Bridge: A bridge offers more features for a busy network. A bridge can act like a repeater to extend the effective length of a network cable, but a bridge has more "intelligence," and can also divide a network to isolate excessive traffic or problem data.

9. **A** Coaxial cable: Thinnet cable is thin (roughly 0.25 inches in diameter), presents a 50Ω impedance to data signals, and can carry electrical signals for over 600 ft. The cable industry refers to this common type of cable as RG-58.

10. **D** 10Mbps Ethernet: 10BaseT is an Ethernet standard designed to support 10Mbps baseband data transmission over Category 3, 4, or 5 twisted-pair cable (UTP).

Network
Software
Concepts

	NEWBIE	SOME EXPERIENCE	EXPERT
ETA	5 hours	3 hours	1 hour

As you learned in the last chapter, networks rely on cabling and communication devices to interconnect the hardware of individual PCs. Still, hardware is not enough to make a network operate. Computers need an operating system to organize the safe sharing of files and equipment, and all of the information shared across a network must use a protocol (or language) that has been approved by one or more international standards organizations. This chapter explains the role of a network operating system and studies the major attributes of today's popular NOS types. You'll also learn how network protocols are used to keep information flowing error free between servers and workstations. You'll even learn about some communication techniques used to connect networks beyond their typical physical limits.

Objective 2.01   Network Operating Systems

Networks are much more than just a series of PCs cobbled together with cabling and communications devices. The whole purpose of networks is to share resources (such as applications, files, messages, printers, scanners, and so on) between those PCs. Sharing requires an operating system (software) that is able to manage the many files and devices that are made available to the network, yet keep those resources secure from intrusion and unauthorized use. This is the role of a *network operating system* (NOS). This part of the chapter introduces the concepts of an NOS and outlines some features that make them different from stand-alone operating systems.

Network Support

The first thing to understand about an NOS is the way network support is added. Some NOS versions simply add networking features "on top" of the PC's existing operating system, while other NOS versions fully integrate network support into the PC's operating system so a stand-alone OS isn't needed. Novell's NetWare 4.x and 5.x are probably the most familiar and popular examples of an NOS where the client computer's networking support is added on top of its existing computer operating system. This means the desktop computer needs *both* operating systems in order to handle stand-alone and networking functions together. By contrast, most operating systems include networking support natively, such as Windows 2000 Server, Windows 2000 Professional, Windows NT Server, Windows NT Workstation, Windows 98, Windows 95, and AppleTalk. While these integrated operating systems have some advantages, they do not preclude using other NOS versions. Keep in mind that either approach has its own unique benefits and limitations, and you'll see more about these trade-offs later in the chapter.

Multitasking Support

Networks are busy places, and users often must wait for access (even though the wait may only be a few milliseconds) while the server tackles one task at a time. If the server could actually work on more than one task simultaneously, network performance could be substantially improved. A *multitasking* operating system provides the means for a server to process more than one task at a time, and a true multitasking operating system can run as many tasks as there are processors. For example, if a server has four processors, a true multitasking OS can run four tasks simultaneously. More commonly, there are more tasks than processors, and the computer must arrange for the available processors to devote a certain amount of time to each task—alternating between tasks until all tasks are completed. With this approach, the computer appears to be working on several tasks at once. There are two primary forms of multitasking:

- **Preemptive**   The operating system can take control of the processor without the task's cooperation. This is often a more versatile approach in a network because the preemptive system can shift CPU activity from a local task to a network task if the situation requires it.
- **Nonpreemptive**   The task itself decides when to give up control of the processor. Programs written for nonpreemptive multitasking systems must include provisions for yielding control of the processor. No other program can run until the nonpreemptive program has given up control of the processor. This is also called *cooperative multitasking*.

Travel Advisory

Preemptive multitasking is the most common and widely used form of multitasking because of its versatility.

Interoperability

Another NOS issue to consider is *interoperability*—the ability of computer operating systems to function and access resources in different environments. This is particularly important when setting up a multivendor network environment. For example, a NetWare server can interoperate with other servers such as Windows NT, and users of Apple computers can interoperate with both NetWare and Windows NT servers. Each NOS addresses interoperability in different ways, so you should understand your own network's interoperability requirements when evaluating each operating system. A peer-to-peer network offers relatively poor security and interoperability because of the limitations inherent in that approach. Security and interoperability is much better on a server-based network.

Local Lingo

Interoperability   The capability of computer operating systems to function and access resources in different environments.

Server Side or Client Side

You'll also need to determine whether interoperability will be provided as a service on the server side or as a client-side application on each networked computer. Server-side interoperability is easier to manage because it is centrally located (like other services). By comparison, client-side interoperability requires software installation and configuration at each computer. This can make interoperability much more difficult to manage. In actual practice, it is common to find both methods (a network service on the server and network client applications at each computer) in a single network. For example, Microsoft Windows network interoperability is achieved with a network client application at each personal computer.

Travel Advisory

You will rarely find only client or server-side interoperability. Most networks provide interoperability features on *both* the server and client side.

Client and Server Software

Normally, a computer's operating system organizes and controls the interaction between the computer hardware and the software (i.e., the applications) that are running. An operating system manages the allocation and use of memory (RAM), processor time, disk access (reading and writing), and peripheral devices (such as video, keyboard, mouse, I/O ports, and so on). In a client/server network environment, this goes a step further, and you'll find that the operating systems used in client and server computers are a bit different. Server network software provides resources to the network clients, and client network software makes those resources available to the client computer. The server and client operating systems are coordinated so that all portions of the network function properly. Network client/server software also offers security by controlling access to data and peripherals.

Client Software

In an individual PC, a user types a command that requires the computer to perform a task. The computer's CPU processes this request. For example, if you want to see a directory listing on one of the local hard disks, the CPU interprets and executes the request and then displays the results in a directory listing in the window. This is a bit different in a network when a user requests a resource that exists on a server in another part of the network. The request has to be forwarded (or redirected) out of the client and onto the network, and from there to the server with the requested resource. This forwarding activity is performed by the *redirector*. A redirector is sometimes referred to as the shell or the requester, depending on the particular networking software. The redirector is a small section of code in the NOS that intercepts requests in the computer and determines if the requests should be handled by the local computer or be redirected over the network to another computer or server.

Local Lingo
Redirector   Part of the NOS that intercepts requests and determines if the requests should be handled by the local computer or be transferred over the network to another computer or server.

Redirection starts in the client computer when a user issues a request for a network resource or service. The user's computer is referred to as a client because it is making a request of a server. The request is intercepted by the redirector and forwarded out onto the network. The server processes the connection requested by the client's redirectors and gives them access to the resources they request. The server fulfills the request made by the client. Using redirection, clients don't need to be concerned with the actual location of data or peripherals, or with the complexities of making a connection. To access data on a network computer, a user only needs to type the drive designator assigned to the location of the resource, and the redirector determines the actual routing.

This offers some powerful advantages. Suppose that you need to access a shared directory, and you have permission to access it. With Windows NT, you could use Windows Explorer to connect to the network drive using the Network Neighborhood icon. You can also map to the drive (*drive mapping* is the assignment of a letter or name to a disk drive so that the operating system or network server can locate it). To map to the drive, right-click the directory icon from the Network Neighborhood icon. A dialog box will allow you to assign an available letter of the alphabet as a drive designator (such as G:). Thereafter, you can refer to the shared directory on the remote computer as G: and the redirector will locate it. The redirector also keeps track of which drive designators are associated with which network resources.

Redirectors can send requests to peripherals as well as to shared directories. The request is redirected away from the originating computer and sent over the network to the target. For example, the target may be a print server for the requested printer. With redirection, LPT1 or COM1 can refer to network printers instead of local printers. The redirector will intercept any print job going to LPT1 and forward it out of the client machine to the specified network printer.

Server Software

With networking software for the server, users at client computers can share the server's data and peripherals (including printers, plotters, directories, and so on). Consider a user requesting a directory listing on a shared remote hard disk. The request is forwarded by the redirector onto the network, where it is passed to the file and print server containing the shared directory. The request is granted and the directory listing is provided back to the client.

In simplest terms, server network software allows sharing and security. *Sharing* is a term used to describe resources made publicly available for access by users on the network. Most network operating systems not only allow sharing, but also determine the degree of sharing. Server software can provide different

| **Exam Tip** |
| A server is not an open book to the network—only server resources that are set up to be "shared" can be accessed across the network. |

resources to users with different levels of access (that is, users with higher access can use more of the server's resources). Server-side software also coordinates access to resources so that two users do not use the same resource at the same time. As an example, suppose an office manager wants everyone on the network to be familiar with a certain document. The document can be placed on the server to be shared, but access can be controlled so that all users can read it, but only users with a certain level of access will be able to edit it.

Network operating systems also provide security by allowing a network administrator to determine which users (or groups) can access network resources. A network administrator can use the server's network software to create user privileges that define who gets to use the network. The administrator can grant or deny user privileges on the network, and remove users from the list of authorized users. By organizing individuals into groups, the administrator can assign privileges to the group (rather than individually). All group members have the same privileges that have been assigned to the group as a whole. When a new user joins the network, the administrator can simply assign the new user to the appropriate group—with its accompanying rights and privileges.

Finally, some advanced server-side network software includes management tools to help administrators keep track of network behavior. If a problem develops on the network, management tools can detect signs of trouble and present the corresponding data in a chart or other suitable format. With these management tools, the network administrator can take corrective action before the problem halts the network.

Novell NetWare

NetWare is one of Novell's most popular network operating systems due to its impressive interoperability. The NetWare operating system employs both network server and network client applications. The client application is designed to run on top of a variety of client operating systems. The server application can be accessed by client computers running under DOS, Windows (3.x, 95, and 98/SE, NT, and Windows 2000), OS/2, AppleTalk, or UNIX. Consequently, NetWare is often the preferred operating system in large networks with mixed operating

Travel Assistance

You can learn more about NetWare features and support from Novell at www.novell.com.

system environments. In small networks, however, NetWare can be difficult and cumbersome for an inexperienced network technician.

NetWare Versions and Features

NetWare version 3.2 is a 32-bit network operating system that supports Windows 3.x/95/98, and NT, along with UNIX, Mac OS, and DOS environments. With NetWare 4.11 (also called IntranetWare), Novell introduced its new Novell Directory Services (NDS). NetWare 5.x addresses the integration of LANs, WANs, network applications, intranets, and the Internet into a single global network.

Novell Directory Services (NDS) provides name services as well as security, routing, messaging, management, Web publishing, and file/print services. Using a directory architecture called X.500, it organizes all network resources (including users, groups, printers, servers, and volumes). NDS also provides a single-point logon for the user, so a user can log on to any server on the network and have access to all their usual user rights and privileges.

File Services   NetWare file services are part of the NDS database. Remember that NDS provides a single-point logon for users, and allows users and administrators alike to view network resources in the same way, but you can also view the entire network in a format that is native to your workstation's operating system. For example, a Windows NT client can map a logical drive to any NetWare file server volume or directory, and the NetWare resources will appear as logical drives on their computer. Such logical drives function just like any other drive in their workstation's computer.

Security Services   NetWare provides extensive security. Logon security provides an authentication of the user's identity based on username, passwords, and time and account restrictions. Trustee rights control which directories and files a user can access (and what they're able to do with them). Directory and file attributes can identify the kinds of actions that can be performed on a file (i.e., read only, write to, copy, share, or delete).

Printing Services   Printing services are totally transparent to the client computer's user. Any print request from a client is redirected to the file server, where it is handed off to a print server and, finally, sent to the printer (though the same computer can serve as both file server and printer server). You can share printers that are attached to the server, attached to a workstation, or attached directly to the network by means of the device's own network interface card (NIC). NetWare print services can support up to 256 printers.

Messaging Services NetWare allows users to send a short message to other users on the network. Messages can be sent to groups as well as to individuals. If all of the intended recipients are in the same group, you'd simply address the message to the group rather than to each individual. Users can also disable or enable the reception for their workstations. When a user disables reception, no broadcast messages will be received by that workstation. Messages can also be handled through the *message handling service* (MHS). MHS can be installed on any server and configured to provide a complete messaging system for e-mail distribution. MHS supports most popular e-mail programs.

NetWare Interoperability

Other operating systems provide client software that supports interoperability with NetWare servers. For example, Windows NT provides Gateway Services for NetWare (GSNW). This service allows a server on the Windows NT network to act as a gateway to the NetWare network. Any workstations on the Windows NT network can request resources or services available on the NetWare network, but they must make the request through the Windows NT server. The server will then act as a client on the NetWare network, passing requests between the two networks. With GSNW service, a Windows NT server can obtain access to NetWare file and print services.

Windows 2000

Built on Windows NT technology, the fully integrated Windows 2000 NOS offers built-in Web and application services, Internet-standard security, and good performance. Released in early 2000, it has quickly become a popular operating system for doing business on the Internet. Windows 2000 readily scales from one or two servers with a few dozen clients to hundreds of servers and thousands of clients. It's also regarded as a reliable operating system. Given the recent release of Windows 2000, it is the best operating system to take advantage of the latest PC hardware (i.e., from small mobile devices to the largest, most powerful servers for e-commerce). Windows 2000 is available in several major variations to best match your particular networking situation:

- **Windows 2000 Professional** Supporting up to two CPUs and 4GB of RAM. A reliable operating system for business desktops and notebook computers that is intended for Internet and mobile users. Windows 2000 Professional does not support clustering.
- **Windows 2000 Server** Windows 2000 Server is an entry-level server software version intended for file, print, intranet, and infrastructure

servers. This version will support up to four CPUs and 4GB of RAM and does not support clustering.

- **Windows 2000 Advanced Server**   Windows 2000 Advanced Server provides improved reliability, availability, and scalability for running e-commerce and line-of-business applications. You'll get support for up to eight CPUs and 8GB of RAM, and clustering support for two-node failover and 32-node network load balancing.
- **Windows 2000 Datacenter Server**   Windows Datacenter Server is the most powerful server operating system offered by Microsoft. Datacenter Server is intended for enterprises that demand the highest levels of availability and scale. You'll be able to use up to 32 CPUs and 64GB of RAM, along with cascading failover among four clustered nodes and 32-node network load balancing.

Travel Assistance

You can learn more about Windows 2000 features and support from Microsoft at www.microsoft.com/windows/default.asp.

Windows 2000 Features

Windows 2000 Professional is easier to deploy, manage, and support. Centralized management utilities, troubleshooting tools, and support for "self-healing" applications all make it simpler for administrators and users to deploy and manage desktop and laptop computers. In turn, these improvements pay off in reduced costs. It combines the power and security of Windows NT Workstation with the traditional ease of use of Windows 98. It also provides more wizards, a centralized location for common tasks, and menus that adapt to the way you work. When you use Windows 2000 Professional in conjunction with Windows 2000 Server, you can take advantage of IntelliMirror technologies. This technology lets you store your important information and desktop settings on a central computer. IntelliMirror lets you work on any computer attached to your network as if you are at your own desk.

    Windows 2000 Professional includes fundamental improvements to reliability (such as modifications to the operating system core to prevent crashes and the ability for the operating system to repair itself) that make it the most reliable desktop operating system Microsoft has ever produced. Windows 2000 also provides comprehensive security features to protect sensitive business data—both locally on your workstation and as it is transmitted over your local area network, phone lines, or the Internet. With its support for Internet-standard security features (such as IP Security, Layer 2 Tunneling Protocol, and Virtual Private Networking), Windows 2000 is considered to be so secure that banks use it.

Windows 2000 Interoperability

The Windows 2000 operating system provides or supports a wide range of protocols. Virtually any other platform client can use Windows 2000 Server–based servers, and clients running Windows 2000 Professional can interoperate with server platforms from Novell, IBM, and others. Windows 2000 interoperability includes support for a number of common communications and security protocols, including Transmission Control Protocol/Internet Protocol (TCP/IP), Lightweight Directory Access Protocol (LDAP), Dynamic Host Configuration Protocol (DHCP), the Domain Name Service (DNS) protocol, and the Kerberos version 5 authentication protocol. With this support, Windows 2000 can communicate with operating systems such as Novell NetWare, Macintosh, HP/UX, Solaris, IBM AIX, and Linux; with directory-based services such as Novell NDS, Lotus Notes, Exchange, and LDAP-based directories; and with database platforms, such as those from IBM, Informix, and Oracle.

Services for UNIX version 2.0 provides components used to integrate Windows 2000 into existing UNIX environments. This add-on software delivers password synchronization, a Network Information Service (NIS) server, an NIS-to-Active Directory Migration Wizard, a username mapping service, and Network File System (NFS) server, client, and gateway software. Microsoft Interix 2.2 provides an environment for running UNIX-based applications and scripts on the Windows NT and Windows 2000 operating systems. For IBM support, the Host Integration Server (a successor to SNA Server) lets you integrate the Windows operating system with other non-Windows enterprise systems running on systems such as IBM mainframes, AS/400, and UNIX.

Services for Macintosh is an integrated component of Windows 2000 Server and includes File Server for Macintosh, Print Server for Macintosh, and support for AppleTalk Protocol and AppleTalk Control Protocol (ATCP). Services for Macintosh makes it possible for computers running the Windows and Macintosh operating systems to share files and printers. A computer running Windows 2000 Server with Services for Macintosh installed can function as a file server, remote access server, and print server for Macintosh client computers. In addition, Windows 2000 Server can perform the functions of an AppleTalk router.

Sold as a separate product, Services for NetWare version 5.0 allows Windows 2000 Professional–based clients (and Windows 2000 Server–based servers) to communicate with NetWare-based servers. Services for NetWare includes File and Print Services for NetWare versions 4.0 and 5.0, Directory Service Manager for NetWare, Microsoft Directory Synchronization Services (MSDSS), and File Migration Utility. In addition, Windows 2000 has several built-in technologies that support NetWare. For example, Client Services for NetWare allows Windows 2000 Professional–based clients to connect to resources on NetWare-based servers. Gateway Service for NetWare allows Windows 2000–based servers to communicate with NetWare-based servers.

Windows NT

Unlike the NetWare operating system, Windows NT combines the computer and network operating systems into one integrated platform. Windows NT Server configures a computer to provide server functions and resources across the network, while Windows NT Workstation provides client functions to the network.

Travel Assistance

You can learn more about Windows NT features and support from Microsoft at www.microsoft.com/windows/default.asp.

Windows NT Versions and Features

Windows NT operates on a domain model—a *domain* is a collection of computers that share a common database and security policy, and each domain has a unique name (you'll find that the idea of domains will be very important when actually setting up accounts and groups in Windows networks). Within each domain, one server must be designated as the primary domain controller (PDC). This PDC server maintains the directory services and authenticates any users that log on. Windows NT directory services can be implemented in various ways by using the account and security database. There are several different domain models to choose from. A *single-domain* network maintains the security and accounts database. A *single-master* network may have several domains, but one is designated as the master and maintains the user account information. A *multiple-master* network includes several domains, but the accounts database is maintained on more than one server. This approach is used for very large organizations. A *complete-trust* network uses several domains, but no single domain is designated as a master. All domains work together smoothly. The combination of Windows NT Server and Windows NT Workstation can provide a powerful suite of file, security, printing, and network services to the system.

File Services   There are two approaches for sharing files on a Windows NT network. First, there is simple file sharing, just as there is on a peer-to-peer network. Any workstation or server can publicly share a directory in the network, and set the attributes of that data (i.e., no access, read only, modify, or full access). One difference between Windows NT and other operating systems (like Windows 95/98) is that in order to share a Windows NT resource, you must have administrative privileges. The other method of sharing takes full advantage of Windows NT security features. You can assign directory-level and file-level permissions, so it's possible to restrict access to specified individuals or groups. You will need to use the Windows NT file system (NTFS). During the installation of Windows NT, you can choose between an NTFS or a FAT16 (DOS) file system. You can install both file systems on different hard drives (or on different partitions of a single hard drive), but when the computer is running in DOS mode, the NTFS directories will be unavailable. Any client not using NTFS can share to the network, but is limited to public sharing and cannot take advantage of NTFS security features.

Exam Tip

Windows 98 uses FAT32 file system. Windows NT is not compatible with FAT32, so NT cannot be installed on a FAT32 system, and will not recognize any files on a FAT32 partition.

Security Services   Windows NT provides security for any resource on the network. A Windows NT network domain server maintains all the account records, manages permissions, and stores user rights. To access any resource on the network, a user must have the rights to complete a task and the permission to use that resource.

Printing Services   In a Windows NT network, any client or server can function as a print server. When sharing a printer on the network, it becomes available to anyone on the network (subject to sharing rules established for the network).

When installing a printer, designate the printer as a local printer (My Computer) or a network printer. If you choose the network printer, a dialog box will appear listing all of the available network printers—simply select the one you want to use. Remember that you can install more than one printer on the network. If you're installing a local printer, you'll be asked if you want to share the printer with the network for others to use.

Network Services   Windows NT provides several services to help facilitate a smooth-running network. Messenger service monitors the network and receives instant messages for you. Alert service sends notifications that are received by the messenger service. Browser service provides a list of servers available on domains and workgroups. Workstation service runs on a workstation and is responsible for connections to servers (this is also referred to as the redirector). Server service provides network access to the resources on a computer.

Windows NT Interoperability

The NWLink network protocol makes Windows NT compatible with NetWare. The first service is Gateway Services for NetWare (GSNW). All Windows NT clients within a domain must contact a NetWare server through a single source, and GSNW provides the gateway connection between a Windows NT domain and a NetWare server. This works well for slow networks, but can impair performance as the number of requests increases. Client Services for NetWare (CSNW) enables a Windows NT Workstation to access file and print services on a NetWare server—it is included as part of GSNW. File and Print Service for NetWare (FPNW) allows NetWare clients to access Windows NT file and print services (this is not a part of the Windows NT package, and must be purchased separately). The Directory Service Manager for NetWare (DSMN) add-on utility integrates

---

Travel Advisory

Computers running Windows 95 or 98/SE will also work well as clients on Windows NT and NetWare LANs. You'll need to install the respective client software. However, Windows 95/98 users cannot fully benefit from Windows NT security features—those features use the NTFS file format, which is not compatible with Windows 95 or 98.

NetWare and Windows NT user and group account information. Finally, the Migration tool for NetWare is used by administrators converting from NetWare to Windows NT—it sends NetWare account information to a Windows NT domain controller.

Objective 2.02   Network Standards

As you've seen, networks are typically collections of hardware and software cobbled together from a number of manufacturers. Because the whole point of networking is *communication*, it is absolutely vital that each vendor creates products that are fundamentally compatible with one another. By adopting a series of standards, the networking industry can ensure product compatibility. With the explosive growth of networks, and the global reach of the Internet, the need for network standards has become more acute than ever. This part of the chapter explores network standards in more detail.

The OSI Model

A network is used to send data from one computer to another. While this might seem like a simple goal, the actual practice of network communication can be a complex process involving numerous tasks at different hardware and software levels. In 1978, the International Organization for Standardization (ISO) authored a set of specifications that described a network architecture for connecting dissimilar devices. This original document applied to systems that were "open" to each other because they could all use the same protocols and standards to exchange information. By 1984, the ISO had updated this model and dubbed it the *Open Systems Interconnection* (OSI) *reference model.*

The OSI reference model represents the seven layers (or levels) at which data is packaged and transmitted from a sending application, through the physical wires of a network, to the receiving application, as shown in Figure 2-1. It describes how network hardware and software work together in order to make communications possible. Today, the OSI model is the best known and most widely used guide for visualizing networking environments. Manufacturers adhere to the OSI reference model when they design network products. The model also helps to troubleshoot problems by explaining how components are supposed to function.

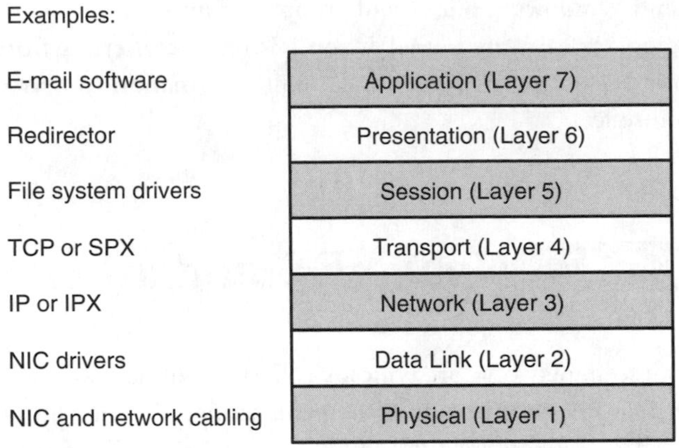

Examples:

E-mail software	Application (Layer 7)
Redirector	Presentation (Layer 6)
File system drivers	Session (Layer 5)
TCP or SPX	Transport (Layer 4)
IP or IPX	Network (Layer 3)
NIC drivers	Data Link (Layer 2)
NIC and network cabling	Physical (Layer 1)

FIGURE 2-1   The OSI reference model

Understanding the Layers

The OSI reference model divides network communication into seven layers, where each layer covers different network activities, equipment, or protocols. The reference model defines how each layer communicates and interacts with the layers immediately above and below it. The following sections describe the purpose of each layer, and identify the services provided to adjacent layers. Normally, the OSI reference model starts at the top (layer 7, or the application layer) and works down to the bottom (layer 1, or the physical layer).

- **Application**   Layer 7 (the application layer) is the highest layer of the OSI reference model. This layer handles the services that directly support user applications (such as software for file transfers, database access, e-mail, and so on). The application layer serves as a window through which applications can access network services. For example, a message to be sent across the network enters the OSI reference model at this point, and exits the OSI reference model's application layer on the receiving computer. Application layer protocols can be programs in themselves such as File Transfer Protocol (FTP), or they can be used by other programs such as Simple Mail Transfer Protocol (SMTP)—which is employed by most e-mail programs to redirect data to the network. Subsequent layers support the tasks that are performed at the application layer (including general network access, flow control, and error detection/recovery).

- **Presentation**   Layer 6 (the presentation layer) describes the format used to exchange data among networked computers. The presentation layer is responsible for converting protocols, translating data, encrypting/decrypting data, changing or converting the character set, and expanding graphics commands. The presentation layer also manages data compression to reduce the number of bits that need to be transmitted. In a sending computer, the presentation layer translates data from the application layer's format into a commonly recognized intermediary format. At the receiving computer, the presentation layer translates this intermediary format back into a format needed by that computer's application layer. The redirector (which redirects I/O operations to resources on a server) operates at this level.

- **Session**   Layer 5 (the session layer) allows two applications on different computers to open, use, and close a connection (called a session)—a structured dialog between two workstations. The session layer is responsible for handling this dialog. It supports name recognition and security features that are needed to allow two applications to communicate over the network. The session layer breaks data into smaller groups for error detection. If the network fails, only the data after the last group has to be resent. This layer also manages the dialog between communicating processes (i.e., which side transmits, when it transmits, and how long it transmits).

- **Transport**   Layer 4 (the transport layer) ensures that packets are delivered error free, in the proper order, and without losses or duplications. At the sending computer, this layer repackages messages by separating long messages into several packets, and collecting small packets together into one package. This process ensures that packets are transmitted efficiently over the network. At the receiving computer, the transport layer opens the packets, reassembles the original messages, and usually sends an acknowledgment that the message was received. If a duplicate packet arrives, this layer will recognize the duplicate and discard it. The transport layer provides flow control and error handling. Transmission Control Protocol (TCP) and Sequenced Packet Exchange (SPX) are examples of transport layer protocols.

- **Network**   Layer 3 (the network layer) addresses messages and translates logical addresses and names into physical addresses. This layer also determines the route from the source to the destination computer. It determines which path the data should take based on network conditions and priorities. The network layer also manages traffic problems on the network (such as switching and routing packets, and easing traffic congestion).

For example, if the network adapter on a router cannot transmit as much data as the source computer sends, the network layer on the router will break the data into smaller units. At the destination system, the network layer reassembles the data. Internet Protocol (IP) and Internetwork Packet Exchange (IPX) are examples of network layer protocols.

- **Data Link**   Layer 2 (the data link layer) sends data frames from the network layer to the physical layer. It controls the electrical signals that travel across the network cable. On the receiving end, the data link layer organizes raw bits from the physical layer into packets. The bit patterns, encoding methods, and tokens are known to this layer only. The data link layer is responsible for providing error-free transfer of these packets from one computer to another through the physical layer. This allows the network layer to enjoy virtually error-free transmission over the network connection. The receiving data link layer detects any problems with the packet that might have occurred during transmission, and packets that were damaged during transmission (or not acknowledged) are then resent.

- **Physical**   Layer 1 (the physical layer, sometimes called the hardware layer) transmits a stream of raw data over a physical medium (i.e., the network cable). The physical layer is entirely hardware, and involves all aspects of establishing and maintaining a physical link between communicating computers. This layer defines how the cable is attached to a NIC. For example, it defines how many pins the connector has and the function of each pin. The physical layer also defines which transmission techniques will be used to send data over the network cable. The physical layer also provides data encoding and bit synchronization.

Exam Tip

It is important to realize that all levels above layer 1 are basically software (for example, firmware on the NIC or programs loaded into RAM).

Data Packets

Information to be sent across the network starts at the application layer and descends through all seven layers. Data packets are also assembled and disassembled according to the OSI reference model, so packet creation begins in the application layer where data is generated. As the packet descends through each layer, information vital to that layer is added to the data. This additional information is intended for the corresponding layer in the receiving computer. You can see how this works in Figure 2-2. For example, a data link layer in the receiving computer will read information added by the data link layer in the sending computer. At the transport layer, the original block of data is broken down into the actual packets where a suitable protocol defines the packet structure used by the two computers. The transport layer adds sequence information that guides the receiving computer in reassembling the data from packets. When the packets finally pass through the physical layer on their way to the cable, they contain information from each of the other six layers.

Most packets on a network are intended for a specific computer, and get the attention of only that particular computer. Each NIC "sees" all the packets sent on its cable segment, but it interrupts the computer for reception *only* if the packet address matches that specific NIC address. A broadcast-type address can also be used. Packets sent with a broadcast address can be received simultaneously by many computers on the network. In large networks that cover entire regions (or even countries) and offer numerous possible communication routes, the network's connectivity and switching components (i.e., bridges and gateways) use the packet's addressing information to determine the best route for addressing individual packets. With *packet forwarding*, computers send a packet on to the next

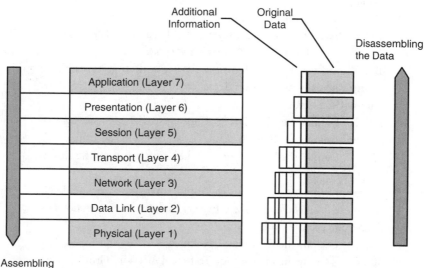

FIGURE 2-2   Adding information through the OSI model

appropriate network component based on the address in the packet's header. With *packet filtering*, computers use criteria (such as a destination address) to select specific packets for reception.

OSI and IEEE 802

Although the bottom two layers of the OSI model (physical and data link layers) refer to network hardware such as the NIC and cabling, there is still a lot of latitude in the way hardware is implemented on a network. In February of 1980, the Institute of Electrical and Electronics Engineers (the IEEE) refined many of the hardware requirements for network applications. These refinements were dubbed the "802 project," and the standards that were eventually developed became known as the IEEE 802.x specifications. IEEE 802.x specifications set standards for network interface cards, WAN components, and components used for twisted-pair and coaxial cable networks. IEEE 802.x also provides enhancements to the OSI model that define the ways that a NIC accesses and transfers data over physical media (i.e., connecting, maintaining, and disconnecting network devices). There are 16 standards implemented by IEEE 802.x, and these are listed here:

- **802.1**   Defines internetworking standards related to network management.
- **802.2**   Defines the general standard for a data link layer. The IEEE divides this layer into two sublayers: the LLC and MAC layers (the MAC layer is detailed further in the next standards).
- **802.3**   Defines the MAC layer for bus networks that use carrier-sense multiple access with collision detection (CSMA/CD)—this is the Ethernet standard.
- **802.4**   Defines the MAC layer for bus networks that use a token-passing scheme (i.e., token bus LAN).
- **802.5**   Defines the MAC layer for token ring networks (i.e., token ring LAN).
- **802.6**   Defines standards for metropolitan area networks (MANs), which are usually characterized by very high-speed connections using fiber-optic cables or other digital media.
- **802.7**   Used by the Broadband Technical Advisory Group.
- **802.8**   Used by the Fiber-Optic Technical Advisory Group.
- **802.9**   Defines integrated voice/data networks.
- **802.10**   Defines network security.
- **802.11**   Defines wireless network standards.

- **802.12**   Defines demand priority access LAN (a.k.a. 100BaseVG or AnyLAN).
- **802.13**   Unused.
- **802.14**   Defines cable modem standards.
- **802.15**   Defines wireless personal area networks (WPANs).
- **802.16**   Defines broadband wireless standards.

Exam Tip

You will frequently see network standards defined by IEEE designations as outlined previously.

LLC and MAC Sublayers

After deciding that more detail was needed at the data link layer, the IEEE 802.x standards committee divided the data link layer into two sublayers: LLC and MAC. The Logical Link Control (LLC) sublayer establishes and terminates links, controls packet traffic, sequences packets, and acknowledges packets. The Media Access Control (MAC) sublayer manages media access, delimits packets, checks packet errors, and recognizes packet addresses.

OSI and Device Drivers

A *driver* (often called a device driver) is a small piece of software that enables a computer's operating system to utilize a particular device such as a NIC. Although a device may be correctly installed on a computer, the operating system cannot communicate with the device until a suitable driver for that device has been installed and configured. The driver tells the operating system how to recognize and use the device so that it performs the job it was intended for. During installation, the driver is stored on the local computer's hard disk. The driver is then read from the disk and loaded into RAM each time the PC starts. Drivers are almost always provided by the device manufacturer, and are included on a diskette or CD accompanying the new device. Because NICs play a critical role in connecting a computer to the physical network, it's helpful to look at device drivers and understand how they relate to the OSI model.

You will recall that a redirector is the part of networking software that accepts I/O requests for remote files and then sends (or redirects) them over the network to another computer. Network drivers provide communication between a NIC adapter and network redirector software running in the computer. NIC drivers reside in the MAC sublayer of the OSI reference model (part of the data link layer). The MAC sublayer provides shared access to the physical layer for the NIC. The NIC drivers provide virtual communication between the computer and the NIC—in turn providing a link between the computer and the rest of the network. It is common for a NIC manufacturer to supply drivers to network software makers so that the drivers can be included with the network operating software.

Travel Advisory

Before purchasing a new hardware device, verify that it contains the correct drivers for the specific computer operating system on which it will be installed. If in doubt, consult the manufacturer before you install the device.

Network Driver Interface Specification (NDIS)

The *Network Driver Interface Specification* (NDIS) standard defines a software interface (the NDIS interface) for communication between the MAC sublayer and the protocol drivers. NDIS supports flexible data exchange by permitting the simultaneous use of multiple protocols and drivers. Protocol drivers use this interface to communicate with the NIC adapter. NDIS is handy because it offers protocol multiplexing, so multiple protocol stacks can be used at the same time. NDIS describes three types of network software:

- A *protocol stack* provides network communications. It creates and disassembles packets (control information and data) that are exchanged with the network.
- An *adapter driver* controls the network interface hardware. It works in the MAC sublayer and moves packets between the protocol stack and the NIC hardware.
- The *protocol manager* controls activity between the protocol stack and the MAC.

Travel Advisory

Microsoft and 3Com jointly developed the NDIS specification for use with OS/2 Warp Server and Windows NT Server. Virtually all NIC manufacturers make their cards support these operating systems by supplying NDIS-compliant software drivers.

Open Data Link Interface (ODI)

The *Open Data Link Interface* (ODI) is an alternative specification adopted by Novell and Apple to ease the driver development for their network operating systems. ODI provides support for multiple protocols on a single NIC. Similar to NDIS, ODI allows Novell NetWare drivers to be written without worrying about the protocol that will be used with them. Many NIC manufacturers can make their boards work with these operating systems by supplying ODI-compliant software drivers.

ODI and NDIS are fundamentally incompatible because they present different programming interfaces to the upper layers of the network software. Novell, IBM, and Microsoft offer ODI-to-NDIS translation software to bridge the two interfaces. Fortunately, most NIC manufacturers provide both NDIS and ODI drivers.

Objective 2.03   Network Protocols

Protocols are basically rules and procedures that govern the communication between two or more computers. There are many protocols. While each protocol supports basic communications, each has different purposes intended to accomplish specific tasks. This means each protocol has its own advantages and limitations. Some protocols work only at a particular OSI layer. For instance, a protocol that works at the physical layer would likely ensure that packets pass through the NIC and out onto the network cable. However, protocols can work together as a set (called a protocol stack). Just as a network incorporates functions at every layer of the OSI model, different protocols can work together at different levels in a single protocol stack. The levels in the protocol stack typically correspond to the layers of the OSI model. This part of the chapter provides an introduction to protocols and explains their function in a networking environment.

Local Lingo

Protocol   The rules and procedures that govern the communication between two or more computers.

Protocol Basics

The process by which data is transmitted over the network consists of discrete systematic steps. Specific actions occur each step along the way, and each step includes its own rules and procedures (or protocol). The protocol must be followed consistently on every computer in the network. In the sending computer, these steps must be executed from the top down. In the receiving computer, these steps must be carried out from the bottom up. Protocols at the sending computer break the data into small sections (called packets) that the protocol can handle. Protocols add addressing information to the packets so that the destination computer on the network can identify it. Finally, protocols prepare the data for transmission through the NIC—and out onto the network cable. Protocols on the receiving computer handle these steps in the reverse order by taking data packets off the cable and bringing the packets into the computer through the NIC. Receiving protocols will strip the data packets of all addressing information and copy data to a buffer for reassembly. Reassembled data is passed to the receiving application. It is important that both sending and receiving computers use the same protocols so that they perform each step in the same way. This ensures data has the same format when it is received as it did when it was sent.

Protocol Stacks

A protocol stack is a combination of protocols. Each layer of the stack involves a different protocol that handles a function or subsystem involved in the communication process—each layer has its own set of rules. The protocols define the rules for each layer in the OSI reference model. For example, protocols lower in the stack specify how manufacturers can make their equipment connect to other manufacturers' equipment (i.e., using NICs from several manufacturers on the same LAN). As long as equipment operates with the same protocols, they'll send and receive data from each other. Protocols higher in the stack usually specify rules for conducting communications sessions (i.e., the time during which two computers maintain a connection) and handling applications. The higher a protocol is in the stack, the more sophisticated the tasks and associated applications become. The networking industry has developed several kinds of "standard" stacks as protocol models. Hardware and software manufacturers can develop their products to meet any one (or several) of these protocols.

> ### Exam Tip
>
> TCP and IP are the most well-known protocols available, often combined as TCP/IP, and used with Internet communication.

There are generally three types of protocols that work across the OSI reference model. These are application protocols, transport protocols, and network protocols. Application protocols work at the uppermost layer of the OSI model by providing data exchange between applications. Popular application protocols include AppleTalk/ AppleShare, FTP, Telnet, and SMTP. Transport protocols handle the communication sessions between computers, and ensure that data is able to move reliably between the computers on a network. Popular transport protocols include TCP, SPX, and NetBEUI. Finally, network protocols provide link services—these protocols handle addressing and routing information, error checking, and retransmission requests. Network protocols also define rules for communicating in a major networking environment such as Ethernet or token ring. Popular network protocols include IP and IPX.

Protocol Binding

Protocols must be connected to each other and the NIC. This is known as *binding*. Protocols and NICs can be mixed and matched on an as-needed basis, so binding allows a lot of flexibility in network configurations. For example, two protocol stacks (i.e., IPX/SPX and TCP/IP) can be bound to one NIC. If there is more than one NIC in the computer, one protocol stack can be bound to either or both NICs. The binding order determines the sequence in which an operating system runs the protocols. When multiple protocols are bound to a single NIC, the binding order selects the protocols that will be utilized in order to attempt a successful connection.

> ### Local Lingo
>
> **Binding** The process of linking or connecting one or more protocols to a network interface card (NIC).

A binding process is normally started when either the operating system or the protocol is initialized. As an example, if TCP/IP is the first protocol to be bound, the network operating system will attempt a network connection via TCP/IP before attempting to use another protocol. If this attempt fails, the computer will attempt to make a connection using the next protocol in the binding order. Binding involves more than just binding the protocol stack to the NIC. Protocol stacks need to be bound with the components above and below them so that data can proceed smoothly through the stack during execution. For example, TCP/IP may be bound to the NetBIOS session layer above, as well as to the NIC driver below it. The NIC driver is also bound to the NIC. Figure 2-3 illustrates a typical Network Binding dialog under Windows.

Protocol Management

In most cases, protocols are installed and removed in much the same way that drivers are added and removed. Essential protocols are installed automatically at the

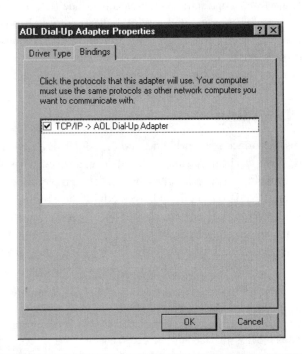

FIGURE 2-3   A typical network binding dialog

same time that the operating system is installed on the computer. To install protocols (such as NWLink) after the initial installation, the network operating system usually includes a utility that leads the administrator through the process. For example, a network operating system setup program might provide a wizard that allows an administrator to install a new protocol, change the protocol binding order, or remove an unneeded or obsolete protocol.

The TCP/IP Protocol

The *Transmission Control Protocol/Internet Protocol* (TCP/IP) is an industry standard suite of protocols that provides communications in a network environment. TCP/IP provides a routable protocol that is suitable for enterprise networking, and even supports access to the Internet and its resources. Designed to be routable, robust, functional, and efficient, TCP/IP has become the de facto standard for *internetworking*—the intercommunication in a network that's composed of smaller networks. Other protocols written specifically to take advantage of TCP/IP's power include SMTP (for e-mail), FTP (for file transfers), and SNMP (for network management).

In actual practice, TCP/IP requires a significant learning curve in order to install and configure it properly. Fortunately, TCP/IP offers several compelling advantages. First, TCP/IP is an industry standard open protocol. This means it is not controlled by a single company and is less subject to compatibility issues. It is the preferred protocol of the Internet. TCP/IP also includes a set of utilities for connecting dissimilar operating systems. This means the ability to communicate between computers does not depend on the network operating system on either system. TCP/IP is scalable, so it can adapt to meet various networking needs. The use of *sockets* (an identifier for a particular service on a given network node) makes the computer operating systems transparent to one another. On the downside, TCP/IP has the disadvantages of relatively large size (and correspondingly slower speed)—though these are not such critical issues on today's operating systems and PC platforms. You can locate more information about TCP/IP standards from www.internic.net.

OSI and TCP/IP

Ideally, TCP/IP should match the OSI reference model, but it does not. Instead of seven distinct layers, TCP/IP uses only four, but each TCP/IP layer corresponds to one or more OSI layers. TCP/IP is broken into the network interface layer, the Internet layer, the transport layer, and the application layer. Taken together, this is known as the *Internet Protocol Suite*. The network interface layer corresponds to the physical and data link layers of the OSI model. This layer communicates directly with the network and provides the interface between the network architecture (i.e., token ring or Ethernet) and the Internet layer. The Internet layer corresponds to the network layer of the OSI model. This layer uses several protocols for routing and delivering packets:

- **Internet Protocol (IP)** IP is a packet-switched protocol that performs addressing and route selection. As a packet is transmitted, this protocol appends a header to the packet so that it can be routed through the network using dynamic routing tables. IP is a connectionless protocol and sends packets without expecting the receiving host to acknowledge receipt. IP is also responsible for packet assembly and disassembly at the physical and data link layers of the OSI model. Each IP packet is made up of a source and a destination address, a protocol identifier, a checksum (an error-checking value), and a TTL (or time to live) value. IP can also determine whether the destination address is local or remote site. If the destination is local, IP will ask the Address Resolution Protocol (ARP) for the hardware address of the destination PC. If the address is remote, the IP checks its local routing table for a route to the destination and sends the packet on its way.

- **Address Resolution Protocol (ARP)** The hardware address of a receiving machine must be determined before an IP packet can be sent. The ARP determines the hardware address (or MAC address) corresponding to an IP address. If ARP does not have the address handy, it requests the address from the network. The packet is then sent on its way, and the new address information is saved.

- **Reverse Address Resolution Protocol (RARP)** A RARP server maintains a database of machine numbers in the form of an ARP table, which is created by the system administrator. Unlike ARP, the RARP protocol provides an IP number to a requesting hardware address. When the RARP server receives a request, it checks its routing table for the machine number and sends the appropriate IP number back to the requester.

- **Internet Control Message Protocol (ICMP)** The ICMP is used by IP to send and receive status reports about information being transmitted. Routers commonly use ICMP to control the flow or speed of data between themselves. If the flow of data is too fast for a given router, it requests that other routers slow down. ICMP messages generally report errors and send queries.

The transport layer corresponds to the transport layer of the OSI model. It is responsible for establishing and maintaining end-to-end communication between network hosts. The transport layer acknowledges receipt, controls data flow, and sequences packets. It also handles the retransmission of packets. The transport layer will generally use TCP or UDP protocols depending on transmission requirements:

- **Transmission Control Protocol (TCP)**   The TCP is responsible for the reliable transmission of data from one node to another. It establishes a connection (aka a session, virtual circuit, or link) between two machines before any data is transferred. To establish a reliable connection, TCP uses a three-way handshake. This establishes the port number and beginning sequence numbers from both sides of the transmission. A requestor sends a packet specifying the port number it plans to use and its initial sequence number (ISN) to the server. The server acknowledges with its ISN, which is typically the requestor's ISN plus 1. The requestor acknowledges the reply. In order to maintain a reliable connection, each packet must contain a source and destination TCP port number, a sequence number for messages, a checksum for error checking, and an acknowledgement number that tells the sending machine which piece(s) of the message have arrived.

- **User Datagram Protocol (UDP)**   The UDP is a connectionless protocol responsible for the end-to-end transmission of data. Unlike TCP, UDP does not establish a connection. Instead, it attempts to send the data and then verify that the destination host actually received the data. UDP is preferred when sending small amounts of data when guaranteed delivery is not critical. UDP ports are different from TCP ports, so they can use the same numbers without interference.

Finally, the application layer connects applications to the network. This corresponds to the session, presentation, and application layers of the OSI model. Two application programming interfaces (APIs) provide access to the TCP/IP transport protocols: Windows Sockets and NetBIOS:

- **Windows Sockets Interface**   Windows Sockets (or simply WinSock) is a networking API designed to support communication among different TCP/IP applications and protocol stacks. It was developed so that applications using TCP/IP could write to a standard interface. WinSock is originally from the sockets created for the BSD UNIX operating system. Today, a WinSock provides a common interface for applications and protocols working near the top of the TCP/IP Protocol Suite—any application written using the WinSock API can communicate with any TCP/IP protocol (and vice versa).

- **NetBIOS**   The Network Basic Input/Output System (NetBIOS) is a session layer communications service used by client and server applications in IBM token ring and PC LAN networks. It provides applications with a programming interface for sharing services and information across a variety of lower-layer network protocols (including IP). The NetBIOS *name service* allows an application to verify that its own NetBIOS name is unique, delete a NetBIOS name that the application no longer requires, and use a server's NetBIOS name to determine the server's network address. The NetBIOS *session service* allows an application to conduct a reliable exchange of messages with another application. The NetBIOS *datagram service* allows an application to exchange datagrams with a specific application (or exchange datagrams with a group). Datagrams allow applications to communicate without establishing a session.

Exam Tip

Windows can be very sensitive to WinSock versions when communicating over the Internet, so be sure that you're using the latest version on your system.

Other Protocols

Of course, TCP/IP is not the only network protocol suite available for networking. As LAN technology has improved over the years, numerous protocols have evolved to support network communication. Many of these lesser-known protocols are still in service, lending their special services to the particular network environment. We'll look at just a few alternative protocols next.

NetWare Protocols

Next to Windows NT/2000, Novell's NetWare remains a popular and powerful network operating system. Like TCP/IP, Novell provides a suite of protocols developed specifically for NetWare. The five principal protocols that make up the NetWare suite include the Media Access Protocol, Internetwork Packet Exchange/Sequenced

Packet Exchange (IPX/SPX), Routing Information Protocol (RIP), Service Advertising Protocol (SAP), and NetWare Core Protocol (NCP). One thing to remember is that the NetWare protocols were developed before the OSI reference model, so NetWare levels do not match OSI layers exactly.

Media Access Protocol (MAP)   Network addressing is implemented in the hardware or NIC, and the MAP defines addressing that distinguishes each node on a NetWare network. The most common MAP implementations are Ethernet (IEEE 802.3), Ethernet 2.0, and token ring (IEEE 802.5). The MAP protocol is responsible for placing the header on the packet, and a header includes the source and destination address. After the packet has been transmitted, each network card checks the address. If their address matches the destination address on the packet (or if the packet is a broadcast message), the NIC copies the packet and sends it up the protocol stack. MAP also provides bit-level error checking in the form of a cyclical redundancy check (CRC).

Internetwork Packet Exchange and Sequenced Packet Exchange (IPX/SPX)   IPX defines addressing used on a NetWare network, and SPX provides security and reliability to the IPX protocol. IPX is a connectionless network layer protocol that is roughly equivalent to IP. It does not require an acknowledgement for each packet sent (any acknowledgement control or connection control must be provided by the protocols above IPX). SPX provides connection-oriented, reliable servers at the transport layer. IPX defines internetwork and intranode addressing. With *internetwork addressing*, the address of a segment on the network is identified by the network number assigned during installation. With *intranode addressing*, the address of a process within a node is identified by a socket number. IPX protocols are used only on networks with NetWare servers, and are often installed along with another protocol suite such as TCP/IP.

Routing Information Protocol (RIP)   RIP facilitates the exchange of routing information on a NetWare network. RIP adds an extra field of data to the packet to improve the decision making when selecting the fastest route to a destination. Routers can request routing information from other routers to update their own internal tables. Routers can also detect a change in the internetwork configuration, and verify that all other routers are aware of the internetwork configuration.

Service Advertising Protocol (SAP)   The SAP allows service nodes (including file servers, printer servers, gateway servers, application servers, and so on) to advertise their services and addresses. Clients on the network are able to obtain the internetwork address of any servers they can access. With SAP, adding and removing services on the network becomes dynamic. By default, a SAP server broadcasts its presence every 60 seconds.

NetWare Core Protocol (NCP)   The NCP defines the connection control and service request encoding that make it possible for clients and servers to communicate. This is the protocol that provides transport and session services. NetWare security is also provided within this protocol.

NetBIOS

Most of the services and applications that run within the Windows network operating system use the NetBIOS interface (dubbed interprocess communication or IPC). NetBIOS originated on LANs, and has developed into a standard interface that applications may use to access networking protocols in the transport layer. NetBIOS interfaces exist for NetBEUI, NWLink, and TCP/IP. NetBIOS requires an IP address and a NetBIOS name to uniquely identify a computer. IBM had originally offered NetBIOS as a separate TSR product. This TSR program is now obsolete, so you should replace it with the Windows NetBIOS interface if you ever encounter one of these systems.

Each workstation on a network has one or more names. NetBIOS maintains a table of names (and any aliases). The first name in the table is the unique name of the NIC, and usernames can be added to provide a user-friendly identification system. NetBIOS then cross-references the names as required. NetBIOS provides a datagram service that allows a message to be sent to any name, group of names, or all users on the network. However, there is no guarantee that the message will arrive at its destination. A NetBIOS session service opens a point-to-point connection between two workstations on the network. One workstation initiates a call to another and opens the connection. Because both workstations are treated as peers, they both can send and receive data concurrently. Finally, the NetBIOS NIC/session status feature provides information about the local NIC, other NICs, and any currently active sessions to any application software using NetBIOS.

NetBEUI

Originally, the NetBIOS Extended User Interface (NetBEUI) was closely coupled to NetBIOS (and considered one protocol). Over the years, network manufacturers separated NetBIOS—a session layer protocol—so that it could be used with other routable transport protocols. NetBIOS acts as an application interface to the network and provides a means for programs to establish a session with another program over the network. By comparison, NetBEUI is a small, fast, and efficient transport layer protocol supplied with all Microsoft network products. NetBEUI sports a small stack size (ideal for systems under DOS), fast data transfer speeds, and compatibility with all Microsoft-based networks. NetBEUI is a good and economical solution for a small peer-to-peer network where all workstations use Microsoft operating systems. The main disadvantage of NetBEUI is that it does not support routing. It is also limited to Microsoft-based networks.

X.25

X.25 is a set of WAN protocols incorporated into a packet-switching network made up of switching services. Packet-switching services were originally established to connect remote terminals to mainframe host systems. The network breaks up each transmission into multiple packets and places them on the network. Each packet can take different routes from the source to the destination. After the packets arrive, they are reassembled into their original data message. The X.25 protocol works in the physical, data link, and network layers of the OSI model, and offers typical data transmission speeds of only 64Kbps. X.25 and TCP/IP are similar in that both use packet-switched protocols. However, TCP/IP only has end-to-end error checking and flow control—X.25 has error checking from node to node. To compensate for this limitation, TCP/IP has a more sophisticated flow control mechanism than X.25.

AppleTalk

AppleTalk is Apple Computer's proprietary protocol stack designed to let Apple computers share files and printers in a networked environment. It was introduced in 1984 as a self-configuring LAN technology, and is generally available on UNIX systems that use third-party freeware and commercial packages. The AppleTalk protocol suite encompasses high-level file sharing using AppleShare, LaserWriter printing services, and print spoolers. The complete suite of AppleTalk protocols are described here:

- **AppleTalk**   This is a collection of protocols that correspond to the OSI reference model. AppleTalk supports LocalTalk, EtherTalk, and TokenTalk.
- **LocalTalk**   This protocol describes the simple STP cable used to connect Apples to other Apples or printers. A LocalTalk segment supports a maximum of 32 devices and operates at a speed of 230Kbps.

- **EtherTalk**   This is basically AppleTalk over Ethernet. It operates at a speed of 10Mbps. The Fast EtherTalk variation operates at a speed of 100Mbps.
- **TokenTalk**   This is AppleTalk over token ring. Depending on its hardware, TokenTalk operates at token ring speeds of either 4Mbps or 16Mbps.

CHECKPOINT

✔ **Objective 2.01: Network Operating Systems**   Networks require a network operating system (NOS) that is able to manage the many files and devices that are made available to the network, yet keep those resources secure from intrusion and unauthorized use. Some NOS versions simply add networking features "on top" of the PC's existing operating system, while other NOS versions fully integrate network support into the PC's operating system. A multitasking operating system provides the means for a server to process more than one task at a time, and a true multitasking operating system can run as many tasks as there are processors.

✔ **Objective 2.02: Network Standards**   The ISO authored a set of specifications that described a network architecture for connecting dissimilar devices and dubbed it the Open Systems Interconnection (OSI) reference model. The OSI reference model represents the seven layers (or levels) at which data is packaged and transmitted from a sending application, through the physical wires of a network, to the receiving application. There are seven levels (or layers): application, presentation, session, transport, network, data link, and physical. Data packets are also assembled and disassembled according to the OSI reference model, so packet creation begins in the application layer where data is generated. As the packet descends through each layer, information vital to that layer is added to the data.

✔ **Objective 2.03: Network Protocols**   Specific actions occur during each step of data transmission, and each step includes its own rules and procedures (or protocol). The protocol must be followed consistently on every computer in the network. The protocols that support multipath LAN-to-LAN communications are known as routable protocols. Several protocols normally need to work together in a network to ensure that the data is properly prepared, transferred, received, and processed. Various protocols must be coordinated, and this process of coordination is known as layering. There are generally three types of protocols that work across the OSI reference model: application protocols, transport protocols, and network protocols.

REVIEW QUESTIONS

1. A server that handles more than one task at a time is running what type of OS?

   A. Multitasking
   B. SNA
   C. Networking
   D. Microsoft

2. Access requests forwarded onto the network are handled by the client's...

   A. Operator
   B. Interface
   C. Redirector
   D. Stack

3. File sharing and security is provided by...

   A. Client-side software
   B. Server-side software
   C. Modem-side software
   D. Protocol stacks

4. The ability of computer operating system to function and access resources in different environments is known as...

   A. Internetability
   B. Interrogation
   C. Interpolation
   D. Interoperability

5. What software enables a Windows NT workstation to access file and print services on a NetWare server?

   A. Print Services for NetWare
   B. Client Services for NetWare
   C. Gateway Services for Netware
   D. None of the above

6. The OSI reference model is comprised of how many levels?

   A. 4
   B. 5
   C. 6
   D. 7

7. Which OSI level ensures that packets are delivered error free, in the proper order, and without losses or duplications?

A. Application

B. Network

C. Transport

D. Physical

8. Which part of the NDIS standard provides network communications?

A. Application driver

B. Protocol manager

C. Adapter driver

D. Protocol stack

9. Which 802 sublayer manages media access, delimits packets, checks packet errors, and recognizes packet addresses?

A. MAC

B. MAP

C. MAIO

D. MCC

10. What process connects protocols to each other and the NIC?

A. Tying

B. Selecting

C. Binding

D. Loading

REVIEW ANSWERS

1. **A** Multitasking: A multitasking operating system provides the means for a server to process more than one task at a time, and a true multitasking operating system can run as many tasks as there are processors.

2. **C** Redirector: A network request has to be forwarded (or redirected) out of the client and onto the network, and from there to the server with the requested resource. This forwarding activity is performed by the *redirector*. A redirector is sometimes referred to as the shell or the requester, depending on the particular networking software.

3. **B** Server-side software: Server network software allows sharing and security. *Sharing* is a term used to describe resources made publicly available for access by users on the network. Most network operating systems not only allow sharing, but also determine the degree of sharing.

4. **D** Interoperability: Interoperability is the ability of computer operating systems to function and access resources in different environments. This is particularly important when setting up a multivendor network environment.

5. **B** Client Services for NetWare: Client Services for NetWare (CSNW) enables a Windows NT Workstation to access file and print services on a NetWare server—it is included as part of GSNW.

6. **D** 7: The OSI reference model divides network communication into seven layers, where each layer covers different network activities, equipment, or protocols.

7. **C** Transport: Layer 4 (the transport layer) ensures that packets are delivered error free, in the proper order, and without losses or duplications.

8. **D** Protocol stack: A protocol stack provides network communications. It creates and disassembles packets (control information and data) that are exchanged with the network.

9. **A** MAC: The Media Access Control (MAC) sublayer manages media access, delimits packets, checks packet errors, and recognizes packet addresses.

10. **C** Binding: Protocols must be connected to each other and the NIC. This is known as binding. Protocols and NICs can be mixed and matched on an as-needed basis, so binding allows a lot of flexibility in network configurations.

Network Planning and Setup

ETA	NEWBIE	SOME EXPERIENCE	EXPERT
	5 hours	3 hours	1 hour

Networks don't simply appear. They are crafted into being with a carefully conceived plan that is based on a solid understanding of the hardware and software elements involved. Implementing a successful network requires an ample amount of planning and selection. If you're working with an existing network, it's imperative that you have access to all of the documents, maps, layouts, and other administrative information available. With this information as your guide, you can select new hardware, software, and cabling that will be compatible with the current network design. Starting a new network from scratch is actually a more difficult endeavor. You'll need to evaluate the needs of your organization and its workers, select the hardware and software to fit the needs (and budget), plan and implement the installation, then establish security with accounts and shares. The bottom line is that good planning and a methodical approach are essential to upgrading an existing network or implementing a new network. In this chapter, you'll learn some elements of network planning, cover basic setup concepts, and see how to protect the network from unauthorized access.

Objective 3.01   Planning a Network

Whether you're updating an existing network or planning a new network, the first step in implementing the work is planning. This may sound painfully obvious, but you'd be amazed at the amount of labor spent correcting oversights and fixing compatibility issues. Proper planning and review will eliminate a *lot* of potential problems (and needless expense) when you're actually doing the work. The planning process can usually be divided into five phases: setting network objectives, evaluating current resources, developing a plan, reviewing the plan, and implementing the plan. Ideally, your implemented plan will meet (or exceed) the objectives set out at the beginning of the project.

Define the Objectives

Surprisingly, setting clear objectives is often the most difficult and frustrating part of the process. The idea here is to identify what needs to be done and what the work will accomplish. While this may not be so critical if you simply need to add a workstation or upgrade a NIC, it is absolutely essential when building or expanding a network—setting objectives will lay the foundation of the entire project. For example, a typical planning process may require you to answer the following questions:

- How many users must be networked together?
- How many existing computers must be connected?
- How many existing devices (i.e., printers) must be connected?
- How many new computers (if any) must be added?
- How many new devices (i.e., printers) must be added?
- Is there a need for future expandability? If so, how many users or devices?
- Are any unusual resources required (i.e., Internet connectivity for a particular user or group)?
- Who is responsible for network maintenance and administration?

Of course, there are countless variations to these questions, and each situation may require more or less information. Ultimately, the goal here is for you to get a clear picture of just what needs to be done, and what your customer expects when the network is completed. By clearly defining your objectives, you can be sure to meet the needs of your customer. The problem with setting objectives is that your customer (perhaps an outside company, or maybe a department head in your own company) may not have a clear knowledge of just what's needed. You may simply be told, "I want everyone in the company (or department) to be on a network." Remember that your customer will probably not know as much about networking as you do, and you may need to ferret out the specific details in order to present a specific plan.

Evaluate Current Resources

Once you've got a clear picture of just what's required of the network, the next step is to evaluate the current hardware and software resources available to work with. Remember that many users in the company or department may already have a computer available to them. In some cases, those computers may even have network cards or network-related software installed, or be part of some preexisting network infrastructure. Before you start buying new equipment, it's important to determine what is already in service. For example, if you're faced with a variety of individual PCs running Windows 95/98, chances are that you'll need to replace or upgrade at least some of the oldest systems, add network cards to the remaining systems, and update the system designated as the server with Windows NT/2000 or NetWare. You will need to take account of hardware, software, connectivity, and network resources.

Exam Tip

Always conduct a complete survey of existing network hardware and software resources before planning network installations or upgrades. Knowing what's available at the start can save money and ease compatibility problems.

Checking Hardware

If you've ever had to check the minimum system requirements on that new game or productivity package, you already know that software makes certain demands on PC hardware. The PC must meet or exceed those minimum levels in order to support the software properly. This is even more important in a network environment. By evaluating the hardware that is available now, you can make informed decisions about which systems must be replaced, upgraded, or added. Knowing the specifications of each system now will prevent serious performance or compatibility problems later on. Identifying specific key devices will also make it easier for you to track down updated drivers, if necessary. For each computer, you will need to gather information such as

- PC make and model (i.e., Gateway Performa 1100).
- Processor manufacturer and speed (i.e., Intel Pentium III 1.1GHz).
- Amount of memory (RAM) installed (i.e., 256MB).
- The manufacturer and size of each hard drive (i.e., C: Maxtor 30GB HDD).
- Details of any other installed drives (i.e., CD-ROM, floppy drive, or Iomega drives).
- Monitor characteristics (i.e., Gateway Vivitron21 21 in).
- Video card characteristics (i.e., Voodoo3 3Dfx 16MB).
- NIC card characteristics (if installed).
- Denote any installed peripherals (i.e., printers or scanners) and see that you have the original installation diskettes or CDs for each.
- Note the system bus (i.e., EISA, ISA, or PCI) and check to see how many slots are free. This will be important if you need to add a network card or upgrade a drive controller.

Checking Software

While you're checking each system's hardware, take some time to survey the software being used on that system. This information can be important because it may affect hardware compatibility. For example, if you updated all the computers to Windows 2000 during network implementation, you might find that some of the existing programs (perhaps used on a daily basis) no longer run. This is particularly tricky when the company or department uses custom-designed or proprietary programs such as accounting databases that have been written especially for the company. Few proprietary programs will run properly on a network (if at all). In other cases, license agreements may not allow network use. You might need to contact the software manufacturer for information about running proprietary programs on the network. Gather the following information for the operating system and each software program:

- Program name.
- Program version number.
- See that you have the original installation diskettes or CDs for each program.
- Check the licensing information for each program (an upgrade may be required to allow use on the network).

It's amazing how software compatibility issues will surface when you actually sit down and see what everyone is using. For example, the accounting department might be using WordPerfect, while the sales department may be using Microsoft Office. You may need to upgrade certain applications in order to standardize on one suite of software for the entire network. This in turn may demand additional training for users that are not familiar with the chosen software.

Checking Connectivity

Today, most networks include some form of telecommunications connectivity in order to use Internet connections or some form of remote access server (RAS—a host on a LAN that includes modems and enables users to connect to the network over telephone lines). Take note of the phone line(s) wired into each office or user location. For example, if a company or department has an electronic telephone system, telephone outlets might be located in every office, but chances are they're not capable of a modem connection—a separate telephone outlet might be required for voice and data communication. Similarly, a digital telephone service (a PBX) may not support standard modems at all. In short, see what's available for telephone connections just in case you need them.

Check Network Resources

A final area to evaluate is the presence of existing network resources. Check for patch panels, RJ-45 or BNC wall outlets, network cabling, or any existing infrastructure that you may be able to use. If the company or department had already been wired for shielded twisted-pair (STP) in every office—perhaps when the building was constructed—this may *greatly* simplify the physical implementation (and reduce the costs) of your network's wiring. Rather than wiring a building from scratch, it may simply be a matter of adding or modifying the cabling in order to support your users. In many cases, you should have a set of building plans available so that you can trace existing wiring and plan new wiring as necessary.

Now is also a good time to consider the physical plant where the network will be installed. Based on the size of the facility, the number of users, and the environment (i.e., office or manufacturing), you can give some thought to how a network will be wired, and what kind of media (i.e., coax or twisted pair) is best suited for your particular situation.

Plan the Work

The next step is to actually plan the work that will be needed to implement your network. Ultimately, a plan will start with the resources that are currently available and detail the work needed to reach the network objectives. Such a plan may include upgrading or replacing existing systems, adding systems for other users, outfitting those systems for network operation, installing the wiring, installing the software, and configuring the network as needed. This planning process usually includes timeframe and budget considerations. In most cases, a plan must be presented to (and approved by) your customer before the actual work can begin.

Logical and Physical Mapping

After deciding on a peer-to-peer or server-based network, you can start to lay out the actual network on paper. This normally involves creating both a physical and logical layout of the proposed network, which includes all of the users and peripheral devices. The physical layout is typically a *map* that illustrates the building layout, the location of each piece of hardware, and a general wiring plan between the server, each PC, and peripheral device(s). If there's a preexisting network infrastructure in place, it should also be included in your layout. You should also create a *logical* layout of the network topology (i.e., bus or star), which also includes the server, each PC, and peripheral devices. Not only will this documentation help when the network is implemented, it will also be a tremendous asset for troubleshooting and network expansion. This documentation will also help other technicians to learn about the network.

Travel Advisory

Carefully document the network plans and keep those plans
up to date as the network evolves.

Selecting Media

Now that you've established a physical and logical layout, it's time to select wiring
(media) for the network. This is an important decision because the labor required
to wire a building is generally quite high—a cost that is exacerbated if inadequate
or inappropriate wiring has to be replaced. Not only must the media be appropriate for your network type—it must also be appropriate for the particular requirements of the location. For example, if several workstations are located in a
manufacturing environment where lots of electrical noise is generated, fiber-optic
cable might be required because it is unaffected by electrical signals. By comparison, ordinary twisted-pair (or shielded twisted pair) cable will usually be appropriate in an office.

The other aspect of network media involves future expandability of the network. Using the minimum cable for your traffic today may save money, but if
users and traffic increase, your wiring may become totally inadequate in the future
and require a time-consuming and expensive rewiring process. As an example, you
might decide to install CAT 3 UTP cable on a small network. This would certainly
support a few workstations, but limit the network speed to 10Mbps. A few years
down the road, that network may have many more workstations, and a 10Mbps
network would become painfully slow. If you look ahead and install CAT 5 UTP
now, you could upgrade the network to 100Mbps at any time in the future without having to rewire the building—and enjoy that capability for just a few cents
more per foot.

Review the Plan

Once you have completed your plan, it's time to sit down and present that plan to
your customer. This type of meeting is often informal, but it is *always* important.
Reviewing the plan ensures that the customer is getting the network that they
need. Weaknesses or oversights in your plan will usually surface during a review,
and any last-minute ideas or requirements can be addressed *before* money is actually spent. It may be necessary for you to go back and tweak some decisions in

order to address all of the network issues and budget constraints, then review the plan once again. It's not uncommon to have several reviews before a final network plan is approved (even more if the network is particularly large or complex). After the customer is satisfied with your plan (and no other issues are raised), it's time to implement the network plan.

Implement the Plan

The next step is to implement the network according to the plan that you've prepared. If you've done an adequate job of planning, you should know exactly what hardware and software to order, and understand the wiring that must be installed to support each device. Typical implementation usually involves installing the wiring, locating each device, connecting the devices, installing the software, and configuring the network.

Wiring Installation

At this point, you (or a professional installation team) will need to run the physical wiring. It's an ideal time to start with the wiring while other equipment is on order. In virtually all cases, this will involve running wiring through walls, ceilings, and floors. For the sake of an example, let's look at the installation of a basic CAT 5 Ethernet cabling system. The simplest way to lay out a network in a small-office environment is to use a physical star topology. The center of any star will be a *patch panel*. A patch panel is a box with an array of RJ-45 female connectors that have terminals for connecting the wires.

A typical patch panel can have 12 or more RJ-45 connectors and a terminal for each of the corresponding 12 cables. If you pay close attention, you'll notice that each terminal has eight connection points—one pin for each of the eight twisted-pair wires. In most cases, connections are color-coded for easy installation. The idea is to mount the patch panel(s) near the hub—usually next to the server—so that you can easily make connections to the network. You'll need to

| **Exam Tip** |

Remember that any cables run above the ceiling or below the floor must meet local construction and fire codes. Use plenum-grade cable where it is required.

install a CAT 5 outlet near the hub and on the other end of each cable so that you
can patch a PC's NIC to the cable.

Device Installation

When wiring is completed and each device is located, it's time to connect the
devices. Connections are straightforward, and are made by attaching a relatively
short patch cable between the NIC port and the RJ-45 outlet in the wall or floor.
If you're using a hub, you will also need a short patch cable to connect the patch
panel to a corresponding outlet on the hub. In other words, to connect a PC to the
network, you need to patch a hub port to an RJ-45 outlet on the wall. That outlet
is cabled to another RJ-45 outlet located near the respective PC. Another patch
cable will connect that RJ-45 outlet on the wall to the PC's NIC. This completes
the path from the PC to the hub. A separate connection then connects the hub to
the server (hopefully located nearby).

Software Issues

After the hardware is installed, you should turn your attention to software issues.
This usually involves the installation of server-side and client-side applications,
drivers, redirectors, and so on. The network must then be configured with permissions and shares (a fundamental aspect of security) so that users can access the
server, exchange messages, and so on.

Objective 3.02   Configuring Network Access

With the network implemented as planned, it's time to configure access for
each of the network's users. In a client/server network, resource sharing is
managed through the use of accounts. By creating accounts (and organizing individual accounts into groups), a network administrator has the tools necessary to
provide a higher level of security. Each workstation must have client software
installed and be configured as a network client. You will have to establish the computer's network identity, enable sharing, and set access privileges for the resources
the computer will share. The actual procedure for installing and configuring client
software depends on the operating system you are using (and the operating system of the network on which you intend to share resources). This part of the

chapter illustrates user and group accounts, highlights the appropriate types of accounts for a given network environment, and outlines the process for creating user and group accounts.

Understanding Accounts

Simply stated, an account provides users with access to files, directories, and devices (such as printers). In a client/server network, accounts are created and managed by the network administrator. An account is composed of a username and logon information established for each user. Logon information can include which computer(s) the user can work at, the days and times during which access is allowed, user passwords, and more. Account information is entered by the administrator and usually stored on the server through the network operating system. A network checks the username and other parameters to verify the account when the user attempts to log on.

Local Lingo

Account   Name, password, and other login information established for each network user.

Group   Sets of similar users organized to share common network rights and tasks.

User Accounts

The first step in enabling a new user is to create an account for that user. An administrator can use a network utility to enter and edit account information for a user. The new user account requires a complete set of information that defines a user to the network security system. This includes a username and password, rights for accessing the system and its resources, and the group(s)—if any—to which the account belongs. Administrators can also configure a number of parameters for a user. Logon times can be entered to restrict access to certain hours of the day. A home directory can be assigned to give a user an area to store private files. And an expiration date can be included to limit a temporary user's access to the network (i.e., a temporary employee).

You should also be familiar with administrator and guest accounts. When a network operating system is first installed, the setup program automatically creates an account with complete network authority. In a Microsoft networking environment, this account is called *administrator*. In the Novell environment, this is the *supervisor* account. Under Linux, it is known as *root*. After logging on as administrator, that user has full control over all network functions. For example, an administrator can start the network, set the initial security parameters, and create other user accounts. By comparison, a guest account is usually a basic default account intended for individuals who do not have a valid user account but need temporary access to some low level of the network.

Group Accounts

Once a user account is created, that account generally has no rights—this is a common default used for security purposes. User accounts are assigned particular rights through group memberships. All user accounts within a particular group will have certain access rights and activities (according to the assigned group). By assigning permissions and rights to a group, an administrator can treat the group as a single account. Groups are commonly used to grant access to resources—the permissions granted to a group are automatically granted to all of its members. Groups also assign rights to perform system tasks (such as to back up and restore files or change the system time). Grouping users together can also simplify communications by reducing the number of individual messages that need to be sent (messages can be sent to the group instead). For example, if an administrator wanted a certain user to have administrative capabilities on the network, the administrator might make that user a member of the Administrators group.

Do not underestimate the power of group accounts. Client/server networks can support hundreds (even thousands) of accounts. There will be occasions when an administrator needs to send messages to large numbers of users notifying them about an event or network policy, or identify every account that has a particular access. If 100 users need a change in their access, the administrator would need to change 100 individual accounts. Clearly, working with individual accounts is a time-consuming and error-prone approach. On the other hand, if those 100 accounts were placed in one group, the administrator would simply send one message to the group account (and each member of the group would automatically get the message). Permissions could be set or changed for the group, and all members of the group would automatically receive the same permissions.

Account Passwords

In most situations, each username is coupled with a password. Passwords help to protect network security by ensuring that each username is authenticated by a secret word (known only to that user and the network). Initially, the password is assigned by the network administrator, but can often be changed later by the user (an administrator can require users to do this automatically by setting a password change time interval for the user). Keep in mind that passwords are not necessarily *required* by a network operating system. In some low-security network environments, it is possible to configure an account so that it no longer needs a password. When selecting a password, avoid obvious choices such as birth dates, social security numbers, or the names of spouses, children, pets, and so on. Never write down the password—memorize it instead. If the password has an expiration date, remember that date so that you can change the password before it expires and locks the user out of the network.

Removing Accounts

When an account is no longer needed, it can generally be disabled or deleted. This will prevent the user from accessing the network. Disabling an account is a handy measure when an account must be stopped temporarily. It will still remain on the network, and can be reactivated later if necessary. For example, if an employee will be on vacation or a leave of absence, their account can be disabled until they return. An account can also be deleted, which will erase the user's information from the network. An account can be deleted when a user leaves the company or moves to another part of the company where no network access is required.

Objective 3.03   **Network Security**

The reason that we build networks at all is to communicate, or to share files and other resources. However, just because networks facilitate communication does not mean that valuable data is free for the taking. In many cases, servers and workstations contain sensitive data that can easily be misused (or even impair your company's ability to do business) if it fell into the wrong hands. As a result, proper network management walks a fine line between allowing adequate access to files and directories, yet protecting those same resources from unauthorized use or malicious intrusion. This is the entire concept behind security. The larger the enterprise, the greater the need for security. In the previous part of the chapter, you looked at ways to access and share resources. In this part of the chapter, you'll examine ways to secure your vital data.

Security Concepts

Modern networks face many different threats, but the most common issues are unauthorized use, tampering, theft, and damage. A network administrator must take adequate precautions to defend the network from these threats but still facilitate easy data access for authorized users. The level of network security also depends on the type of environment. For example, a network that stores data for a major bank requires more extensive security than a LAN that links the computers in a small community volunteer organization. This balance between security and accessibility is difficult to achieve, and becomes even more complicated as the network grows.

- **Unauthorized Use** Every user on the network must have a valid account. When an individual logs on with another user's account, or a valid user attempts to access resources that are not permitted, that is considered to be *unauthorized use* of the network.
- **Tampering** Generally speaking, *tampering* is any effort to interfere with the proper operation of a network. Tampering also includes the uploading of a worm or virus to the network. Tampering may be perpetrated by malicious users, or unauthorized users that have acquired the logon information of an authorized user.
- **Theft** In virtually all cases, *theft* involves the transfer of data to an unauthorized or inappropriate location (maybe a remote workstation, maybe a floppy disk, maybe even out of the network to the Internet).
- **Damage** The idea of *damage* involves any physical damage to servers, wiring, or workstations. In most situations, damage is caused by major disasters such as fire, flood, or earthquake.

Physical Security

One of the first steps toward securing a network is to secure the physical server(s). Since most of a network's critical data is stored in one or more servers, you'll notice that many medium-to-large server rooms are kept locked at all times, and server rooms are often equipped with high-performance air handling and fire suppression systems. Locking the servers in a protected location will ensure that only network administrators and trained technicians have access to the equipment—no one will be tempted to tinker if problems arise.

In some cases, the network cabling must also be secured. Remember that copper wiring (such as coaxial cable) emits electronic signals that mimic the information it carries. Information carried in these signals can be monitored with electronic listening equipment. Copper cable can also be tapped so that information can be stolen directly from the original cable. As a rule, cable runs that carry sensitive data should be accessible only to authorized people (i.e., run along locked conduit). Often, just planning the cable runs carefully (i.e., through ceilings, walls, and floors) will be very effective.

Securing Data

Once the major physical elements of the network have been secured, an administrator can focus on protecting the network resources from unauthorized access. As you saw in the last part of this chapter, data is often secured by assigning permissions to the various network resources. Client/server networks use *access permissions* (or user-level security). Setting up a carefully conceived suite of permissions is usually the first line of defense against unauthorized use.

Password-Protected Shares   When using password-protected shares, you'll need to assign a password to each shared resource. Access is granted to the shared resource when a user enters the correct password. In operating systems such as Windows, resources can be shared with different types of permissions, such as read only, full access, or depends on password. If a share is set up as read only, users who know the password only have *read* access to the files in that directory. For example, they can view files, copy them to their PC, and print them, but they cannot change the original files. With *full access*, users who know the password have complete access to the files in that directory—they can view, modify, add, and delete the shared directory's files. When access *depends on password*, you're setting up a share that uses two levels of passwords (read-only and full access). Users who know the read-only password have read access, and users who know the full access password have full access. Ultimately, the password-protected share approach is a simple security method that allows anyone who knows the password to obtain access to that particular resource. This is often adequate for peer-to-peer networks where security is not such an issue, but is often inappropriate for larger server-based networks.

Access Permissions   With access permission, certain rights are assigned on a user-by-user basis. A user types a name and password when logging on to the network. The server validates this username and password combination, and uses it to grant (or deny) access to resources by checking access to each resource against an access database on the server. This approach provides a higher level of control over access rights. After a user has been authenticated and allowed onto the network, the security system gives that user access to the appropriate resources. While users have passwords, resources have *permissions*. Users with higher permissions are allowed to do more with a resource than others. The administrator determines which users should be allowed particular permissions. Permissions under Windows NT can be set to the following:

- **Read-Only**   Reads and copies files in the shared directory
- **Execute**   Runs (a.k.a. executes) the files in the directory
- **Write**   Creates new files in the directory
- **Delete**   Deletes files in the directory
- **No Access**   Prevents the user from accessing directories, files, or resources

Group Permissions   The most efficient way to give users appropriate permissions to a resource is through groups (especially in a large organization with many users). Permissions for groups work in the same way as they work for individuals—an administrator reviews the permissions required by each account and assigns the accounts to the proper group(s). Grouping is the preferred method of assigning permissions because it is far easier than assigning permissions to each account individually.

For example, giving the *All* group full control of the public directory might not be a good choice because full access would allow anyone to delete or modify the contents of the files in the public directory. Instead, the All group can be granted read access to the directory public. Members of the All group can read files in the public directory, but not delete or modify them. The administrator could then create a group called *Editors* and grant full access permissions to the files in that directory. So any user in the Editors group could alter the files in the public directory.

Objective 3.04   Supplemental Hardware

There are several other pieces of hardware that you should consider during network planning and setup: a KVM switch, a UPS, and a tape drive. A KVM (keyboard, video, mouse) switch is a device used to control several PCs, but still use a single monitor, keyboard, and mouse. An uninterruptable power supply (or UPS) is a vital device used to maintain the operation of a PC during a power interruption. A tape drive allows you to back up and restore applications and files. This makes tape drives a vital part of your maintenance and disaster recovery planning processes. This part of the chapter introduces the essential ideas of each device, and explains some important installation issues.

KVM Switches

Even the most complex server is still a computer, and you'd operate it with an every-day keyboard and mouse, then view the system's operations on a monitor—just as you would any other PC. But just imagine what would happen when several servers are on the network (perhaps many servers). Think of all those monitors and key-boards. Where would you put them all? How would you even keep track of them? In actual practice, a server needs surprisingly little interaction once it's installed and con-figured. This means it's often a waste to leave monitors and input devices attached. Yet it's a real hassle to try disconnecting and reconnecting this hardware. KVM switches address this problem by allowing one monitor, keyboard, and mouse (per-haps located at a central maintenance station) to safely switch between computers on demand with the touch of a button. You can see a typical KVM switch in Figure 3-1.

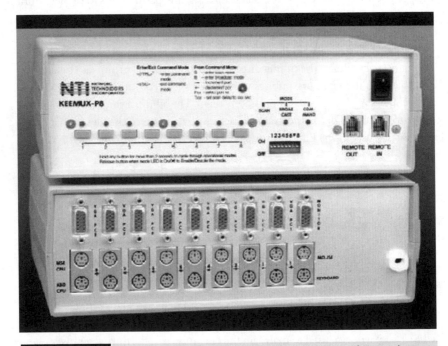

FIGURE 3-1   An NTI KEEMUX-P8 KVM switch (Courtesy of Network Technologies, Inc.)

Travel Assistance

You can learn technical details about the KEEMUX-P8 KVM
switch at www.networktechinc.com/srvsw-pc.html.

KVM Connections

Dedicated internal microprocessors emulate keyboard and mouse presence to each
attached PC all of the time, so all computers boot error free and won't lock up when
another system is selected. This offers a powerful convenience to network administrators because many (even all) servers can be operated from a single location—
saving the clutter, confusion, and power consumption of many monitors and
input devices. In many cases, KVM switches can even be cascaded together to
operate up to 128 computers (maybe even more). Generally speaking, a KVM
switch interconnects with devices and systems using adapter cables. For example,
a PC uses male/male cables to connect the female keyboard, mouse, and video
ports to the KVM switch. The male ends of the monitor, keyboard, and mouse
then attach to the KVM switch.

Installation Guidelines

The following steps outline the steps used to install a typical KVM switch. Keep in
mind that your particular switch may be different, so be sure to read the instructions and precautions with your own unit before proceeding.

1. Before connecting the keyboard, monitor, and mouse switch to your computers, make sure all computers, the monitor, and the switch are turned off.
2. If you're cascading units together, configure the unit according to the manufacturer's direction.
3. Disconnect the monitor cable from the computer and connect the monitor
   cable to the connector labeled "Monitor" on rear of the switch.
4. Disconnect the keyboard cable from the computer and connect the keyboard
   cable to the connector labeled "Keybd" on the rear panel of the switch.
5. Disconnect the mouse cable from the computer and connect the mouse
   cable to the connector labeled "Mouse" on the rear panel of the switch.
6. If you're using an optional wired remote, plug it into the connector labeled
   "Remote In" on the front panel of the switch (or rear panel for rack units).
   Do this before powering the unit on.

7. Connect each computer to the keyboard, monitor, and mouse switch using keyboard, monitor, and mouse interface cables. For example, group the keyboard, monitor, and mouse interface cables from each computer. Make sure that the cables connected to your first computer are attached to the Kybd Port 1, Video Port 1, and Mouse Port 1, connectors. The second computer's cables should connect to Kybd Port 2, Video Port 2, and Mouse Port 2 connectors, and so on.

8. Turn the KVM switch power on first, then turn then monitor power on.

9. Turn on all of the computers that you need.

The switches on the front panel are configurable for several tasks. Some switches are used for cascading actions and some switches are used for keyboard configurations. Keyboard configuration switches usually come preset in the off position (you should not change these settings because the PS/2 keyboard will not work). If these switches are set in the on position, you'll need to power down the entire system (including each system), change the switches back to the off position, then power the system back up. If you need to replace a PS/2 keyboard with another one, it can be hot swapped without powering down. The PS/2 KVM switch can be expanded to access up to 128 systems by cascading multiple units together. The KVM switch connected to the monitor and keyboard must be configured as the master unit, and any KVM switches connected to the master must be configured as slave units. The only additional hardware required is a set of keyboard, monitor, mouse extension cables for each slave unit.

UPS Systems

Networks rely on the constant operation of servers, workstations, and other devices. In many cases, equipment is running continuously. Operation depends on an adequate supply of commercial power (the ac from a wall outlet). Unfortunately, power distribution is not perfect, and interruptions such as brownouts, blackouts, surges, and spikes do occur. Power interruptions can cause erratic server operation or reboots. In more extreme cases, power problems can corrupt data, and even damage your network equipment. The uninterruptable power supply (UPS) is a device used to provide power when an interruption occurs (see Figure 3-2). The UPS is inserted inline between an ac outlet and the computer equipment that you need to protect. When a power problem occurs, the UPS switches over to a battery-based power source that will keep the equipment running—at least long enough to save data and initiate an orderly shutdown. In most cases, a UPS also contains protective circuitry that will prevent sudden voltage surges or spikes from passing into the computer equipment.

| **FIGURE 3-2** | A Tripp Lite BCPro 850 UPS (Courtesy of Tripp Lite) |

Travel Assistance

You can learn more about the BCPro 850 UPS at
www.tripplite.com.

Understanding the UPS

There are basically two types of UPS designs: online and offline. An *online* UPS
is a system where the *inverter* (the circuit that changes dc power to ac power) is
constantly operating and powering the computer equipment. In effect, the PC
is constantly running from battery power even though ac is readily available
and keeping the UPS batteries charged. The ac from the wall is translated into
dc, which charges the batteries, and then that dc battery voltage is inverted back
into ac to run the computer equipment. This is often referred to as a "double
conversion" UPS, and both voltage and frequency can be highly regulated. A
second type of online UPS became popular by 1990. This is referred to as a
"single-conversion," "delta conversion," or "parallel online" UPS. In this design,

only a portion of the output power of the UPS has been processed by the ac-to-dc-to-ac process.

By comparison, an *offline* UPS only runs (provides battery power) when ac is lost. These are traditionally referred to as a "battery backup system" or "standby UPS." When ac fails, the UPS inverter kicks in and runs the PC equipment entirely from battery power. This type of UPS is a bit simpler to design and maintain, but it's hard on the batteries because they are often heavily discharged to support the attached PC load. In normal applications, a standby UPS is used to protect less critical loads for short periods of time (i.e., a workstation).

Line interactive UPS systems are a dramatic improvement over standby systems because they are capable of correcting modest undervoltage (brownout) or overvoltage (surge) conditions without depleting the batteries. By using a boost function to raise utility voltage up, or a buck function to reduce incoming voltage, the line interactive UPS postpones using battery power until the voltage is substantially out of range. A line interactive UPS typically includes a display showing the percent of load, percent of battery capacity remaining, and other status information. They are excellent choices for almost any critical load.

Travel Advisory

UPS systems are almost always battery based. However, some advanced UPS systems may use gasoline-powered generators to supplement battery power and provide greatly extended running time.

Running Time

As you might expect, the batteries in a UPS cannot power a load forever. This means a UPS can only power certain pieces of equipment for a limited amount of time. The exact amount of time depends on the *load* (the amount of equipment) that you've attached to the UPS and the size (capacity) of the UPS itself. For a UPS of any given capacity, a higher load will result in shorter running time. Lightening the load (or using a larger-capacity UPS) will increase the running time. The real trick is to determine your running time by checking the load that you're planning to attach.

All UPS systems are rated in terms of *volt amperes* (VA), which is a more technical indication of power (usually measured in watts, or W). The power requirements of your equipment should be less than or equal to the VA capacity of the UPS. For example, an IBM OfficePro 700 UPS provides 700VA capacity. A VA capacity will generally operate a load at that level for about 8–10 minutes. That means the 700VA UPS should power 700VA worth of PC equipment for about 10 minutes. If you're using half the load (350VA), the UPS should operate for twice as long (i.e., 16–20 minutes). If you're using a quarter of the load (175VA), the UPS should operate for four times as long (i.e., 35–40 minutes), and so on. In practice, the actual amount of running time will be a bit longer if the load is measurably lower than the UPS capacity (i.e., the UPS is overrated for the load).

The real trick is to calculate the load that you're attaching. All PC equipment makers list a load rating for their devices. This rating is usually listed on the nameplate or label near the line cord on the rear of the device. The rating may be in VA, in watts (W), or in amps (A). Ideally, all loads should be denoted in VA so that the loads can simply be added together. If a load is in watts, convert to VA by multiplying W × 1.4. If a load is in amps, convert to VA by multiplying A × 120 (for a 120V device) or A × 230 (for a 230V device). Suppose you want to use a UPS to run a monitor, PC, and tape drive. A typical example may be as follows:

Computer VA	=	120V x 2A	=	240VA
Monitor VA	=	100W x 1.4	=	140VA
Tape drive VA	=	120V x 1A	=	120VA
Total			=	**500VA**

In this example, a 500VA UPS will run this load for about 8–10 minutes, or a 1,000VA UPS will run this equipment for about 20 minutes.

> **Travel Advisory**
>
> Do not connect laser printers to a UPS! The power requirements of a typical laser printer are much larger than the requirements of other computer peripherals, and may trip the UPS system's protective circuit breaker. Plug laser printers into a quality surge suppressor. Print jobs can always be requeued when the power is restored.

Testing the UPS

After the UPS has had several hours to recharge its batteries, turn on the UPS system's power control and switch on your computer equipment. The UPS indicator should be illuminated and your equipment should operate normally. To test the operation of a UPS, simply unplug its input cord (or press and hold the Test/Alarm Disable switch on units so equipped) to simulate a utility blackout. The UPS will immediately transfer your equipment to power from the UPS internal battery. During this time, the UPS will emit a beep once every few seconds to remind you that your equipment is operating from a source of power that is limited in duration. Restore power to the UPS by plugging in the line cord (or releasing the Test control switch). Observe that your equipment operates normally during the transfer from and to ac power. Repeat this test four or five times to ensure proper operation.

If the total power requirement of your attached equipment is much greater than the capacity of the UPS, the rear circuit breaker on the UPS may trip—this is an overload situation. Once the circuit breaker trips, the UPS will attempt to operate the load using its internal batteries, but this may result in an unexpectedly short runtime. If the overload is severe, the UPS will immediately shut down and cease to power the load. In this case, the UPS will emit a loud tone to alert you of the overload. If this occurs during your test, turn off the UPS and disconnect any nonessential equipment from the UPS. The circuit breaker may be reset when the overload is removed.

Tape Drives

No matter how reliable your network is, you will invariably experience periods of unexpected downtime. When downtime results in data loss or corruption, the consequences to your business can be terrible. Even with the use of RAID and redundant (clustered) servers, tape drives remain one of the most economical and reliable means of backing up your important data safely. In many cases, backups are the only means of recovering your network from disasters (i.e., fire, flood, or earthquake). In this part of the chapter, we'll look at the installation and use of a typical SCSI 40/80GB digital linear tape (DLT) drive as shown in Figure 3-3. For best performance, look for tape drives that support Fast SCSI-2 (Wide), Wide-Ultra SCSI, or Ultra-2 SCSI.

Capacity and Data Compression

Generally speaking, a DLT tape drive (such as the Compaq 40/80 DLT drive) will read and write in both uncompressed (that is, native) and Digital Lempel-Ziv (DLZ) compressed data formats. The Compaq DLT drive features a native for-matted capacity of 40GB and a sustained native data transfer of 6.0 MB/s. When operating in compressed mode, data capacity is affected by how much the data can be compressed—most data can be compressed at roughly a 2:1 ratio. This would

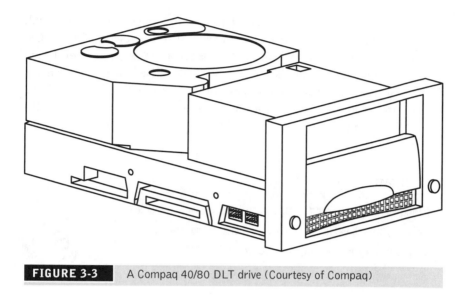

FIGURE 3-3   A Compaq 40/80 DLT drive (Courtesy of Compaq)

provide the 40/80 DLT drive with a compressed capacity of 80GB and a compressed data transfer up to 12 MB/s. When installing a DLT drive, check to see if
the drive ships from the factory with data compression enabled for writing. If so,
data is always compressed when writing to the tape, but the drive is capable of
reading both compressed and uncompressed tapes. For the drive to write uncompressed data, the data compression setting must be changed through the tape drive
software. Some drives allow the recording density to be adjusted through a Density
Select button on the front panel, but this only works during a given session (and
defaults back to the drive's preset values the next time it is used).

DLT Drive Installation

Internal DLT drive installation is generally not a difficult process, but it does
require a particular attention to detail—especially when working with internal
SCSI drive installation and termination. After you check the drive and set its SCSI
ID, you'll need to shut down the server and all peripheral devices in order to install
the actual drive. When you reassemble the server and power it (and its peripherals) back up, you'll need to install the drivers and backup software.

1. Set the SCSI ID and terminator power. Before beginning the installation
    process, the drive's SCSI ID must be set. As you'll see in Chapter 7, each SCSI
    device on the same SCSI bus must have a unique SCSI ID. Use the jumper

block located on the left side of the tape drive to configure an ID. The default SCSI ID is usually ID 6. Remember that SCSI ID 7 is reserved for the SCSI controller card. If a SCSI ID other than the default is used, the Remote ID pin must have a jumper installed on it. A SCSI DLT drive usually ships from the factory with terminator power (TERM PWR) disabled. This allows only the controller to provide power for SCSI termination. If enabled, the TERM PWR setting allows the drive (in addition to the controller) to provide the termination power.

Exam Tip

Electrostatic discharge (ESD) can easily damage electronic components such as those found in a server. Be sure that you are properly
grounded before beginning this procedure.

2. Prepare the server. To prepare a server for DLT drive installation, perform a normal system shutdown (you will probably need to schedule this downtime in advance). Turn off the server and all peripheral devices. Disconnect ac power from the server and from all peripheral devices. Disassemble the server chassis to expose an available drive bay. You might need to check the server's user manual for proper disassembly instructions.

3. Install the drive .Now it's time to actually install the DLT drive. If you're using drive rails to adapt the drive for the chassis opening, install the rails first, then slide the drive into a suitable bay. Secure the drive into the bay with the rec-ommended screws. In many cases, this will require four screws, but some chassis only use two screws from the front of the drive. Connect an available power cable and the appropriate SCSI signal cable. Be sure that the SCSI chain is properly terminated.

4. Reassemble the server. To reassemble the server, replace the chassis access panels and secure the enclosure, and then reconnect the peripheral device(s) to the server. Reconnect the ac power cord to the server and any peripheral devices; then turn on the server and devices. The server hardware should boot normally.

5. Install the drivers. After the server's operating system boots, you can install the drivers. For example, the Compaq 40/80 DLT drive supports Windows NT/2000, Novell NetWare, Tru64 UNIX, and OpenVMS network operat-ing systems. Drivers are located on the Compaq SmartStart and Support Software CD, the Support Software Diskettes, and the Tape Drive Supplemental

Driver CD in the Storage Management Solutions package that came with the tape drive. You can use SmartStart to create Support Software Diskettes for specific operating systems.

Starting the Drive

When power is initially applied to the server, the DLT drive performs its own *power on self test* (POST). This self test starts a sequence of events indicated by the front-panel LEDs. For the Compaq 40/80 DLT drive, this sequence of events includes the following:

- All left-side LEDs illuminate for approximately three seconds, then shut off.
- The Operate Handle, the Write Protect, and the Use Cleaning Tape LEDs turn off.
- The Tape in Use LED blinks while the cartridge drive initializes.
- After initializing, if a cartridge is not loaded in the drive, the Tape in Use LED turns off, and the Operate Handle LED illuminates.
- The drive is now ready for operation.

Travel Advisory

POST will not complete until the operate handle is in the down position. If POST is waiting for the handle to be put down, the Operate Handle LED will flash.

Loading and Unloading the Drive

The following steps outline the loading of a DLT tape cartridge:

1. When the Operate Handle LED is illuminated, lift the cartridge insert/release handle.
2. Insert a tape cartridge and push the cartridge completely into the drive.
3. Lower the handle to lock the cartridge in place.
4. Cartridge initialization begins once a cartridge is inserted, and the Tape in Use LED flashes.
5. When the tape reaches the *beginning of tape* (BOT) marker, the Tape in Use LED illuminates.
6. The cartridge is now ready for use.

The following steps outline the unloading of a DLT tape cartridge:

1. Press the Unload button (or issue an "eject" command in the software application).
2. After a few moments, the Operate Handle LED illuminates.
3. Lift the handle, remove the cartridge, and lower the handle.

DLT Cartridge Protection

A DLT tape cartridge has a write-protect switch to prevent accidental erasure of data. Before loading the cartridge into a drive, position the write-protect switch on the front of the cartridge. For example, by moving the switch to the left, the cartridge is write-protected. By moving the switch to the right, the cartridge is write-enabled. If you move the cartridge write-protect switch to the left while the cartridge is in a DLT drive, the drive illuminates the write-protect LED immediately. If the drive is writing to the cartridge, write-protect does not begin until the current write command completes.

Exam Tip

For best protection, store backups in a fire/flood-proof location away from the network.

Updating DLT Drive Firmware

From time to time, the tape drive manufacturer may release firmware updates for the drive. These may be necessary to improve drive performance, extend compatibility with drive backup software, or improve operation under new operating systems. Depending on your particular drive, you may be able to update firmware through a downloadable file, or through a file on a tape cartridge. For example, let's look at a Compaq 40/80 DLT drive upgrade using a cartridge:

1. Exit all tape cartridge application software before proceeding with a firmware upgrade.
2. Put the DLT subsystem into the Firmware Update mode. Remove any cartridge that is in the target DLT drive and close the handle (down position).
3. Press the Unload button on the drive front panel and hold the button (for about 6 seconds) until the Write Protect LED blinks. This indicates that the DLT has requested the firmware update and is ready to proceed.

Exam Tip

When performing a firmware update, be sure to prevent a power failure. A power failure when the new firmware image is being programmed into the FLASH EEPROMs causes the tape drive to be unusable.

4. When the Write Protect LED blinks, release the Unload button and press it again within 4 seconds.
5. The Tape in Use and Write Protect LEDs blink to indicate that the date drive has entered the firmware update mode.
6. After the firmware update mode has been selected, insert the firmware cartridge into the drive. This automatically reads the cartridge, examines the data, and verifies the data is a valid DLT firmware image.
7. If the firmware image is valid, the update proceeds automatically. If the code is the same as the cartridge to be updated, the drive firmware is not updated. If the drive code is different, the drive firmware will be updated (usually a process taking 2–3 minutes). While the drive code goes through the update, the Write Protect and Tape in Use LEDs flash alternately.
8. When the drive firmware update is complete, the drive resets and goes through initialization. The initialization process waits until the cartridge is rewound to the beginning of the tape.
9. Wait until the Unload LED is illuminated, then remove the firmware cartridge. This should complete the drive's firmware update.

CHECKPOINT

✔ **Objective 3.01: Planning a Network**   Setting clear objectives will lay the foundation of the entire project. Evaluate the current hardware and software resources available to work with (if any). The next step is to actually plan the work that will be needed to implement your network. Review the plan to ensure that the customer is getting the network that they need. Finally, implement the network according to the plan that you've prepared—including the installation of wiring and devices.

✔ **Objective 3.02: Configuring Network Access**   In a client/server network, resource sharing is managed through the use of accounts. By creating accounts (and organizing individual accounts into groups), a network administrator has the tools necessary to provide a higher level of security. An account provides users with access to files, directories, and devices (such as printers). User accounts are assigned particular rights through group memberships. All user accounts within a particular group will have certain access rights and activities according to the assigned group.

✔ **Objective 3.03: Network Security**   Proper network management allows adequate access to files and directories, yet protects those same resources from unauthorized use or malicious intrusion. Each username is coupled with a password. Passwords help to protect network security by ensuring that each username is authenticated by a secret word known only to that user and the network. When an account is no longer needed, it can generally be disabled or deleted.

✔ **Objective 3.04: Supplemental Hardware**   KVM switches allow one monitor, keyboard, and mouse to safely switch between numerous computers on demand with the touch of a button. The uninterruptable power supply (UPS) is a device used to provide power when an interruption occurs. The UPS is inserted inline between an ac outlet and the computer equipment that you need to protect. Tape drives remain one of the most economical and reliable means of backing up your important data safely. In many cases, backups are the only means of recovering your network from disasters (i.e., fire, flood, or earthquake).

REVIEW QUESTIONS

1. What is the first thing you should do when planning a network?

   A. Check the budget
   B. Update your resume
   C Define your objectives
   D. Purchase the parts you might need

2. In a client/server network, resource sharing is managed through the use of...

   A. Shares
   B. Accounts
   C NT
   D. Integration

3. The first step in enabling a new user is to…

 A. Assign the new user to a group
 B. Delete old or expired users
 C. Create an account for that user
 D. Update the server software

4. In order to ease the configuration and maintenance of individual users, accounts are usually organized into…

 A. Shares
 B. Groups
 C. Files
 D. Directories

5. A password is usually first assigned by the…

 A. User
 B. Manager
 C. Director
 D. Administrator

6. Which of the following is *not* a typical threat to network security?

 A. Unauthorized use of the network
 B. Tampering with files or hardware
 C. Theft of data
 D. Software updates

7. When a network account is no longer needed, it should be…

 A. Deleted
 B. Detailed
 C. Reversed
 D. Retired

8. What type of compression is frequently used by DLT drives?

 A. ROM
 B. DLZ
 C. MAC
 D. UPS

9. Which of the following devices will a KVM switch *not* support?

    A. A keyboard

    B. A mouse

    C. A monitor

    D. A tablet

10. UPS systems are rated in terms of…

    A. Watts (W)

    B. Volt amperes (VA)

    C. Running time (RT)

    D. Amps (A)

REVIEW ANSWERS

1. **C** Define your objectives: The planning process can usually be divided into five phases: setting network objectives, evaluating current resources, developing a plan, reviewing the plan, and implementing the plan.

2. **B** Accounts: An account provides users with access to files, directories, and devices (such as printers). In a client/server network, accounts are created and managed by the network administrator.

3. **C** Create an account for that user: The first step in enabling a new user is to create an account for that user. An administrator can use a network utility to enter and edit account information for a user. The new user account requires a complete set of information that defines a user to the network security system.

4. **B** Groups: Groups are commonly used to grant access to resources—the permissions granted to a group are automatically granted to all of its members. By assigning permissions and rights to a group, an administrator can treat the group as a single account.

5. **D** Administrator: The first step in enabling a new user is to create an account for that user. An administrator can use a network utility to enter and edit account information for a user.

6. **D** Software updates: Typical security threats include unauthorized use of the network, tampering with files or hardware, and theft of data. Software updates are not typical security issues.

7. **A** Deleted: When an account is no longer needed, it can generally be disabled or deleted. This will prevent the user from accessing the network.

8. **B** DLZ: Generally speaking, a DLT tape drive (such as the Compaq 40/80 DLT drive) will read and write in both uncompressed (that is, "native") and Digital Lempel-Ziv (DLZ) compressed data formats.

9. **D** A tablet: A typical KVM switch will support a keyboard, monitor, and mouse, but will not support a serial device such as a tablet.

10. **B** Volt amperes (VA): All UPS systems are rated in terms of volt amperes (or VA), which is a more technical indication of power (usually measured in watts, or W). The power requirements of your equipment should be less than or equal to the VA capacity of the UPS.

Server
Configuration
Issues

NEWBIE	SOME EXPERIENCE	EXPERT
4 hours	2 hours	0.5 hour

Even after a network is assembled and operational, it's unlikely that your network configuration will remain the same for very long. Hardware often needs to be upgraded as the network expands, defective devices must quickly be replaced (or reconfigured) to maintain reliability, and software should be periodically upgraded to take advantage of bug fixes or performance patches. As the server (and your overall network) matures, you'll need to make these hardware and software adjustments. Once you've made your changes, it's imperative that you document any changes and establish a new server performance baseline. In this chapter, we'll examine some of the issues involved with server configuration.

Objective 4.01   Server CMOS Configuration

A network server is basically a PC that's been souped up with advanced communication and data handling and features. Like any PC, the server must be configured in order to use the various hardware devices in the system. The motherboard BIOS provides a simple menu-driven interface that allows you to view and edit these hardware options, and each selection is held in a small amount of nonvolatile RAM (NVRAM) on the motherboard. We typically refer to this menu-driven interface as the CMOS Setup (though many PC makers call this the BIOS Setup, System Setup, or simply the Setup). The main advantage of a BIOS-based setup routine is self-diagnostics. When the server starts, it compares the hardware configuration listed with the hardware actually found in the system. If the two match, the server's POST assumes that the hardware is working properly, and the operating system is allowed to load. If the two do not match, the server's POST reports an error, and the boot process halts until the problem is corrected. For example, you'd run the CMOS Setup to identify a floppy drive, enable a parallel port for IEEE 1284 operation, enable a serial (COM) port, set the date/time, identify a hard drive, set up the hardware boot sequence, and so on.

Exam Tip

The CMOS Setup (or simply, the setup) should not be confused with the server's *system setup utility* (SSU). The SSU is a utility run from a floppy diskette that is usually intended to enter or change information about specific expansion cards.

Accessing the Setup

Because the CMOS Setup is a hardware-level routine that is operating system independent, you can only access it in the few moments after POST starts, but before the operating system starts to load. For example, if you see a message such as "Starting Windows," you've waited too long to invoke the CMOS Setup routine. After the POST completes its memory count, you can invoke the CMOS Setup by pressing one or more keys (such as F2). In many cases, you'll see a brief message below the BIOS banner that tells you which key(s) to press (i.e., "Press F1 for Setup"). If you have cleared the CMOS RAM using the Clear CMOS motherboard jumper (i.e., after upgrading the BIOS), or if the CMOS RAM contents are lost (often due to a low backup battery), you will automatically enter the CMOS Setup so that you can reconfigure the server hardware.

Travel Advisory

If your floppy disk drive is not configured properly, and you cannot use the CMOS Setup to correct the problem, you might need to clear the CMOS RAM using the motherboard's Clear CMOS jumper.

Setup Menus

Once the CMOS Setup starts, you can select from one of the menu options that appears. In most cases, the CMOS Setup routine can be divided into six major menus: Main menu, Advanced menu, Security menu, Server menu, Boot menu, and Exit menu. Keep in mind that the options found in the CMOS Setup can easily vary between systems. These are the menu and submenus that allow you to configure the drive controllers and processor settings:

- **Main Menu**   The Main menu generally allows you to set the date, time, and drive setup.
- **Advanced Menu**   The Advanced menu usually allows for control of the PCI bus (including embedded controllers), integrated peripherals, ports, and advanced chipset settings.
- **Security Menu**   The Security menu allows you to configure the server's security features such as passwords, case protection, and lockout features.

- **Server Menu**   The Server menu lets you adjust network-specific settings such as system management, console redirection, emergency management, and platform event paging.
- **Boot Menu**   The Boot menu allows you to configure boot device priority, hard drive setup, and removable device configurations.
- **Exit Menu**   This menu lets you choose how to handle the changes you've made to the CMOS RAM (if any).

> ### Travel Advisory
>
> As you navigate the various setup menus, you may find that some options are shown but cannot be changed. This usually means that the option is autoconfigured or autodetected, you must use a different Setup screen to change it, or you must use the *System Setup Utility* (SSU) diskette to make the necessary changes.

Changing the Boot Device

The *boot order* is the sequence in which BIOS checks the available drives in the system for boot information. For example, a typical PC might check the floppy drive first, then check the hard drive, and then check the CD-ROM drive. You may find it necessary to change the boot order in order to improve boot performance or troubleshoot possible drive problems. Fortunately, you can change the boot order using the CMOS Setup routine.

| Objective 4.02 |

RAID Controller Configuration

An important task of any server is to protect the valuable data that is being handled on the network. RAID techniques are employed to provide redundant data storage, and to enhance the transfer of data to and from the server. After you install (or replace) a RAID controller, you'll need to configure the RAID system for proper operation. In many cases, the RAID controller may attempt to "autoconfigure" itself, but you should understand the techniques involved with manual configuration in the event that you even need to tweak the controller's installation yourself.

> **Local Lingo**
>
> **RAID (redundant array of independent disks)**   Drive technology that protects data by mirroring information between disks, or improves disk performance by splitting data between multiple disks.

System Configuration Utility

In most cases, your RAID controller is shipped with a configuration utility that can be run directly from the RAID controller's driver/software CD. In other cases, the RAID configuration utility may already be copied to the server's boot disk. Be sure that you've installed the very latest versions of the RAID driver and support software before attempting to configure the RAID controller. If you're not sure, use the configuration software on the controller's CD. If your server does not have a bootable CD-ROM drive, it may be possible for you to create setup diskettes from the CD on another system, then use those diskettes to configure the RAID controller. Otherwise, start the RAID configuration software according to the manufacturer's instructions.

Controller Order

Chances are that large servers or data subsystems will include more than one RAID controller (perhaps many controllers). You can select the order in which each particular RAID controller—and other hard drive controllers—will be recognized at boot time. The first controller is always set to the primary hard drive controller that is managing the boot disk. Remember that the first disk drive on this controller is the one the server will boot from. Then it's a matter of setting subsequent controllers with an appropriate place in the order. Some systems will support up to 15 disk controllers. For example, if the boot disk is being handled by a RAID controller, you'll need to set the controller to "first" (and other controllers to subsequent numbers). You can also rearrange the order of other controllers as well.

When installing a RAID controller in a system with an existing array controller, you can either place the new controller at the end of the controller order or reorder the controllers. Keep in mind that reordering the controllers will change the current drive letter assignments for all drives on the system. To avoid changing the drive letter assignments, place the new controller at the end of the controller order. When you've finished setting the controller order, save your changes and exit. The server will reboot. Remove the RAID controller's software CD and verify that the system boots normally without POST errors.

RAID Configuration Utility

Once you've configured the new RAID controller in the server's system configuration utility (as shown previously), you'll need to run the RAID controller's configuration utility in order to set up the controller card itself. The configuration utility allows a wide range of disk array management controls such as adding more disk drives, selecting RAID levels, creating new arrays, expanding and extending capacity, changing stripe sizes, and other key RAID features.

Exam Tip

Depending on the network operating system in use, you might need to take the network offline before using the configuration utility.

Using Configuration Wizards

If your RAID controller offers Configuration Wizards, you can check and optimize your drive array almost automatically. When you start the RAID controller's configuration utility, the software checks the configuration of the controller and its drive array(s). If the arrays are unconfigured or the configuration is less than optimal, the Configuration Wizard tool can often guide you through the configuration process. This provides a particularly handy tool when setting up new RAID installations. A RAID controller with a Configuration Wizard (such as the SmartArray 4250ES) recognizes the following conditions:

- **Unconfigured Controller** When the configuration utility detects an unconfigured controller, the Configuration Wizard leads you through the controller configuration process.
- **Unused Physical Drives** When the configuration utility detects unused physical drives, the Configuration Wizard provides an easy way to add them to an array. For example, the capacity expansion capability of the SmartArray 4250ES allows the configuration utility to add new physical drives to an existing array without destroying data on the existing logical drives.

- **Unused Space On an Array**   If the configuration utility detects unused capacity in an array, the Configuration Wizard leads you through the process of configuring the space into one or more logical drives.

Manual Configuration

Rather than using the Configuration wizards to enable your drive array, you can use the RAID controller's configuration utility to manually configure the controller and your drive array. The procedures below outline the techniques used with a popular RAID controller to create a new array, expand an array, extend a logical drive, alter the stripe size, and alter the RAID level.

Creating a New Array

To create a new drive array, you'll need to choose a RAID controller to manage the array, group selected drives (of the same size) into the array, then create logical drives from the physical array. Suppose that you have four 4.3GB drives and two 9.1GB drives connected to your SCSI RAID controller. You'd probably create two arrays. Array A would consist of three 4.3GB drives (with the fourth 4.3GB drive used as a spare), and array B would be the two 9.1GB drives. The fault-tolerance method for all logical drives in array A might be RAID 5 (distributed data guarding), and the fault-tolerance method for all logical drives in array B may be RAID 1 (drive mirroring). Let's review the steps to set up this type of example manually:

1. Start the RAID controller's configuration utility. In the Main Configuration screen, select the Controller Selection box.
2. Select one of the listed controllers. If there is only one RAID controller in the server, only one controller should be listed.
3. Click the Controller Settings button, and the Controller Settings screen appears (see Figure 4-1).
4. Select the correct operating system.
5. Click the Create Array button, and the Create Drive Array screen appears (see Figure 4-2).
6. Select the three drives you want to make up array A from the drives listed (for example, SCSI IDs 0, 1, and 2). Remember to always group physical drives of the *same* size—if you mix drive sizes, the capacity of the larger drives is wasted.
7. Click the Assign Drive(s) to Array button.

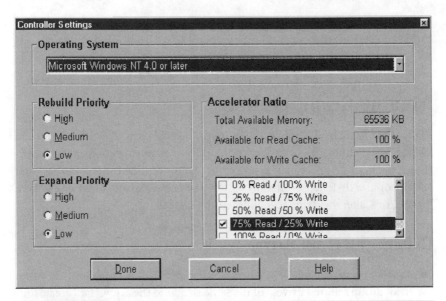

FIGURE 4-1   The Controller Settings dialog box

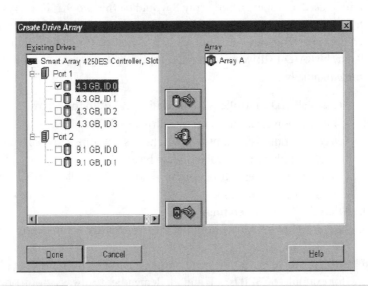

FIGURE 4-2   The Create Drive Array dialog box

8. Select the last 4.3GB drive (ID 3) and click the Assign Spare to Array button. Remember that the same spare drive may be assigned to multiple arrays, but spare drives should have the same (or greater) capacity as the drives in the array.

9. Click the Done button to return to the Main Configuration screen.

10. Select the controller again; then click the Create Array button to create array B.

11. Assign both 9.1GB drives to the array and click the Done button.

12. Select array A (or the Unused Space icon under array A) in the Logical Configuration view.

13. Click the Create Logical Drive button (see Figure 4-3).

14. Select your RAID level. For our example, click the Distributed Data Guarding (RAID 5) option button.

15. Click the Array Accelerator Enable button (if your controller provides array acceleration).

16. Select your stripe size. Stripe size can be left at the default for the selected RAID level, or set to another value.

17. Size your logical drive. The Logical Drive Size area includes a graphical representation of the storage capacity available. To create a single logical drive across this array, accept the default values.

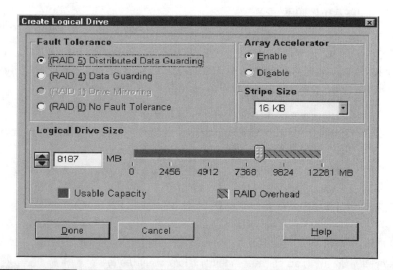

FIGURE 4-3   The Create Logical Drive dialog box

18. Click the Done button.
19. Click array B (or the Unused Space icon under array B) in the Logical Configuration view.
20. Repeat these steps to create a single logical drive on array B—this time selecting RAID 1 fault tolerance. This should complete the basic configuration of your drive array(s).

Expanding Capacity

Capacity expansion involves adding storage capacity (drives) to an array that has already been configured. If an existing array is nearly full of data, you can expand the capacity *without* disturbing the existing data. When you run the RAID controller's configuration utility, the program checks the drive hardware and configuration. If the configuration utility discovers a physical drive that is not being used, the Configuration Wizard leads you through the steps for adding the drive, or you can expand the capacity manually:

1. Install the new physical drive(s). Always group physical drives of the same size—if you mix drive sizes, the capacity of the larger drives is wasted.
2. Assign the new physical drive(s) to an existing array. Existing logical drive(s) will automatically expand across the physical drives (including the newly added ones).
3. Create a new logical drive to use the extra space on the expanded array.

Consider a configuration similar to the previous example: three 4.3GB drives in array A (no spare), and two 9.1GB drives in array B. If a fourth 4.3GB drive is added later, you can expand array A to include the fourth drive:

1. Select array A and click the Expand button.
2. Select the unassigned 4.3GB drive; then click Assign Drive(s) to Array.
3. Click the Next button at the bottom of the screen.
4. Click the Create Logical Drive button.

Exam Tip

In the event of power loss, capacity expansion information is temporarily stored in the array accelerator's memory. To prevent the loss of data in the expanding logical drive, do not interchange RAID controllers or array accelerator boards during a capacity expansion process.

5. Set the fault tolerance, enable the array accelerator, set the stripe size, and set the size for logical drive 2.
6. Click Done.
7. On the main screen, select Controller and Save Configuration from the menu bar. This saves the new settings for logical drive 2 and starts the capacity expansion process.

Extending Capacity

Logical drive extension allows you to increase the size of existing logical drives without disturbing the data on those logical drives. Keep in mind that logical drive extension is *not* supported by all operating systems. If an existing logical drive is full of data, you can extend the logical drive when there is free space in the array. If there is no free space available, you can add drives to the array and proceed to extend the logical drive:

1. Click the logical drive that you want to extend.
2. Click the Drive menu.
3. Select Extend Logical Drive.
4. The Extend Logical Drive screen displays the current capacity and RAID overhead of the selected logical drive.
5. Click the slider control to change (increase) the size of the logical drive. You cannot reduce the size of the logical drive from this screen.
6. Click Done.
7. Save the logical drive by opening the Controller menu and selecting the Save Configuration option.
8. The logical drive will be restructured so that its data will be preserved.
9. Make the extended space of the logical drive available for use by creating a new partition in the extended space of the logical drive, or by increasing the size of existing partition(s) in the extended logical drive.

Changing RAID Level and Stripe Size

Use the Online RAID Level dialog box to reconfigure a currently configured logical drive to a new fault-tolerance (RAID) level, or use the Stripe Size Migration dialog box to change an existing logical drive's stripe size to a new stripe size. Both processes can be accomplished online without causing any data loss:

1. Select a logical drive from the Logical Configuration view.
2. Select the Drive menu.
3. Click the Migrate RAID/Stripe Size option button (see Figure 4-4).

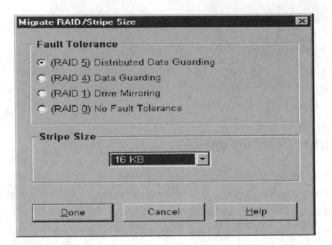

FIGURE 4-4   The Migrate RAID/Stripe Size dialog box

1. Select a new RAID level (i.e., click the RAID 5 Distributed Data Guarding button).
2. The stripe size can be left at the default for the selected RAID level, or set to another value. For example, you can set the stripe size to 16KB.
3. Click Done.

Objective 4.03   SCSI Controller Configuration

Whether added as an expansion device or integrated into your server's motherboard, the vast majority of SCSI host adapters will employ onboard firmware to configure the adapter's various operations. In most cases, the default settings of your SCSI BIOS are adequate, and you should not need to change the default configuration of the host adapter. However, you may decide to alter these default values if there is a conflict between device settings, or if you need to optimize the system's performance. This part of the chapter outlines the default settings of a common SCSI host adapter, and explains many of the SCSI BIOS settings that you may encounter.

Using Setup Menus

The version number of your SCSI BIOS appears in a banner displayed on your computer monitor during boot. If a configuration utility is available, a message similar to the following also appears on your monitor:

```
Press Ctrl+C to start Symbios Configuration Utility...
```

This message remains on your screen for about five seconds, giving you time to start the utility. If you decide to press CTRL-C, the message changes to

```
Please wait, invoking Symbios Configuration Utility...
```

After a brief pause, your computer monitor displays the Main menu of the Symbios SCSI BIOS configuration utility.

> **Exam Tip**
>
> Not all devices detected by the configuration utility can be controlled by the BIOS. Devices such as tape drives and scanners require that a device driver specific to that peripheral be loaded. The device manufacturer provides those device drivers.

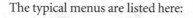

The typical menus are listed here:

- **Main Menu** When you start the Symbios SCSI BIOS configuration utility, the Main menu appears. This menu displays a list of up to four Symbios PCI to SCSI host adapters in the system and information about each of them. To select an adapter, use only the arrow keys and ENTER key. You can then view or change the current settings for that adapter and the SCSI devices attached to it. Select an adapter only if its Current Status is On. If any settings are altered, the system reboots upon exit from the configuration utility when you use the Quit option.
- **Change Adapter Status** The Change Adapter Status option allows you to activate or deactivate a host adapter and all SCSI devices attached to it. When this option is used to make a change, the change takes place after a reboot once you exit from the utility. To change an adapter's status, select

it and press ENTER. Press the ESC key to exit from this menu and return
to the Main menu.

- **Adapter Boot Order**   The Adapter Boot Order option allows you to
  set the order in which host adapters will boot (when more than one
  SCSI host adapter is in the system). When this option is selected, the
  Boot Order menu appears. To change an adapter's boot order, select
  it and press ENTER. The system prompts you to enter the new boot
  sequence number. To remove an adapter from the boot order, press
  ENTER again rather than entering a new sequence number. Only four
  adapters can be assigned a boot order, starting with boot sequence
  number zero (0). If an invalid number is entered, an error message
  appears. When the adapters are ordered properly, press the ESC key
  to exit from this menu.

- **Additional Adapter Configuration**   The Additional Adapter
  Configuration option allows you to configure an adapter that is
  not assigned a boot order. When this option is selected, the Adapter
  Configuration menu appears. Highlight the adapter to be configured
  and press ENTER. The message "Resetting adapter, please wait" appears,
  and then the system scans for devices. Finally, the Utilities menu
  appears and lists the available options.

- **Display Mode**   The Display Mode option determines how much information about your host adapter(s) and SCSI devices appear on the computer monitor during boot. For more complete information, choose
  the verbose setting. For a faster boot, choose the terse setting.

- **Mono/Color**   The Mono/Color option allows a choice between a
  monochrome or color display for the SCSI BIOS configuration utility.
  Choose the mono setting to get a more readable screen on a monochrome monitor (if necessary). In most cases, the color option will
  yield the best results on color displays.

- **Language**   When the Language option is enabled, you can select from
  one of several different languages (i.e., English, German, French, Italian,
  and Spanish).

- **Utilities Menu**   When you select a host adapter on the Main menu, the
  Utilities menu appears. Choose Adapter Setup to view and change the
  selected adapter settings. Choose Device Selections to view and change
  settings for the devices attached to the selected adapter. After making
  changes to the configuration of any host adapter or connected SCSI
  device, the system returns to the Utilities menu. Before you exit this
  menu, you're prompted to save or cancel any changes.

Adapter Setup Menu

The settings in this menu are global settings that affect the selected host adapter and all SCSI devices attached to it. One of these choices can be selected by highlighting it and pressing ENTER:

- **SCAM Support**   The Symbios BIOS version 4.xx and above supports the SCSI PnP protocol called SCAM (SCSI Configured AutoMatically). SCAM support by default is off in versions 4.09 and later for the SYM53C875 controller. You may choose to turn this feature on *only* if the system drivers do not require SCAM to be off.
- **Parity**   The Symbios PCI SCSI host adapters always generate parity, but some older SCSI devices do not. You're offered the option of disabling parity checking. When disabling parity checking, it's also necessary to disable disconnects for all devices, as parity checking for the reselection phase is not disabled. If a device does not generate parity and it disconnects, the I/O cycle never completes because the reselection never finishes.
- **Host SCSI ID**   The host adapter's SCSI ID (logical unit number or LUN) is a unique number used to identify the device on the SCSI bus. In general, it's suggested that you *not* change the host adapter ID from the default value of 7 (this ID gives the SCSI adapter the highest priority on the SCSI bus). Also please note that if you have 8-bit SCSI devices (narrow), they *cannot* see host IDs greater than 7.
- **Scan Order**   This option allows the user to tell the SCSI BIOS and device drivers to scan the SCSI bus from low to high (0 to Max) SCSI ID, or from high to low (Max to 0) SCSI ID. If there is more than one device on the SCSI bus, changing the scan order changes the order in which drive letters are assigned by the system. Drive order may be reassigned differently in systems supporting the BIOS Boot Specification (BBS). This scan order option may conflict with operating systems that automatically assign a drive order.
- **Removable Media Support**   This option defines the removable media support for a specific drive. When this option is selected, a window appears with three choices: None, Boot Drive Only, and With Media Installed. None indicates there is no removable media support. Boot Drive Only provides removable media support for a removable hard drive if it is first in the scan order. With Media Installed provides removable media support wherever the drive actually resides. One of these choices can be selected by highlighting it and pressing ENTER.

- **CHS Mapping**   This option defines the cylinder head sector (CHS) values that will be mapped onto a disk without preexisting partition information. SCSI PnP Mapping is the default value. To support interchange with non-compatible systems, there is another option that can be selected by choosing CHS Mapping and then selecting Alternate CHS Mapping. Neither of these options will have any effect after the disk has been partitioned with the FDISK command. To remove partitioning, two options are available: Reformat the Disk Using the Format Device option and Use the FDISK /MBR Command at the C:\ Prompt, where MBR is the master boot record. After clearing the partitions and data, it is necessary to reboot and clear memory or the old partitioning data will be reused, thus nullifying the previous operation.
- **Spinup Delay (seconds)**   This option allows you to stagger spinups for a longer period of time to balance the total current load. The default value is 2 seconds—with choices between 1 and 10 seconds. This is a power management technique designed to accommodate disk devices that may have heavy current loads during power up. If multiple drives are being powered up simultaneously and drawing heavy current, this option staggers the spinups to limit startup current.

Device Selections Menu

The settings in this menu affect individual SCSI devices attached to the selected host adapter. Changes made from this menu do not cause the system to reboot upon exit from the SCSI BIOS configuration utility:

- **Sync Rate (MB/s)**   This option defines the maximum data transfer rate at which the host adapter will attempt to negotiate. The host adapter and a SCSI device must agree to a rate they can both handle.
- **Width (bits)**   This option defines the maximum SCSI data width at which the host adapter will attempt to negotiate. The host adapter and a SCSI device must agree to the data width they can both handle. Only host adapters that can handle 16-bit data transfers have this option enabled.
- **Disconnect**   SCSI devices have the capability to disconnect from the initiator during an I/O transfer. This disconnect option frees the SCSI bus to allow other I/O processes. It also tells the host adapter whether to allow a device to disconnect. Some devices run faster with disconnects enabled (mostly newer devices), while some run faster with disconnects disabled (mostly older devices).
- **Read Write I/O Time-Out (seconds)**   This option sets the amount of time the host adapter waits for a read, write, or seek command to complete

before trying the I/O transfer again. Because this provides a safeguard allowing the system to recover if an I/O operation fails, it is recommended that you always set the time-out to a value greater than zero. A zero value allows unlimited time for an operation to complete and could result in the system being hung-up.

- **Scan for Device at Boot Time**   Set this option to No if there is a device that you do not want to be available to the system. On a bus with only a few devices attached, you can speed up boot time by changing this setting to No for all unused SCSI IDs.

- **Scan for SCSI Logical Units (LUNs)**   Set this option to No if problems arise with a device that responds to all LUNs whether they are occupied or not. For example, if a SCSI device with multiple LUNs is present on your system but you do not want all of those LUNs to be available to the system, then set this option to No. This will limit the scan to LUN 0 only.

- **Queue Tags**   If the device driver supports this capability, this option allows you to enable or disable the issuing of queue tags during I/O requests.

- **Initial Boot**   This option allows any device attached to the first adapter to become the boot device. It provides the users of non-BBS personal computers with some of the flexibility of a BBS machine.

- **Format Device**   If enabled, this option allows the user to low-level format a magnetic disk drive. Low-level formatting will completely and irreversibly erase all data on the drive. Formatting will default the drive to a 512-byte sector size even if the drive had previously been formatted to another sector size.

- **Verify**   This option allows the user to read all the sectors on a disk looking for errors. When selected, this option displays the following message: "Verify all sectors on the device. Press ESC to abort. Press any key to continue."

- **Restore Default Setup**   This option resets all device selections back to their default settings. Select this option to restore all manufacturing defaults for the specified adapter. Note that all user-customized options will be lost upon saving after restoring default setup.

Objective 4.04   Handling Software Updates

As you saw in Chapter 2, a server is also highly dependent on software for proper operation. An operating system provides the user interface, launches applications, and manages resources. Drivers allow the operating system to recognize and use hardware and features that the operating system may not directly support. From time to time, software bugs, compatibility problems, security holes, and other issues will surface, and you'll need to update the operating system and drivers. This part of the chapter highlights the general process involved with OS and driver updates.

OS Update Considerations

The operating system is an important platform that manages applications and resources on the server. Consequently, OS upgrades are not something to be undertaken lightly. Even the relatively minor processes of patching and fixing can have a profound impact on compatibility and system reliability. Before upgrading or patching an OS, consider some of the following issues:

- **What does the update offer or fix?** Updates are intended to serve a particular purpose. It's important that you have a clear understanding of the features and fixes offered by an update. In some cases, you may not need to perform an update if you're not affected by the issues that the fix corrects—this can save unnecessary work.
- **How is the update provided (i.e., CD or download)?** Downloads may take a great deal of time, and can impair server operation during the download process. Distribution on CD may be a bit more convenient—especially if you must update a large number of systems.
- **What does the update cost (if any)?** In many cases, upgrades (i.e., a Windows NT to Windows 2000 upgrade) can cost several hundred (perhaps several thousand) dollars, but updates (i.e., a service pack or patch) are usually available for free. Ordering an update on CD usually carries a cost for shipping and handling. Make sure that you have the appropriate license to install the upgrade/update on each system.
- **What support is available?** There will undoubtedly be questions and issues during the update process. You should check to see if FAQs or other support resources are available to help you overcome potential problems.
- **How long is the download?** Downloads take time—often a long time—and may prevent Internet access while the download is taking place. You may need to plan a download at times of low server utilization.
- **How long does it take to install?** It takes time to install an OS upgrade or patch, so you'll need to plan the necessary amount of server downtime in order to install the new software. You may need to plan an installation at times of low server utilization.

- **What happens to the current server information?**   Your server is configured with user accounts, permissions, security settings, and so on. You should verify that all of your server information is maintained (transferred) when the upgrade or update is installed. If not, this may seriously interfere with network's operation, and you'll need to reenter that information. This can be a time-consuming and error-prone process that can dramatically increase server downtime.
- **Are there any software compatibility issues?**   Remember that applications are the reason that we use PCs and networks in the first place, and applications are designed for certain operating systems. If you plan to upgrade or update an operating system, you should verify that your main applications are unaffected. If they are, you may need to update those application(s) to ensure compatibility.
- **Are there any hardware compatibility issues?**   As with software, hardware drivers are often OS-specific. When upgrading or updating an operating system, you may need to update the drivers for key devices (such as RAID controllers or SCSI controllers). It may be necessary to download updated drivers well before any planned OS update.
- **Will a server backup be required?**   It's usually a good idea to perform a complete system backup before attempting an OS update. This requires time and tape drive resources, and the time needed to perform the backup may interfere with other routine backup functions.

Driver Update Considerations

A device driver (or simply a driver) is a small program that allows an operating system to use that particular device, and make its resources available to applications. While a device may be physically installed on the computer, an operating system cannot communicate with the device until the driver for that device has been installed and configured. The driver tells the computer how to work with the device so that the device can perform its job properly. For example, a driver is necessary so that you can operate the video card in high resolutions, color depths, or refresh rates (among other attributes). Modern PCs use drivers for just about every type of peripheral including

- Input devices (i.e., mice and keyboards)
- Drive devices (i.e., floppy drives, hard drives, CD drives, and removable media devices)
- Drive controllers (i.e., IDE, SCSI, and RAID controllers)

- Network controllers
- Multimedia devices (i.e., video cards, sound cards, capture cards, and so on)
- Output devices (i.e., printers and plotters)

Printers are another great example of driver importance. Printers are built by many different manufacturers and each has a wide array of features and functions. It would be impossible for computer and operating system manufacturers to prepare a computer with all the software needed to identify and use with every type of printer. Instead, computers are often prepared for a small range of popular or generic printers, and printer manufacturers make drivers available for each of their printers. Before your computer can send documents to a printer, you must install (a.k.a. load) the drivers for that printer so your computer will be able to communicate with it.

In virtually all cases, the manufacturer of each component or device is responsible for supplying the drivers for their equipment. For example, NIC manufacturers are responsible for making drivers available for their cards. Drivers are usually included on a diskette or CD that accompanies the device, or can be downloaded from the manufacturer's Web site.

Exam Tip

Device drivers allow the operating system to communicate with a vast array of hardware devices. Keeping drivers updated can resolve compatibility issues and improve a device's functionality.

Hardware Compatibility

Because drivers form the interface between operating systems and hardware devices, each driver is generally designed for a specific OS (or family of operating systems). For example, a different driver version may be required for Windows 98, Windows NT, or Windows 2000. When you're planning to purchase a device, you must check to see that a suitable driver is available for your particular operating system; otherwise, the device may not work. For example, you generally cannot use USB adapters under Windows NT. One way to check compatibility is to investigate the *hardware compatibility list* (HCL) maintained by the

OS maker. The HCL lists drivers that have been tested (and often included) with the operating system.

Driver Management Tips

Drivers must be installed, configured, updated, and sometimes removed. Each operating system uses its own methods for accomplishing these functions, but most employ a graphical user interface with a series of dialog boxes that walk you through each process. For the sake of this discussion, let's consider driver management under Windows NT.

- **Driver Installation**   End-user oriented operating systems like Windows 98/ME use Plug-and-Play (PnP) technology to automatically identify new devices and begin the driver installation process. By comparison, Windows NT is not well suited to PnP operation. With Windows NT, you'll need to start the Control Panel and proceed with a manual identification of new devices, then install the drivers from diskette of CD.

- **Driver Configuration**   Most devices typically offer a suite of options that must be set correctly in order for the device to function properly. Among these options are the system resources (i.e., IRQs, I/O ranges, DMA channels, and so on) necessary to configure the device alongside other devices in the PC. Where PnP operating systems can automatically assign resources to a device, Windows NT may require you to set resource assignments manually.

- **Driver Removal**   It is sometimes necessary to remove drivers in order to relieve conflicts with other devices, or when devices are being removed/replaced. In many cases, you should also remove existing drivers before installing updated drivers to prevent possible conflicts between similar driver versions. The process of removing a driver is similar to that of installing a driver—you simply select the desired device and click Remove. It may be necessary to turn off or reboot the system to unload the old driver from memory (RAM).

- **Driver Updates**   As you have seen, a manufacturer will frequently incorporate additions or changes to a driver to improve the device's performance or ease compatibility issues. You can almost always locate updated drivers on the device manufacturer's Web site where they can be downloaded and installed. You may need to remove the old driver first and reboot the system. Once the old driver is gone, you can then install the new driver. In some cases, the new driver will be in the form of an executable file, and you need simply run the executable file to install the updated driver. Always check for any README or other document files that accompany the updated driver. Documentation will detail the update process and list any important precautions to follow.

Objective 4.05   Documenting a Network

Regardless of your role in network support, your ultimate success in maintaining, upgrading, or repairing a network depends on your understanding of the network. Being familiar with the network's organization, hardware, and software significantly eases your workload and worries. Another consideration is network performance. Measuring normal network activity allows you to establish a baseline for your network—and subsequent changes in activity and performance levels can be used to identify problems or justify upgrades. This part of the chapter offers a series of guidelines that can help you document and establish an operating baseline for your network.

Obtaining Documentation

Over time, even simple networks can evolve into complicated arrangements of servers, workstations, and media. While the individual workstation and server PC hardware may be well understood, the interconnections and setup of various hardware components may be obscured. As a result, all technicians should have access to a comprehensive collection of network documentation. The actual documents can vary quite a bit between companies, but at its core up-to-date documentation provides information about how the network should look and perform, as well as where to seek help if there are problems. Documentation provides those "need to know" details that show you where to find solutions to the

---

Travel Advisory

Documentation is an essential troubleshooting tool. Always keep network documentation available, and keep it up to date as the network matures and grows.

problems that may occur, and will always pay off when you need to repair or update a network. Documentation should generally contain the following:

- A map of the entire network, including the locations of all hardware and cabling. This may be accompanied by a logical layout of the network (i.e., a star topology), though that is not always necessary.
- Complete information on each server, such as the make, model, and included hardware devices. This should also include the schedule and locations of all backups. Similar information on each workstation is also helpful, but often does not require the same level of detail.
- Complete information on each repeater, hub, bridge, and router. Often, this merely involves denoting their locations in the network map and including a copy of their respective user manuals.
- Complete NOS and application software information, including versions, licensing, and support details (as well as the location of all installation CDs).
- A complete index of vendors, suppliers, contractors, and other related contacts. If equipment is maintained by manufacturers or outside organizations, be sure to have a current copy of each respective service agreement.
- A detailed repair record of all problems, including symptoms and solutions, event dates, contacts, troubleshooting procedures, and overall results.

Do not underestimate the importance of thorough, well-organized documentation. Any experienced technician can relate tales of woe when the last network guru left the company without leaving meaningful records or training a successor. Overcoming poor documentation can be a painful (and sometimes overwhelming) process.

Creating a Baseline

Understanding how a healthy network functions is sometimes more important than knowing how to resolve problems if the network fails. When a network is implemented, it is common practice to establish a *baseline* in order to document the network's typical operating levels. By establishing a baseline, you can identify normal network performance. More importantly, changes in the baseline can help you to identify network problems and plan upgrades to the server or network. As a rule, a baseline is updated whenever users, hardware, or software are changed (i.e., added to or removed from) the network. After a baseline is established, all network activities can be compared to it as part of the ongoing monitoring process. A baseline is especially helpful in identifying and understanding the following information.

- Daily and weekly patterns of network utilization
- Patterns of heavy network usage
- Traffic and data transfer bottlenecks
- Traffic patterns involving various protocols

It is important to establish a baseline only after your network is documented and operating properly. Do not establish a baseline until you have verified that all network connections are correct, all hardware is operational, and any necessary system fine-tuning has been accomplished. It is a common error (especially among novice technicians) to take a baseline as quickly as possible—overlooking network problems or configuration errors that may impair performance right from the beginning. Measure network performance and set your baseline after the performance is determined to be acceptable. Network performance involves elements of the entire network such as

- Server hardware
- Workstation hardware
- Communication hardware (hubs, routers, bridges)
- Network interface cards (NICs)
- Cable media (a.k.a. cable runs)
- Cable connection schemes (i.e., RJ-45 wall plates and patch panels)

When you're ready to set your baseline, it's a matter of selecting and using the proper tool to make your measurements. Fortunately, there is a selection of tools available to help technicians document network performance (including network monitors, protocol analyzers, and other utilities).

Exam Tip

Ping is an ideal tool for testing network connections to see if they are intact.

Baselines vs. Benchmarks

Many technicians often confuse the terms *baseline* and *benchmark*; they are not the same thing. A benchmark is a program or utility that measures one or more attributes of a system's performance (i.e., the ServerBench utility can measure data transfer speeds), but a benchmark does not indicate whether those results are normal for your network. By comparison, a baseline is a collection of test results that are judged to represent typical (or normal) network/server performance. In many cases, a benchmark or other monitoring utility is used to measure performance levels in order to help you set the baseline. By rerunning benchmark or monitoring software regularly, those results can then be compared against the baseline. It's a subtle but important difference that all technicians should understand.

Local Lingo

Baseline   A collection of test results that is judged to represent typical (or normal) network/server performance.

Benchmark   A program or utility that measures one or more attributes of a system's performance.

Identifying Performance Bottlenecks

Network operation doesn't happen in a vacuum—it is the result of carefully coordinated actions between devices in the server (or workstation). For example, each device in the server takes a certain amount of time to do its job. When each device is able to do its job effectively, it stands to reason that the network can perform at an optimum level. Unfortunately, there are many times when one or more devices do not operate at their best. A *bottleneck* occurs when a device is unable to handle the load placed on it. The device might not be configured for most efficient operation, or it may just be too slow for the job (and need to be upgraded). Processors, memory (RAM), NICs, disk controllers, and network cabling are just a few places where network performance bottlenecks commonly occur. Regular performance monitoring can help identify bottlenecks. For example, if network performance is faltering, and monitoring reveals that the server's processor utilization is very high, this can be an indication of a processor bottleneck. Adding another processor, upgrading the existing processor, or even adding another server may help to relieve the bottleneck. Generally speaking, bottlenecks usually indicate that an upgrade is necessary.

System Management

Network size and complexity has exploded over the last few years, and it's becoming increasingly difficult for a technician or administrator to keep track of the entire system. Vendors have responded to this by developing powerful utilities that are designed to aid in the management of WANs and larger LANs by providing a means of centralized administration—in effect, these system management tools take performance monitoring to a system-wide level. System management tools are often capable of collecting hardware and software inventory information, distributing and installing software, sharing network applications, and troubleshooting hardware and software problems. Let's look at some of the features found in Microsoft's Systems Management Server:

- **Inventory Management**   Inventory management (IM) software collects and maintains an inventory of the hardware and software for each computer in the network, and stores the inventory in a database. Typical inventory items include the type of CPU, amount of RAM, hard-disk size(s), operating system versions, and application software for each component installed.

- **Software Distribution**   Once a computer's inventory has been entered into the database, a software distribution utility can install and configure new software (or upgrade previously installed software) directly on a client. This distribution mechanism can also be used to run commands or utilities (i.e., virus scans) on specific clients.

- **Shared Application Management**   Shared applications can also be installed to a server for clients to access as needed. When a user logs on to the network, the management software builds a program folder on each client, which contains more folders that include the program icons representing the shared applications available to that user. To launch the shared application, the user selects an icon from the program folder displayed on the local workstation—though the application is actually stored on the server.

- **Remote Control and Network Monitors**   A systems management server can also provide help desk and diagnostic utilities that allow you to control and monitor remote clients directly. The diagnostic utilities let you view the client's current configuration, and help desk utilities provide direct access to a remote client.

CHECKPOINT

✔ **Objective 4.01: Server CMOS Configuration**   The motherboard BIOS provides a simple menu-driven interface that allows you to view and edit these hardware options, and each selection is held in a small amount of nonvolatile

RAM (NVRAM) on the motherboard. This menu-driven interface is called the CMOS Setup. If the setup values in memory are lost, the server may refuse to start. This means you should always make the effort to record each of the CMOS Setup entries, and keep those values with the server's documentation. After the POST completes its memory count, you can invoke the CMOS Setup by pressing one or more keys (such as F2).

✔ **Objective 4.02: RAID Controller Configuration**   After you install (or replace) a RAID controller, you'll need to configure the server for proper operation. A RAID controller is shipped with a configuration utility that can be run directly from the RAID controller's driver/software CD. You can select the order in which each particular RAID controller will be recognized by the server at boot time. The first controller is always set to the primary hard drive controller that is managing the boot disk. You'll then need to run the RAID controller's configuration utility in order to set up the controller card itself. You can create a new array, extend capacity, expand capacity, and change the RAID level or stripe size of the array.

✔ **Objective 4.03: SCSI Controller Configuration**   The vast majority of SCSI host adapters will employ onboard firmware to configure the adapter's various operations. In most cases, the default settings of your SCSI BIOS are adequate, and you should not need to change the default configuration of the host adapter. However, you might decide to alter these default values if there is a conflict between device settings, or if you need to optimize the system's performance.

✔ **Objective 4.04: Handling Software Updates**   Even the relatively minor processes of patching and fixing can have a profound impact on compatibility and system reliability. A device driver (or simply a driver) is a small program that allows an operating system to use that particular device, and make its resources available to applications. The driver tells the computer how to work with the device so that the device can perform its job properly. Because drivers form the interface between operating systems and hardware devices, each driver is generally designed for a specific OS (or family of operating systems).

✔ **Objective 4.05: Documenting a Network**   Success in maintaining, upgrading, or repairing a network depends on your understanding of the network. Measuring normal network activity allows you to establish a baseline for your network—and subsequent changes in activity and performance levels can be used to identify problems or justify upgrades. Technicians should have access to a comprehensive collection of network documentation. The actual documents can vary, but should provide information about how the network should look and perform, as well as where to seek help if there are problems.

REVIEW QUESTIONS

1. The drives on a server are typically configured using the...

   A. CMOS Setup

   B. SSU

   C. EMP

   D. PEP

2. If there is a problem with the floppy drive, you can boot from the CD-ROM by changing the...

   A. CMOS Setup

   B. Boot order

   C. Floppy drive

   D. CD-ROM drive

3. The PCI bus would generally be enabled and configured through which setup menu?

   A. Security

   B. Hot-Plug PCI

   C. Advanced

   D. Primary IDE master/slave

4. To add storage capacity (drives) to an existing RAID array, you would invoke...

   A. Capacity expansion

   B. Central extension

   C. Array calibration

   D. Automatic reset

5. To increase the size of existing logical drives without disturbing data in a RAID array, you would...

   A. Expand the drive

   B. Recalibrate the drive

   C. Rearrange the drive

   D. Extend the drive

6. By default, most SCSI controllers have the bus parity checking…

    A. Enabled

    B. Disabled

    C. Removed

    D. Overridden

7. Most SCSI controllers use a SCSI ID of…

    A. 4

    B. 5

    C. 6

    D. 7

8. Which of the following would *not* be a major OS update consideration?

    A. The issues fixed by the update

    B. The time needed to download the update

    C. The release date of the update

    D. The time needed to install the update

9. Getting a device to work under a new operating system may require updating the…

    A. Device hardware

    B. Motherboard

    C. Device firmware

    D. Device driver

10. Normal network/server operation can be recognized by establishing a…

    A. Benchmark

    B. Baseline

    C. Base memory

    D. Basic utility

REVIEW ANSWERS

1.   **A**   CMOS Setup: In most cases, the CMOS Setup routine can be divided into six major menus: Main menu, Advanced menu, Security menu, Server menu, Boot menu, and Exit menu. These are the menu and submenus that allow you to configure the drives, controllers and processor settings.

2. **B** Boot order: Boot order is the sequence in which BIOS checks the available drives in the system for boot information. For example, a typical PC may check the floppy drive first, then the hard drive, then the CD-ROM drive. You may find it necessary to change the boot order in order to improve boot performance or troubleshoot possible drive problems.

3. **C** Advanced: The Advanced menu usually allows for control of the PCI bus (including embedded controllers), integrated peripherals, ports, and advanced chipset settings.

4. **A** Capacity expansion: Capacity expansion involves adding storage capacity (drives) to an array that has already been configured. If an existing array is nearly full of data, you can expand the capacity without disturbing the existing data.

5. **D** Extend the drive: Drive extension allows you to increase the size of existing logical drives without disturbing the data on those logical drives. If an existing logical drive is full of data, you can extend the logical drive when there is free space in the array. If there is no free space available, you can add drives to the array and proceed to extend the logical drive.

6. **A** Enabled: By default, most SCSI controllers have the bus parity checking enabled.

7. **D** 7: Most SCSI controllers use a SCSI ID of 7.

8. **C** The release date of the update: OS update considerations are affected by the issues fixed by the update, the time needed to download the update, and the time needed to install the update. It is *not* affected by the release date of the update.

9. **D** Device driver: When you update or upgrade an operating system, you may need to install corresponding driver updates so that you may continue to use each device. If a driver update is not available for a piece of critical hardware, you might need to delay the OS update until a suitable driver (or alternative device) becomes available.

10. **B** Baseline: A baseline is a collection of test results that are judged to represent typical (or normal) network/server performance.

Server
Maintenance and
Upgrade Issues

CHAPTER

5

ETA	NEWBIE	SOME EXPERIENCE	EXPERT
	6 hours	3 hours	1 hour

Networks are used to connect busy people. When network servers fail, everyone using that network comes to a halt. Regardless of your network's size, server problems typically result in lost productivity—and often lost data. In order to minimize the impact of network problems, servers must be maintained in a prompt and professional manner. The idea of server maintenance is not new, but its many roles often vary from company to company (and even between networks in the same company) depending on the size and traffic being supported. For our purposes, server maintenance involves the creation, verification, and restoration of system tape backups. Maintenance also includes all types of upgrades and routine replacement tasks such as BIOS upgrades, CPU and memory upgrades, UPS battery replacement, drive replacement and retirement, virus checking, and all types of network expansions (i.e., adding a workstation). This chapter is intended to familiarize you with the essential requirements for these general maintenance tasks.

Objective 5.01 Server Maintenance Guidelines

Server maintenance is often more of an art than a science—there is no one way to do it right. Still, a good technician should understand the server, be familiar with its components, and have the tools available to boot and restore the server when trouble strikes. The following guidelines may help you to prepare for server maintenance tasks a bit more clearly.

Know the Server

A network server is essentially a powerful PC. As with any PC, you should know the various components that your server can accept, as well as the parts currently installed. For example, if the server can accept two Pentium III CPUs up to 1.4GHz, but only one Pentium III 1GHz CPU is installed, you should know this. Such knowledge will make it easier to identify and gather up replacement parts quickly and effectively—especially if the server is at a remote site. Write this information in your notebook or maintenance log where it is easily accessible. As a minimum, record the following:

- CPU speed (installed and maximum)
- Number of CPUs installed/supported

- CPU step (version designation)
- Amount of RAM (installed and maximum)
- Configuration of installed RAM (i.e., PC133 SDRAM 256MB DIMMs)
- BIOS manufacturer and version number
- Manufacturer and size(s) of your system drive(s)
- RAID controller make and model (and its firmware version number)
- SCSI controller make and model (and its firmware version number)
- NIC adapter make and model (and its firmware version number)

If the server was purchased "off the shelf," you should also record the system's make and model, as well as its service tag/serial number, along with the manufacturer's technical support telephone number.

Know the Software

Network hardware is useless without the network operating system and applications. You should make it a point to identify the critical software installed on your server. This can be particularly important when planning the installation of service packs or maintenance patches, and can help you prevent software compatibility problems. As a minimum, record the following:

- System operating system version (with any service packs or updates installed)
- Network operating system version (with any service packs or updates installed)
- Driver versions for the RAID and NIC adapters
- Any system diagnostics, virus checkers, or other tools needed for network support

It's usually a good idea to have all of the installation CDs or diskettes for this software at your disposal. Be sure to have a current boot diskette that can start the server in the event of an unrecoverable drive failure.

Check and Tune Drives Regularly

Hard drives are generally quite reliable, but they are certainly not infallible. Common disk problems include lost clusters and cross-linked files. File fragmentation is also an issue. Part of your routine maintenance policy should be to run ScanDisk and Disk Defragmenter (or other suitable disk tools) to check for file problems, surface defects, and efficient file organization. You may elect to wait for such procedures until hours of low network use (such as evenings or weekends), or until other routine procedures are required such as drive installations.

Backup Reliably

Select a backup system based on your needs and the sensitivity of your data. Busy corporate networks or sales entry systems may require daily backups (perhaps several times per day). The main issue to consider is that after you develop a backup plan, you must implement that plan consistently. Be sure to *verify* your backup. A poor or incomplete backup is worse than no backup at all—there's nothing worse than trying to restore a damaged or incomplete backup. Backups should ideally be stored off-site in a protected location, but you should periodically plan on practicing a restoration procedure to keep your skills sharp. Remember that time is money, so the ability to recover from a disaster is one of the most valuable maintenance skills available.

Check for Viruses

Networks are ideal for transferring viruses, especially if your network allows access to the Internet. Your network software should certainly include a comprehensive network virus checker, and that virus checker should be updated regularly to include the latest signature files and patches. Be sure to scan all files when the virus checker is first installed, then scan files that change (or new files) on the network. Users should be briefed on proper safety procedures regarding file downloads and even e-mail.

Maintain the Environment

Servers are normally stored in closets or rooms where they are protected from casual access. However, servers can dissipate a great deal of heat from the CPUs and drives in the system. Be sure that your server location provides adequate cooling and power. Excessive dust and heat can be detrimental to system cooling. When extensive network equipment is involved, dust filters and air conditioning equipment may be needed to maintain suitable levels of temperature and humidity.

Keep Your Maintenance Logs

Each time that work is performed on a server, that service should be entered into a permanent written log. It is very important for maintenance logs to be kept up-to-date as service and upgrades are performed. Careful records help to keep system maintenance current, prevent duplicated effort, and serve as a guide to future upgrades. It also makes technicians accountable for their work. Maintenance logs should be kept with the server and other network equipment.

Objective 5.02 Tape Backups

When trouble strikes, it usually strikes without warning, and our vital data is usually caught in the crossfire. While it's easy for a technician to replace failed components or rewire damaged cabling, lost data is virtually impossible to re-create—it must be replaced. More than one company has lost income (and even gone out of business) after losing important data. Disasters can be caused by a wide range of natural or man-made events, including the following:

- Component failure (i.e., NIC adapter failure)
- Computer viruses (introduced by file transfers or infected applications)
- Data deletion and corruption (i.e., sabotage by a disgruntled employee)
- Fires caused by arson or electrical mishaps
- Natural disasters (i.e., lightning, floods, tornadoes, or earthquakes)
- Power supply failure and power surges
- Theft and vandalism

Consequently, the techniques of making, verifying, and restoring backups are essential parts of network maintenance. The simplest, most inexpensive way to avoid such a disastrous loss of data is to implement a schedule of periodic backups (preferably using storage facilities off-site). Using a tape backup is still one of the few simple and economical ways to ensure that important data remains safe and usable. A reliable backup strategy minimizes the risk of losing data by maintaining a *current* backup—copies of existing files—so that files can be recovered if the original data is lost or damaged. This part of the chapter explores the concepts and practices of tape backups.

Scheduling Backups

So, when should backups be performed? It's not a simple answer because each network situation is different. When selecting a backup schedule, follow a simple rule: *If you cannot get along without it, back it up.* Critical data should be backed up daily, weekly, or monthly—it really depends on how critical the data is and how frequently it is updated. It is best to schedule backup operations during periods of low system use (i.e., during late evening or weekend hours). Users should be notified when the backup will be performed so that they will not be using the server during the backup period.

Backup Techniques

There is no single way to back up a server. You can choose from several common backup practices, and most administrators will use a combination of these techniques:

- **Full Backup**   A full backup is used to save and mark selected files regardless of whether or not they have changed since the last backup. This provides the most complete and convenient data protection, but it takes the longest to implement.
- **Copy**   A copy backs up all selected files without marking them as being backed up.
- **Incremental Backup**   This process saves and marks selected files only if they have changed since the last time they were backed up.
- **Daily Copy**   This is a variation of copy that saves only those files that have been modified that day, without marking them as being backed up.
- **Differential Backup**   This saves selected files only if they have changed since the last time they were backed up, without marking them as being backed up.

For example, you may choose to start a backup cycle on Monday with a full backup, then perform an incremental backup each day through the rest of the week to preserve the files that have changed, and then repeat the cycle again on the following Monday. Of course, the actual frequency of your backups will depend on your particular network needs. Most backup strategies will involve numerous tapes rotated on a regular basis.

Backups are useless if they cannot be restored, and any experienced technician will tell you to test (aka verify) a backup. Network administrators will periodically perform disaster recovery drills by making a backup, deleting files, restoring the data, and attempting to use that data. These drills are used to verify that the necessary files are indeed backed up, and that a reliable recovery procedure is in place.

Regardless of what backup plan you adopt, don't skimp on tape quality. Tapes cannot be reused indefinitely, so selecting a quality, name-brand product that is recommended for your particular tape drive will help you to achieve the most uses and longest data retention.

Backup Logs

Backup procedures should also be logged (either as a separate record or as part of your server maintenance log). A complete backup record can be critical for proper data recovery later, and should include the following information:

- Date of the backup
- Tape set number (or other identifier)
- Type of backup performed (i.e., full, incremental, and so on)
- Which computer/server was backed up
- Which drives/files were backed up
- Who performed the backup
- The physical location of the backup tapes (if the tapes are stored off-site)

Tape Rotation Tactics

Tape cartridges are certainly the most common medium for backup systems. Although the number of backups you perform per week or per month will depend entirely on the amount of activity on your system or network, backup integrity is limited by the tapes themselves. By using more than one tape as part of your backup regimen, you will not find yourself writing over a current backup (potentially disastrous if the backup process is interrupted). Tape rotation is a common tactic that helps to ensure that data is protected and integral at all times. Small organizations may use only two tapes, while large busy organizations may use ten tapes or more.

Backup Problems

While backups are usually considered to be a cost-effective form of data archiving and a reliable means of data protection, backups are hardly perfect. There is a wide range of issues that can adversely affect your backup efforts (or those of your customer). This part of the chapter illustrates some common pitfalls to look out for when planning and executing backups:

- **Backups are Performed Irregularly or Inconsistently**   This is probably the single most troublesome problem when implementing a backup strategy. In order to be effective, backups must be performed regularly. All too often, users make some initial backups on schedule, but fail to follow through with subsequent backups. Before long, the backups that *were* made fall so far out-of-date that they become useless. When trouble occurs, the investment in equipment and media just does not pay off. Make it a point to implement regular backups and follow through with them consistently.

- **Backups Are Poorly Labeled and Stored**   This problem is typical of large tape rotations. Often, tapes and other backup media are left strewn around an office or department with little or no idea what is on them. Effective backup strategies demand that each tape be marked and identified clearly so that no one will accidentally discard or overwrite it. Groups of tapes should always be kept together in a secured drawer or on a shelf the same way you would organize volumes of books. It's hard enough to keep regular backups without having to search for the tapes and guess which ones to use. Make it a point to keep tapes (and all magnetic media) away from telephones, monitors, power supplies, excessive heat, extreme cold, and all forms of moisture.

- **Inadequate Disaster Preparation**   Here's another real impediment to successful backups. Too often, businesses invest serious money in backup equipment—only to leave the tapes sitting on top of the backed-up system. If you rely on backups to store your vital files, those tapes should be stored in a location that is reasonably safe from disasters (i.e., fire, flood, theft, or sabotage). Often, a fireproof safe or file cabinet will perform quite well. The same concern is true for off-site storage.

- **Inadequate Testing and Maintenance**   Some businesses are so preoccupied with *performing* a backup that they do not check to confirm that the backup is any good. When trouble strikes, they are horrified to find that the backup lacks vital files, is unreadable, or does not restore properly—leaving the backup virtually useless. After a backup is made, it should be tested using a "compare" or "verify" function of the backup software to check the tape contents against the disk files. Although this takes a bit longer, it need not be done each time a backup is made. When errors are indicated, it usually means that the drive is failing or has not been routinely cleaned as required. Try cleaning the backup drive as recommended by the manufacturer and perform the backup again. Every so often, it may be worth testing your backup capability with a backup drill.

- **Inadequate Attention to the Media**   Like diskettes, tapes are magnetic media. Unfortunately, magnetic media does not last forever. One of the big problems with frequent backups is that users mistake backup or compare errors as a problem with the drive or backup software, where it is actually the *tape* that has worn out. As a general rule, plan on replacing your tapes at least once a year. If you are performing frequent backups, plan on replacing your tapes even more frequently. Tape life is also dependent on tape quality—high-quality tapes last longer than low-quality tapes. It is often more prudent to spend a bit more for a reliable, good-quality tape than save a little money on a low-cost tape—only to find that the tape wears out much sooner, or loses data when it's needed.

Backup and Restore Examples

Ultimately, you'll need to install and use backup software on your server(s). There are many different tape backup products available today, and you'll need to select a product that suits the needs of your particular network environment. For this example, we'll review the basic installation, backup, and restoration of files using UltraBac for Windows NT/2000. As with all software, you should familiarize yourself with the user manuals and other product documentation before proceeding—your own tape backup software may be very different.

Travel Assistance

You can download UltraBac and its documentation from www.ultrabac.com/support/default.asp.

Installing UltraBac

After you select a tape backup product, you'll need to install it on your network. The following outlines some typical installation steps:

1. Select Start | Run and enter the path to your tape backup installer (i.e., **d:\setup.exe**), and then click OK to start the installation.
2. When given a choice of destination, keep the installation at root of the OS partition.
3. Choose Typical installation.
4. After the installation, you may start UltraBac by selecting Start | Programs | UltraBac | UltraBac.

A prompt will ask you if you want to start the BEI Scheduler. Choose Yes if you want to schedule unattended backups. You will be prompted to create an account called *Ultrabac*. You can use an existing account if the existing account has appropriate privileges.

Planning a Backup

In order to back up, you need to create a backup set that includes the files that should be backed up (including such elements as the Registry). The following steps highlight a wizard-driven backup process:

1. Open the UltraBac software. The New Backup Wizard should start. If the New Backup Wizard doesn't automatically start, select Backup and New from the menu bar.
2. Once you're in the wizard (see Figure 5-1), choose Back Up All Local Fixed Drives and Registry.
3. Choose Next.
4. Now you'll need to create a new backup set (see Figure 5-2). Give the set of backup files a name under Set Description.
5. Choose File Selection Logic, and then select All Files from the drop-down menu.
6. You can also run other programs or batch files before and after this set to stop or start other services on the machine you're backing up.

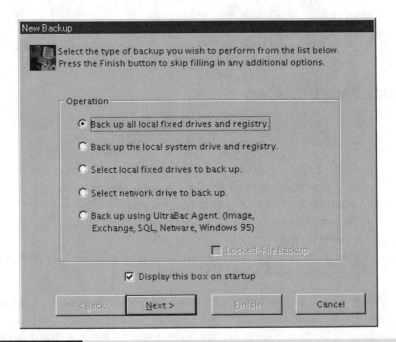

| FIGURE 5-1 | Configuring the New Backup Wizard |

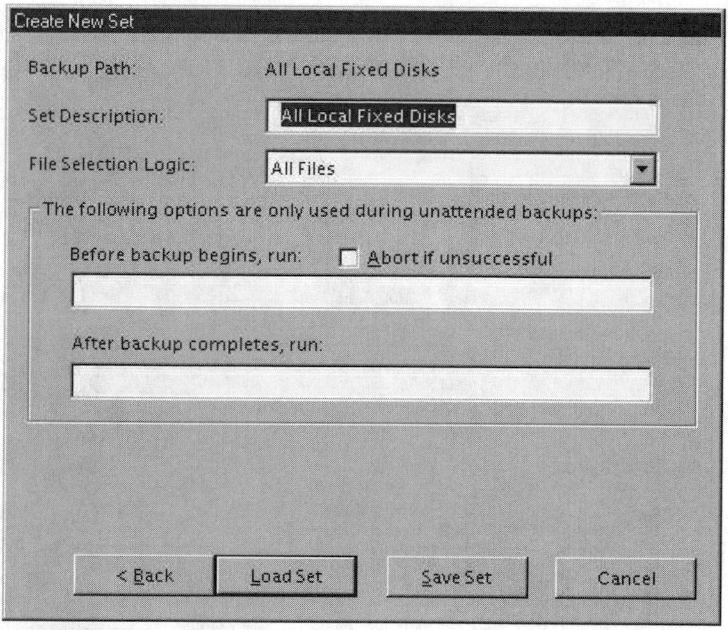

FIGURE 5-2 Defining the backup set

7. Choose Save Set. Either browse to another computer to save the set there, or choose save to save the set on the local machine. For now, do not browse—just save the set locally.

8. Give the file a .UB extension. You will now be able to create another new backup set. Choose Cancel.

Scheduling/Running a Backup

Once you've installed the backup software and planned the backup process, you'll need to schedule and run the actual backup. Follow these steps to schedule and run a typical backup process:

1. Open the UltraBac software.
2. Select Scheduler and Schedule Backups from the menu bar (see Figure 5-3).
3. To add a set under Scheduled Backups, choose a set in the Available Sets window and click Add.
4. To remove a set, choose the set and click Remove.
5. Once you have selected all desired sets, choose Options.

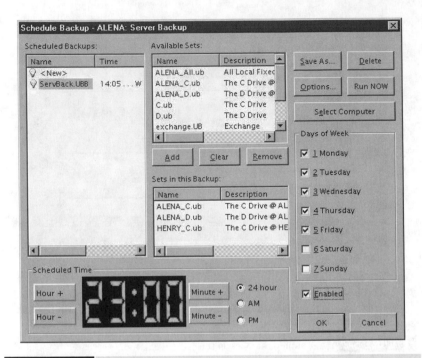

FIGURE 5-3   Scheduling and executing a backup

6. Type in a backup description and select the desired options (it is recommended that you *always* verify after backup).

7. Choose OK.

8. Select the days of the week you would like this backup to run unattended.

9. If you don't want a backup to run unattended, uncheck the Enabled box.

10. Choose Save As to save the scheduled backup.

11. You can also click Run Now to execute the selected backup sets immediately.

Planning the Restoration

Using products like UltraBac, you can restore individual files or selected files, and even restore a failed operating system. The following steps highlight these basic procedures:

1. Open the UltraBac software.

2. Choose Mode | Restore on the drop-down menu (the menu will allow the mode of the system to change between doing backup, restore, or verify).

system administrator can be informed when power events occur, and an orderly system shutdown can be invoked.

> **Exam Tip**
>
> While most UPS systems use batteries as the source of backup power, some more sophisticated systems supplement the battery power with a gasoline generator that can keep a server running for hours.

UPS Battery Testing

Batteries are electrochemical devices. This means a battery will eventually wear out after an ample number of charge and discharge cycles, and you'll need to replace them. As a rule of thumb, you can expect to change your batteries every 3–5 years under normal use. Other circumstances such as bad commercial power sources, elevated temperatures where the batteries are stored, and improper maintenance procedures can all reduce the working life of a battery. You should suspect battery problems when they cannot hold a charge (i.e., you experience short runtimes and "low battery" alarms even after ample charging time). The UPS internal diagnostics will typically report battery problems as they develop. For example, a battery service indicator may appear on the UPS, or UPS software on the server may report battery trouble. In many cases, you can test batteries yourself using steps similar to those shown below (for +12Vdc batteries):

- Make sure that your BPS or UPS is connected correctly, and has at least 50 percent of its total load devices plugged in (desktop unit, monitor, scanner, and so on).
- Turn the system and attached peripherals on, and allow the PC to boot normally.
- Simulate a power outage by disconnecting the BPS or UPS line cord.
- Use a standard digital voltmeter and measure each individual battery voltage.
- Each +12Vdc battery should read between +11.5Vdc and +12.5Vdc. Any battery measuring outside of that range should be considered defective and should be replaced.
- All batteries should measure about the same. Any battery that differs more than 0.4 volts from the rest of the batteries should be considered bad and replaced.

- Wait about five minutes and repeat test (looking for one weak battery to discharge faster than the others). If any battery appears to be discharging faster than the others, it should be considered bad and replaced.

UPS Battery Replacement

If you find that battery replacement is required, you can use the following guidelines to replace the UPS batteries. Remember that you *must* replace batteries with the exact same make and model as the original batteries, or use a suitable substitute recommended by the UPS manufacturer. If you must substitute batteries, it may be necessary to replace all of the batteries in that UPS (even if only one is weak). Be sure to consult with the UPS manufacturer for their recommendations.

> **Travel Advisory**
>
> Older batteries may register as fully charged but still be incapable of providing adequate backup for load devices. This means the battery charge LEDs may indicate the batteries are fully charged, while the UPS diagnostics have determined that the batteries need to be replaced.

Testing the Battery Pack

After the new battery pack is installed, run a UPS self-test or diagnostic (i.e., press the Test/Alarm Reset button). Refer to the documentation that accompanied your specific UPS for self-test or diagnostic instructions. Remember that most UPS systems will not invoke a self-test until the new batteries are 90-percent charged or more, so you may need to wait a little while until the new battery pack is charged. If there are problems with the new installation, one or more battery warning displays (i.e., a battery service indicator) will light. You may need to go back and check your terminal connections.

Objective 5.04   # Network Upgrades

Networks are surprisingly dynamic systems—they're constantly growing, changing, and improving as users and resources are brought to bear. The need for upgrades is often unclear, but changes in performance and user feedback will help to indicate when upgrades warrant consideration. For example, an eventual decline in network data transfer performance may indicate that an upgrade is needed. This means a large portion of your maintenance efforts will focus on network upgrades and enhancements. In most cases, upgrades are intended to improve the network's performance (i.e., increase throughput), increase storage or add fault tolerance, and add support for more users. This part of the chapter will examine BIOS, processor, memory, NIC, and storage upgrades.

Network Architecture and Media

Two important considerations in the design and implementation of a network are the architecture and the media. The *architecture* is the network's structure or topology (i.e., ring or bus). The *media* is the cabling that connects network devices (i.e., copper or fiber). There may be situations when it's necessary to make upgrades to the network architecture or media. While such upgrade processes are beyond the scope of this book, you should consider these upgrades when fundamental network performance upgrades are needed. Consider the following examples:

- If a network has been designed using a bus topology (and its users are complaining of frequent network crashes), it might be necessary to upgrade to a star or ring topology.
- If the size and number of networked buildings is expanding, upgrading to fiber-optic media for the network backbone could be a worthwhile investment. Fiber-optic media can also be used for cable runs between remote buildings.
- If the network was configured with copper-based media (and devices have been added that create large amounts of electrical interference), it might be necessary to upgrade using fiber-optic media.
- If online conferencing or advanced Web-based applications at the desktop are being introduced, the network could also benefit from an upgrade to fiber-optic cable.

There are other factors to consider before making an architecture or media upgrade decision (such as cost). Although the price of fiber-optic media is dropping,

Local Lingo
Topology   The physical setup (interconnection scheme) of a network. The three common topologies are bus, ring, and star.

the installation of fiber-optic cable requires a trained technician—an added expense. Remember that the network interface cards, hubs, and other network hardware will need to be upgraded at the same time, so there may be additional upgrade procedures that need to be conducted at the same time.

Hardware Compatibility

One of the most important issues of network upgrades is hardware compatibility, especially when working with business-oriented operating systems such as Windows NT or 2000. Because networking is so hardware-dependent, verifying the correct choice of hardware is an important step in network planning. Otherwise, hardware purchases may not function as expected (if at all). This part of the chapter explains the importance of compatibility checking prior to implementing an upgrade, and offers some suggestions for resolving compatibility issues.

Identifying Problems

In today's computer industry, hardware and software incompatibilities are simply a fact of life. Hundreds of manufacturers develop hardware and software. Even with well-established standards and protocols, each developer has a unique perspective on the best way to accomplish the same task, and each will provide a unique solution. This is a mixed blessing—competition between developers keeps prices low and selection high, but not all products work together. Consequently, evaluating and selecting suitable products is a major part of planning for network implementation.

If you have the luxury of designing a network from the ground up, you can generally just choose your product vendors and place the burden of compatibility on them. The best way to avoid problems is to research your key items *before* you make purchases. You might consider giving your vendors a list of the hardware and software you plan to use and ask them to certify that those items are compatible with that vendor's products. For example, if you are considering the purchase of two devices, ask both vendors if their product is compatible with the other. Compare the responses you get, because they may help you to find an incompatibility you would otherwise fail to detect.

In most cases, you'll need to create a network out of an existing collection of hardware, and the likelihood of problems developing from incompatible hardware is very high. The most common incompatibilities occur between existing hardware and new software, or new hardware and existing software. Changing or upgrading a computer or network operating system can lead to major compatibility problems.

For example, Windows 98/SE provides excellent support for USB ports, but Windows NT does not. If you need to use Windows NT in order to create a network, and you're relying on that USB printer for the network, you may find that the Windows NT upgrade has effectively disabled your printer.

Checking Documentation and Requirements

The manuals that accompany a product can yield valuable information about compatibility issues. This is especially true for product Web sites where manufacturers can quickly post known issues (and any workarounds that have been discovered). Online product FAQs can often address a wide range of common questions and problems. You must also verify that your system meets the minimum (preferably the recommended) system requirements for any hardware or software that you plan to install. Issues of processor speed, memory (RAM), and available disk space are particularly important.

Checking the HCL

Operating systems and network operating systems are extensively tested with a vast array of hardware devices. If you're planning a hardware upgrade, or need to verify that a NOS upgrade will continue to support your existing hardware, you can check the hardware compatibility list (HCL) for your NOS. If your hardware is not listed in the HCL, it may still work with third-party or manufacturer-specific drivers, but at least this might alert you to the possibility of trouble.

When you install a new computer or network operating system, the installation routine will usually attempt to detect the hardware in the system during the installation process, then load the appropriate drivers for each device. Check the list of detected hardware and ensure that it matches what is already in the machine. For example, if you're installing Novell's IntranetWare, the install utility will automatically scan your computer for devices such as hard drives, CD-ROM drives, and NICs. Detection should also occur when a new device is added to an

Travel Assistance

For example, Microsoft maintains a comprehensive HCL for Windows 2000 at www.microsoft.com/windows2000/server/ howtobuy/upgrading/compat/default.asp.

existing network operating system. If the devices are recognized, the appropriate drivers will be loaded for the recognized devices. If a device is not detected, check to see if a manufacturer-specific driver or other supporting software is available. Otherwise, you may not be able to use the device.

BIOS Upgrades

BIOS is *firmware*—software that has been permanently recorded onto one or more memory chips and is used to operate the PC. When bugs are corrected, compatibility issues are resolved, and performance is tweaked in the BIOS code, it may be necessary for you to update the BIOS in your own server to the latest version available. Traditionally, updating the BIOS required you to physically replace the chip(s) or even update the entire motherboard. Today, virtually all PCs use flash BIOS, which allows the BIOS to be reprogrammed on the chip right in the system. This means you can download the updated BIOS file and flash loader utility from the motherboard maker's Web site and install it yourself.

Local Lingo

Firmware   Program code that has been recorded onto permanent memory devices such as flash ROM chips. Firmware can usually be upgraded as needed.

Checking Your BIOS Version

Before you attempt a BIOS upgrade, it's important to determine the current version of your BIOS. Once you know the version that's on your system, you can ensure that you're installing a later/better version. BIOS is identified in the moments following the initial power up, but before the operating system starts to load—usually while the memory count is taking place. Keep in mind that the BIOS ID string only appears for several seconds, so you may need to reboot the system more than once in order to get the entire code. Although the BIOS ID may appear as a jumble of codes, you should pay particular attention to the BIOS maker and its release date. For example,

```
Example BIOS 4.65 12/25/2000
```

When selecting a BIOS upgrade, be sure that the BIOS is correct for your exact server. If you install the wrong BIOS version, your system may fail to run properly (if it starts at all).

Preparing the Upgrade Process

BIOS upgrades require a little bit of preparation. You'll need to download the appropriate flash file to a bootable floppy diskette, then decompress the flash file into its constituent files (usually a flash loader utility, a new BIOS data file, and a README file. These following steps cover a basic example:

Travel Advisory

Please review the specific instructions distributed with the flash loader upgrade utility before attempting a BIOS upgrade.

1. Make a clean bootable diskette using either DOS or Windows 98/SE.
2. The BIOS upgrade file is usually a compressed self-extracting archive that contains the files you need to upgrade the BIOS. Copy the BIOS upgrade file to a temporary directory on your hard disk.
3. From the C prompt, change to the temporary directory.
4. To extract the upgrade file, type the name of the BIOS upgrade file. For example,

   ```
   10006BC1.EXE
   ```

5. Press ENTER and the file will decompress. The extracted file will include files such as

   ```
   LICENSE.TXT
   README.TXT
   BIOS.EXE
   ```

6. Read the LICENSE.TXT file, which contains the instructions for the BIOS upgrade on your specific system.
7. Insert the bootable floppy disk into drive A.

8. Extract the flash loader (i.e., BIOS.EXE) file to the floppy disk, change to the temporary directory containing the flash loader file, and type **BIOS A:**
9. Press ENTER.
10. The bootable diskette now holds the BIOS upgrade and recovery files.

Completing the Upgrade Process

Once you've prepared your diskette for the BIOS upgrade, use the following steps as a guideline for the new BIOS installation:

1. Boot the computer with the floppy disk in drive A. The BIOS Upgrade Utility screen appears.
2. Select Update Flash Memory From a File.
3. Select Update System BIOS and press ENTER.
4. Use the arrow keys to select the correct .BIO file and press ENTER.
5. When the utility asks for confirmation that you want to flash the new BIOS into memory, select Continue with Programming and press ENTER.
6. When the utility displays the message "Upgrade is Complete," remove the floppy disk and press ENTER.
7. As the computer boots again, check the BIOS identifier (the BIOS version number) to verify that the upgrade was successful.
8. To enter the CMOS Setup program, observe the BIOS banner such as

   ```
   Press <F2> Key if you want to run SETUP
   ```

9. For proper operation, load the CMOS Setup program defaults and press ENTER to accept the defaults.
10. Reset any critical entries in the CMOS Setup.
11. Accept and save the settings, then turn off the computer and reboot.

NIC Upgrades

As users come onto the network and traffic levels increase, you may need to improve the data transfer capacity (throughput) of your network. This means

> ### Exam Tip
>
> Remember that most computers protect the BIOS with one or more jumpers (i.e., the BIOS Write Enable jumper). You should configure the server to accept the new BIOS file before booting the system.

you'll need to replace your NIC adapter. The upgrade process is virtually identical to the installation of any other PnP PCI expansion device, and follows four basic steps: remove the existing card, install the new card, connect the network cable, and configure the new card.

Removing the Old Drivers

If you're replacing or upgrading a NIC device (or upgrading the drivers), it is often necessary to remove the older NIC drivers first. This ensures that there is no software conflict between the older and newer software. This example shows you how to remove the Windows NT drivers for an Adaptec DuraLAN NIC:

1. Double-click My Computer on your desktop.
2. Double-click Control Panel.
3. Double-click the Network icon.
4. In the Network window, click the Adapters tab.
5. In the Network Adapters list, click the NIC you want to remove (i.e., Adaptec DuraLAN NIC), and then click Remove.
6. When asked if you want to continue, click Yes.
7. Repeat the previous two steps until all of the related drivers (i.e., Adaptec DuraLAN) drivers are removed.
8. When you're finished, click OK.
9. Click Close to close the Network window.
10. Click Yes to restart your computer.

Travel Advisory

When you restart Windows NT, a message might indicate that at least one service failed to start. This message should not appear after you add the new driver, so simply click OK.

Removing the Existing Card

After the old drivers are removed, it's time to uninstall the old NIC. Follow these steps to remove your old NIC adapter:

1. Turn off the power to your PC and disconnect the power cord from the wall outlet. During the removal, you should ground yourself by touching any unpainted surface of the PC case.

2. Remove the outer cover from your computer according to the manufacturer's instructions.
3. Disconnect the network cabling from your existing NIC.
4. Remove the screw holding the NIC in place, then gently remove the card from its slot.

Travel Advisory

Before shutting down the PC to remove the NIC, it might be necessary to remove the NIC driver(s) and supporting software.

Installing the New Card

With the old NIC out of the system, go ahead and install the new NIC using the following steps:

1. You should ground yourself by touching any unpainted surface of the PC case.
2. Carefully remove the new NIC from its antistatic container. Verify the model by looking at the model name on the NIC itself (you may place the old NIC in the antistatic container).
3. Check the NIC for any visible signs of damage that may have occurred during shipping or handling. If you find a problem, immediately notify your network supplier and the shipping service that delivered your NIC—you'll need to arrange for a replacement NIC.
4. Because the PC is already opened, locate an unused expansion slot (a PCI slot in this case). Remove the bracket screw and remove the expansion slot bracket that covers the card slot's opening.

Exam Tip

PCI slots and NICs come in two varieties: 3.3 volt, and the more common 5 volt. PCI NICs generally support 5-volt slots. Some models also support 3.3-volt slots. To improve performance with multiport NICs, install these NICs in PCI bus slot 0.

5. Insert the NIC into the PCI expansion slot—press down firmly and evenly until the bus contacts are seated in the slot.
6. Secure the NIC in the expansion slot with the bracket screw you removed earlier.
7. Replace the computer's outer cover on the computer.
8. Reconnect any other devices that you might have removed during the installation.

Reconnecting and Reconfiguring

Carefully reconnect the network cabling to the new NIC adapter (after the NIC drivers are installed, the card's selection of cabling should normally be automatic). Depending on your particular system, you may need to configure the card through the server's CMOS Setup. You may also need to adjust the card's configuration through its own on-board setup.

Installing the New Drivers

After installing, connecting, and configuring the new NIC hardware, you must install the appropriate NIC driver for your particular network operating system. Before proceeding, it's usually a good idea to check for driver updates and patches with the NIC manufacturer. This section of the chapter illustrates the typical installation process for an Adaptec DuraLAN NIC under Windows NT:

1. Start the system to Windows NT.
2. From the Start menu, choose Settings | Control Panel.
3. In the Control Panel, double-click the Network icon.
4. In the Network window, click the Adapters tab.
5. In the Adapters tab, click Add.
6. In the Select Network Adapter window, click Have Disk.
7. At the Insert Disk window, insert the driver diskette (i.e., Duralink64 for Windows NT diskette), then click OK.
8. In the Select OEM Option window, click the NIC model that's installed (i.e., DuraLAN NIC); then click OK.
9. In the installation window that appears (i.e., Adaptec DuraLAN NIC Driver Installation window), select the desired driver and click OK.
10. Continue on to install the standard driver, the failover driver, or the port aggregation driver.

Storage Upgrades

Networks rely on a great deal of storage for the many files and applications that are needed. This means you'll be adding and replacing drives to accommodate the server's storage needs. Servers typically use removable media and hot-pluggable drives to provide storage. Removable media drives include floppy, tape, and CD type drives. Hot-pluggable drives include all types of SCSI hard drives—usually configured for RAID applications.

Removable Media Drives

Removable media drives can typically be removed from a rack-mounted server using the these steps:

1. Extend the server out from the rack to the locked position and remove cover plate.
2. Remove the Y brace and card bracket brace.
3. Slide the base frame back to access cables in the drive cage.
4. Lift the protective cover and disconnect power and signal cables to the drive.
5. Remove the media trim piece retaining screws (two of them) from the front bezel.
6. Remove the storage device retaining screws (two of them) and slide the drive out.

Simply reverse these steps to install the drive. It's important to remember that not all drives are supported in every bay. For example, a 1.44MB 3.5-in floppy drive may only work in bays 5 and 6, while a CD-ROM drive may only work in drive bay 5, and a TurboDAT drive may only work in bay 7. You should research the server's documentation to be certain that you know which drives are compatible in each of the server's drive bays.

Hot-Pluggable Drives

Hot-pluggable drives can be removed and replaced while the server power is still applied. In most cases, it is not necessary to set the SCSI ID jumpers on a replacement hot-pluggable hard drive—the SCSI ID is set automatically by the motherboard and the hot-pluggable tray when the drive is installed. When a drive (configured for fault tolerance) is replaced, the replacement drive will automatically begin being restored after the installation is replaced. While a drive is being restored, the online LED will flash green. The LED will continue to flash until the drive is completely restored. The following guidelines must be followed when replacing hot-pluggable hard drives:

- **Never remove more than one drive at a time**   When a drive is replaced, the controller uses data from the other drives in the array to reconstruct data on the replacement drive. If more than one drive is removed, a complete data set is not available to reconstruct data on the replacement drive(s).

- **Never remove a working drive when another drive has failed**   Drives that have been failed by the controller are indicated by an amber drive failure LED on the drive tray. Permanent data loss will occur if a working drive is removed when replacing a failed drive.

- **Never remove a drive while another drive is being rebuilt**   A drive's online LED will flash green whenever it is being rebuilt. A replaced drive is restored from data stored on the other drives.

- **Never turn off a drive (storage) system while the controlling server is powered on**   This would cause the server's SMART controller to mark all the drives as failed—this could result in permanent data loss.

- **If an online spare drive is installed, wait for it to finish rebuilding before replacing the failed drive**   When a drive fails, the online spare will become active and begin being rebuilt as a replacement drive. Once the online spare has finished being rebuilt, the failed drive should be replaced with a new replacement drive. Do not replace the failed drive with the online spare.

- **A POST error message (i.e., code 1786) will occur during server power up if a drive has been replaced while the system is off**   When this occurs, you'll be prompted to continue booting and rebuild the replaced drive, or continue booting and not rebuild (this will result in data loss).

It's a relatively simple matter to replace a hot-pluggable hard drive. In most cases, drives are accessed from the front of the rack and do not require that the server be extended from the rack. To remove the drive, press the releases on the ejector levers and swing the levers out (see Figure 5-6). This will pull the drives out of the backplane connector. Slide the hot-pluggable hard drive out of the chassis. To replace the drive, slide the hot-pluggable hard drive all the way into the drive cage. Mate the drive with the backplane connector and swing the ejector levers back into place. When routing cables, always make sure that the cables are not in a position where they will be pinched or crimped.

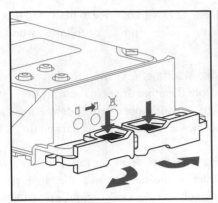
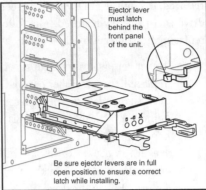

Ejector lever must latch behind the front panel of the unit.

Be sure ejector levers are in full open position to ensure a correct latch while installing.

FIGURE 5-6   Installing a hot-pluggable hard drive (Courtesy of Compaq)

Travel Advisory

In many cases, SCSI hard drives on the same SCSI bus must be internal (within the server) or in an external storage system, but not both. A configuration with both internal and external SCSI hard drives requires more than one single-channel SCSI controller. A multichannel controller (such as the Compaq SMART SCSI Array Controller) supports both internal and external SCSI hard drives on separate SCSI buses.

Memory Upgrades

Server memory is often installed in the form of DIMMs (dual inline memory modules), and a typical server motherboard will support 768MB to 1GB (or more) of fast Synchronous DRAM (SDRAM) memory across up to four DIMM slots (i.e., four 256MB DIMMs). Some servers will employ Rambus memory (RDRAM) fitted into RIMM (Rambus Inline Memory Module) slots. As server complexity and traffic increase, more memory may be necessary to handle the larger number of open files. Because you might need to upgrade memory in an existing configuration, let's look at DIMM removal first:

1. Open the server (if it's not already open) and locate the DIMM slot(s).
2. Gently push the plastic ejector levers out and down to eject the selected DIMM from its slot.

Travel Advisory

All forms of memory are extremely sensitive to accidental damage from ESD. Use all antistatic precautions when handling a DIMM or RIMM.

3. Hold the DIMM only by its edges (careful not to touch its components or gold edge connectors) and carefully lift it away from the socket. Store the old DIMM in an antistatic package.
4. Repeat to remove other DIMMs as necessary.

Travel Advisory

Use extreme care when removing or installing a DIMM or RIMM—too much pressure can damage the slot (and ruin the motherboard). Apply only enough pressure on the plastic ejector levers to release or secure the module. Modules are keyed to allow insertion in only one way.

Refer to the motherboard's documentation and select one or more DIMMs to provide an adequate amount of memory for the server. DIMMs must be selected based on capacity (i.e., 128MB), memory type (i.e., SDRAM), speed (i.e., 8ns cycle time), and error checking (i.e., parity, nonparity, ECC, or non-ECC). Let's review the process for DIMM installation:

Exam Tip

DIMMs and sockets may use tin or gold in the connectors, but mixing dissimilar metals (i.e., a DIMM with gold contacts into a DIMM slot with tin contacts) may cause later memory failures—resulting in data corruption. Only install DIMMs with gold-plated edge connectors in gold-plated sockets.

1. Open your server (if it's not already open) and locate the DIMM slot(s).
2. Hold a DIMM only by its edges, and remove it from its antistatic package.
3. Orient the DIMM so that the two notches in the bottom edge of the DIMM align with the keys in the slot.
4. Insert the bottom edge of the DIMM into the slot, and press down firmly on the DIMM until it seats correctly and fully in the slot.
5. Gently push the plastic ejector levers on either end of the slot to the upright (locked) position.
6. Repeat to install other DIMMs as necessary.

Local Lingo

ECC (error checking and correction)   A technique used to detect single-bit and multibit errors in memory, and even correct single-bit errors on the fly. Many mission-critical servers use memory with ECC.

CPU Upgrades

A server motherboard will normally accommodate two or four (or more) processors. While one processor should work fine for most end users, network servers can employ additional processors to manage more users and open files. You'll need to attach an appropriate heat sink/fan unit to each processor being installed now, and have a termination card available for other unused processor slot(s). Refer to the documentation that accompanied the server motherboard and verify the type and speed of compatible processors (i.e., one or two 1GHz Pentium III processors). If you're adding a second processor, be sure that the new processor(s) match the existing one (including the processor's manufacturing revision if necessary), or is otherwise suitable for use with the original CPU.

Select one or more suitable processors for the motherboard, and verify that their heat sink/fan units are properly attached. Locate the corresponding CPU slots (or sockets) on the motherboard, and also locate the small fan connectors

Exam Tip

All processors are extremely sensitive to accidental damage from ESD. Use all antistatic precautions when handling a processor.

Travel Advisory

If the server has been running, any installed processor and heat sink will be hot. To avoid possible burn injury, allow the system to remain off for at least 15 minutes before servicing the processors.

near each slot (or socket). Virtually all modern server motherboards will autodetect the processor and configure the bus speed, multiplier, and CPU voltage automatically. This means you rarely need to set jumpers to prepare a motherboard for new CPUs. Let's cover the essentials of processor installation now:

1. Open your server (if it's not already open) and locate the processor slot(s).
2. If your server has one processor and you're adding another, you must remove the termination card from the next processor(s) slot. Carefully pull back the tab of the retention mechanism until the termination card can be rotated out of the slot. Grasp the card on the side closest to the retention mechanism tab and rotate the one side of the card out of the slot. Once that side is free, you can pull the other side out of the slot.

Exam Tip

You generally must install a termination card into any vacant processor slot to ensure reliable system operation. A termination card contains AGTL+ termination circuitry and clock termination. The server may not boot unless all vacant processor slots contain a termination card.

3. If your server has one processor and you're replacing it, leave the termination card in place in the empty secondary slot. Remove the processor you want to replace.
4. If your server has two processors and you're replacing one or both, remove the appropriate one(s).
5. Remove the new processor from its antistatic package and orient the processor in its slot (or socket) using special care to align pin 1 properly.

Exam Tip

The grounded retention mechanisms (GRMs) are not compatible with SECC-type processor packaging—the new GRMs only support SECC2-type (i.e., Pentium II/III Xeon) processors. If you plan on using SECC-type (i.e., ordinary Pentium II/III) processors, you must use a universal retention mechanism (URM).

(For cartridge-type processors, slide the processor into the retention mechanism. Push down firmly, with even pressure on both sides of the top, until the processor is seated. It should click into place.)

6. For socket-type processors, seat the processor fully into the socket, then close and lock the ZIF lever.
7. Attach the fan power cable to the three-pin connector on the server board.
8. Close the server and secure the outer cover (make sure that any intrusion switch is closed).
9. Connect any remaining external cables and attach the ac power cord.
10. Turn on the monitor and then power up the server. Start the server's CMOS Setup routine to configure the new server motherboard, memory, and CPU(s).

Processor Card Notes

In some cases, rack-mounted servers (especially older servers such as the Compaq ProLiant 4500) might include the processor(s) on a removable card as shown in Figure 5-7. Such a processor card typically includes the BIOS and many of the core processing elements normally found on an ordinary motherboard. This approach allows designers to simplify the rack's main board, and install the processor card as an expansion card, which can easily be replaced for repairs or upgrades. Today, the high-frequency signaling used with modern processors does not lend itself well to processor card technology, so processors are included on the motherboard (much the same way that CPUs are installed on desktop PCs).

Processor Matching Notes

Even processors with identical speed and voltage ratings may be slightly different internally. Such changes occur when bugs are fixed and performance enhancements

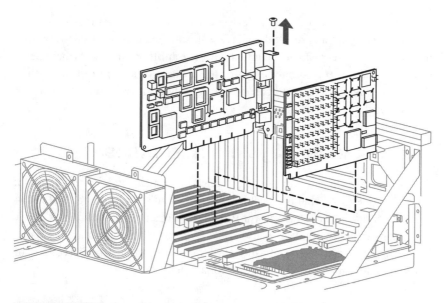

FIGURE 5-7   Removing processor and option card(s) from a rack-mounted server (Courtesy of Compaq)

are made to the processor's design. In many cases, the processors used in a typical network server should be matched. So, not only should the processors use the same speed and voltage, they should all be of the *same* engineering revision level. For example, Intel processors use "S-spec" numbers to represent the revision level. Matching is not required on every server motherboard (the newest server motherboards are more tolerant of CPU mismatches), but matching is generally regarded as the best default configuration policy. If matching is required for your server, but you cannot match new processors (i.e., because the engineering level of the existing processors is too old and stock is no longer available), you may need to install an entirely new suite of processors that are matched.

Objective 5.05   Conflict Detection and Resolution

E very device installed in the server (i.e., an NIC or video card) uses system resources in order to obtain the system's attention and communicate data with memory or the CPU. All PCs (including servers) offer only a limited amount of resources, and no two devices can use the same resources; otherwise, a *hardware conflict* will result. Low-level software (such as device drivers) that use system resources can also conflict with one another during normal operation. This part of the chapter explains the concept of system resources, then shows you how to detect and correct conflicts that can arise in both hardware and software.

Understanding System Resources

The key to mastering and eliminating conflicts is to understand the importance of each system resource that is available to you. PCs and servers provide three typical types of resources: interrupts (or IRQs), DMA channels, and I/O areas. Many controllers and network devices also utilize BIOS, which requires memory space. Do *not* underestimate the importance of these resource areas—conflicts can occur anywhere, and carry dire consequences for a system.

Interrupts

An *interrupt* is probably the most well-known and best understood type of resource. Interrupts are used to demand attention from the CPU. This allows a device or subsystem to work in the background until a particular event occurs that requires system processing. Such an event may include receiving a character at the serial port, striking a key on the keyboard, or any number of other real-world situations. An interrupt is invoked by asserting a logic level on one of the physical *interrupt request* (IRQ) lines accessible through any of the motherboard's expansion bus slots. AT-compatible computers provide 16 IRQ lines (noted IRQ 0 through IRQ 15).

After an interrupt is triggered, an interrupt-handling routine saves the current CPU register states to a small area of memory (called the *stack*), then directs the CPU to the *interrupt vector table*. The interrupt vector table is a list of program locations that correspond to each interrupt. When an interrupt occurs, the CPU will jump to the interrupt handler routine at the location specified in the interrupt vector table and execute the routine. In most cases, the interrupt handler is a device driver associated with the board generating the interrupt. For example, an IRQ from a network card will likely call a network device driver to operate the card. For a hard disk controller, an IRQ calls the BIOS ROM code that operates the drive. When the handling routine is finished, the CPU's original register contents are popped from the stack, and the CPU picks up from where it left off without interruption.

DMA Channels

The CPU is very adept at moving data. It can transfer data between memory locations, I/O locations, or from memory to I/O and back with equal ease. However, PC designers realized that transferring large amounts of data (one word at a time) through the CPU is a hideous waste of CPU time. After all, the CPU really isn't *processing* anything during a data move—it's just shuttling data from one place to another. If there were a way to off-load such redundant tasks from the CPU, data could be moved faster than would be possible with CPU intervention. Direct memory access (DMA) is a technique designed to move large amounts of data from memory to an I/O location, or vice versa, without the direct intervention by the CPU. In theory, the DMA controller chip acts as a stand-alone data processor, leaving the CPU free to handle other tasks.

A DMA transfer starts with a DMA request (DRQ) signal generated by the requesting device (such as the floppy disk controller board). If the channel has been previously enabled through software drivers or BIOS routines, the request will reach the corresponding DMA controller chip on the motherboard. The DMA controller will then send a HOLD request to the CPU, which responds with a Hold Acknowledge (HLDA) signal. When the DMA controller receives the HLDA signal, it instructs the bus controller to effectively disconnect the CPU from the expansion bus and allow the DMA controller chip to take control of the bus itself. The DMA controller sends a DMA Acknowledge (DACK) signal to the requesting device, and the transfer process may begin. After the transfer is done, the DMA controller will reconnect the CPU and drop its HOLD request—the CPU then continues with whatever it was doing without interruption.

As with interrupts, a DMA channel is selected by setting a physical jumper or DIP switch on the particular expansion board (or through Plug and Play). When the board is installed in an expansion slot, the channel setting establishes a connection between the board and DMA controller chip. Often, accompanying software drivers must use a command-line switch that points to the corresponding hardware DMA assignment. Also, DMA channels cannot be shared between two or more devices. If more than one device attempts to use the same DMA channel at the same time, a conflict will result.

I/O Space

All computers provide space for I/O (input/output) ports. An I/O port acts very much like a memory address, but it's not for storage. Instead, an I/O port provides the means for a PC to communicate directly with a device—allowing the PC to efficiently pass commands and data between the system and various expansion devices. Each device must be assigned to a unique address (or address range).

I/O assignments are generally made manually by setting jumpers or DIP switches on the expansion device itself (or automatically through the use of Plug and Play). As with other system resources, it is vitally important that no two devices use the same I/O port(s) at the same time. If one or more I/O addresses overlap, a hardware conflict will result. When a conflict occurs, commands meant for one device may be erroneously interpreted by another. Keep in mind that while many expansion devices can be set at a variety of addresses, some devices cannot.

Memory Assignments

Memory is another vital resource for the PC. While early devices relied on the assignment of IRQ, DMA channels, and I/O ports, most current devices (i.e., SCSI controllers, network cards, video boards, modems, and so on), are demanding memory space for the support of each device's on-board BIOS ROM (their firmware). No two ROMs can overlap in their addresses; otherwise, a conflict will occur.

Recognizing and Dealing with Conflicts

Fortunately, conflicts are almost *always* the result of a PC upgrade gone awry. Thus, a technician can be alerted to the possibility of a system conflict by applying the Last Upgrade rule. The rule consists of three parts:

- A piece of *hardware* and/or *software* has been added to the system very recently.
- The trouble occurred *after* a piece of hardware and/or software was added to the system.
- The system was working fine *before* the hardware and/or software was added.

If all three of these common-sense factors are true, chances are very good that you are faced with a hardware or software conflict (rather than a defective device). Unlike most other types of PC problems, which tend to be specific to the faulty subassembly, conflicts usually manifest themselves as much more general and perplexing problems. The following symptoms are typical of serious hardware or software conflicts:

- The system locks up during the POST or operating system initialization.
- The system locks up during a particular application.
- The system locks up when a particular device (i.e., a TWAIN scanner) is used.

- The system locks up randomly or without warning regardless of the application.
- The system might not crash, but the device that was added may not function (even though it seems properly configured). Devices that were in the system previously may still work correctly.
- The system may not crash, but a device or application that was working previously no longer seems to function. The newly added device (and accompanying software) may or may not work properly.

What makes these problems so generic is that the severity and frequency of a fault (as well as the point at which the fault occurs) depend on such factors as the particular *devices* that are conflicting, the *resource(s)* that are conflicting among the devices (i.e., IRQs, DMAs, or I/O addresses), and the *function* being performed by the PC when the conflict manifests itself. Because every PC is equipped and configured a bit differently, it is virtually impossible to predict a conflict's symptoms more precisely.

Confirming and Resolving Conflicts

Recognizing the possibility of a conflict is one thing, but proving and correcting it is another issue entirely. However, there are some very effective tactics at your disposal. The first rule of conflict resolution is *last in first out* (LIFO). The LIFO principle basically says that *the fastest means of overcoming a conflict problem is to remove the hardware or software that resulted in the conflict*. In other words, if you install board X and board Y ceases to function, board X is probably conflicting with the system, so removing board X should restore board Y to normal operation. The same concept holds true for software. If you add a new application to your system, then find that an existing application fails to work properly, the new application is likely at fault. Unfortunately removing the offending element is not enough. You still have to install the new device or software in such a way that it will no longer conflict in the system.

Dealing with Software Conflicts

Device drivers present a potential conflict problem. Some server hardware upgrades require the addition of one or more real-mode (a.k.a. DOS) device drivers. Such drivers are called from the CONFIG.SYS file during system initialization (or loaded with Windows), and use a series of command-line parameters to specify the system resources that are being used. This is often necessary to ensure that the driver operates its associated hardware properly. If the command-line options used for the device driver do not match the hardware settings (or overlap the settings of another device driver), system problems can result. If you suspect that a device driver is causing the problem, find its reference in the CONFIG.SYS file and disable it by placing the command REM in front of its command line, such as

```
REM DEVICE = C:\DRIVERS\NEWDRIVE.SYS /A360 /I:5
```

The REM command turns the line into a "REMark," which can easily be removed later if you choose to restore the line. Remember that disabling the device driver in this fashion will prevent the associated hardware from working, but if the problem clears, you can work with the driver settings until the problem is resolved. Remember to reboot the computer so that your changes will take effect. Finally, consider the possibility that the offending software is buggy or defective. Try contacting the software manufacturer. There may be a fix or undocumented feature that you are unaware of. There may also be a patch or update that will solve the problem.

Dealing with Hardware Conflicts and Error Codes

Consider an example. A PC user recently added a CD-ROM and adapter board to their system. The installation went flawlessly using the defaults—a 10-minute job. Several days later, when attempting to back up the system, the user noticed that the parallel port tape backup did not respond (although the printer that had been connected to the parallel port was working fine). The user tried booting the system from a clean bootable floppy disk (no CONFIG.SYS or AUTOEXEC.BAT files to eliminate the device drivers), but the problem remained. After a bit of consideration, the user powered down the system, removed the CD-ROM adapter board, and booted the system from a clean bootable floppy disk. Sure enough, the parallel port tape backup started working again.

Stories such as this remind technicians that hardware conflicts are not always the monstrous, system-smashing mistakes that they are made out to be. In many cases, conflicts have subtle, noncatastrophic consequences. Since the CD-ROM was the last device to be added, it was the first to be removed. It took about five minutes to realize and remove the problem. However, *removing* the problem is only part of conflict troubleshooting—reinstalling the device without a conflict is the real challenge.

Fortunately, Windows provides a Device Manager that tracks the devices in your system and identifies the resources and drivers assigned to each device. As an example, under Windows 98/SE, when you open the Device Manager, double-click the Computer entry at the top of the device list. The Computer Properties dialog box will open. Select the View Resources tab (see Figure 5-8) and you can check the assignments for IRQs, DMA, I/O, or memory. By reviewing these entries, you can quickly determine which resources are assigned and which are free.

The Windows 95/98/2000 Device Manager is a very powerful resource that's designed to help you inspect the configuration and settings of almost every device in your system. When a problem occurs, the Device Manager can often identify the problem and provide valuable clues that will help you resolve the trouble. Before we start working through the conflict resolution process, let's learn to find typical Device Manager errors. Check your Device Manager for error codes:

1. Choose Start | Settings | Control Panel.
2. In the Control Panel, double-click the System icon.
3. Click the Device Manager tab.
4. Double-click a device type (i.e., Mouse) to see the devices in that category.
5. Double-click a device to view its Properties dialog box.
6. If an error code has been generated, the code appears in the Device Status box on the General tab. In some cases, there will be a Solution button (Windows 98 only).

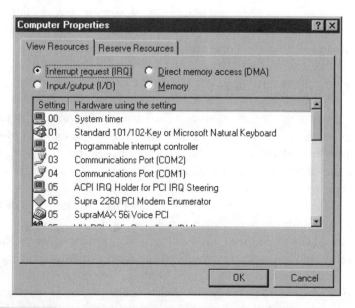

FIGURE 5-8   Determining resource assignments under Windows 98/SE

Objective 5.06 **Computer Virus Issues**

Computer viruses are rogue software designed to load and run without the user's knowledge, often hiding in normal programs. Viruses also execute their functions without prompting users for permission, they do not warn of potential dangers to the system, and they do not produce error messages when problems are encountered. Essentially, a computer virus is a fragment of executable code that runs secretly and is capable of cloning itself in other programs. Once activated, a virus can be a simple annoyance or completely catastrophic in its effect. Viruses are written by people with the intent to do harm.

Types of Viruses

As you might have suspected, all virulent code is not created equal. Viruses are as varied as legitimate application software, and each technique provides the virus author with an array of advantages and disadvantages. Some viral techniques are preferred because they are more difficult to detect and remove, but require extra resources to develop. Other viral techniques are easier to develop, but lack the stealth and sophistication that more powerful viruses demand. Still other viral techniques stand a better chance of infecting multiple systems.

Boot-Sector Viruses

Early PCs loaded their operating systems from floppy disks. Virus authors quickly discovered that they could substitute their own program for the executable code present on the boot sector of every floppy disk formatted with DOS—whether or not it included system files. Unsuspecting users thus loaded the virus into memory every time they started their computers with an infected disk. Once in memory, a virus can copy itself to boot sectors on other floppy or hard disks. For example, those who unintentionally loaded the "Brain" virus from an infected floppy found themselves reading an advertisement for a computer consulting company in Pakistan. With that advertisement, Brain pioneered another characteristic feature of modern viruses—the "payload." The payload is the prank or malicious behavior that (if triggered) causes effects that range from annoying messages to data destruction. It's the virus characteristic that draws the most attention. Many virus authors now write their viruses specifically to deliver their payloads to as many computers as possible.

For a time, sophisticated descendants of this first boot-sector virus represented the most serious virus threat to computer users. Variants of boot-sector viruses also infect the master boot record (MBR), which stores partition information. Nearly every step in the boot process (from reading the MBR to loading the operating system) is vulnerable to viral sabotage. Some of the most tenacious and destructive viruses still include the ability to infect your computer's boot sector or MBR. Loading a boot-sector virus at boot time can give a virus a chance to do its work before your antivirus software has a chance to run. Some antivirus tools anticipate this possibility by allowing you to create an emergency disk that you can use to boot your computer and remove infections.

File Infector Viruses

At about the same time as the authors of the Brain virus found vulnerabilities in the DOS boot sector, other virus writers found out how to use existing software to help replicate their creations. An early example of this type of virus showed up in computers at Lehigh University in Pennsylvania. The virus infected part of the DOS command interpreter (COMMAND.COM), which it used to load itself into memory—once there, it spreads to other uninfected COMMAND.COM files each time a user enters any standard DOS command that involves disk access. Early iterations of this virus limited its spread to floppy disks that contain a full operating system.

Later viruses quickly overcame this limitation—sometimes with fairly clever programming. For example, virus writers might have their virus add its code to the beginning of an executable file. When users start a program, the virus code executes immediately, then transfers control back to the legitimate software (which runs as though nothing unusual has happened). Once it activates, the virus "hooks" or "traps" requests that legitimate software makes to the operating system and substitutes its own responses. Particularly clever viruses can even subvert attempts to clear them from memory by trapping the CTRL-ALT-DEL keyboard sequence for a warm reboot, then faking a restart. Sometimes the only outward indication that anything on your system is amiss (before any payload detonates) might be a small change in the file size of infected legitimate software.

Stealth, Mutating, Encrypted, and Polymorphic Viruses

As unobtrusive as they might be, changes in file size and other scant evidence of a virus infection usually gives most antivirus software enough of a clue to locate and remove the offending code. One of the virus writer's principal challenges is to find ways to hide their handiwork. The earliest disguises were a mixture of innovative programming and obvious giveaways. For instance, the Brain virus redirected requests to see a disk's boot sector away from the actual location of the infected sector to the new location of the boot files, which the virus had moved. This "stealth" capability enabled this and other viruses to hide from conventional search techniques.

Because viruses needed to avoid continuously reinfecting host systems (doing so would quickly balloon an infected file's size to easily detectable proportions, or would consume enough system resources to point to an obvious culprit), virus authors also needed to tell them to leave certain files alone. They addressed this problem by having the virus write a code "signature" that would flag infected files with the software equivalent of a "do not disturb" sign. Although that kept the virus from giving itself away immediately, it opened the way for antivirus software to use the code signatures themselves to find the virus.

In response, virus writers found ways to conceal the code signatures. Some viruses would mutate, or write different code signatures with each new infection. Others encrypted most of the code signature or the virus itself—leaving only a couple of bytes to use as a key for decryption. The most sophisticated new viruses employ stealth, mutation, and encryption to appear in an almost undetectable variety of new forms. Finding these polymorphic viruses required software engineers to develop very elaborate programming techniques for antivirus software.

Macro Viruses

By 1995 or so, the virus war had come to something of a standstill. New viruses appeared continuously (prompted in part by the availability of ready-made virus kits that enabled even some nonprogrammers to whip up a new virus in no time). Most existing antivirus software could easily be updated to detect and dispose of the new virus variants, which consisted primarily of minor tweaks to well-known templates.

But 1995 marked the emergence of the "concept" virus, which added a new and surprising twist to virus history. Before concept, most virus researchers thought of data files (the text, spreadsheet, or drawing documents created by the software you use) as immune to infection. Viruses, after all, are programs, and as such, needed to be run the same way executable software did in order to do their damage. On the other hand, data files are simply stored information that you entered when you worked with your software.

That distinction melted away when Microsoft began adding macro capabilities to Word and Excel—the flagship applications in its Office suite. Using a stripped-down version of its Visual BASIC language, users could create document templates that would automatically format and add other features to documents created with Word and Excel. Virus writers seized the opportunity that this presented to conceal and spread viruses in documents that you, the user, created yourself. The exploding popularity of the Internet and of e-mail software that allows users to attach files to messages ensured that macro viruses would spread very quickly and very widely. Within a year, macro viruses had become the most potent virus threat ever.

Java and ActiveX

Programs based on Java and ActiveX come in a variety of forms. Some are special-purpose miniature applications (or applets) written in Java—a new programming language first developed by Sun Microsystems. Others are developed using ActiveX—a Microsoft technology that programmers can use for similar purposes. Both Java and ActiveX make extensive use of prewritten software modules (or objects) that programmers can write themselves, or take from existing sources and fashion into the plug-ins, applets, device drivers, and other software needed to power the Web. Java objects are called "classes," while ActiveX objects are called "controls." The principle difference between them lies in how they run on the host system. Java applets run in a Java virtual machine designed especially to interpret Java programming and translate it into action on the host machine, while ActiveX controls run as native Windows programs that link and pass data between existing Windows software.

The overwhelming majority of these objects are useful (even necessary) parts of any interactive Web site. But despite the best efforts of Sun and Microsoft engineers to design security measures into them, determined programmers can use Java and ActiveX tools to plant harmful objects on Web sites, where they can lurk until visitors unwittingly allow them access to vulnerable computer systems. Unlike viruses, harmful Java and ActiveX objects usually don't seek self-replication as their primary goal—the Web provides them with plenty of opportunities to spread to target computer systems, while their small size and innocuous nature makes it easy for them to evade detection. In fact, unless you specifically tell your browser software to block them, Java and ActiveX objects automatically download to your system whenever you visit a Web site that hosts them.

Instead, harmful objects exist to deliver their equivalent of a virus payload. For example, programmers have written objects that can read data from your hard disk and send it back to the Web site you visited. These objects can "hijack" your e-mail account and send out offensive messages in your name, or can watch data that passes between your computer and other computers.

Recognizing an Infection

As any doctor will tell you, the first step toward recovery is *diagnosis*—recognizing the subtle (and not so subtle) signs of viral activity can give you an edge in stopping the activities of a virus, and save you a substantial amount of time in needless hardware troubleshooting. The following part of this chapter illustrates some of the more important signs of virus activity:

- **You see a warning generated by a virus scanner**   Your antivirus package has detected a virus either in memory, or in one or more executable files. More comprehensive tools may flag infected e-mail attachments or prevent Java/ActiveX Web items. Once the antivirus package has completed its infection report, go ahead and attempt to disinfect as many files as possible. Many of today's viruses cannot be removed without damaging the executable file, so be prepared to restore the infected files from a backup or original installation disks. After the system is cleaned (and damaged files restored), go ahead and check for viruses again. Repeat this procedure until the entire system is clear.

- **You see some sort of bizarre message (i.e., "legalize marijuana" or "your computer is stoned")**   Unfortunately, when a virus reveals itself in this way, it has probably already done its damage to your system. Launch your antivirus software as soon as possible and remove any occurrences of the virus. Be prepared to restore damaged executable files and corrupted data files.

- **You notice that your machine is acting strangely for no apparent reason**   This may happen especially on holidays and other important days of the year. Applications may freeze, crash, or produce unusual error messages without warning. You may notice excessive or random disk access where there was none before. The system may behave unusually slowly files and programs may take a long time to load. Familiar applications may not respond to the keyboard or mouse properly. Leave the application as soon as possible and run your antivirus tools.

- **The computer starts to boot, but freezes before displaying a DOS prompt**   Chances are that you've got a command processor infection. Boot the system from a clean, write-protected floppy disk, then try switching to the infected hard drive. If you cannot access the hard drive, it may be defective, or the virus may have affected the drive's partition table. Run an antivirus package to check the system and eliminate any virulent code.

- **Programs and data files become erased or corrupted without warning**   This is a classic sign of a virus at work. It is highly unlikely that the random loss of a single file is due to a hardware defect. DOS drive access works in terms of clusters, and most files require several clusters. If a cluster— or a sector within that cluster—were to fail, the file would still appear in the directory. Run your antivirus package and check for viruses in memory as well as on disk.

- **You see an error message indicating a problem with the file allocation table or the partition table**   While this may indeed be the result of a hard drive fault, you should make it a point to boot the system from a write-protected floppy disk and check for viruses. If the system checks clear, go ahead and try a package like Drive Pro by MicroHouse to check and reconstruct the damaged boot areas.

- **Programs access more than one disk drive where they did not before**   It is exceptionally rare for a program to try accessing more than one drive unless it is explicitly instructed to do so by you. For example, if you save your new word processing document to drive C, there will be no reason for the program to access drive A. This kind of behavior suggests that a virus is attempting to slip its operations into normal disk access activities. Leave your application and run a virus checker.

- **The number of bad disk sectors increases steadily**   It is not uncommon for viruses to create bad disk sectors and hide within them to escape detection. Since DOS is designed to step over bad sectors, some antivirus programs will not detect viruses using that tactic—leaving you to back up as much of the drive as possible and perform a new low-level format of the drive. Before resorting to that tactic, however, try an antivirus package.

- **The amount of available system RAM suddenly or steadily decreases**   DOS provides the MEM function that allows you to peek at conventional, upper, extended, and expanded memory. If you find that certain programs no longer have enough memory to run, consider the possibility of a memory-resident virus or replicator or some sort. Try your antivirus package. If you have a memory-resident antivirus product available, try loading that on the system for a while.

- **Memory maps (such as the DOS MEM function) reveal strange TSRs not loaded by CONFIG.SYS or AUTOEXEC.BAT**   You can use the MEM function to reveal any drivers or TSRs loaded in the system. If you see a strange or unexpected TSR, you may be faced with a memory-resident virus. Run your antivirus package. If you have a memory-resident antivirus product available, try loading that on the system for a while.

- **File names, extensions, attributes, or date codes are changed unexpectedly**   This is another classic sign of viral activity that is usually attributable to older virulent code that lacked the sophistication to hide its own actions. A reliable antivirus program should be able to deal with any viruses effectively.

- **Unknown files mysteriously appear**   This is a tough call for technicians new to a system, but as a computer user, you are generally pretty aware when a new data file is created on your own system (i.e., a new word processor document or a new spreadsheet). However, when unknown executable files are created, a virus may be at work. Newly created files may be hidden, so use a directory tool that displays hidden files (such as Windows Explorer). Try your antivirus software to locate and eliminate potential viruses.

Travel Advisory

None of the symptoms here guarantee the presence of a virus, and might often be caused by other harmless system conditions.

Dealing with an Infection

Even with the best antivirus tools, regular testing, and consistent backups, systems can still be susceptible to the ravages of computer viruses. When dealing with viruses, you must understand what can and cannot be infected. Programs can be infected—*that's all* (though macro viruses can infect data files such as documents or spread sheets). Programs are any files that have an extension of .EXE, .COM, .BAT, .SYS, .BIN, .DRV, .OVL, .DLL, or .VXD, and of course the two hidden system files that compose the DOS kernel. With the rise of macro viruses, data files such as Microsoft Word and Excel files can also be infected—spreading their havoc when the file's macro is run. Other data files such as images certainly can be corrupted, damaged, or completely destroyed, but they cannot be infected. For example, if you download an Internet image (i.e., a .JPG file), it cannot contain a virus. It is not impossible to infect programs inside an archive (such as .ZIP, .ARC, .ARJ, .LZH, or .ZOO), but it is extremely unlikely because a virus does not want you to know it's there—but the programs may have been contaminated before being placed in the archive. When you suspect the presence of a virus in the system, the following procedures can help you optimize the damage control:

- **Boot from a Clean, Write-Protected Floppy Disk**   One of the most fundamental rules of virus defense is that a virus is harmless until it is launched by the boot sector, command processor, or application. If you can *prevent* the virus from loading in the first place, you stand a good chance of running an antivirus tool successfully. Make sure that the boot disk is prepared on a virus-free PC. The disk should also contain a copy of your antivirus package (most are designed to run from a floppy disk). Do not attempt to launch applications from the questionable hard drive until it has been checked and cleaned.

- **Use Your Antivirus Tools**   If the system booted properly from your write-protected floppy disk, the virus(es) in your system should now be neutralized. Start the antivirus tool contained on your floppy disk and run a comprehensive test of all system files. Also make it a point to check the boot sector and command processor. If your current tool does not support boot sector or command processor testing, you should consider using a second tool that does. When viruses are detected (chances are that more than one file will be infected), attempt to remove as many instances as possible. With luck, you can remove viruses without damaging the infected file, but this is often not possible with today's viruses. When a file cannot be cleaned, it should be erased. Be sure to log each erased file and directory path so that you can replace only those files rather than restore entire subdirectories.

- **Start a Quarantine on Your Computer**   Because many viruses propagate by infecting floppy disks, any disks that have been in your computer should be assumed to have the virus on them. By assuming the worst-case situation, you are possibly saving many others from getting and spreading the virus even further. Gather up as many disks as you can find and check each for viruses. Also, do not share disks between other systems until your system has run for a while and proven itself to be virus-free.

- **Restore the Backups**   It is likely that you had to destroy one or more executable files. Systematically reload any files that were erased during the cleaning process. In most cases, you can restore the damaged files from their original, write-protected installation disks. A tape backup is another popular backup source. Try to avoid reinstalling the entire application unless there is no other alternative.

- **Recheck the Backup**   After the deleted files have been destroyed, it is vitally important to restart your antivirus tool and check the suspect disk again. It is not uncommon for recent backups to be contaminated as well. Verify that the drive is still virus-free. If you locate new viruses introduced in the restored files, remove the viruses again and restore the files from original, write-protected floppy disks.

- **Minimize the Collateral Damage** Immediately notify anybody who you have given any software, sent e-mail (with attachments) to, shared bootable disks with, or if you have even read their disks on your computer. If you have uploaded any programs to a BBS or the Internet, notify the Sysop or Webmaster of that system immediately.

CHECKPOINT

✔ **Objective 5.01: Server Maintenance Guidelines** Servers must be maintained in a prompt and professional manner. Server maintenance generally involves the creation, verification, and restoration of system tape backups. Maintenance also includes all types of upgrades and routine replacement tasks such as BIOS upgrades, CPU and memory upgrades, UPS battery replacement, drive replacement and retirement, virus checking, and all types of network expansions.

✔ **Objective 5.02: Tape Backups** Tape backups are vital because lost data is virtually impossible to re-create. The simplest, most inexpensive way to avoid such a disastrous loss of data is to implement a schedule of periodic backups (preferably using storage facilities off-site). It is best to schedule backup operations during periods of low system use (i.e., during late evening or weekend hours). Backup procedures should also be logged (either as a separate record or as part of your server maintenance log).

✔ **Objective 5.03: UPS Maintenance** Uninterruptible power supply (UPS) systems are designed to keep a server running in the event of a power problem. If ac power is interrupted briefly, the UPS keeps power levels steady and prevent server crashes. If ac power fails completely, the UPS continues to provide power for several minutes, and allows an orderly save and shutdown of the server. Batteries will eventually wear out after an ample number of charge and discharge cycles, and you'll need to replace them.

✔ **Objective 5.04: Network Upgrades** Upgrades are intended to improve the network's performance (i.e., increase throughput), increase storage or add fault tolerance, and add support for more users. One of the most important issues of network upgrades is hardware compatibility, especially when working with business-oriented operating systems such as Windows NT or 2000.

It may be necessary for you to update the BIOS in your own server to the latest version available. You'll need to replace your NIC adapter as users come onto the network and traffic levels increase. You'll also be adding and replacing drives to accommodate the server's storage needs. As server complexity and traffic increase, more memory (RAM) and additional CPUs may be necessary to handle the larger number of open files.

✔ **Objective 5.05: Conflict Detection and Resolution** All PCs (including servers) offer only a limited amount of resources, and no two devices can use the same resources; otherwise, a hardware conflict will result. Interrupts are used to demand attention from the CPU. This allows a device or subsystem to work in the background until a particular event occurs that requires system processing. Direct memory access (DMA) is a technique designed to move large amounts of data from memory to an I/O location, or vice versa, without the direct intervention by the CPU. An I/O port provides the means for a PC to communicate directly with a device.

✔ **Objective 5.06: Computer Virus Issues** Computer viruses are rogue software designed to load and run without the user's knowledge, often hiding in normal programs. There are many different types of viruses to contend with. Use the latest antivirus software on your network, and keep it updated aggressively. Recognizing the subtle (and not so subtle) signs of viral activity can save you a substantial amount of time in needless hardware troubleshooting.

REVIEW QUESTIONS

1. When should you perform a backup process?

    A. Once a day
    B. Once a week
    C. Once a month
    D. As needed by your use of the network

2. After completing a backup process, the backup must be...

    A. Calibrated
    B. Formatted
    C. Verified
    D. Replicated

3. A backup technique that saves and marks selected files only if they have changed since the last time they were backed up is known as…

    A. Full
    B. Incremental
    C. Differential
    D. Copy

4. What routine maintenance should you generally perform on a UPS?

    A. Periodic replacement of the batteries
    B. Periodic replacement of the display panel
    C. Calibration of the output voltage
    D. None of the above

5. Upgrading a network's media means upgrading/replacing the network's…

    A. Drives
    B. Cabling
    C. Video card
    D. Printer

6. Network hardware upgrade problems can be reduced by verifying…

    A. Cable length
    B. Driver versions
    C. Hardware compatibility
    D. Manufacturer's warranty

7. If you need to improve the performance and compatibility of a motherboard, you can sometimes accomplish this by upgrading the…

    A. Bus slots
    B. DIMMs or RIMMs
    C. Tape backup drive
    D. Motherboard BIOS

8. When upgrading a NIC, it is often most helpful to first remove the old…

    A. Operating system
    B. NIC drivers
    C. Network media
    D. NIC adapter

9. Selecting multiple processors with identical speed, voltage, and revision levels is known as...

    A. Processor selection
    B. Processor amplification
    C. Processor matching
    D. Processor filtering

10. Devices that use the same system resources may cause a...

    A. Hardware conflict
    B. Short circuit
    C. Power problem
    D. BIOS fault

REVIEW ANSWERS

1. **A** As needed by your use of the network: When selecting a backup schedule, follow a simple rule: If you cannot get along without it, back it up. Critical data should be backed up daily, weekly, or monthly—it really depends on how critical the data is and how frequently it is updated.

2. **C** Verified: Backups are useless if they cannot be restored, and any experienced technician will tell you to test (aka verify) a backup. Network administrators will periodically perform disaster recovery drills by making a backup, deleting files, restoring the data, and attempting to use that data.

3. **B** Incremental: The incremental backup process saves and marks selected files only if they have changed since the last time they were backed up.

4. **A** Periodic replacement of the batteries: Batteries are electrochemical devices. This means a battery will eventually wear out after an ample number of charge and discharge cycles, and you'll need to replace them. As a rule of thumb, you can expect to change your batteries every 3–5 years under normal use.

5. **B** Cabling: The media is the cabling that connects network devices (i.e., copper or fiber). There may be situations when it's necessary to make upgrades to the network architecture or media.

6. **C** Hardware compatibility: One of the most important issues of network upgrades is hardware compatibility especially when working with

business-oriented operating systems such as Windows NT/2000. Because networking is so hardware-dependent, verifying the correct choice of hardware is an important step in network planning. Otherwise, hardware purchases may not function as expected (if at all).

7. **D** Motherboard BIOS: When bugs are corrected, compatibility issues are resolved, and performance is tweaked in the BIOS code, it may be necessary for you to update the BIOS in your own server to the latest version available.

8. **B** NIC drivers: If you're replacing or upgrading a NIC device (or upgrading the drivers), it is often necessary to remove the older NIC drivers first. This ensures that there is no software conflict between the older and newer software.

9. **C** Processor matching: In many cases, the processors used in a typical network server should be matched. So, not only should the processors use the same speed and voltage, they should all be of the same engineering revision level. For example, Intel processors use "S-spec" numbers to represent the revision level.

10. **A** Hardware conflict: All PCs (including servers) offer only a limited amount of resources, and no two devices can use the same resources; otherwise, a *hardware conflict* will result.

IDE
Technology

	NEWBIE	SOME EXPERIENCE	EXPERT
ETA	4 hours	2 hours	0.5 hour

Whether you're working with a server or a workstation, you're going to need storage—lots of storage—in order to handle the vast number of applications, data, e-mail, multimedia streams, and gigabytes of other traffic that flows across a typical network. Common low-end servers and workstations will use the advanced IDE (Integrated Drive Electronics) type of hard drives and optical drives such as CD-ROMs. The well-established IDE interface is known for its respectable performance, low cost, and ease of installation/use, and is regarded as standard equipment with regular PCs. This chapter discusses basic IDE hard drive and controller concepts, and outlines a wide selection of troubleshooting solutions for technicians.

Objective 6.01 Basic IDE Drive Concepts

In order to use any kind of drive properly, you should understand some of the characteristics involved in drive configuration and management. You'll need to install an IDE drive properly, and prepare the drive so that the system "sees" it adequately. This part of the chapter explains the difference between physical and logical drives, covers several important drive attributes that you should be familiar with, and outlines the typical interface versions that you will probably encounter.

Binary Megabytes versus Decimal Megabytes

Most folks know that hard drive sizes are measured in megabytes (MB) and gigabytes (GB); however, beginners and experienced technicians alike are often confused by the difference between binary megabytes and decimal megabytes (as well as for gigabytes). For example, you'll notice that when you install a new 4GB hard drive, utilities like the CMOS Setup, FDISK, and Windows Explorer will report only about 3.72GB, but other utilities like CHKDSK report about 4GB. This difference is often confusing, but it's due to the way in which manufacturers and software makers calculate drive capacity. *Technically*, hard drive capacity is calculated by multiplying the number of cylinders, sectors, and heads times 512, such as this:

Capacity = Cylinders × Heads × Sectors × 512 (bytes/sector)

So, if you're using an AC2850 drive with 1,654 cylinders, 16 heads, and 63 sectors, you'd wind up with

$1,654 \times 16 \times 63 \times 512 =$ **853,622,784 bytes**

By comparison, an AC34000 drive with 7,752 cylinders, 16 heads, and 63 sectors would yield

$7752 \times 16 \times 63 \times 512 =$ **4,000,776,192 bytes**

The problem is that hard drive manufacturers use the notion of decimal megabytes (or decimal gigabytes) to determine the size of their hard drives. To calculate drive sizes in decimal megabytes, just divide the drive size by 1,000,000 (or 1,000,000,000 for GB). For the AC2850, you'd get this:

853,622,784 / 1,000,000 = **853.6MB**
For the AC34000, you'd get
4,000,776,192 / 1,000,000,000 = **4.0GB**

Makes sense, right? The problem is that many software makers will use binary megabytes (or binary gigabytes) to calculate drive sizes. A binary megabyte is 1,048,576 bytes, and a binary gigabyte is 1,073,741,824 bytes, so here's how a lot of software will report the AC2850:

853,622,784 bytes / 1,048,576 = **814MB**

And here's the calculation for the AC34000:

4,000,776,192 bytes / 1,073,741,824 = **3.72GB**

These are simply two slightly different ways of representing the same drives, so *both* methods are correct. The important issue here is that you recognize the difference, and do not mistake that difference as being a problem with the drive.

Drive Parameters and Translation

A host computer must know the key parameters of its installed hard drive before the drive can be used. There are six parameters that a system must know: the number of cylinders, heads, and sectors, as well as the track where write precompensation begins, what track the landing zone is on, and the drive's total formatted capacity. These parameters are stored in the computer's CMOS RAM and configured with the CMOS Setup utility. If a new drive is installed, the CMOS setup can easily be updated to show the changes. You can tell a lot about a drive by reviewing its parameters. Consider the Maxtor 88400D8—with 16 heads, 63 sectors per track, and 16,278 tracks (cylinders), the capacity works out as (16,278 × 16 × 63 × 512) 8,401,010,688 bytes (or 8.4GB).

There are two interesting things to note about modern drives. First, the write precompensation and landing zone entries are essentially unused. In most cases, the landing zone is now an automated feature of the particular drive. The second issue to consider is that these numbers are *logical*, and not *physical*. Just imagine that with two heads per platter, you'd need 8 platters to support 16 heads—not too likely in today's small form-factor drives. Also, in actual practice, the number of sectors per track can differ because of zoned recording techniques. What this means is that the drive parameters you are entering into CMOS are *translation parameters*. The electronics on the drive itself actually convert (or translate) those parameters into actual physical drive locations.

Local Lingo

Drive translation The process where the system converts a logical drive location into a physical drive location.

Start Time

Booting a computer can take up to 30 seconds, and often more. Some of this time is an artificial delay needed to initialize the hard drive. From the moment power is applied to the hard drive, it can take anywhere from 7–10 seconds for the drive's on-board controller to start and initialize the drive where it can be recognized by the system POST (power on self test). This is known as the drive's *start time*. Boot problems with a new hard drive are frequently caused by an insufficient delay at boot time. The BIOS attempts to check for the presence of a hard drive that has not yet had time to initialize. The start time can be adjusted through the CMOS Setup (i.e., Power On Boot Delay).

Power Mode Definitions

Modern hard drives are not simply "on" or "off." They operate in any one of several modes, and each mode makes different power demands on the host system. This is particularly important because today's desktops and workstations are becoming ever more power conscious, so the ability to control drive power is an integral part of PC power conservation systems. Typical hard drives operate in any of five different power modes:

- **Spin-up** The drive is spinning up following initial application of power and has not yet reached full speed. This demands about 14W, and is particularly demanding of the power supply (if the supply is marginal or overloaded, the hard drive may not spin-up properly).

- **Seek**   This is a random access operation by the disk drive as it tries to locate the required track for reading or writing. This demands about 8.5–9.0W.
- **Read/Write**   A seek has been completed, and data is being read from or written to the drive. This uses about 5.0W.
- **Idle**   This is a basic power conservation mode where the drive is spinning and all other circuitry is powered on, but the head actuator is parked and powered off. This drops power demands to about 4W, yet the drive is capable of responding to read commands within 40ms.
- **Standby**   The spindle motor is not running (the drive spins down). This is the main power conservation mode that requires just 1W. It may take up to several seconds for the drive to leave this mode (or spin-up) upon receipt of a command that requires disk access.

Latency

As fast as a hard drive is, it cannot work instantaneously. There is a finite period of delay between the moment that a read or write command is initiated over the drive's physical interface and the moment that desired information is available (or placed). This delay is known as *latency*. More specifically, latency refers to the time it takes for needed bytes to pass under a R/W head. If the head has not quite reached the desired location yet, latency can be quite short. If the head has just missed the desired location, the head must wait almost a full rotation of the disk platters before the needed bits are available again, so latency can be rather long. In general, a disk drive is specified with *average latency* that (statistically) is the time for the spindle to make half of a full rotation. For a disk rotating at 3,600 rpm (or 60 rotations per second), a full rotation is completed in [1/60] 16.7ms. Average latency would then be [16.7/2] 8.3ms. Disks spinning at 5,200 rpm offer an average latency of 5.8ms, and so on. As a rule, the faster a disk spins, the lower its latency will be. Ultimately, disk speed is limited by centrifugal forces acting on the platters.

Local Lingo

Average latency   The time required for one half a rotation of the disk platters.

Objective 6.02   Understanding the Interface

The Integrated Drive Electronics (IDE) interface was developed in 1988 in response to an industry push to create a standard software interface for SCSI peripherals. The industry consortium, known as the Common Access Method Committee (or CAMC), attempted to originate an AT Attachment (ATA) interface that could be incorporated into low-cost AT-compatible motherboards. The CAMC completed its specification, which was later approved by ANSI. The term "ATA interface" generally refers to the controller interface, while "IDE" refers to the drive. Today, "IDE" simply refers to an interface type, and can be applied to either the drive or controller (such as Figure 6-1). For example, an IDE drive will require an IDE controller.

Travel Advisory

Even though there are numerous iterations of the IDE family today (such as EIDE, UDMA/66, and UDMA/100), the family is still commonly referred to as "IDE-type."

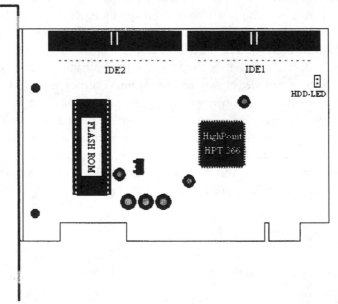

FIGURE 6-1   A typical IDE-type controller

IDE/ATA

IDE (Integrated Drive Electronics) and ATA (AT Attachment) are basically one and the same thing—a disk drive scheme designed to integrate the controller onto the drive mechanism itself instead of relying on a stand-alone controller board as older MFM and RLL drives did. This approach reduces interface costs and makes drive firmware implementations easier. IDE proved to be a low-cost, easily configured system—so much so that it created a boom in the disk drive industry. Although the terms "IDE" and "ATA" are sometimes used interchangeably, ATA is the formal standard that defines the drive and how it operates, while IDE is really the "trade name" that refers to the 40-pin interface (and the 40-pin cable shown in Figure 6-2) and drive controller architecture designed to implement the ATA standard.

The AT Attachment interface was submitted to ANSI for approval in 1990, and was finally published in 1994 as ANSI standard X3.221-1994, titled "AT Attachment Interface for Disk Drives." This standard is sometimes called ATA-1 to distinguish it from its successors. The original IDE/ATA standard defines the following features and transfer modes:

- The specification calls for a single channel in a PC, shared by two devices that are configured as master and slave.
- ATA includes support for PIO modes 0, 1, and 2.
- ATA includes support for single-word DMA modes 0, 1, and 2, and multiword DMA mode 0.

ATA does not include support for enhancements such as ATAPI support for non-hard-disk IDE/ATA devices, block mode transfers, logical block addressing,

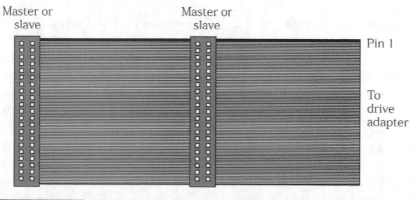

Master or
slave

Master or
slave

Pin 1

To
drive
adapter

FIGURE 6-2 A typical 40-pin IDE signal cable

Ultra-DMA modes, or other advanced features. The ATA-1 standard is now completely obsolete, and drives developed to meet this standard are no longer made. At the recommendation of the T13 Technical Committee, ATA-1 was withdrawn as an official ANSI standard in 1999.

ATAPI

Originally, the IDE/ATA interface was designed to work only with hard drives. Other devices such as CD-ROMs and tape drives used proprietary interfaces (often implemented on sound cards), the floppy disk interface (which is slow and cumbersome), or SCSI. In the early 1990s, designers realized that there would be enormous advantages to using the standard IDE/ATA interface to support devices other than hard drives. The intention was not to replace SCSI, but rather to eliminate proprietary interfaces and the slow floppy interface for tape drives.

Unfortunately, given the ATA command structure, it wasn't possible to put non-hard drive devices on the IDE channel and expect them to work. A special protocol was developed, called the AT Attachment Packet Interface or ATAPI. The ATAPI standard is used for devices like CD, tape and removable media drives. It enables them to use the standard IDE cable used by IDE/ATA hard drives, and be configured as master or slave just like a hard drive. When you see a CD-ROM or other non-HDD peripheral denoted as an "IDE device," it is really using the ATAPI protocol. Internally, the ATAPI protocol is not at all similar to the standard ATA command set used by hard drives. The name "packet interface" suggests that commands to ATAPI devices are sent in groups called packets. In some ways, ATAPI resembles SCSI more than IDE in terms of its command set and operation. The first ATAPI standard document was called SFF-8020 (later renamed INF-8020), which is now quite old and obsolete. In the late 1990s, the T13 Technical Committee took over control of the ATAPI command set and protocol, combining it with ATA into the ATA/ATAPI-4 standard.

A special ATAPI driver is used to communicate with ATAPI devices—this driver must be loaded into memory before the device can be accessed (though most newer operating systems such as Windows support ATAPI internally and load their own drivers for the interface). The actual data transfers use regular PIO or DMA modes—just like hard disks—though support for the various modes differs widely by device. For the most part, ATAPI devices will coexist with IDE/ATA devices. From the user's perspective, ATAPI devices behave as if they are regular IDE/ATA disks on the channel. Newer BIOS versions will even allow the system to boot from ATAPI CD-ROM drives.

ATA-2, Fast-ATA, and EIDE

By the early 1990s, it became clear that ATA architecture would soon be over-whelmed by advances in hard drive technology. The ATA interface committee responded by developing the ATA-2 standard that essentially combined the features and attributes defined by marketing programs created at Seagate, Quantum and Western Digital. This standard was published in 1996 as ANSI standard X3.279-1996, called the AT Attachment Interface with Extensions. ATA-2 is largely regarded as a significant improvement to ATA. It defines faster PIO (Programmed I/O) and DMA (Direct Memory Access) data transfer modes, adds more powerful drive commands (such as the Identify Drive command to support auto-identification in CMOS), adds support for a second drive channel, handles block data transfers (Block Transfer Mode), and defines a new means of addressing sectors on the hard drive using *Logical Block Addressing* (LBA). LBA has proven to be a very effective vehicle for overcoming the traditional 528MB hard drive size limit. Yet ATA-2 continues to use the same 40-pin physical interface used by ATA, and is backward compatible with ATA (IDE) drives.

Along with ATA-2, you'll probably find two additional terms: EIDE (*Enhanced IDE*) and *Fast-ATA*. These are not standards—merely different implementations of the ATA-2 standard. EIDE represents the Western Digital implementation of ATA-2 that builds upon both the ATA-2 and ATAPI standards. This has been *so* effective that EIDE has become the "generic" term. Seagate and Quantum have thrown their support behind the Fast-ATA implementation of the ATA-2 standard. However, Fast-ATA builds on ATA-2 only. For all practical purposes, there is no significant difference between ATA-2, EIDE, and Fast-ATA, and you'll probably see these three terms used interchangeably (though this is not *technically* correct).

ATA-3

A more recent implementation of the ATA standard is ATA-3, which was published in 1997 as ANSI standard X3.298-1997 called AT Attachment 3 Interface. It does not define any new data transfer modes, but it does improve the reliability of

---

Exam Tip

ATA-3 does *not* define any of the Ultra-DMA modes—these were first defined with the **ATA/ATAPI-4** standard. **ATA-3** is also not the same as **ATA-33** (often used as a slang term for Ultra-DMA/33).

PIO mode 4. It also offers a simple password-based security scheme, more sophisticated power management features, and "Self-Monitoring Analysis and Reporting Technology" (SMART). ATA-3 is also backward compatible with ATA-2, ATAPI, and ATA devices. Since no new data transfer modes are defined by ATA-3, you may also see the generic term "EIDE" used interchangeably (though this is also not technically correct).

Travel Advisory

You may see a "PIO mode 5" described in some places with the claim that it was introduced in ATA-3. This mode was suggested by some controller manufacturers, but never approved and never implemented. It is not defined in any of the ATA standards and only exists in some BIOS versions.

ATA/ATAPI-4 (Ultra-ATA/33)

The next significant enhancement to the ATA standard saw the ATA Packet Interface (ATAPI) feature set merged with the conventional ATA command set and protocols to create ATA/ATAPI-4. This standard was published by ANSI in 1998 as NCITS 317-1998, AT Attachment with Packet Interface Extensions. Aside from combining ATA and ATAPI, this standard defined several other significant enhancements and changes:

- High-speed Ultra-DMA modes 0, 1, and 2 were created, defining transfer rates of 16.7, 25, and 33.3MB/s.
- A 40-pin/80 conductor IDE cable was first defined in this standard. It was thought that the higher-speed Ultra-DMA modes would require the use of this cable in order to eliminate signal problems caused by the higher speed. The use of this cable was left optional for this standard, though it became mandatory under the faster UDMA modes defined in ATA/ATAPI-5.
- Cyclical redundancy checking (CRC) was added to ensure the integrity of data sent using the faster Ultra-DMA modes.
- The command set was cleaned up and several older, obsolete commands removed, and special command queuing and overlapping protocols were defined.

Obviously, the Ultra-DMA (UDMA) modes were the most exciting part of this new standard. Ultra-DMA modes 0 and 1 were never really implemented by hard disk manufacturers, but UDMA mode 2 made a real impression since it doubled the throughput of the fastest transfer mode then available to 33.3MB/s. Ultra-DMA mode 2 was quickly dubbed "Ultra-DMA/33," and drives conforming to ATA/ATAPI-4 are often called "Ultra-ATA/33" drives (which is technically inaccurate).

In actual practice, you'll need an Ultra-ATA drive, controller, and BIOS to support an Ultra-ATA drive system, but it is fully backward compatible with previous ATA standards. You can use ordinary 40-pin IDE-type cables for UDMA/33 unless any of the following issues occur:

- The standard cable is low quality, damaged, or weakened by many installs.
- The system suffers from excessive signal noise—these systems may have multiple drives, dual power supplies, or an integrated CRT.
- The system is overclocked (or otherwise configured beyond the manufacturer's supported specifications).

ATA/ATAPI-5 (Ultra-ATA/66)

With the rapid adoption of ATA/ATAPI-4, the T13 committee immediately began work on its next generation of interface standard dubbed ATA/ATAPI-5. This standard was published by ANSI in 2000 as NCITS 340-2000, called the AT Attachment with Packet Interface–5. The changes defined in ATA/ATAPI-5 include the following:

- More high-speed Ultra-DMA modes 3 and 4, defining transfer rates of 44.4 and 66.6 MB/s respectively.
- The 40-pin/80-conductor IDE cable that was optional in ATA/ATAPI-4 is made mandatory for UDMA modes 3 and 4. ATA/ATAPI-5 also defines a method by which a host system can detect if an 80-conductor cable is in use, so it can determine whether or not to enable the higher-speed transfer modes.
- Numerous interface commands were changed, and some old ones were deleted.

Like ATA-3, not that many changes were made in ATA/ATAPI-5. However, the main change was certainly important—another doubling of the throughput of the interface to 66.6MB/s. Many companies quickly labeled ATA/ATAPI-5 drives running Ultra-DMA mode 4 as "Ultra-ATA/66." During late 1999 and early 2000, new IDE/ATA drives conforming to this standard began appearing on the market.

You'll need an Ultra-ATA/66 drive, controller, and BIOS to support an Ultra-ATA/66 drive system, but it is fully backward compatible with previous ATA standards. Unlike the Ultra-ATA/33 approach, you'll need a specially designed 40-pin/80-conductor cable (typically provided with UDMA/66 drives). Also keep in mind that the operating system must also be enabled for DMA transfers. Keep the following issues in mind when implementing a UDMA/66 system:

- Make sure that the signal cable is Ultra-ATA/66 capable. An Ultra-ATA/66-compliant cable is a 40-pin/80-conductor cable with a black connector on one end, a blue connector on the other end, and a gray connector in the middle. In addition, pin 34 on the cable should be notched or cut (though this may be difficult to see with the human eye).
- Make sure the system board (motherboard) controller is capable of supporting Ultra-ATA/66. An Ultra-ATA/66-capable controller has a detect circuit that can detect line 34 missing on the cable. If there is no detect circuit, the system can wrongly detect the presence of an Ultra-ATA/66 cable, and try to configure the device for a higher transfer rate.
- Some system board (motherboard) controllers may not successfully handle Ultra-ATA/66 on both the primary and secondary channels. If you have difficulty with a UDMA/66 device on the secondary controller channel, consider troubleshooting with the device in the primary master position.
- If you have trouble getting a UDMA/66 system configured properly, contact the system board (motherboard) or controller card manufacturer for the latest BIOS upgrade (and any Ultra-ATA/66 device drivers or patches).
- Make sure the operating system is "DMA-capable," and verify that the DMA mode is activated. For Windows 9x/Me, check the drive's Properties dialog box in the Device Manager.
- Make sure the Ultra-ATA/66-capable drive has been configured to run at Ultra-ATA/66 transfer rates. Some drives ship with the UDMA/66 mode disabled by default, and require a jumper change and/or software utility in order to activate the UDMA/66 mode.

ATA/ATAPI-6 (Ultra-ATA/100)

At the time this edition is being written, the T13 Technical Committee is working on he next version of the ATA standard dubbed ATA/ATAPI-6. It is likely that this standard will be completed in 2001, and published sometime later that year or early in 2002. Since this standard is still in development, it is impossible to say exactly what features and changes it will include. One addition to the standard will almost certainly be the new Ultra-DMA mode 5, which increases transfer throughput to 100MB/s (now available in drives dubbed UDMA/100). Some possible new features for the next standard include the following:

- LBA address size expansion to overcome the traditional 28-bit LBA scheme (limiting drive sizes to 137GB, and a possible size barrier in the next year or two). An addressing mode will probably be included in ATA/ATAPI-6 that expands the address width from 28-bits to either 48 or 64 bits.
- Hard drive noise reduction (acoustic management) may be included that allows the mechanics of the drive to be modified under software control—allowing the user choose between higher performance or quieter operation.
- Additional ATA commands may be added to support audio and video streaming (or other multimedia operations).

Travel Advisory

Ultra-DMA/100 drives are currently available, and may be standardized with the release of ATA/ATAPI-6.

Data Transfer Modes

Data transfer rates play a major role in drive performance. In practice, there are two measures of data transfer: the rate at which data is taken from the platters, and the rate at which data is passed between the drive and controller. The *internal* data transfer between the platters and drive buffer is typically the slower rate. Older Ultra-ATA drives like the Maxtor DiamondMax 2160 run at 14MB/s, but their newer DiamondMax 80 (UDMA/100) drives can move information between the buffer and media up to 46.7MB/s. The *external* data transfer between the drive and controller (the "interface rate") is often the *faster* rate. Older ATA-2 (EIDE) drives can operate up to 16MB/s using PIO mode 4, but Ultra-DMA/66 drives can burst data from the buffer to the interface at 66MB/s, and Ultra-DMA/100 drives can handle burst data transfers of 100MB/s.

The modern standards of external data transfer are listed as PIO (or Programmed I/O) and DMA (Direct Memory Access) modes. PIO modes are managed by the system processor. The PIO mode specifies how fast data is transferred to and from the drive as shown in Table 6-1.

TABLE 6.1	Data Transfer Speed for PIO Modes		
PIO Mode	Cycle Time (ns)	Transfer Rate (MB/s)	Notes
0	600	3.3	These are the old ATA (IDE) modes.
1	383	5.2	
2	240	8.3	
3	180 IORDY	11.1	These are the newer ATA-2 (EIDE) modes.
4	120 IORDY	16.6	

You may notice that the EIDE-specific modes (PIO-3 and PIO-4) use the IORDY hardware flow control line. This means that the drive can use the IORDY line to slow down the interface when necessary. Interfaces without proper IORDY support might cause data corruption in the fast PIO modes (so you'd be stuck with the slower modes). When choosing an EIDE drive and controller, always be sure to check that the IORDY line is being used.

By comparison, DMA data transfers mean that the data is transferred *directly* between the drive and memory without using the CPU as an intermediary (as is the case with PIO). In true multitasking operating systems like OS/2, Windows NT, or Linux, DMA transfers leave the CPU free to do something useful during disk transfers. In a DOS or Windows environment, the CPU will have to wait for the transfer to finish anyway, so in these cases DMA transfers don't offer that much of a multitasking advantage. There are two distinct types of direct memory access: ordinary DMA and bus-mastering DMA. Ordinary DMA uses the DMA controller on the system's motherboard to perform the complex task of arbitration, grabbing the system bus, and transferring the data. With bus-mastering DMA, all this is done by logic in the drive controller itself. DMA transfer modes are listed in Table 6-2.

Block Mode Transfers

Traditionally, an interrupt (IRQ) is generated each time a read or write command is passed to the drive. This causes a certain amount of overhead work for the host system and CPU. If it were possible to transfer *multiple* sectors of data between the

DMA Mode	Cycle Time (ns)	Transfer Rate (MB/s)	Notes
Single Word 0	960	2.1	Also in ATA
1	480	4.2	
2	240	8.3	
Multi Word 0	480	4.2	Also in ATA
1	150	13.3	
2	120	16.6	
3	—	33.0	Ultra-DMA/33
4	—	66.0	Ultra-DMA/66
5	—	100.0	Ultra-DMA/100

TABLE 6.2 Data Transfer Speed for DMA Modes

drive and host without generating an IRQ, data transfer could be accomplished much more efficiently. Block mode transfers allow up to 128 sectors of data to be transferred at a single time, and can improve transfers as much as 30 percent. However, block mode transfers are not terribly effective on single-tasking operating systems like DOS—any improvement over a few percent usually indicates bad buffer cache management on the part of the drive. Finally, the block size that is optimal for drive throughput isn't always the best for system performance. For example, the DOS FAT file system tends to favor a block size equal to the cluster size.

Ideas of Bus Mastering

Bus mastering is a high-performance enhancement to the drive controller interface on your system (you may see some motherboards or chipsets mention bus master support as BM-IDE). When configured properly, bus mastering uses DMA data transfers to reduce the CPU's workload when it comes to saving or recalling data from the IDE/UDMA drive (such as a hard drive or ATAPI CD-ROM). By comparison, programmed I/O (PIO) data transfer modes are very CPU-intensive.

Bus mastering is particularly useful if you have multiple disk-intensive applications running simultaneously. Most modern PCs support bus mastering, but to make the most of bus master performance, your system must have *all* of the following elements:

- The motherboard (drive controller) must be bus master IDE compliant.
- The motherboard BIOS must support bus mastering.
- You need a multitasking operating system (OS) such as Windows 95/98/2000.
- A bus mastering *device driver* is needed for the operating system.
- You need a bus mastering-compatible IDE/UDMA device (disk drive, CD-ROM) that supports DMA multiword modes.

You can use bus master IDE and nonbus master IDE devices in the same system, but the nonbus master IDE devices will reduce the overall performance of the bus mastering devices. However, bus mastering IDE is not a cure-all for system performance problems. In fact, bus mastering will probably not benefit the system significantly if you run DOS applications, work with only single applications at a time, or use multiple applications that are not disk-intensive.

SMART Technology

SMART (Self-Monitoring Analysis and Reporting Technology) is a self-diagnostic system that enables the PC to predict the impending failures of devices such as disk drives. With a given failure prediction, the user or system manager can back up key data, replace a suspect device prior to data loss, and avoid undesired downtime. SMART is a key for improving data integrity and data availability of the PC.

SMART goes by a variety of names in the computer industry. The term *predictive failure analysis* (PFA) was given to SMART technology by its inventor IBM. PFA is implemented into all of IBM's mainframe computer systems. Compaq was one of the first companies to implement SMART in their hard

---

Travel Assistance

You can learn more about SMART from Maxtor at www.maxtor.com/technology/whitepapers/smart0.html. You can also check with StorageSoft at www.storagesoft.com for detailed information on their SMART utility.

drives, and this was dubbed "drive failure prediction (DFP)." The initial Compaq Computer SMART specification was modified and submitted for general industry consideration by the Small Form Factor Committee. SMART is now being standardized by ANSI in the ATA-4 (ANSI X3T13 ATA\ATAPI-4) specification. To implement SMART, the host computer must have BIOS or device driver support that is capable of sending SMART commands to and from the ATA interface registers. SMART technology is growing in popularity, and all current Maxtor drives are SMART ready.

Drive Caching

Ideally, a drive should respond instantaneously—data should be available the moment it's requested. Unfortunately, the instant access and transfer of data is impossible with even today's magnetic (and optical) storage technologies. The inescapable laws of physics govern the limitations of mechanical systems such as spindles and head stepping, and mechanical delays will always be present (to some extent) in drive systems. The problem now facing computer designers is that mechanical drive systems—as fast and precise as they are—still lag far behind the computer circuitry handling the information. In the world of personal computers, a millisecond is a very long time. You often must wait for disk access to be completed before DOS allows another operation to begin. Such delays can be quite irritating when the drive is accessing huge programs and data files typical of current software packages. Drives use a technique called *drive caching* to increase the apparent speed of drive systems.

Caching basically allocates a small amount of solid-state memory that acts as an interim storage area (or buffer) located right on the drive. A cache is typically loaded with information that is *anticipated* to be required by the system. When a disk read is initiated, the cache is checked for desired information. If the desired information is actually in the cache (a *cache hit*), that information is transferred from the cache buffer to the core logic at electronic rates—no disk access occurs, and very fast data transfer is achieved. If the desired information is not in the cache (a *cache miss*), the data is taken from the hard disk at normal drive speeds with no improvement in performance. Today's hard drives use as much as 256KB of modern high-performance memory for on-board drive cache. A variety of complex software algorithms are used to predict what disk information to load and save in a cache.

Although the majority of caches are intended to buffer read operations, some caches also buffer write operations. A write cache accepts the data to be saved from core logic, then returns system control while the drive works separately to save the information. Keep in mind that a cache does not accelerate the drive itself. A cache merely helps to move your system along so that you need not wait for drive delays. In terms of general implementation, a cache can be located on the hard drive itself or on the drive controller board. For most computers using system-level hard drive interfaces (UDMA or SCSI), any cache is usually located on the drive itself.

Objective 6.03 Drive Preparation Essentials

You can imagine a disk drive as being a big file cabinet. When the drive is first installed, the "file cabinet" is completely empty—there are no dividers or folders or labels of any kind to organize information. In order to make the drive useful, it must be *partitioned* and *formatted*. There are basically two steps to the format process: partitioning, and formatting. Each of these steps is critically important for the proper operation of a drive.

Physical versus Logical Drives

When working with hard drives, you should be familiar with the idea of *physical* and *logical* hard drives. It's important for you to realize that these are *not* necessarily the same thing (even though they may be on the same drive). The physical hard drive is the actual drive device that you take out of the box and install in the PC. However, just because you install a hard drive in the PC is no guarantee that the operating system (i.e., Windows NT or Windows 98/SE) will recognize the drive. Because an operating system only deals with logical volumes, you must convert the physical drive into one or more logical drives. Logical volumes are placed on the physical drive through the *partitioning* process (using FDISK). You can place up to four partitions on one logical drive using the FDISK utility, and each partition must be formatted with the FORMAT utility before an operating system can use it.

Partitioning

Where low-level formatting is a hardware-specific process, *partitioning* is an operating system–specific process. After low-level formatting is complete, the drive must be partitioned before an OS file system or boot information is written to the drive. Also, partitioning allows a large physical drive to be divided up into several smaller *logical* drives. There are several file systems in service today, but DOS and Windows 9x/Me continue to use the file allocation table (FAT) system. Network operating systems such as Windows NT and 2000 support the NT File System (NFTS). The main criticism of the FAT system is that sectors are grouped and assigned as clusters. This is a wasteful use of drive space (especially for large drives where up to 64 sectors—32KB—may be in a single cluster). One of the newly created partitions will be assigned as the boot partition, and a *master boot sector* (MBS) containing a special boot program and partition table will be written to the first sector. The MBS is often referred to as the *master boot record* (MBR). FDISK is the DOS utility used for drive partitioning. Different operating systems carry their own partitioning limitations:

- Versions of MS-DOS and PC-DOS after 3.30 (but before 4.0) have a 32MB per partition limit.
- All versions of DOS have a 1,024-cylinder limitation. To access more cylinders, you'll need a device driver or a controller card that offers a translate mode (i.e., LBA).
- DOS and Windows 95 using FAT16 are limited to 2.1GB per partition.
- Versions of Windows NT 4.0 and earlier are limited to a 4.2GB boot partition.
- Windows 95 OSR2 and Windows 98 use FAT32 partitions that can support up to 2TB partitions.

High-Level (DOS) Formatting

Even after partitioning, an operating system cannot store files on a drive. A series of data structures must be written to the drive. A *volume boot sector* (VBS), two copies of the *file allocation table* (FAT), and a *root directory* are written to each logical partition. High-level formatting also checks and locks out bad sectors so that they will not be used during normal operation. FORMAT is the DOS utility used for high-level formatting. It is interesting to note that the FORMAT utility will perform both low-level and high-level formatting for a floppy disk, but *not* for a hard drive.

Local Lingo
FAT (file allocation table)   The way in which files are stored on a hard drive by organizing disk sectors into groups called clusters.

FAT Basics

As you saw previously, Microsoft DOS and Windows can use a FAT to organize files on the drive. Sectors are organized into groups called *clusters*, and each cluster is assigned a number. Early drives (i.e., floppy drives) used a 12-bit number (known as FAT12), but hard drives typically used a 16-bit number (called FAT16). The newest releases of Windows 95 (OSR2) and Windows 98/SE/Me assign a 32-bit number to each cluster (called FAT32). By assigning each cluster with its own number, it is possible to store files in any available (unused) clusters throughout the drive without worrying about the file's size. As files are erased, those clusters become available for reuse. Overall, the FAT system has proven to be a versatile and reliable file management system.

The problem with the FAT system is that you can only have as many clusters as can be specified by the number of bits available. For a 12-bit FAT, you can only have 4,096 (2^{12}) clusters. For a 16-bit FAT, you can have 65,536 (2^{16}) clusters. If the drive is 120MB, each cluster must then be about (120MB / 65,536) 1.8KB (2KB in actual practice). If the drive were 500MB, each cluster must be about (540MB / 65,536) 7.6KB (8KB in actual practice). Because only *one* file can be assigned to any given cluster, the *entire* space for that cluster is assigned (even if the file is very small). So if you were to store a 2KB file in an 8KB cluster, you'd waste (8KB–2KB) 6KB! This wasted space is known as *slack space*. Of course, the FAT12 system was long since abandoned while hard drives were still about 32MB, but you get the idea that very large drives can waste a serious amount of space when using a FAT system.

Another frequent complaint about the FAT file system is the phenomenon of *file fragmentation*. Because clusters are all independent, and clusters are assigned wherever they can be found, a file requiring more than one cluster can be scattered anywhere on the disk. For example, suppose you're editing a large image (it can take several MB). The file may use the 20 available clusters on track 345, two more available clusters on track 1012, 50 available clusters on track 2011, and so on. In theory, fragmentation is simply a harmless side effect of the FAT system. But in practice, badly fragmented files can force the hard drive to work unusually hard chasing down the various clusters associated with the file. Not only does this slow the drive's effective performance, but the extra work required of the drive may ultimately shorten its working life. The best way to correct this issue is to periodically defragment the disk with a utility like Disk Defragmenter (simply called Defrag). Defragmenting the disk will rearrange all the clusters so that all the clusters for any given file will be contiguous.

FAT16

DOS (including the DOS under Windows 95/NT) uses the FAT16 file system to store data. The FAT16 system uses 16-bit-cluster address numbers that allow up to 65,536 clusters. Under FAT16, a cluster can be as big as 32KB, which translates into a maximum partition size of (65,536 x 32,768) 2,147,483,648 bytes (2.1GB). While a 16-bit cluster number is much more efficient than a 12-bit cluster number, every file *must* take up at least one cluster even if the file size is much smaller than the cluster. For the very large drives we have today, the correspondingly large clusters can result in a significant amount of *slack space*. If the physical drive is larger than 2.1GB, you must create subsequent logical partitions to utilize the additional space. For example, if you have a 3.1GB drive, you can create one 2.1GB partition, then create a second 1.0GB partition. One way to reduce slack space is to create a larger number of smaller logical partitions. This results in smaller clusters, but generates a larger number of logical drives and corresponding drive letters.

FAT32

Obviously, the limitations of FAT16 are presenting a serious issue with hard drives over 6GB. Microsoft has responded by developing a 32-bit FAT system to implement in a service release of Windows 95 (called OSR2)—and now in Windows 98/SE. The upper 4 bits are reserved, so the system will actually access (2^{28}) 268,435,456 clusters (over 256 million clusters). This allows single partitions of 8GB with clusters only 4KB in size—the maximum size of any given partition is 2TB (yes, *terabytes*—thousands of gigabytes). FAT32 also eliminates the fixed size for a root directory, so you can have as many files and directories in the root as you want.

   On the surface, this probably sounds like a great deal, but there are some major problems that you'll need to consider before updating to FAT32. First, DOS applications (without being rewritten) can only access files up to 2GB, and Win32 applications can work with files up to 4GB. By itself, that's not so bad, but FAT32 partitions are *only* accessible through the OSR2-enhanced Windows 95, Windows

---

Exam Tip

Windows NT does *not* support FAT32, so servers running Windows
NT will be limited to FAT16 partitions.

98/SE, and the corresponding DOS 7.X. No other operating system can read the partitions (including Windows NT). Also, any disk utilities written for FAT16 won't work for FAT32 (and can seriously damage your data).

Even though the OSR2 release ships with FAT32 versions of FDISK, FORMAT, SCANDISK, and Defrag, the version of DriveSpace 3 will *not* support FAT32. So if you're using drive compression, you're out of luck. Further, there are older APIs (application programming interfaces) in service that simply won't support FAT32, so some programs may refuse to work outright until the software is recompiled with FAT32-compliant APIs. DOS device drivers (such as those needed to support SCSI devices) will also have to be updated for FAT32. In other words, you'll lose your SCSI drives until suitable drivers become available.

NTFS

The *NT File System* (NTFS) is the preferred file system under Windows NT, largely because of the security and large partition sizes offered by NTFS. NTFS should generally be considered when security is needed for servers and workstations. NTFS is the only file system under Windows NT that allows permissions to be assigned to individual files and folders. NTFS also maintains a transaction log file as files are moved and updated. This makes it much easier to recover lost, damaged, or deleted information. NTFS supports cluster remapping so that faulty clusters are replaced with good (spare) clusters on the drive.

When using NTFS, you should also understand some of its disadvantages. As a rule, you should avoid using NTFS on a volume that is smaller than about 400MB. The amount of overhead space involved in NTFS prohibits this. Overhead is in the form of NTFS system files that typically use at least 4MB of drive space on a 100MB partition. There is no file encryption built into NTFS, so a user can boot to DOS (or another operating system) and use a low-level disk editing utility to view data stored on an NTFS volume. Finally, it is not possible to format a floppy disk with the NTFS file system. Windows NT formats all floppy disks with the FAT file system.

Converting to NTFS   Windows NT includes an executable file called CONVERT.EXE that can be used to convert an existing FAT hard drive partition to NTFS. Converting from FAT to NTFS preserves all of the data on that partition, so converting is often easier than repartitioning and reformatting the drive, then reinstalling applications and data.

1. Choose Start | Programs; then choose Command Prompt.
2. At the command line, type **convert <drive> /f:ntfs**, and then press ENTER.

3. The conversion process will start. If another program or process is currently using the drive, conversion will not be allowed, so you may need to reboot the system so that the conversion will begin.

4. To check the file system after conversion, right-click My Computer | Explore. When Windows NT Explorer starts, right-click the drive icon that you just converted, and then click Properties. The file system should be listed as NTFS.

Exam Tip

Remember that FAT-to-NTFS conversion is a one-way process, and you cannot return to a FAT file system without repartitioning and reformatting the drive for FAT.

Creating a Boot Disk for Windows NT/2000   A network server or workstation will normally boot from a local hard drive. When trouble occurs with the drive or its partition information, it may be necessary for you to start the Windows NT/2000 system from a bootable diskette. Under Windows 2000, you can simply use the MAKEBOOT.EXE utility in the \Bootdisk folder of your Windows 2000 CD:

1. Insert the Windows 2000 CD in the CD-ROM drive.
2. Choose Start | Run.
3. In the Open box, type *drive*:\bootdisk\makeboot a: and then press ENTER (where *drive* is the letter of your CD-ROM drive). This will create your boot disk.

Remember that you don't need to be running Windows 2000 to create boot disks—you could start your computer with a Windows 98/SE Startup disk, and then run MAKEBOOT.EXE from the Windows 2000 CD. Under Windows NT, the process is a little more involved:

1. Format a floppy disk using the Windows NT format utility (or the Disk Administrator).
2. Format a floppy disk by using the Full Format option in the Windows NT format utility in order to properly rewrite any boot sector content on the floppy disk.
3. Copy NTLDR from the Windows NT CD, Windows NT floppy, or a computer running the same version of Windows NT as the computer you want to access with the boot floppy. In Windows NT 4.0, you can copy this file from the Windows NT 4.0 CD.

4. Copy the NTDETECT.COM file to the disk.
5. Create a BOOT.INI file (or copy one from a running Windows NT computer) and modify it to match the computer you are trying to access, such as

```
[boot loader]
timeout=30
Default= scsi(0)disk(0)rdisk(0)partition(1)\winnt
[operating systems]
scsi(0)disk(0)rdisk(0)partition(1)\winnt="Windows NT"
```

6. If your computer starts from an IDE, EIDE, or ESDI hard drive, replace the scsi(0) with multi(0).
7. If you're using scsi(x) in the BOOT.INI, copy the correct device driver for the SCSI controller used on the computer and rename it to NTBOOTDD.SYS. If you're using multi(x) in the BOOT.INI file, you don't need to do this.
8. Start using the floppy disk, and then log on to Windows NT.

Objective 6.04   Understanding Drive Capacity Limits

Capacity limitations are encountered whenever a computer system BIOS (and operating system) is unable to identify (or *address*) physical locations on a hard drive. This is not a problem with the design or structure of the hard drive itself, but rather a limitation of the system's BIOS and/or operating system. For the BIOS, it is not capable of translating the addresses of the sectors beyond a certain number of cylinders, thus limiting the capacity of the hard drive to less than it's full amount. For the operating system, the file structure (file allocation table, or FAT) is limited in the number of physical locations (or addresses) that can be entered in the FAT. Drive manufacturers first encountered BIOS limitations in 1994 with the release of 540MB (ATA-2/EIDE) hard drives. Operating system limitations were discovered with the release of hard drives larger than 2.1GB. Your exact limitations vary depending on your BIOS version and the operating system. Today, you'll probably encounter BIOS with limitations at 2.1GB, 4.2GB, 8.4GB, and 32GB levels. Operating systems like DOS and Windows 95 have a 2.1GB partition size limitation (because of FAT16), and Windows NT has a 4.2GB partition size limit, but Windows 95 OSR2 and Windows 98/SE can access much larger drives using the FAT32 file system. This part of the chapter is intended to help you understand and correct these drive size limitations.

Overcoming Capacity Limits

Since 1994, the PC industry has been working hard to overcome the drive size limits imposed by BIOS and operating systems. Unfortunately, drive size limits still plague older systems. This is particularly prevalent because many systems a few years old are now being upgraded with the huge hard drives that are on the market. As a result, drive size support problems are the most frequent issues encountered during drive upgrades. Still, there are several tactics that have become available for technicians, as briefly described here.

The 528MB Limit

Supporting large (EIDE) hard drives over 528MB will clearly require a system upgrade. There are three possible solutions to the problem: upgrade the motherboard BIOS to support LBA, upgrade the drive controller with one using an on-board BIOS that supports LBA, or partition the drive with a drive overlay utility like Disk Manager or EZ-Drive. If the system is older than 1994, a new drive controller and on-board BIOS will probably yield a noticeable drive system performance improvement. If price is the primary concern, drive overlay software is free (included with most new hard drives) and requires no invasive hardware upgrade.

2.1GB, 4.2GB, 8.4GB, and 32GB Limits

The difficulty with these limits is that there are several possible symptoms that can crop up:

- **Truncation of Cylinders** Cylinder truncation is when the BIOS limits the number of cylinders reported to the operating system to 4,095. The BIOS may display the drive as having more than 4,095 cylinders, but it still only reports a total of 4,095.
- **System Hang-Up at POST** A system hang-up occurs when the BIOS has a problem truncating the cylinders, and locks the system up during power on self test (POST). This is most frequently caused by the Autodetect feature some BIOS versions have implemented.
- **Cylinder Wrap** Cylinder wrapping is when the BIOS takes the remaining number of cylinders from the maximum allowed (4,095) and reports it to the operating system. For example, if the drive listed 4,096 cylinders, the BIOS would report only one cylinder to the operating system.
- **System Hangs at Boot Time** This usually occurs for drives larger than 4.2GB (i.e., 8GB or 32GB drives). A system hang is when the operating

system hangs up during initial loading (either from floppy diskette or existing hard drives). This can be caused by the BIOS reporting the number of heads to the operating system as 256 (100h). The register size DOS and Windows 95/98 uses for the head count has a capacity of two hex digits (equivalent to decimal values 255).

In virtually all cases, these symptoms represent a BIOS compatibility problem, and can be corrected by a BIOS upgrade. You should contact the system or motherboard maker to inquire if a BIOS update is available. If you cannot upgrade the motherboard BIOS directly, you can install a new drive controller with a current LBA-compatible BIOS that will support additional cylinders.

You might also be able to adjust the drive's "translation" to overcome BIOS cylinder limits. You may find that these huge hard drives seem to autodetect correctly in BIOS, and the problem crops up when trying to partition the drive. The partition may seem to be created properly through FDISK, but the system hangs when rebooting. Although this is an operating system limitation, it appears that the appropriate way to deal with this problem is to account for it in the system BIOS. Fortunately, there is a temporary workaround to the problem (until you get the BIOS upgraded).

Exam Tip

You should first verify that you have a new enough BIOS to handle drives *over* 2GB, 4GB, 8.1GB, or 32GB correctly.

To set up a drive over 4GB (under an older BIOS), follow these steps:

1. Autodetect the drive in CMOS Setup.
2. Manually adjust the number of heads from 16 to 15.
3. Multiply the number of cylinders by [16/15] (rounded down to whole number). Since 16/15 is 1.06667, the simplest way to multiply by [16/15] would be to multiply by 1.06667 (and then round down to a whole number).

Travel Advisory

The important thing to keep in mind using the previous workaround is that you must keep a record of the translation values used so that they can be reentered if the contents of CMOS RAM are lost, or if the drive is moved to another system. Write the values on masking tape, and stick the tape on the drive itself.

4. Adjust the number of cylinders to this larger amount.

5. Write down these adjusted values for cylinders, heads, and sectors.

6. Save changes to CMOS, and then partition and format the drive.

Operating System Limits

You basically have two solutions for overcoming drive size limits through an operating system. If you continue to use FAT16, you'll need to create partitions equal to or smaller than 2GB. If the drive is larger than 2GB, you can make multiple partitions on the drive. This makes more than one logical drive for the system to deal with, but it will allow you to use the entire drive capacity.

But there are some other issues. For example, hard disks and other media greater than 32GB in size are not supported in any version of Windows 95. Media at this capacity were not available at the time Windows 95 and OSR versions were developed. If you want to use media larger than 32GB in size, you should upgrade to Windows 98/SE or Microsoft Windows NT. Note that you must use Windows NT 4.0, Service Pack 4 (or newer) to address this capacity limitation.

Also, the protected-mode (Windows) version of ScanDisk may misreport cluster sizes on IDE hard drives whose capacity exceeds 32GB. The resulting symptoms may also include an inability to access areas of the hard drive beyond the first 32GB. You can correct this problem by downloading the file 243450US8.EXE (release date 12/10/99) from the Microsoft Web site (see Microsoft Knowledge Base article Q243450 for more information). Note this problem does not occur if the BIOS uses true logical block addressing assist translation instead of BitShift translation.

Objective 6.05

IDE Controller Installation/ Replacement Guidelines

In many cases, you'll find that the motherboard will provide a primary and secondary drive controller channel that will suit a wide variety of drives in the market at the time the system was manufactured. Over time, new drive types, larger drive capacities, and enhanced data transfer modes may require you to upgrade the motherboard's controller feature. It might also be necessary to install a new controller in the event that an existing controller fails. This part of the chapter highlights the major points involved in IDE-type controller installation using a Promise Ultra66 controller (see Figure 6-3).

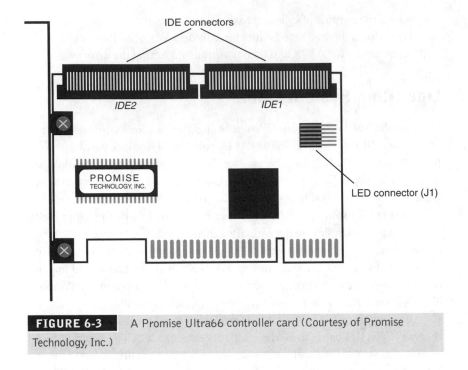

FIGURE 6-3   A Promise Ultra66 controller card (Courtesy of Promise Technology, Inc.)

Preparing for a New Controller

Although a new drive controller should work with your existing drives, there may be some circumstances where a new controller may cause problems. This happens most frequently when the old controller is not removed or disabled properly, or the new controller uses an addressing scheme that is not compliant with the drive's current setup. Before you start unwrapping that new controller, take some time to prepare your system:

- **Back Up the Drive(s)**   Before performing any type of drive-related work, you should protect your valuable data by creating a complete backup of the drive(s) on your system to tape, CD-R, Iomega Jaz, or other suitable media. Boot to the CMOS Setup and record the geometry settings for each drive (you might need to reenter them later).
- **Ready Your Software**   You should have your Windows 98 CD handy in the event you need to reinstall the operating system or load new drivers when the controller is installed. If there were drivers with the new controller, you should also have that disc on hand (or download the newest driver versions from the controller's manufacturer).

- **Review Your Current Controller** You'll need to eventually remove or disable the current controller, so take a moment to review the documentation for your system, and understand the required methods for disabling the current controller. If the controller is currently integrated into your motherboard, it can typically be disabled through the CMOS Setup (older motherboards may use a jumper instead). Controllers that are implemented on stand-alone expansion cards can usually just be removed.
- **Preconfigure Your New Controller** Study the documentation that comes with your new controller card. If the controller offers a number of controller features (i.e., a floppy controller, game port, COM ports, or other features), you should make it a point to disable any features that are not going to be used. Remember that each feature will demand system resources, so don't allow those extra features to remain enabled and conflict with similar features still operating on the motherboard.
- **Check the BIOS Version** It's not uncommon for firmware updates to change frequently. Check with the new controller's manufacturer to see if there's a new firmware version that should be updated after you've installed the new controller.

Installing the New Controller

There's certainly no magic to successfully installing a new controller card, but there are a few minor wrinkles that you should be aware of:

1. Turn off and unplug the system, then unbolt the outer housing and remove it. Set the housing and screws aside in a safe place.
2. Locate the old drive controller and gently disconnect the 40-pin cables from the controller end (leave them connected to the drives). You may choose to label the signal cables so that you can easily locate the primary and secondary channels.
3. Remove the old controller card (if there is one), and insert the new controller card into its expansion slot; otherwise, unbolt the bracket from another appropriate expansion slot and insert the new controller there (use the bracket to cover up the unused slot). Bolt the new controller card to the chassis. If the original controller is integrated onto the motherboard, there is nothing to remove, but you will need to disable the controller through a motherboard jumper or the system's CMOS Setup once you reboot the system again.

4. If your computer case offers a hard drive activity LED, you can generally connect this cable to the small activity header on the new controller card. However, this is generally optional, and you may leave the activity LED connected to a drive if you want.

5. Locate the new drive controller headers. The primary channel may be labeled "Pri-IDE" or "IDE 0". The secondary channel may be labeled "Sec-IDE" or "IDE 1." Connect the primary and secondary drive cables to their corresponding headers on the controller.

Exam Tip

Remember that UDMA/66 and UDMA/100 drives and controllers must be connected via a 40-pin/80-conductor cable specially intended for UDMA/66 or UDMA/100 use. If you're upgrading drives along with the controller, be sure to use this cable.

Configuring the New Controller

Once the new controller is secure and connected, it's time to start up the computer and make any necessary configuration changes needed to use the new controller and avoid system conflicts. Leave the computer's housing off for the time being and follow the tips here:

- **Adjust the Motherboard's CMOS Setup**   Boot the system directly to the CMOS Setup. If your old controller was integrated into the motherboard, you may need to disable the controller(s). However, because we're not changing drives in this exercise, you should verify the drive geometry settings, or reenter them if necessary. No changes are needed for CD-ROM (or other ATAPI) drives that are attached to the controller. The motherboard will automatically assign the IRQ and I/O resources to the new controller. Save your changes and reboot the system.

- **Access the New Controller's BIOS**   Because virtually all drive controller cards use their own on-board BIOS chip, chances are that you'll see a BIOS banner for the controller's BIOS. If you press the key listed in the controller's BIOS banner while rebooting the system, you can access the controller's BIOS and configure specific attributes of the controller's operation. Refer to the controller's manual for specific options and suggested settings. Most installations work just fine with default settings, and you never need to change the controller's internal configuration.

Software Installation

The new controller's on-board BIOS should fully support normal system operation in the real mode (DOS). However, Windows NT/2000 will probably require the installation of numerous drivers to support the controller (especially the UDMA/66 or UDMA/100 DMA drivers). The previous steps highlight a general installation scenario for Windows NT 4.0:

Travel Advisory

Be sure to review the installation instructions of your new controller before installation. Some controllers require that you *not* connect the hard drive before installing the drivers. If this is the case, you'll need to leave the old controller enabled (and hard drives attached) alongside the new controller while you install the drivers for the new card.

---

1. Allow Windows NT to boot normally.
2. Choose Start | Settings | Control Panel.
3. Double-click the SCSI Adapters icon to open the SCSI Adapters dialog box.
4. Select Drivers | Add.
5. In the Install Drivers dialog box, click Have Disk.
6. When the Install From Disk window appears, insert the new controller's driver diskette in drive A and then click OK.
7. When the Install Driver dialog box appears, select the manufacturer (i.e., Promise Technology, Inc., ULTRA100 Controller) and click OK.
8. When the Select SCSI Adapter Option dialog box appears, click Install.

After successful installation, the SCSI Adapter Setup box will show that the new controller (i.e., a "Promise Technology, Inc., ULTRA100 Controller") driver has been installed. Power off your system, and then attach the hard drives to the controller card if necessary.

IDE Hard Drive Installation/ Replacement Guidelines

Objective 6.06

Hard drives must be installed when building new PCs, adding supplemental drives to an existing system, or replacing outdated or failed drives. The installation process is not terribly complicated, but it can be confusing to the novice. This part of the chapter offers some basic guidelines for IDE-type drive installation and preparation under Windows NT 4.0.

Selecting Jumper Configurations

An IDE-type drive may be installed as a master or slave device on any hard drive controller channel. These master/slave settings are handled through one or two jumpers located on the rear of the drive (right next to the 40-pin signal cable connector). You can see an example of this in the Maxtor drive of Figure 6-4. One of your first decisions when planning an installation should be to decide the drive's configuration:

- If you're installing only one hard drive in the system, it must be jumpered as the master device. Note that the master drive on the primary drive controller channel will be the boot drive (i.e., drive C:).

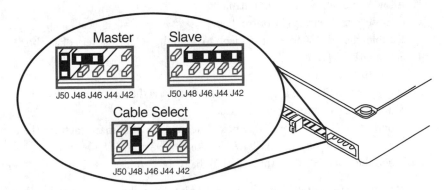

Rear View of Hard Drive / Jumper Detail

FIGURE 6-4   Setting jumpers on a Maxtor DiamondMAX Plus drive (Courtesy of Maxtor Corp.)

- If you're installing a second hard drive alongside the first, that second drive must be jumpered as the slave device.
- If you're installing a second hard drive on the second drive controller channel, it should be jumpered as the master device (any other device should be reconfigured as a slave device).

Travel Advisory

Refer to the documentation that accompanies your particular hard drive in order to determine the exact master/slave jumper settings. If you do not have the drive documentation handy, check the drive manufacturer's Web site for online information.

Attaching Cables and Mounting the Drive

Once the drive is jumpered as needed, you'll need to connect the signal and power cables, then physically bolt the drive into the system. In some cases, it may be easier to mount the drive first, then attach the cables. The overall steps are covered here:

1. Turn off and unplug the PC, and then remove the outer cover to expose the computer's drive bays.
2. Attach one end of the 40-pin drive interface cable to the drive controller connector on your motherboard (or drive controller card). Remember to align pin 1 on the cable (the side of the cable with the blue or red stripe) with pin 1 on the drive controller connector.
3. Locate an available drive bay for the hard drive. Remove the plastic housing covering the drive bay, then slide the drive inside. Locate the four screw holes needed to mount the drive. In some cases, you may need to attach mounting rails to the drive so that the drive will be wide enough to fit in the drive bay.

Exam Tip

A 40-pin/80-conductor cable is required to run in Ultra-DMA/66 or Ultra-DMA/100 mode. Attach the blue end of the connector to the drive controller end, the black connector to the master (or single) drive, and the gray connector (if there is one) to the slave drive.

You can mount the drive horizontally (usually with the circuit board down) or vertically.

4. Attach the 40-pin signal cable and the 4-pin power connector to the new drive, then bolt the drive securely into place. Do not overtighten the screws since this may damage the drive. If you do not have an available 4-pin power connector, you may use an appropriate Y splitter, if necessary, to split power from another drive (preferably the floppy drive).

Configuring the CMOS Setup

Before you attempt to partition or format your new drive, you must configure your computer's BIOS to accept the drive (through the CMOS Setup):

1. Turn the computer on. As your computer starts up, watch for a message that describes how to run the CMOS Setup (i.e., Press F1 for Setup). Press the appropriate key to start the CMOS Setup program.
2. Select the hard drive settings menu. To set the drive parameters, choose the primary master or primary slave (or secondary master/slave, depending on how you've physically installed the drive).
3. Select automatic drive detection if available—this option automatically configures the computer for your new drive. If your BIOS does not provide automatic drive detection, select user-defined drive settings and enter the appropriate geometry values from the drive documentation. As a rule, Write Precomp and Landing Zone parameters are set to zero.
4. Verify that the LBA mode is enabled for your drive. Many BIOS versions use the logical block addressing (LBA) mode to access drives with capacities greater than 528MB. Most BIOS will automatically set this mode during the autodetection process.
5. Enable the Ultra-DMA mode if it is available (and both the drive and controller support it).
6. Save the settings and exit the CMOS Setup program. Your computer will automatically reboot.

Finishing the Drive Preparation

You can prepare the disk with a real-mode boot disk. Start the system with a boot disk containing FDISK and FORMAT. You will use these utilities to partition and format the drive, respectively. Partition the disk with FDISK. If you use a FAT16 version of FDISK, you cannot create partitions greater than 2.1GB. If you use the

FAT32 version of FDISK, you can create extremely large partitions. Now use FOR-MAT to prepare the drive for your operating system. Again, use the proper version of the FORMAT utility, depending on which FAT system you plan on using. If you would prefer, you can use the Windows NT Disk Administrator and create and format the drive's partitions once the system restarts.

Reassembling the Computer

Double-check all your signal and power cables to verify that they are secure, and then tuck the cables gently into the computer's chassis. Check that there are no loose tools, screws, or cables inside the chassis. Now reattach the computer's outer housing(s).

Objective 6.07   Drive Testing and Troubleshooting

Fortunately, not all hard drive problems are necessarily fatal. True, you might lose some programs and data (back up your hard drive frequently!), but many drive problems are recoverable without resorting to drive replacement. Instead of focusing on repairing a hard drive's electronics or mechanics, today's repair tactics focus on repairing a drive's *data*. By reconstructing or relocating faulty drive information, it is often possible to recover from a wide variety of drive problems. If that fails, the drive (and/or its controller) must be replaced. Before you begin any sort of drive troubleshooting, you should take the following steps:

1. Gather a DOS boot disk or startup disk. If you don't have a boot disk on hand, you should make one now before continuing.
2. Gather your DOS installation disk(s) or OS installation CD—if you need to reinstall the operating system or any of its components at some point, these will be invaluable.
3. Gather any hard drive/controller diagnostics that you'll need.
4. Back up as much as you can from your hard drive(s) before attempting any sort of drive service.

General Troubleshooting Guidelines

Although most drive installations and replacements will proceed flawlessly, there are many times when problems will crop up. If you've installed a hard drive and it does not function properly, perform the following basic checks before examining specific symptoms:

- **Turn Off Power and Eliminate Static**   Always turn off the computer before changing jumpers or unplugging cables and cards. Wear an anti-static wrist strap (or use other antistatic precautions) while working on your computer or handling a drive.
- **Verify Compatibility**   Verify that the drive controller and drive are appropriately matched to each other (and to your computer). For example, an Ultra-DMA/100 drive will not run at top speed on an Ultra-DMA/33 controller.
- **Check All Cards**   Verify that all expansion cards (including the drive controller card) are seated in their slots on the motherboard, and are secured with mounting screws. Often one or more cards may be displaced when a PC is opened for service.
- **Check All Connectors and Cables**   Make sure that all ribbon and power cables are securely connected. Ribbon cables are easily damaged (especially at the connectors). Try a new cable that you know is good. Make sure no connector pins are bent. Verify that pin 1 on the interface cable is aligned with pin 1 on the drive and the controller.
- **Verify Drive Jumper Settings**   Review the instructions in your drive's manual (and in your host adapter installation guide), and see that all appropriate jumpers are installed—or removed—as necessary. Incorrect or duplicated jumper settings (i.e., two master drives on the same channel) can easily interfere with drive operation.
- **Check Your Power Supply Capacity**   Each time you add a new device to your computer, make sure your computer's power supply can support the total power demand. Install a larger (higher wattage) power supply if necessary.
- **Verify the Drive Settings in Your CMOS Setup**   The drive settings in the CMOS Setup must not exceed the physical specifications of your drive. Also, the settings must not exceed the limitations set by the operating system and BIOS. Try the CMOS Setup's autodetect feature to identify the drive, or consider upgrading the BIOS and/or drive controller.
- **Check for Viruses**   Before you use an unknown diskette in your system for the first time, scan the diskette for viruses. Also scan the system for viruses periodically.

Drive Not Recognized by the Operating System

There are some circumstances when a hard drive is recognized correctly by the BIOS (i.e., the drive is properly autodetected), but it is not properly identified by the operating system. In virtually all cases, the problem can be traced to installation issues or drive software (code-related) issues. Check the essential installation points first:

- Check the parameters in the CMOS Setup and verify that the drive parameters *and* translation mode are set correctly.
- Contact the system or motherboard manufacturer to verify potential BIOS capacity limitations. For example, you might need a BIOS upgrade to accommodate the drive sizes that you're using.
- Ensure that newly installed EIDE or UDMA controller cards do not conflict with the existing system BIOS. You may need to disable the motherboard's existing drive controller channel(s) through the CMOS Setup before the new controller card will be recognized by the OS.
- Systematically step down the enhanced features of your BIOS (i.e., block mode, multisector transfers, 32-bit transfers, PIO mode settings, and so on) to their minimum values, or disable the features entirely. You may also try the BIOS Default settings in your CMOS Setup.
- If your motherboard uses ISA bus slots, check AT BUS Clock speed in your CMOS Setup and verify that it's set between 8–10MHz (ideally 8.33MHz).
- Increase the boot process time in your CMOS Setup—you can enable Floppy Seek At Boot, Test Memory Above 1MB, and/or set the Boot Sequence" to "A then C".
- Set Boot Speed to its lowest value in the CMOS Setup, and set the Boot Pre-delay entry (if present) to its highest value.
- Double-check your partitions using FDISK or another utility such as Disk Administrator. If the drive was not previously partitioned, create a primary DOS partition on the drive. Use option 2 to set the partition "active". Exit FDISK and reboot. Format the new partition and install the system files. If the drive was previously partitioned, make sure the first partition is "PRI DOS" and its Status is "A". Compare the sum of all partition sizes to the Total Disk Space—this should be same within about 1MB. If the total is different, correct the drive parameters or translation mode in CMOS Setup and repartition the drive.
- Double-check the master/slave jumpers on all drives using the primary controller.

- Install (set) the jumper for I/O Channel Ready on the drive (if that option is present).
- If you're using a SCSI drive, verify that the parity jumper is installed.
- Check all of your cable connections, and try a shorter replacement cable (or connect the drive to the middle cable connector).
- Replace the drive controller card.
- Remove the slave drive (if present) to determine the presence of any compatibility issues.

Travel Advisory

If the drive was previously partitioned, but no partitions are currently seen in FDISK, do *not* attempt to create new partitions if data on the drive is to be saved.

You might also need to check for data corruption or errors on the drive:

- Clean boot the system to a boot diskette and execute FDISK /MBR and SYS C:. Make sure the DOS version on the floppy diskette is the *same* version as on the hard drive before using the SYS command.
- Bypass CONFIG.SYS and AUTOEXEC.BAT to check for problems in your startup files. If this works, use the step-by-step boot mode in the Windows Startup menu to walk through each step of these files until the problem is found, then edit both the CONFIG.SYS and AUTOEXEC.BAT files and comment out the statement(s) causing the problem.
- Check for drive compression, and try removing the compression drivers if there is no important data on the drive.
- Delete the partition using FDISK, then repartition and reformat the drive.
- Replace the hard drive.

Dealing with Drive Noise

All hard drives make a certain amount of noise during normal operation, and the noise level will vary depending on whether the drive is spinning or accessing. However, when the drive makes substantial or abnormal noises, this may indicate an impending failure. The trick here is to tell the normal noises from the abnormal noises. A drive makes three basic sounds:

- A whining noise during the drive spin-up (and a mild whir while the system is on).
- Regular clicking or tapping sounds during drive access (the R/W heads stepping across the platters).
- Hard clicks when the drive heads park before power off.

You should develop a keen ear for abnormal drive sounds:

- A high-pitched whining sound (such as a screech or squeal) can be an indication of problems.
- Noises (vibrations) caused by mounting issues. This is due to either a high-frequency vibration in the mounting hardware or a potential drive failure.
- Repeated regular tapping, grinding, or beeping. When the hard drive is suspect, it is always important to make an immediate backup of your data.

Exam Tip

To isolate the drive for noise, try disconnecting the drive's signal cable and power the system up. If the noise persists, the drive should be backed up and replaced at your earliest convenience. If the noise stops, there may be an issue with the cable or controller that you should investigate further.

Dealing with Spin Problems

All hard drives must spin their platters at a constant rate of speed, so any spin problems can render the drive inaccessible. Spin problems can usually be broken down into three types:

- **Drive Does Not Spin at All**   When a system is turned on, the characteristic hard drive wind-up sounds are not present. This can also occur if the hard drive spins down (without cause) after working for a period of time.
- **Drive Spins Up and Spins Down Again**   This normally occurs during the initial power up. The hard drive will start spinning, and then slow down again (or it cycles up to a point and ceases to spin).
- **Drive Spins Down Following Period of Inactivity**   The hard drive fails to spin up when access is attempted.

Check for any installation errors first:

- Check the jumper settings on all hard drives attached to the same interface cable. For example, check the master/slave jumpers on each drive; then check for energy management or deferred spinup jumpers. Most SCSI (and a few IDE) hard drives contain one or both jumper options.
- Check all the power supply cable connections.
- Check the interface (ribbon) cable connections.
- Check for any system software for power management, and disable or uninstall that software if necessary.

Next, check for "green" or power management features that might be set improperly:

- Disable your drive-related power management features in the CMOS Setup.
- Disable the power management jumper on your hard drive (if present).
- Some overlay software has the capability to set power management features. For example, you can disable power management under Maxtor's MaxBlast software (versions 7.04–7.12) by removing the /E switch. Clean boot the system if other power management software is the suspected culprit.
- Windows can enable power management. This feature will need to be disabled through the operating system's Power Management icon in the Control Panel.

Finally, check for hardware failures with the drive and/or its controller:

- Try installing drive in another system—this will verify the problem is with the drive, not the system.
- Use a different power supply plug.
- Use a different interface (ribbon) cable.
- Use a different drive controller (i.e., try a PCI drive controller card).
- Disconnect ribbon cable from drive.
- Replace the drive outright.

CHECKPOINT

✔ **Objective 6.01: Basic IDE Drive Concepts**   The well-established IDE interface is known for its respectable performance, low cost, and ease of installation/use, and is regarded as standard equipment with regular PCs. Although the terms "IDE" and "ATA" are sometimes used interchangeably, ATA is the formal standard that defines the drive and how it operates, while IDE is really the trade name that refers to the 40-pin interface.

✔ **Objective 6.02: Understanding the Interface Classical**   IDE drives were limited to 528MB in size, but logical block addressing and improvements to the Int 13 BIOS calls allowed for advances in IDE speed and size with iterations including EIDE, Ultra-DMA/33, Ultra-DMA/66, and Ultra-DMA/100. Ultra-DMA drives can handle burst data transfers of 33MB/s, 66MB/s, and 100MB/s, respectively. Bus mastering must be supported on the PC to allow for optimum UDMA data transfers.

✔ **Objective 6.03: Drive Preparation Essentials**   Drives must be prepared before they can be used. Preparation includes creating one or more logical partitions on the drive, then formatting each partition for the necessary operating system. Most servers will use drives with FAT16 or NTFS partitions. Bootable drives include a master boot record as part of the partition information that directs the boot process to start loading the operating system.

✔ **Objective 6.04: Understanding Drive Capacity Limits**   Very large hard drives may not be usable on all PCs because the BIOS (as well as the operating system) may not recognize the entire drive size. When a system cannot access the entire drive size, a BIOS upgrade, new drive controller, or drive overlay software can be used.

✔ **Objective 6.05: IDE Controller Installation/Replacement Guidelines**   Although a new drive controller should work with your existing drives, there may be some circumstances where a new controller may cause problems. This happens most frequently when the old controller is not removed or disabled properly, or the new controller uses an addressing scheme that is not compliant with the drive's current setup.

✔ **Objective 6.06: IDE Hard Drive Installation/Replacement Guidelines**   Hard drives must be installed when building new PCs, adding supplemental drives to an existing system, or replacing outdated or failed drives. The installation process includes setting jumpers, connecting the drive, and entering the drive in the CMOS Setup.

✔ **Objective 6.07: Drive Testing and Troubleshooting**   Many drive problems are recoverable without resorting to drive replacement. Instead of focusing on repairing a hard drive's electronics or mechanics, today's repair tactics focus on repairing a drive's data. By reconstructing or relocating faulty drive information, it is often possible to recover from a wide variety of drive problems. If that fails, the drive (and/or its controller) must be replaced.

REVIEW QUESTIONS

1. The term "IDE" means...

   A. Integrated Drive Electronics
   B. Illustrated Drive Electronics
   C. Intelligent Disk Elements
   D. Integrated Disk Errors

2. A disk size based on binary megabytes bases a megabyte (MB) on...

   A. 1,000,000 bytes
   B. 1,048,576 bytes
   C. 1,033,556 bytes
   D. 994,345 bytes

3. The time it takes for needed bytes to pass under a drive's R/W head is referred to as...

   A. Access time
   B. Partition size
   C. Sector skewing
   D. Latency

4. To make an IDE drive the first (or primary) device on a controller channel, it must be configured/jumpered as...

   A. SMART
   B. Master
   C. Slave
   D. Cable Select (CSEL)

5. The early extension of the ATA (IDE) interface designed to allow non–hard drive devices to plug into an ordinary ATA (IDE) port is known as...

   A. ATA-3
   B. ATAPI
   C. ATA
   D. Ultra-DMA

6. The Ultra-ATA standard for ATA/ATAPI-4 will support burst data transfers up to...

   A. 16MB/s
   B. 33MB/s
   C. 66MB/s
   D. 100MB/s

7. The self-diagnostic system that enables the PC to predict the impending failures of disk drives is known as...

   A. SMART
   B. Bus mastering
   C. BIOS
   D. POST

8. An ATA (IDE) interface uses which cable?

   A. 34-pin cable
   B. 68-pin cable
   C. 50-pin cable
   D. 40-pin cable

9. How can you overcome drive capacity limitations imposed by older BIOS versions?

   A. Upgrade the BIOS
   B. Upgrade the drive controller
   C. Install drive overlay software
   D. All of the above

10. What is the first thing you should check when a drive is completely dead?

    A. Check the system power
    B. Check the drive power
    C. Check the CMOS Setup
    D. Check the drive jumpers

REVIEW ANSWERS

1. **A** Integrated Drive Electronics: The term *IDE* means *Integrated Drive Electronics.*

2. **B** 1,048,576 bytes: A disk size based on binary megabytes bases a megabyte (MB) on 1,048,576 bytes.

3. **D** Latency: The time it takes for needed bytes to pass under a drive's R/W head is referred to as latency.

4. **B** Master: To make an IDE drive the first (or primary) device on a controller channel, it must be configured/jumpered as master.

5. **B** ATAPI: Unfortunately, given the ATA command structure, it wasn't possible to put non-hard drive devices on the IDE channel and expect them to work. A special protocol was developed, called the AT Attachment Packet Interface or ATAPI. The ATAPI standard is used for devices like CD, tape, and removable media drives.

6. **C** 66MB/s: UDMA mode 2 made a real impression since it doubled the throughput of the fastest transfer mode then available to 33.3MB/s. Ultra-DMA mode 2 was quickly dubbed "Ultra-DMA/33", and drives conforming to ATA/ATAPI-4 are often called "Ultra-ATA/33" drives.

7. **A** SMART: SMART (Self-Monitoring Analysis and Reporting Technology) is a self-diagnostic system that enables the PC to predict the impending failures of devices such as disk drives. With a given failure prediction, the user or system manager can back up key data, replace a suspect device prior to data loss, and avoid undesired downtime.

8. **D** 40-pin cable: An ATA (IDE) interface uses a 40-pin cable.

9. **D** All of the above: You can overcome drive capacity limitations by upgrading the BIOS, upgrading the drive controller, or installing drive overlay software (all of the above).

10. **B** Check the drive power: The first thing you should check when a drive is completely dead is to check the drive power.

SCSI
Technology

	NEWBIE	SOME EXPERIENCE	EXPERT
ETA	4 hours	2 hours	0.5 hour

PC designers have always sought ways to connect more devices to fewer cables, and achieve faster data transfer between the system and its peripheral devices. In the early 1980s, it became clear that a more versatile and intelligent interface would be needed to overcome the myriad of proprietary interfaces appearing at the time. By 1986, PC designers responded with the introduction of the Small Computer System Interface (SCSI, pronounced *scuzzy*). SCSI proved to be a revolution for PC power users. With it, a single adapter could operate a number of unique devices simultaneously, all daisy-chained to the same signal cable. Common low-end PCs needed one adapter for hard drives, one adapter for the CD-ROM, another adapter for a tape drive, and so on. But a system fitted with a SCSI adapter (shown in Figure 7-1) could handle all of these devices (and more), and achieve data throughputs that other interfaces of the day couldn't even dream of.

Today's PC industry has changed. Proprietary interfaces have been essentially abandoned in favor of the standardized interfaces (such as UDMA/66 and UDMA/100), and these standard interface schemes now support a variety of devices while offering low cost and performance levels rivaling traditional SCSI. Yet, SCSI has endured and evolved, and it remains the interface of choice for multitasking, servers, and other high-end computer systems. This chapter will provide an overview of the SCSI interface, cover the essential installation and setup of a SCSI host adapter, and show you how to deal with a series of troubleshooting problems. You'll also learn about two advanced serial SCSI techniques: FireWire and FibreChannel.

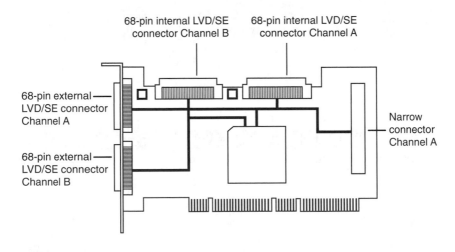

FIGURE 7-1   A typical SCSI host adapter (Courtesy of Adaptec)

Local Lingo

SCSI (Small Computer System Interface) A bus and device-level command architecture designed to operate numerous PC devices with a uniform controller.

Objective 7.01 # Understanding SCSI Concepts

Ideally, peripheral devices should be *independent* of the microprocessor's operation. The computer should only have to send commands and data to the peripheral, and wait for the peripheral to respond. Printers work this way. The parallel and serial ports are actually *device-level* interfaces. The computer is unconcerned with what device is attached to the port. In other words, you can take a printer built 12 years ago and connect it to a new AMD Athlon-based system, and the printer will work just fine because only data and commands are being sent across the interface. Very simply put, this is the concept behind SCSI. Computers and peripherals can be designed, developed, and integrated without worrying about hardware compatibility—such compatibility is established entirely by the SCSI interface.

Device Independence

From a practical standpoint, SCSI is a *bus* and a *command set*. The bus is an organization of physical wires and terminations where each wire has its own name and purpose. The command set is a limited set of instructions that allow the computer and peripherals to communicate over that physical bus. The SCSI bus is used in systems that want to achieve device independence. For example, all hard disk drives look alike to the SCSI interface (except for their total capacity), all optical drives look alike, all printers look alike, and so on. For any particular type of SCSI device, you should be able to replace an existing device with another device without any system modifications, and new SCSI devices can often be added to the bus with little more than a driver upgrade. Because the intelligence of SCSI resides in the peripheral device itself and not in the computer, the computer is capable of employing a small set of standard commands to accomplish data transfer back and forth to the peripheral.

SCSI Variations

At this point, let's take a look at the evolution of the SCSI interface, and examine the ways in which it has evolved and proliferated. SCSI began life in 1979 when Shugart Associates (PC old-timers might remember them as one of the first PC hard drive makers) released their Shugart Associates Systems Interface (or SASI) standard. The X3T9.2 committee was formed by ANSI in 1982 to develop the SASI standard (later renamed SCSI). SCSI drives and interfaces that were developed under the evolving X3T9.2 SCSI standard were known as SCSI-1, though the actual SCSI-1 standard (ANSI X3.131-1986) didn't become official until 1986. SCSI-1 provided a system-level 8-bit bus (referred to as "narrow") that could operate up to eight devices and transfer data at up to 5MB/s. However, the delay in standardization led to a lot of configuration and compatibility problems with SCSI-1 setups. Table 7-1 compares the specifications of each SCSI standard.

> ### Exam Tip
>
> Although SCSI-1 was supposed to support all SCSI devices, manufacturers took liberties with the evolving standard. This frequently led to installation and compatibility problems between SCSI-1 devices that should theoretically have worked together perfectly. Today, all obsolete SCSI-1 adapters should be upgraded to SCSI-3 installations.

Earlier in 1986 (even before the SCSI-1 standard was ratified), work started on the SCSI-2 standard that was intended to overcome many of the speed and compatibility problems encountered with SCSI-1. By 1994, ANSI blessed the SCSI-2 standard (X3.131-1994). SCSI-2 was designed to be backward compatible with SCSI-1, but SCSI-2 also provided for several variations. Fast SCSI-2 (Fast SCSI) doubles the SCSI bus clock speed and allows 10MB/s data transfers across the 8-bit SCSI data bus. Wide SCSI-2 (Wide SCSI) also doubles the original data transfer rate to 10MB/s by using a 16-bit data bus instead of the original 8-bit data bus (the SCSI clock is left unchanged). To support the larger data bus, Wide SCSI uses a 68-pin cable instead of the traditional 50-pin cable. Wide SCSI can also support up to 16 SCSI devices. Designers then combined the attributes of fast and wide operation to create Fast Wide SCSI-2 (Fast Wide SCSI), which supports 20MB/s data transfers across a 16-bit data bus. Whenever you see references to Fast SCSI, Wide SCSI, or Fast Wide SCSI, you're *always* dealing with a SCSI-2 implementation.

TABLE 7.1	Comparison of SCSI Conventions

Terms	Name	MHz	Bus Width	MB/s	Mbps
SCSI-1	SCSI-1	5	8	5	40
Fast SCSI	SCSI-2	10	8	10	80
Fast-Wide SCSI	SCSI-2/ SCSI-3	10	16	20	160
Ultra SCSI	SCSI-3	20	8	20	160
Ultra-Wide SCSI	SCSI-3	20	16	40	320
Ultra2 SCSI	SCSI-4	40	8	40	320
Ultra2-Wide SCSI	SCSI-4	40	16	80	640
Ultra3 SCSI	Ultra 160	40*2[1]	8	80	640
Ultra3-Wide SCSI	Ultra 160	40*2[1]	16	160	1280
Ultra4 SCSI	Ultra 320	Undefined			
Ultra4-Wide SCSI	Ultra 320	Undefined			

[1]*Ultra3 features the same base frequency as Ultra2 (40MHz), but transmits 2 bytes per data clock, thus doubling the total throughput.*

But SCSI advancement hasn't stopped there. ANSI began development of the SCSI-3 standard in 1993 (even before SCSI-2 was adopted). SCSI-3 is intended to be backward compatible with SCSI-2 and SCSI-1 devices, and there are many SCSI devices and controllers that are making use of the advances offered by SCSI-3 development. These typical SCSI-3 devices are generally known as Fast-20 SCSI (or Ultra SCSI-3, also termed Ultra SCSI). Ultra SCSI uses a 20MHz SCSI bus clock with an 8-bit data bus to achieve 20MB/s data transfers. By using a 16-bit data bus, SCSI-3 offers Wide Fast-20 SCSI (or Ultra Wide SCSI-3, also termed Ultra Wide SCSI), which handles 40MB/s data transfers. SCSI development continued with the SCSI-4 implementations. The SCSI-4 standard covers Fast-40 SCSI (called Ultra2 SCSI-4 and Ultra2 SCSI) using a 40MHz bus clock to provide 40MB/s data transfers with an 8-bit data bus. The 16-bit data bus version is known as Wide Fast-40 SCSI (called Ultra2 Wide SCSI-4, or Ultra2 Wide SCSI), which is supposed to support 80MB/s data transfers. Whenever you see references to Ultra2 or Fast-40, you're almost certain to be faced with a SCSI-4 setup.

But SCSI advances have not stopped there. The Ultra3 SCSI standard (known as Ultra160) employs a 40MHz bus clock that is "double transitioned." This allows twice the effective data transfer on the same 40MHz clock, yielding data transfers up to 80MB/s. The Ultra3 Wide SCSI standard offers 16 data bits rather than 8. On the same double-transitioned 40MHz clock, Ultra3 Wide SCSI can achieve data transfers up to 160MB/s. While Ultra360 (Ultra4) SCSI standards have not yet been fully defined, you can be sure that even faster SCSI implementations are on the horizon. Also keep in mind that SCSI has traditionally been a *parallel* bus—that is, 8 or 16 bits of data are transferred at a time across parallel data lines. SCSI-3 is proposing three new *serial* connection schemes. You'll see these noted as Serial Storage Architecture (SSA), FibreChannel, and IEEE P1394 (a.k.a. FireWire). These serial schemes will offer faster data transfers than their parallel bus cousins, but are *not* backward compatible with SCSI-2 or SCSI-1.

Bus Length

As you're already aware, SCSI devices are daisy-chained together with a 50-pin or 68-pin cable. The total length of this cable makes up the overall SCSI bus. When there are only *internal* SCSI devices, the bus length is measured from the SCSI host adapter to the last internal SCSI device on the chain (the terminated device). When there are only *external* SCSI devices, the bus length is measured from the SCSI host adapter to the last external SCSI device on the chain (it should also be terminated). When there are *both* internal and external SCSI devices, the bus length is measured from the last external device to the last internal device. There are finite limits on the length of your SCSI bus. As SCSI implementations have become faster over the years, that effective bus length has shortened. Table 7-2 illustrates the maximum SCSI bus lengths for single-ended, differential, and low-voltage differential (LVD) signaling approaches.

Initiators and Targets

There are basically two types of devices on the SCSI bus: initiators and targets. An *initiator* starts communication when something has to be done, and a *target* responds to the initiator's commands. The important thing for you to understand here is that this master/slave relationship is not a one-way arrangement—an initiator may become a target at some point in the data transfer cycle, and the

TABLE 7.2	Maximum SCSI Bus Lengths		
Terms	**Single-Ended**	**Differential**	**LVD**
SCSI-1	6m	25m	12m[2]
Fast SCSI	3m	25m	12m[2]
Fast Wide SCSI	3m	25m	12m[2]
Ultra SCSI	1.5m–3m	Up to 25m	Up to 12m
Wide Ultra SCSI	Up to 3m	Up to 25m	Up to 12m
Ultra2 SCSI	1	25m	12m
Wide Ultra2 SCSI	1	25m	12m
Ultra3 SCSI	1	25m	12m
Wide Ultra3 SCSI	1	25m	12m

[1] *Single-ended and high-powered differential are not defined at Ultra2 and Ultra3 speeds.*
[2] *Only if all devices on the bus support LVD.*

target may become the initiator at other points. A SCSI bus can support up to eight devices simultaneously, but there *must* be at least one initiator and one target in the system. A SCSI host adapter card is typically the initiator, and all other devices (i.e., hard drives or CD-ROMs) are usually targets, but that is not necessarily the only possible case. Many kinds of computer peripherals are candidates for the SCSI bus. Each peripheral offers unique characteristics and applications, but each also requires different methods of control. By adding SCSI "intelligence" to these devices, they can all be made to share the same bus together. The SCSI nomenclature groups similar devices together into specific device types.

Local Lingo

initiator The SCSI device that starts communication.
target The SCSI device that the initiator communicates with.

Synchronous and Asynchronous

As a system-level interface, SCSI requires an operating *handshaking protocol* that organizes the transfer of data from a sending point to a requesting point. There are typically three handshaking protocols for SCSI: asynchronous, synchronous, and fast synchronous. The *asynchronous* protocol works rather like a parallel port. Each byte must be requested and acknowledged before the next byte can be sent. Asynchronous operation generally results in very reliable (but slow) performance. *Synchronous* and *fast synchronous* operations both ignore the request/acknowledge handshake for data transfer only. This allows slightly faster operation than an asynchronous protocol, but a certain fixed amount of time delay (sometimes called an *offset*) must be allowed for request and acknowledge timing. The fast synchronous protocol uses slightly shorter signals, resulting in even faster speed. An important point to remember is that SCSI systems can typically use any of these three protocols as desired. The actual protocol that is used must be mutually agreed to by the initiator and the target through their communications. SCSI systems normally initialize in an asynchronous protocol.

Disconnect and Reconnect

There are a number of instances when it would be desirable to allow a target to operate offline while the initiator is occupied elsewhere. Tape rewind time is just one example. An important feature of SCSI is the ability to *disconnect* two communicating devices, then *reconnect* them again later. Disconnect and reconnect operations allow several different operations to occur simultaneously in the system and are the main reasons why SCSI architecture is so desirable in a multitasking environment. It is up to the initiator to grant a disconnect privilege to a target.

Single-Ended and Differential

The signal wiring used in a SCSI bus has a definite impact on bus performance. There are two generally used wiring techniques for SCSI: single-ended and differential. Both wiring schemes have advantages and disadvantages.

The *single-ended* (SE) wiring technique is just as the name implies—a single wire carries the particular signal from initiator to target. Each signal requires only one wire. Terminating resistors at each end of the cable help to maintain acceptable signal levels. A common ground (return) provides the reference for all single-ended signals. Unfortunately, single-ended circuitry is not very noise resistant, so single-ended cabling is generally limited to about 6 meters at data transfer speeds of 5MHz or less. At higher data transfer speeds, cable length can be as short as 1.5 meters. In spite of the disadvantages, single-ended operation is simple and popular because of its simplicity.

The *differential* (DIF) wiring approach uses *two* wires for each signal (instead of one wire referenced to a common ground). A differential signal offers excellent noise resistance because it does not rely on a common ground. This allows much longer cables (up to 25 meters) and higher-speed operation (10MHz). An array of pull-up resistors at each end of the cable helps to ensure signal integrity. The problem with differential wiring is that it is more complicated than single-ended interfaces. *Low-voltage differential* (or LVD) SCSI is an emerging standard defined in the SPI-2 document of SCSI-3 that runs on 3.3Vdc rather than 5Vdc. The goal of LVD is to allow higher data rates while combining the benefits of single-ended and differential SCSI bus schemes. LVD is less sensitive to electromagnetic noise and allows high data rates at greater cable lengths than a single-ended bus. LVD is the interface specified for use with Ultra-2 SCSI and Ultra160/m specifications. While LVD is not directly compatible with single-ended wiring, the devices will use multimode driver circuits that automatically detect the type of bus used and switch to the appropriate mode of operation. This will allow you to use an LVD/SE device on a single-ended bus without having to set any switches or jumpers. Therefore, LVD has been introduced gradually without the loss of the current investment in single-ended devices. Still, the advantages of LVD are lost when an LVD/SE device is used in a single-ended bus—as soon as one single-ended device is connected to LVD/SE bus, the whole bus switches to single-ended mode (with all its limitations).

Terminators

When high-frequency signals are transmitted over adjacent wires, signals tend to degrade and interfere with one another over the length of the cable. This is a very normal and relatively well-understood electrical phenomenon. In the PC, SCSI signal integrity is enhanced by using powered resistors at each end of the data cable to "pull up" active signals. Built-in pull-up resistors at drives and controller cards already terminate most high-frequency signal cables in the PC. The small resistor array is known as a *terminator*. Since there is a distinct limit to the number of devices that can be added to a floppy drive or IDE cable, designers have never made a big deal about termination—they just added the resistors and that was it. With SCSI, however, up to eight devices can be added to the bus cable. The SCSI cable also must be terminated, but the location of terminating resistors depends on which devices are added to the bus, and *where* they are placed. As a result, termination is a much more vital element of SCSI setup and troubleshooting. Poor or incorrect termination can cause intermittent signal problems. Later on, you'll see how to determine the proper placement of terminating resistors.

Termination is typically either active or passive. Basically, *passive* termination is simply plugging a resistor pack into a SCSI device. Passive resistors are powered by the TERMPWR line. Passive termination is simple and effective over short distances (up to about 1 meter) and usually works just fine for the cable lengths inside a PC, but can be a drawback over longer distances. *Active* terminators provide their own regulated power sources, which make them most effective for longer cables (such as those found in external SCSI devices like page scanners) or Wide SCSI systems. Most SCSI-2 implementations (and later) use active terminators. A variation on active termination is *forced perfect termination* (or FPT). FPT includes diode clamps that prevent signal overshoot and undershoot. This makes FPT effective for long SCSI cable lengths.

SCSI IDs and LUNs

A typical SCSI bus will support up to eight devices, called *logical units*, and these devices are each identified using an ID. This means each device on the bus must have its own unique ID number (0–7)—if two devices use the same ID, there will be a conflict. IDs are typically set on the SCSI adapter and each SCSI device using jumpers or DIP switches (see Figure 7-2). Typically, the SCSI adapter is set for ID7, the primary SCSI hard drive is set to ID0, and a second SCSI hard drive is ID1. Other devices can usually be placed anywhere from ID2–ID6.

Logical unit numbers (LUNs) are similar to SCSI IDs because both identify SCSI devices. However, LUNs indicate devices within devices—divisions within IDs. Every SCSI ID from 0–7 can have up to eight LUNs (64 LUNs in SCSI-3), or eight subdevices for every given device ID. Suppose you needed to use more than eight devices on a SCSI bus. You could cause your device to respond to a SCSI ID, and have each device using the ID respond to a different LUN. For example, if you had three hard drives E:, F:, and G:, you could have all three drives use ID2, but E: could be assigned LUN0, F: could be assigned LUN1, and G: could be assigned LUN2. This is often the case with SCSI RAID systems where there are far more drives than available SCSI IDs. Unfortunately, a SCSI user cannot arbitrarily decide to use LUN assignments—the hardware must be designed for that purpose. Also, LUNs are seldom used, and many SCSI adapters don't check for them. This shortcut speeds bus scanning a bit. If you have a device that uses LUNs (i.e., a CD jukebox), you may need to enable LUN support in the host adapter's BIOS or device driver.

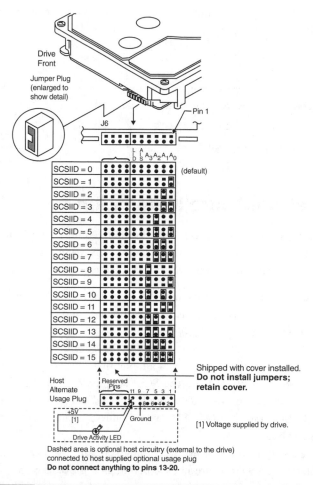

FIGURE 7-2   Setting a SCSI ID jumper (Courtesy of Seagate)

Objective 7.02   Installing a SCSI System

Today, virtually all SCSI host adapters are Plug-and-Play (PnP) devices that are designed for automatic detection and resource assignment in a motherboard's PCI slot. Still, most SCSI host adapter problems *start* when the card is first installed in the system—usually because of inadequate or incorrect installation of the hardware and software. This part of the chapter offers an overview of the SCSI adapter installation process and SCSI BIOS setup so that you can check your own installation for missing steps.

> **Travel Advisory**
>
> If your server motherboard incorporates a SCSI host adapter, you can generally skip the installation steps and focus on the SCSI setup and configuration issues.

Internal Hardware Installation

Implementing SCSI on your server or workstation requires that you install a SCSI host adapter (a.k.a. a controller) and at least one SCSI device. The following steps outline the installation of a typical SCSI host adapter:

1. Shut down your system, then turn off and unplug the computer.
2. Unbolt the outer case, then remove the housing and set it (and the screws) aside in a safe place.
3. If you're replacing an existing SCSI host adapter with a newer, faster model, you'll need to remove the old SCSI adapter first. Disconnect the internal and external SCSI cable(s) from the SCSI adapter. Unbolt the old SCSI card bracket from the chassis and remove the old SCSI adapter from its expansion slot. Be sure to set the old SCSI adapter aside on a static-safe surface, or in an antistatic bag.
4. Locate a slot for the new SCSI host adapter card. Most current SCSI host adapter devices will require a PCI slot, though some older SCSI cards will use an ISA slot. Find an available bus-mastering PCI slot that's appropriate for your SCSI adapter card. Remove the cover for the slot you intend to use (if it's not already removed), and save the screw for the mounting bracket.
5. Insert the SCSI host adapter card. Push the card in firmly and evenly until it's fully seated in the slot. Replace the screw to secure the bracket of your SCSI card to the computer's chassis.
6. If you're connecting any internal SCSI devices, plug the 50-pin or 68-pin SCSI connector on the end of the internal SCSI ribbon cable into the SCSI card's header. Make sure to align pin 1 on both connectors.
7. Connect your computer's drive activity LED cable to the appropriate connector on the SCSI card (if desired). This is designed to operate the front panel LED found on most PC cabinets to indicate activity on the SCSI bus.

8. Make any external SCSI bus connections that may be required (i.e., from your SCSI scanner or external SCSI drives).

The SCSI bus requires proper termination, and no duplicate SCSI IDs. Before you attempt to reboot the computer, verify the SCSI IDs for each SCSI device, and double-check the SCSI termination at the end(s) of your SCSI chain. If your server's motherboard provides an onboard SCSI host adapter, remember that the onboard adapter may be terminated by default.

> **Exam Tip**
>
> If you cannot disable the onboard adapter's termination, you may be limited to using only internal or external SCSI devices, but not both. See your motherboard's documentation for specific limitations.

Software Installation

Now that the physical hardware for your new SCSI host adapter card has been installed, it's time to install the SCSI adapter drivers and application software that you'll need to identify the device under the operating system. The following steps illustrate a typical procedure for Windows NT, but check the adapter's recommendations for other operating systems. Leave the computer's housing off for now, but reconnect the ac cord to the computer and prepare to start the system again.

1. Open the Control Panel and double-click the SCSI Adapters icon.
2. The SCSI Adapters dialog box opens. Select the Drivers tab.
3. In the Install Driver dialog box, click Have Disk.
4. The Install From Disk dialog box will open and ask for the path to the drivers. If you're installing from a floppy disk, specify **a:** and if you're installing from the HDD, specify the path to the HDD such as **c:\advansys**.

> **Travel Advisory**
>
> Always refer to the README file on the SCSI adapter card's driver disc to obtain the very latest feature descriptions and software installation guidelines for your particular card.

5. The Install Driver dialog box will return and list the drivers available for installation. Highlight the appropriate driver (i.e., AdvanSys Windows NT SCSI HBA Driver) and click OK. Windows NT may ask you to repeat the path to the drivers.

6. Drivers are now copied to the NT system. Remove the driver disk from the system and reboot Windows NT.

You can then confirm driver installation under Windows NT:

1. Open the Control Panel and double-click the SCSI Adapters icon.

2. The SCSI Adapters dialog box opens. Select the Devices tab.

3. One of the entries will list the SCSI driver (i.e., AdvanSys Window NT SCSI HBA Driver) as in Figure 7-3. If you expand this entry, you should see all the active SCSI devices connected to the card.

Managing the SCSI BIOS

Whether added as an expansion device or integrated into your server's mother-board, the vast majority of SCSI host adapters will employ BIOS (a.k.a. *firmware*) to configure the adapter's various operations. In most cases, the default settings of your SCSI BIOS are adequate, and you should not need to change the default configuration of the host adapter. However, you may decide to alter these default values if there is a conflict between device settings, or if you need to optimize the system's

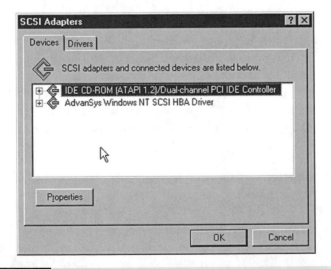

FIGURE 7-3   Checking a SCSI controller

performance. Typical default settings are listed in Table 7-3. The global settings affect your host adapter and all SCSI devices that are connected to it, but the device settings affect only *individual* SCSI devices.

The version number of your SCSI BIOS appears in a banner displayed on your computer monitor during boot. If a configuration utility is available, the following message (or something similar) also appears on your monitor:

```
Press Ctrl-C to start Symbios Configuration Utility...
```

This message remains on your screen for about five seconds, giving you time to start the utility. If you decide to press CTRL-C, the message changes to

```
Please wait, invoking Symbios Configuration Utility...
```

After a brief pause, your computer monitor displays the Main menu of the Symbios SCSI BIOS Configuration Utility.

TABLE 7.3	Typical Default Settings for a SCSI Host Adapter
Global Default Settings	
SCAM Support	Off (applies to BIOS version 4.09 and later
Parity Checking	Enabled
Host Adapter SCSI ID	7
Scan Order	Low to High (0–Max)
Device Default Settings	
Synchronous Transfer Rate (MB/s)	40
Data Width	16
Disconnect	On
Read/Write I/O Time-out (seconds)	10
Scan for Devices at Boot Time	Yes
Scan for SCSI LUNs	Yes
Queue Tags	On

The SCSI BIOS Configuration Utility is a powerful tool. If you somehow disable all of your controllers while using it, pressing CTRL-A (or CTRL-E on version 4.04 or later) after memory initialization during reboot allows you to re-enable the defaults and reconfigure your SCSI BIOS.

Exam Tip

Not all devices detected by the Configuration Utility can be controlled by the BIOS. Devices such as tape drives and scanners require that a device driver specific to that peripheral be loaded. The device manufacturer provides the device drivers.

Objective 7.03 SCSI Considerations

Whether you're considering adding SCSI support to your own computer or planning an upgrade for a customer, there are four essential elements that you must consider: the SCSI peripheral(s), the SCSI host adapter, the SCSI cable assembly, and the SCSI software driver(s). If any one of these four elements is missing or ill planned, your installation is going to run into problems.

SCSI Peripherals

The first items to be considered are the SCSI peripherals themselves. You first need to know what types of devices are needed (such as a SCSI hard drive or CD-ROM). The peripheral should be compatible with the architecture of your controller (i.e., SCSI-3 or SCSI-4). You may also find a growing base of Ultra160/m-compliant

---

Exam Tip

Ideally, a SCSI-4 host adapter should support SCSI-3 and SCSI-2 devices. If you have any intention of employing SCSI-4 devices, be sure to use a SCSI-4 adapter.

adapters and peripherals. Each SCSI peripheral device should also have a wide range of available SCSI ID settings. SCSI typically handles eight IDs (0–7) and the peripheral should have the flexibility to run on virtually any ID. If only a few IDs are available, you may be limited when it comes time to add other SCSI devices. Peripherals should support SCSI parity.

SCSI Host Adapter

The next item to be considered is the SCSI host adapter (often just called a host or HA) that fits in the PC expansion bus. Make sure to choose an adapter that is compatible with the PC bus in use (i.e., either ISA or PCI). Bus-mastering 32/64-bit PCI SCSI adapters will provide superior performance if your system will support them. Like the peripheral itself, the adapter should also be designed to support the SCSI-3 standard (or SCSI-4 if possible). Although most adapters are assigned a SCSI ID of 7, the adapter should be flexible enough to work with any ID from 0–7. The host adapter will also require a device driver for using devices other than hard drives. Make sure that the host device driver uses the same standard as the peripheral(s) (ASPI, CAM, or LADDR). It is important to note here that the driver standard has nothing to do with the choice of SCSI-2, SCSI-3, or SCSI-4. It is only important that the peripherals and the adapter use the *same* driver standard.

SCSI Cables and Terminators

Check that you select the proper cabling for the SCSI level you are using. Although SCSI cabling is now highly standardized, some older cables may use slight modifications for particular peripherals (a typical trick used with SCSI-1 devices). Be certain that you know of any specialized cabling requirements when choosing peripherals. Try to avoid specialized cabling if at all possible, but if you *must* use specialized cabling, you should determine what impact the cabling will have on any other SCSI peripherals that may be installed (or may be installed later). Use

Travel Advisory

Remember that SCSI host adapters integrated onto server motherboards may have fixed termination enabled, and you may not be able to run both internal and external devices from that controller.

good-quality SCSI cables specifically intended for the SCSI level you are using (probably SCSI-3/4), and keep the cables short to minimize signal degradation.

SCSI cables must be terminated at the beginning (host adapter) and end (after the last device) of the SCSI chain. Try to choose internal peripherals that have built-in terminators. Also try to select a host adapter and peripherals that use the same type of terminator resistor network. SCSI-2 and later systems use active terminator networks. You will see much more about cabling and termination a bit later in this chapter.

SCSI Drivers

Device drivers provide the instructions that allow the SCSI host adapter to communicate with the PC, as well as the peripherals in the SCSI chain (or the SCSI *bus*). The host adapter itself will require a device driver, as will every peripheral that is added. For example, a SCSI system with one CD-ROM will need a driver for the host adapter and a driver for the CD-ROM. Make sure that driver standards (ASPI, CAM, or LADDR) are the *same* for the host adapter and peripherals. The only exception to the device driver requirement (at this time) is the SCSI hard drive, which may be supported by the SCSI adapter's BIOS ROM.

Real-mode device drivers are added by including them in your PC's CONFIG.SYS and AUTOEXEC.BAT files. One issue to keep in mind when adding device drivers is that drivers use *conventional* memory (unless you successfully load the drivers into *high* memory). The more drivers that are added, the more memory that will be consumed. It is possible that a large number of device drivers may prevent certain memory-demanding DOS applications from running. To keep as much conventional memory (the first 640KB in RAM) as free as possible, use the DOS devicehigh and loadhigh features to load the drivers into upper memory (from 640KB–1MB in RAM). Windows 95/98/NT avoids this problem by using protected-mode drivers for the host adapter and devices.

Tips for a Smooth Installation

SCSI is not a terribly difficult technology to implement properly, but the subtle considerations and inconsistencies that have always been a part of SCSI implementations can result in confusion and serious delays for you and your customer. The following tips should help to ease your upgrades:

- **Add Only Add One SCSI Device at a Time**   By adding one device at a time and testing the system after each installation, it becomes much easier to determine the point where problems occur. Imagine what happens when you add an adapter, hard drive, and CD-ROM. If the system fails to function, you will have to isolate and check each item to locate the fault. On the other hand, by adding the adapter and testing it, then adding the hard drive and testing it, then adding the CD-ROM and testing it, installation troubleshooting becomes a much simpler matter (although it may take a bit more time overall).

- **Record the Host Adapter's Resources**   One of the most difficult aspects of troubleshooting is determining what the configuration of a system is. This is especially important during an upgrade since you *must* know the interrupts (IRQs), DMA channel(s), and I/O ranges used by other expansion devices in the PC. Any overlap in the use of these system resources will eventually result in a hardware conflict. When you install a SCSI host adapter, make it a point to record its IRQ, DMA, and I/O settings along with the SCSI ID settings of all devices that are installed. Tape the record to the inside of the PC's cover—next time the PC returns for service or upgrade, you'll have the information right at your fingertips.
- **Use Good-Quality Cabling**   Using the correct terminators and cables can have a profound effect on the performance of your SCSI installation. Good-quality cables and terminators provide electrical characteristics that support good signal transfer. This results in good data reliability between the host controller and peripherals. If cable quality is substandard or terminators are not correct for the SCSI level being used, the cable's electrical characteristics and data transfer will be degraded.

Cabling and Termination

Once the host adapter and peripheral are configured and installed, you must connect them with a cable. Internal devices are typically connected with a 68-pin IDC (insulation displacement connector) ribbon cable (a P-cable). By placing multiple connectors along the length of cable, daisy chaining can be achieved with a single connector on each internal device. External devices typically connect to an external 68-pin connector on the rear of the SCSI adapter, and each device offers two connectors, which allows daisy chaining to additional devices. Most commercial adapter and drive kits are packed with an appropriate cable.

The cable(s) must be terminated. There are internal and external SCSI cable terminators, along with SCSI devices that have terminating resistor networks already built in. The concept of termination is reasonably simple: Achieve the desired signal cable characteristics by *loading* each end of the SCSI chain with resistors. If the chain is not terminated properly, signals will not be carried reliably (which invariably results in system errors). For technicians and end users alike, the trouble usually arises in determining where the ends are. A number of examples will help to clarify how to determine the chain ends.

For a single SCSI drive and adapter as shown in Figure 7-4, the ends are easy to see. One end should be terminated at the host adapter (which usually has terminating resistors built in). The other end should be terminated at the SCSI hard drive (which also usually has terminating resistors built in). In this type of situation, you need only connect the cable between both devices and verify that the terminators are in place.

When a second SCSI peripheral is added, as shown in Figure 7-5, termination becomes a bit more complex. Suppose a CD-ROM is added with a SCSI ID of 6. The terminator on the existing SCSI hard drive is no longer appropriate—it should be removed and the termination should be made on the CD-ROM, which is now the *last device* in the SCSI chain. In most cases, a terminator network can be deactivated by flipping a DIP switch or changing a jumper on the peripheral itself. If the terminator cannot be shut off, it can almost always be removed by gently easing the resistor network out of its holder using needlenose pliers. If you remove a terminator, place it in an envelope and tape it to the inside of the PC enclosure. If it is simply impossible to remove the existing terminator on the hard drive, place the CD-ROM between the adapter and hard drive and remove the CD-ROM's terminator (rearrange the chain). The SCSI host adapter must remain terminated.

So what happens if an *external* device is used (such as a scanner), as in Figure 7-6? An external cable connects the adapter to the scanner. Because the scanner

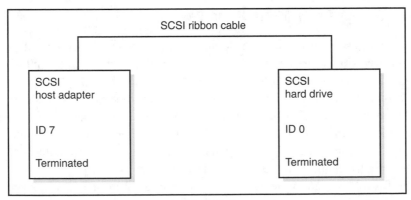

FIGURE 7-4　Terminating an internal SCSI adapter and hard drive

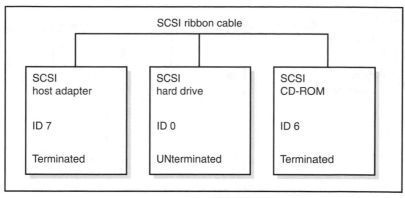

FIGURE 7-5   Terminating an internal SCSI adapter, HDD, and CD-ROM

(ID 6) and adapter (ID 7) are the only two points in the chain, both are terminated. Most external devices designed for SCSI-2 compatibility allow the active terminator built into the peripheral to be switched off, if necessary.

Suppose both an internal *and* an external SCSI device are being used, as shown in Figure 7-7. The SCSI host adapter (ID 7) is no longer at an end of the chain, so its terminator should be switched off or removed. It is the internal hard drive (ID 0) and external scanner (ID 6) that now form the ends, so both devices should be terminated. Since both peripherals should ideally support internal termination,

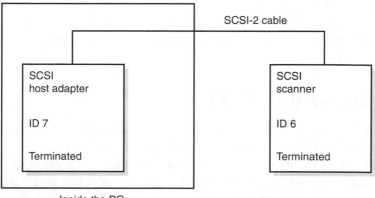

FIGURE 7-6   Terminating an external SCSI device

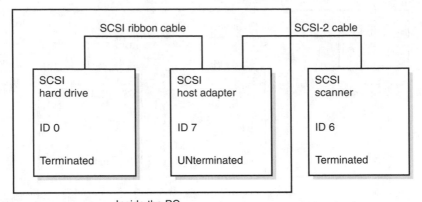

FIGURE 7-7 Terminating mixed internal and external SCSI devices

nothing needs to be done except to confirm that the terminators are in place and switched on.

Objective 7.04 SCSI Troubleshooting

As far as the *bus* is concerned, there is very little that can go wrong—wires and connectors do not fail spontaneously. However, it never hurts to examine the wiring, connectors, and terminator network(s) to ensure that the physical connections are intact (especially after installing or configuring new devices). The most likely areas of trouble are in the installation, setup, and operation of the devices residing on the bus.

Isolating Trouble Spots

Assuming that your SCSI devices have been installed correctly, problem scenarios can occur during normal operation. The first indication of a problem usually comes in the form of an error message from your operating system or application program. For example, your SCSI hard drive may not be responding, or the host PC may not be able to identify the SCSI host controller board, and so on.

The advantage to SCSI architecture is that it is reasonably easy to determine problem locations using intuitive deduction. Consider a typical SCSI system with one initiator (a host controller) and one target (i.e., a hard drive). If the hard drive fails to function, the trouble is either in the host controller or the drive itself. When you see drive access being attempted but an error is generated, the trouble is probably in the drive. If no drive access is attempted before an error is generated, the error is likely in the host controller. As another example, consider a setup with one initiator and two or more targets (i.e., a hard drive and CD-ROM). If *both* the hard drive *and* CD-ROM become inoperative, the problem is likely in the host controller card since the host adapter controls both targets. If only *one* of the devices becomes inoperative (and the other device works just fine), the trouble is likely in the particular device itself.

General Troubleshooting Tips

No matter how many precautions you take, you cannot always prevent problems from striking during SCSI installations or replacements. Fortunately, if you are installing devices one by one as suggested, you will have far fewer problem areas to check. Your first diagnostic for a SCSI installation should be the host adapter's SCSI BIOS initialization message. If you see no initialization message when the system powers up, the problem is likely with the host adapter itself. Either it is not installed properly or it is defective. Make sure that the adapter is set to the desired ID (usually 7). Try a new or alternate SCSI adapter. If the adapter provides its initialization message as expected, the problem is probably related to driver installation. Check the installation and any command-line switches for each device driver. When installing a SCSI hard drive instead of IDE hard drives, you must ensure that any previous hard drive references are "mapped out" of the CMOS setup by entering "none" or "not installed." If preexisting drive references are not removed, the system will try to boot from IDE drives that aren't there.

Be aware that faulty SCSI ID settings can result in system problems such as "ghost" disks—disks that the system says are there but that cannot be read from or written to. Some peripherals may also not work properly with the ID that has been assigned. If you have problems interacting with an installed device, try the device with a different ID, and make sure that there are no two devices using the *same* ID. Don't be surprised to find that certain types of cables don't work properly with SCSI installations. Make sure that everything is terminated correctly. Also be sure that any external SCSI devices are powered up (if possible) before the PC is initialized. If problems persist, try different cables. A quick-reference checklist is outlined here:

- Check the power to all SCSI devices (make sure that the power supply has enough capacity to handle all of your attached SCSI devices).

- Check the 50/68-pin signal cable to all SCSI devices. It should be a good-quality cable that is attached securely to each device.
- Check the orientation of each connector on the SCSI cable. Pin 1 must always be in the proper orientation.
- Check the SCSI ID of each device. Duplicate IDs are *not* allowed unless you're using LUN designations—this can occur when using a large number of SCSI devices such a RAID system.
- Check that both ends of the SCSI cable are properly terminated, and that the terminators are active.
- Check SCSI host adapter BIOS. If you're not booting from SCSI hard drives, you can often leave the SCSI BIOS disabled. This will also simplify the device configuration. You may be able to upgrade the host adapter's BIOS to resolve performance problems or compatibility issues.
- Check the CMOS Setup for drive configurations. When SCSI drives are in the system and IDE/EIDE drives are not, be sure that the drive entries under CMOS are set for None or Not Installed.
- Check the PCI bus configuration in the CMOS Setup. See that the PCI slot containing the SCSI host adapter is active, and is using a unique IRQ (usually named IRQ A). PCI bus mastering should also be enabled.
- Check for the protected-mode drivers under Windows 98/NT/2000. If you're working under Windows, see that any needed protected-mode drivers for the host adapter and SCSI devices are installed. The SCSI host adapter should be properly identified in the SCSI Adapters Wizard.

Objective 7.05

Understanding FireWire and FibreChannel

SCSI has traditionally been an 8-bit or 16-bit "parallel" standard allowing a wide variety of devices to communicate with the host computer at high speeds. Although designers constantly struggle to improve SCSI performance, it's clear that technical issues in cabling and controllers present some serious challenges to faster parallel SCSI. As part of today's SCSI-3 standards, designers have developed two serial SCSI approaches: FireWire (IEEE 1394) and FibreChannel (FC). This part of the chapter explores the main ideas behind FireWire and FibreChannel.

About FireWire

Simply put, the IEEE 1394 interface is a remarkably fast and effective high-speed ser-ial SCSI interface that is intended to support peripheral data transfers between demanding peripheral devices. This technology was originally developed by Apple, but was eventually adopted by the IEEE as an official industry standard. Operating at speeds up to 400Mbps (megabits per second), systems supporting IEEE 1394 have 30 times more bandwidth than USB (though USB is not in the SCSI family). IEEE 1394 also includes automatic configuration *without* the need for device IDs or terminators, hot swapping of peripherals, and support for up to 63 devices (on cables up to 15 feet long). It's easy to see that this technology permits the addition of a virtually unlimited amount of data storage capacity through the use of multiple external hard drives.

Given its high speed, IEEE 1394 technology is perfectly suited for multimedia peripherals, hard drives, and printers. It's becoming the interface of choice for mov-ing audio files and the images from video camcorders and digital cameras. More and more computer users are employing IEEE 1394 for their multimedia, home entertainment, and data processing applications. IEEE 1394 is gaining support as a solution for many applications outside of the computer industry. FireWire is offered as a standard interface on many new consumer digital devices, including camcorders, still cameras, and even the newest game consoles. When redefining the MIDI standard with MIDI 2, music manufacturers have chosen IEEE 1394 as the new-generation interface for electronic musical instruments and high-performance editing systems. IEEE 1394 has also been adopted as the video interface for its next generation of products by a group of VCR manufacturers. The Video Electronics Standards Association has selected IEEE 1394 for its home-distribution network in such systems as set-top boxes and high-definition television.

FibreChannel (FC)

FibreChannel (FC) is another powerful variation of the serial SCSI-3 standards allowing for very fast data transfers between devices over a relatively simple cop-per or fiber cable. Bandwidth is the main advantage of FibreChannel. Remember

---

Travel Assistance

You can learn about Adaptec's line of FireWire products at www.adaptec.com/worldwide/product/prodtechindex.html? cat=%2fTechnology%2fFireWire-1394.

that the peak bandwidth of UltraWide SCSI is 40MB/s, and UltraWide2 SCSI offers a maximum bandwidth of 80MB/s. However, FibreChannel offers a current bandwidth of 100Mb/s, and is expected to achieve 200Mb/s and 400Mb/s in the future. Another significant advantage of FibreChannel is increased transmission distance. With parallel SCSI, the maximum distance between a host server and an external storage device is 12 ft (or 3.5m). Using fiber-optic cable, a FibreChannel interconnect can easily achieve transmission distances of about 500m. With more advanced fiber-optic equipment, FibreChannel can transfer data for distances of up to about 10km. Such huge distances allow for remote mirroring of data at very high data rates—effectively providing off-site data storage. The longer communication links of FibreChannel also allow multiple systems to share the same storage facilities.

Given its speed and distance advantages, FibreChannel is expected to be a key technology for high-speed storage interconnections (i.e., processor-to-storage and storage-to-storage communications) and for the serial drive interface (i.e., high-performance disk systems). It allows for the integration of primary and secondary storage, as well as for shared storage among multiple servers. FiberChannel has also become a serious player in Gigabit Ethernet—a high-speed extension to Ethernet. It leverages the physical advantages and encoding used in FibreChannel data transfers. Gigabit Ethernet provides the high-speed local area network (LAN), while FibreChannel provides the high-speed storage area network (SAN). A FibreChannel storage area network allows a client attached to a specific processor to access data in any storage device within the storage area network because all storage devices are accessible to all processors. A typical FibreChannel card is shown in Figure 7-8.

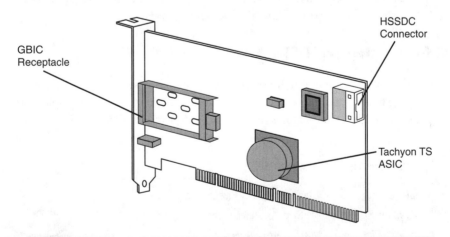

GBIC
Receptacle

HSSDC
Connector

Tachyon TS
ASIC

FIGURE 7-8   A typical FibreChannel host adapter (Courtesy of Adaptec)

CHECKPOINT

✔ **Objective 7.01: Understanding SCSI Concepts**   The Small Computer System Interface (SCSI) is a device-level interface designed to support a wide range of devices using a single bus architecture. "Wide" SCSI variations normally use a 16-bit data bus (rather than 8 bits), and "Fast" SCSI variations use an accelerated clock for higher data transfer speeds. Each device on the SCSI bus must be identified with a unique number (or SCSI ID), and no two devices can have the same ID. Signals on the SCSI bus are kept from "bouncing" back across the cable through the use of *terminators.* Terminators may be active or passive.

✔ **Objective 7.02: Installing a SCSI System**   Adding SCSI support generally involves installing a SCSI host adapter (usually an expansion card) and installing drivers for the host adapter. Once the host adapter is recognized by the system, individual devices can be installed (along with any necessary device drivers).

✔ **Objective 7.03: SCSI Considerations**   SCSI systems are based on a SCSI controller (host adapter), which is normally installed as a PCI adapter card. The SCSI host adapter can be adjusted through its own firmware setup utility. After installing the adapter and installing the SCSI adapter drivers, individual SCSI devices may be added to the SCSI bus.

✔ **Objective 7.04: SCSI Troubleshooting**   SCSI problems can usually be traced to issues with the SCSI host adapter or drivers. Troubles with individual SCSI devices are often caused by compatibility problems, SCSI ID settings, driver conflicts, or outright device failures.

✔ **Objective 7.05: Understanding FireWire and FibreChannel**   There are two forms of "serial" SCSI: FibreChannel and FireWire, which are part of the SCSI-3 standard. FireWire (IEEE 1394) operates up to 400Mb/s, and FibreChannel operates up to 100Mb/s.

REVIEW QUESTIONS

1. The term SCSI stands for...

    A. Standard Common System Integration

    B. Small Computer System Interface

    C. Simple Control System Integrator

    D. Server Control System Interface

2. The technique of balancing SCSI signals is known as...

   A. Termination

   B. Interconnection

   C. Interfacing

   D. Tinning

3. The data transfer rate for an Ultra3 SCSI interface is...

   A. 10MB/s

   B. 20MB/s

   C. 40MB/s

   D. 80MB/s

4. "Ghost" disks that the system says are there but that cannot be read from or written to are often caused by...

   A. Defective disks

   B. Outdated or buggy drivers

   C. Incorrect SCSI ID settings

   D. Defective SCSI adapter

5. SCSI adapter cards work best in what kind of bus slot?

   A. ISA

   B. EISA

   C. PCI

   D. AGP

6. The SCSI protocol that can ignore request/acknowledge handshakes for data transfer is known as...

   A. Asynchronous

   B. Synchronous

   C. Calibrated

   D. Segmented

7. How many SCSI IDs can be supported on a standard SCSI bus?

   A. 5

   B. 6

   C. 7

   D. 8

8. FireWire is part of the serial standard known as…

   A. SCSI-1
   B. SCSI-2
   C. SCSI-3
   D. SCSI-4

9. FireWire can support data transfers up to…

   A. 200Mbps
   B. 400Mbps
   C. 600Mbps
   D. 800Mbps

10. FibreChannel supports an initial bandwidth of…

   A. 100Mbps
   B. 200Mbps
   C. 325Mbps
   D. 400Mbps

REVIEW ANSWERS

1. **B** Small Computer System Interface: The term SCSI stands for Small Computer System Interface.

2. **A** Termination: In the PC, SCSI signal integrity is enhanced by using powered resistors at each end of the data cable to "pull up" active signals. Built-in pull-up resistors at drives and controller cards already terminate most high-frequency signal cables in the PC. The small resistor array is known as a terminator.

3. **D** 80MB/s: The data transfer rate for an Ultra3 SCSI interface is 80MB/s.

4. **C** Incorrect SCSI ID settings: Be aware that faulty SCSI ID settings can result in system problems such as "ghost" disks—disks that the system says are there but that cannot be read from or written to. Some peripherals may also not work properly with the ID that has been assigned.

5. **C** PCI: Today, virtually all SCSI host adapters are Plug-and-Play (PnP) devices that are designed for automatic detection and resource assignment in a motherboard's PCI slot.

6. **B** Synchronous: Synchronous and fast synchronous operations both ignore the request/acknowledge handshake for data transfer only. This allows slightly faster operation than an asynchronous protocol, but a certain fixed amount of time delay (sometimes called an *offset*) must be allowed for request and acknowledge timing.

7. **D** 8: A standard SCSI bus can support up to eight SCSI IDs (0 through 7) with ID 7 usually reserved for the SCSI host adapter.

8. **C** SCSI-3: As part of today's SCSI-3 standards, designers have developed two serial SCSI approaches: FireWire (IEEE 1394) and FibreChannel (FC).

9. **B** 400Mbps: Operating at speeds up to 400Mbps (megabits per second), systems supporting IEEE 1394 have 30 times more bandwidth than USB (though USB is not in the SCSI family).

10. **A** 100Mbps: FibreChannel offers a current bandwidth of 100Mb/s, and is expected to achieve 200Mbps and 400Mbps in the future.

RAID
Technology

	NEWBIE	SOME EXPERIENCE	EXPERT
ETA	5 hours	2 hours	1 hour

Networks are intended to handle huge amounts of valuable data, but networks are hardly infallible. Hardware failures and software incompatibilities can easily interrupt network operations. Such interruptions can compromise data transfers and secure transactions, and cause countless other faults that will interfere with your day-to-day business. Networks try to overcome potential problems *before* they occur using techniques of fault tolerance. One of the most common fault-tolerance techniques available to network planners is RAID—a *redundant array of independent disks*. RAID allows you to use multiple physical drives to create a variety of logical volumes that can mirror drives or share data across several physical drives. This chapter reviews the essential concepts of RAID systems, outlines RAID installation and configuration, and presents common troubleshooting issues.

Travel Advisory

Keep in mind that RAID can be implemented with IDE or SCSI drives depending on which type of RAID controller is selected. Small business servers often save money using IDE RAID, but large high-end servers will normally implement SCSI RAID. This chapter will present both types of RAID controllers.

Objective 8.01   RAID Primer

In simplest terms, a *disk array* is formed from a group of two or more physical disk drives that appear to the system as a single drive. The advantage of an array is to provide better performance and data fault tolerance. Better performance is accomplished by sharing the data transfer workload in parallel among multiple physical drives. Fault tolerance is achieved through data redundant operation, where if one (or more) drives should fail (or suffer a sector failure), a mirrored copy of the data can be found on another drive(s). For optimal results, select identical drives for installation in disk arrays. The drives' *matched performance* allows the array to function better as a single drive. The individual disk drives in an array are called *members*. Each member of a specific disk array is coded in its reserved sector with configuration information that identifies the drive as a member of the given array.

Logical Drives

A *logical drive* is storage space that is distributed across multiple physical drives in an array (except for online spares). Distributing the storage space in this way provides some significant advantages. For example, data can be accessed on all the physical drives at once, resulting in much higher performance data storage and retrieval. Fault-tolerant RAID levels may be used to protect your data against hardware failures. Finally, an array can consist of several logical drives, each spanning multiple physical drives in the array. (For maximum space efficiency, all physical drives in each array should also be the same size.)

Disk Array Adapter (DAA)

This is the generic term used for the RAID controller—the device that supports your mirrored drive(s), which are generally termed the *disk array*. Most RAID controllers are implemented using the SCSI interface, but Promise offers the FastTrack100, which supports RAID functions for UDMA/66 or UDMA/100 hard drives. The controller will virtually always incorporate a BIOS that fully supports the drive operations (i.e., SCSI or UDMA/100), and provide a setup feature (similar to the CMOS Setup) that will allow you to configure the RAID controller's many features.

Reserved Sector

Vital information is saved in a special location, called the *reserved sector*, on each disk member. This area contains array configuration data about the drive and other members in the disk array. If reserved data on any member of the array becomes corrupted or lost, the redundant configuration data on the other members can be used for automatic rebuilds. As a rule, disk array members do not have specific drive positions. This allows drives to be placed on different RAID controller connectors or cards within the system without reconfiguring or rebuilding the array.

Distributing Data and Striping

Distributing data makes it possible to access data concurrently from multiple drives in an array. This yields I/O rates many times faster than conventional nonarrayed drives. *Data striping* distributes data across the drives, and is automatically handled on a RAID controller in order to store data. A stripe is a collection of contiguous data that is distributed evenly across all the physical drives of a logical drive. The width of the stripe (the amount of data stored on each physical drive) is selected to optimize the performance of the operating system, but striping is *not* fault tolerant. For example, consider an operating system that typically requests data in 32-sector blocks (a sector contains 512 bytes of data). A RAID controller (i.e., the Compaq Smart Array 4250ES) distributes the data so that the first 32 sectors of data are on the first drive in the array. The controller continues distributing the next 32 sectors on the second drive, the next 32 sectors on the third drive, and so on. Evenly distributing the user data across all drives in an array results in improved performance by allowing data access to all drives simultaneously.

Depending on your particular RAID controller, you may be able to change the stripe size either during the initial configuration of the system or later after the system has been in use for some time. It may also be done online if the new stripe size fits within the existing format. Because data is rewritten to the drives in a different format, the battery-supported *write cache* must be enabled to protect the data in the event of power loss during the stripe change. Also, the RAID array accelerator memory must be large enough to support the least common multiple of the two different full stripe sizes. For example, suppose you expand the stripe size from an 11-drive RAID 5 volume (the default is 32 sectors, so a full stripe is 320 sectors) to a 14-drive RAID 1 volume (the default is 256 sectors, so a full stripe is 1,792 sectors). The least common multiple of a full stripe would require 8,960 sectors (4,480KB) available in the array accelerator.

Keep in mind that the number of sectors on the physical drives cannot be increased. An error can occur as the result of a request to increase stripe size—the newly selected stripe size would not be allowed. For example, if you try to change the stripe size from 32 to 256 sectors, there may not be enough sectors at the end of the disks for a complete stripe of the larger size. Because a partial stripe cannot be supported, the request would not be allowed. To select the new stripe-size, the current drive configuration would have to be deleted and the array configured with the new stripe-size. Since the data would be destroyed when the configuration is deleted, you'd need to back up the data and restore it after the array is reconfigured.

Disk Array Types

A typical RAID controller will support four general operating modes: striping, mirroring, stripe/mirror, and spanning. The choice of RAID mode will affect your drive capacity, drive performance, or fault tolerance. To appreciate the versatility of RAID, you should understand a little more about each of these RAID modes.

> ### Exam Tip
>
> Remember that all disk members in a formed disk array are generally recognized as a single logical drive volume to the host system—though the array can be broken up into more than one logical drive.

Striping (RAID 0)

In this mode, sectors of data are interleaved between multiple drives—effectively forming one large drive from two or more smaller ones. Striping is regarded as a performance enhancement rather than fault tolerance. Performance is better than a single drive since the read/write workload is distributed between the array members, and this array type is encountered in high-performance systems. Identical drives are recommended for performance (as well as data storage efficiency). The disk array data capacity is equal to the number of drive members times the smallest member capacity. For example, one 1GB and three 1.2GB drives will form a 4GB (4×1GB) disk array. The weakness with RAID 0 is that there is no redundancy—when any disk member fails, it affects the entire array because some portion of the overall drive is lost. You may consider assigning RAID 0 to drives that require large capacity and high speed but do not contain critical data.

Mirroring (RAID 1)

This approach writes duplicate data onto a pair of drives, while reads are performed in parallel (improving read performance). IDE-type RAID 1 is fault tolerant because data is duplicated, and each drive of a mirrored pair is installed on separate connectors. The RAID controller (i.e., FastTrack66) performs reads using data-handling techniques that distribute the workload in a more efficient manner than using a single drive. When a read request is made, the controller selects the drive positioned closest to the requested data, then looks to the *idle* drive to perform the next read access.

If one of the mirrored drives suffers a mechanical failure (i.e., a spindle failure) or does not respond, the remaining drive will continue to function (this is called *fault tolerance*). If one drive has a physical sector error, the mirrored drive will also continue to function. On the next reboot, the RAID software utility will display an error in the array and recommend to replace the failed drive. Users may choose to continue using their PC; however, it's often best to replace the failed drive as soon as possible.

Due to redundancy, the drive capacity of the array is half the total drive capacity. For example, two 1GB drives that have a combined capacity of 2GB would have 1GB of usable storage. With drives of different capacities, there may be unused capacity on the larger drive. To improve performance in configurations with more than two drives, the data is striped across the drives (this is also referred to as RAID 0+1 or RAID 10).

Exam Tip

If two drives being mirrored to each other fail, the volume is failed and data loss may occur.

Spare Drive

Under a RAID 1 configuration, an extra *hot spare* drive can be attached to the RAID controller but not assigned to the array. In this case, the spare drive will be put on standby. This drive will be activated to replace a failed drive that is part of the mirrored array. In most cases, a rebuild is performed automatically in the background to mirror the good drive onto the spare. At a later time, the system can be powered off, and the failed drive can be physically removed and replaced. Spare drives must be the same or larger capacity than the smallest array member.

Striping/Mirror (RAID 0+1)

This is a combination of the array types detailed previously. It can increase performance by reading and writing data in parallel while protecting data with duplication. A minimum of four drives needs to be installed. With a four-drive disk array, two pairs of drives are striped, and each pair mirrors the data on the other pair of striped drives. The data capacity is similar to a standard mirroring array with half of the total capacity dedicated for redundancy.

Striping/Mirror (RAID 1+0 or "10")

This is an alternative combination of mirroring (RAID 1) and striping (RAID 0). As with RAID 0+1, it can increase performance by reading and writing data in parallel while protecting data with duplication. A minimum of four drives needs to be installed. However, with a four-drive disk array, only one pair of drives is striped, and one pair mirrors the data on the other pair of striped drives. This provides RAID 1–type fault tolerance, and high I/O rates are provided by striping those RAID 1 elements. This type of configuration is most frequently seen in database servers where high performance and fault tolerance are vital. RAID 0+1 should *not* be confused with RAID 1+0.

Spanning (JBOD)

A spanning disk array (also aptly named JBOD for "just a bunch of drives") is equal to the sum of all drives when the drives used are of different capacities. Spanning stores data onto a drive until it is full, then proceeds to store files onto the next drive in the array. There are no major performance or fault-tolerance array features in this mode. When any disk member fails, the failure affects the entire array.

Spanning may be considered for performance in certain instances. With striping, array performance is affected directly by the stripe block size. Block size should be tailored to the typical I/O on the drive whether drive access is generally more random or sequential. However, if there is no predictability as to the type of I/O access, and both random and sequential I/Os occur unpredictably, the performance of a striped array will fluctuate. In the end, this may result in no overall performance gain. With spanning, the performance factor simply reflects a single drive's performance level. This offers a more predictable transfer rate, and allows the use of mismatched drives.

Disk Striping with ECC (RAID 2)

When a block of data is written, the data is broken up and distributed (interleaved) across all of the data drives (see "Striping (RAID 0)" earlier in this chapter) along with error-checking data. Error checking and correction (ECC) requires a larger amount of disk space than parity checking.

Disk Striping with Parity (RAID 3)

When a block of data is written, the data is broken up and distributed (interleaved) across all of the data drives (see "Striping (RAID 0)" earlier in this chapter) along with error-checking data. However, parity checking is used instead of ECC. Since parity data does not require as much space as ECC, parity can be stored more conveniently.

Data Guarding (RAID 4)

Data guarding (also called RAID 4) assures data reliability while using only a small percentage of the logical drive storage capacity. A single designated drive contains *parity* data. If a drive fails, the controller uses the data on the parity drive—and the data on the remaining drives—to reconstruct data from the failed drive. This allows the system to continue operating with slightly reduced performance until you replace the failed drive. Data guarding requires a minimum of *three* drives (two data drives and one parity drive) in an array, and allows the maximum number of drives allowed by the server. For example, in an array containing three physical drives, data guarding uses only 33 percent of the total logical drive storage capacity for fault tolerance. By comparison, an 18-drive configuration (17 data drives and one parity drive) uses only 6 percent.

Travel Advisory

Given the reliability of a particular generation of hard drive technology, the probability of an array experiencing a drive failure increases with the number of drives in an array.

Distributed Data Guarding (RAID 5)

Distributed data guarding (also called RAID 5) stores parity data across all the drives in the array. Spreading the parity across all the drives allows more simultaneous read operations and higher performance than data guarding (RAID 4). If a drive fails, the controller uses the parity data and the data on the remaining drives to reconstruct data from the failed drive. This allows the system to continue operating with a slightly reduced performance until you replace the failed drive. Distributed data guarding requires an array with a minimum of three physical drives, and allows the maximum number of drives allowed by the server. In an array containing three physical drives, distributed data guarding uses only 33 percent of the total logical drive storage capacity for fault tolerance, while an 18-drive configuration uses only 6 percent.

Changing the Array Storage Capacity

For a given disk array, you can normally adjust capacity by expanding or extending the array. These are subtle differences that you should understand. *Capacity expansion* means increasing the size of an array by adding physical drives and creating additional logical drives. By comparison, *capacity extension* means increasing the size of an array by adding physical drives and "growing" your existing logical drive(s) without adding more logical drives. In either case, more hard drives must be added to the server. Capacity can be adjusted through the RAID controller's configuration utility. The RAID controller will redistribute data in the original logical drive to a logical drive that spans *all* the physical drives in the array (including the added drives). The room left over is then used to increase the size of a logical drive (extending) or to create additional logical drives that also span the physical drives (expanding). The resized (extended) logical drive is within the larger drive array. When logical drives are added (expanded), the logical drives are then included in the larger drive array. Altering the capacity of an existing logical drive can be done offline by backing up all data, reconfiguring the array, and then restoring the data. To alter capacity online (with the server running), your operating system *must* support a logical drive increasing in size.

Exam Tip

The RAID controller's configuration utility will typically allow you to increase the size of existing logical drives under any operating system.

In certain cases, the RAID controller and its configuration utility may support making storage capacity changes online *without* downing the server or storage system. These features are available if you're using either Windows NT or NetWare operating system (NetWare 3.11 not supported) along with hot-pluggable drives. Hot-pluggable drives are required for online storage changes because conventional (non-hot-pluggable) drives require that the server be powered down to add or remove the drive(s). To use hot-pluggable drives, your server (i.e., a Compaq ProLiant server) must support hot-pluggable drives.

Travel Assistance

Windows NT 4.0 and OS/2 allow you to resize a partition inside the extended (bigger) logical drive using third-party tools like Partition Magic 3.0 or later (www.powerquest.com).

Using Larger Hard Drives

Additional storage space in a fault-tolerant configuration may be obtained with the same number of physical drives by systematically replacing your existing drives with higher-capacity drives. By replacing the drives one at a time, the data on the new drive is re-created from redundant information on the remaining drives. After each new drive has been rebuilt, the next drive can be replaced. When all drives have been replaced and rebuilt, the additional capacity on each drive can be utilized by increasing an existing logical drive (extension) or adding a new logical drive (expansion). The RAID controller's configuration utility automatically recognizes the unused space and guides you through the procedures to use it.

Controller Fault-Management Features

Depending on your particular RAID level, your server can realize faster data access and fault tolerance (often both). The problem is that failures are usually assumed to occur with the hard drives—the RAID controller itself is often overlooked as a source of system problems. Today, RAID controllers offer the intelligence and features that can help identify and correct problems in the drive array, as well as the controller itself. This part of the chapter highlights some of the fault management features found in a typical SCSI RAID controller and supported by network operating systems.

Redundant Controllers

Controllers are often the weak link in a RAID setup. However, advanced servers support a *redundant controller* arrangement. One controller is used as the primary controller, while the second controller operates in an active standby mode. If the primary controller fails, the active standby controller immediately assumes control of the disk array with no data loss or interruption in server operation. For example, Compaq SmartArray 4250ES SCSI RAID controllers have this capability when used on servers with 64-bit PCI and extended SCSI connectors. The SCSI buses are routed to both extended SCSI connectors so that either controller can read or write to the disk array. Another SCSI channel is routed between the two connectors, and this provides an intercontroller link for the two controllers to monitor each other's status and maintain cache integrity between them. Both controllers send status information to each other. In the unlikely event of one controller failing, the operating system is notified by the other controller. If the primary controller fails to respond, the secondary controller will take over operation of the drive array. If the secondary controller fails to respond, the primary controller would simply notify the operating system that redundancy is no longer available.

Autoreliability Monitoring

Automatic reliability monitoring (ARM) is a background process that scans for bad sectors on hard drives within fault-tolerant logical drives. ARM also verifies the consistency of parity data in drives with data guarding or distributed data guarding. This routine process assures that you can recover all data successfully if a drive failure occurs in the future. ARM operates only when you select RAID 1, RAID 4, or RAID 5.

Dynamic Sector Repairing

It's not uncommon for age and use to affect the integrity of drive sectors. A RAID controller that supports on-demand *dynamic sector repairing* (DSR) can automatically remap any sectors with media faults that are detected either during normal operation or during autoreliability monitoring.

Drive Parameter Tracking

Drive parameter tracking (also known as *drive performance tracking*) is a feature that monitors numerous drive parameters and functional tests. For RAID controllers such as the Compaq Smart Array 4250ES, this includes monitoring parameters such as "read/write/seek errors," "spin-up time," "cable problems," and functional tests such as "track-to-track seek time," "one-third stroke seek time," and "full stroke seek time." Drive parameter tracking allows the RAID controller to detect drive problems and predict drive failures before they actually occur.

Interim Data Recovery

If a drive fails in RAID 1(or higher) fault-tolerant configuration, the system continues to operate in an *interim data recovery* mode. For example, if you selected RAID 5 for a logical drive using four physical drives, and one of the drives fails, the system continues to process I/O requests, but at a reduced performance level. Replace the failed drive as soon as possible to restore performance and full fault tolerance for that logical drive.

Automatic Data Recovery

After you replace a failed drive, *automatic data recovery* reconstructs any lost data and places it on the replacement drive. This feature allows the rapid recovery of operating performance without interrupting normal system operations. In general, the time required for a rebuild is approximately 15 minutes per gigabyte (GB). However, the actual rebuild time depends on the rebuild priority set for the amount of I/O activity occurring during the rebuild operation, the disk drive speed, and the number of drives in the array (RAID 4 and RAID 5). For example, in RAID 4 and RAID 5 configurations, the rebuild time varies from 10 minutes/GB for three drives to 20 minutes/GB for 18 drives (using 9GB SCSI Ultra Wide hard drives).

Travel Advisory

You must specify RAID 5, RAID 4, or RAID 1 through the RAID controller's configuration utility in order to make the recovery features available.

Hot-Pluggable Drives

You can install or remove hot-pluggable drives without turning off the system power. This greatly speeds service time because the system does not need to be shut down, opened, serviced, then brought back online. This feature operates independently of the network operating system and requires a RAID controller used with a server chassis that supports "hot-pluggable" drives.

Exam Tip

Never turn off the hot-pluggable server when removing or installing the pluggable replacement drives. If you turn off the storage subsystem while server power is on, the RAID controller marks all the drives as "failed," and that could result in permanent data loss when the storage system is turned back on.

Controller Duplexing

Some operating systems support *controller duplexing*, a fault-tolerance feature that requires two RAID controllers. Using duplexing, the two controllers each have their own drives that contain identical data. In the unlikely event of a RAID controller failure, the remaining drives and RAID controller service all requests.

> **Travel Advisory**
>
> Since both RAID controllers would be connected to the same SCSI buses, controller duplexing is an operating system feature that is not supported by all RAID controllers. For example, the Compaq SmartArray 4250ES does not support controller duplexing.

Software-Based Drive Mirroring

Some operating systems support software-based *drive mirroring* as a fault-tolerance feature. Software drive mirroring resembles hardware-based drive mirroring (RAID 1), except that the operating system mirrors logical drives instead of physical drives. The problem with software-based drive mirroring is that the operating system believes each logical drive is a separate physical drive. If you mirror logical drives in the same array and a physical drive fails, both logical drives in the mirrored pair will fail, and you will not be able to retrieve your data. If you choose software-based drive mirroring, create at least two arrays with RAID 0 to achieve maximum storage capacity. When configuring your drive mirroring through the operating system, mirror logical drives residing in different arrays.

Objective 8.02   Installing and Configuring a RAID Controller

Before you can use a RAID controller, you'll need to install it in the server. This part of the chapter outlines the general process for installing and configuring a typical SCSI RAID controller card in a server both with and without PCI hot-plug support. If you're installing a second RAID controller (i.e., a Compaq SmartArray

4250ES) to provide array controller redundancy, make sure that both of the controllers have been upgraded to the latest firmware version, and see that the system BIOS has been upgraded to the latest version. Also see that the firmware version is the same on both controllers. Start with some preinstallation steps:

Exam Tip

If your RAID controller uses 64-bit PCI slots with extended SCSI connectors, be sure to install the controllers *only* into those slots. Installing the controller in slots without these connectors will cause the system to malfunction.

---

1. Always start by backing up data from any hard drive(s) that will be moved to the new controller.
2. Upgrade the existing array controller firmware and system BIOS.
3. Remove the server access panels for the PCI and SCSI bus connectors (i.e., the 64-bit PCI bus with extended SCSI connectors).
4. Install additional internal drive cages in the server, if necessary.
5. Attach the preinstalled SCSI RAID controller 68-pin Wide SCSI ribbon cables to the appropriate internal drive cage(s).
6. Connect the ports to the drives (i.e., SCSI port 1 to drive cage 1, port 2 to drive cage 2, and so on).
7. Install drives in the drive cages.

If your server supports hot-plug operation, you do not have to power off the server to install the RAID controller:

1. Unlock and open the server's hot-plug access panel(s).
2. Use the PCI Hot Plug button (or software application) to turn off power to the desired slot. A green LED will flash during the power-down transition and will turn off when power-down is complete.
3. Press the top of the appropriate expansion slot release lever and open the lever toward the rear of the expansion slot. Be sure to use the correct expansion slot.
4. Position the RAID controller board into the appropriate expansion slot alignment guides.
5. Insert the RAID controller until it's resting on the top of the slot connector.
6. Secure the controller board by pushing the ejector levers down.

7. Close the expansion slot release lever from the rear of the unit to secure the board. Make sure the lever latches into the closed position.

8. Activate power to the slot through the PCI hot-plug application (or by pressing the PCI Hot Plug button associated with the corresponding PCI slot).

9. Review the LEDs for slot status—a green LED flashes during the power-up transition, and will turn on when the power-up is complete.

10. Close and lock the server hot-plug access panels.

11. Run the server's configuration utility and the RAID controller's configuration utility as required to set up the RAID card.

Travel Advisory

Make sure that the appropriate hot-plug drivers are installed for your operating system. If they are *not* installed, the system will halt when a controller is removed or inserted.

If your server does *not* support hot-plug operation, you *will* have to power off the server (and allow internal devices to cool) before installing the RAID controller:

1. Back up all data from any hard drives that will be moved to the new controller.

2. Power down the server and disconnect the power cord(s).

3. Remove the server access panels for the PCI and SCSI bus connectors (i.e., the 64-bit PCI bus with extended SCSI connectors).

4. Position the RAID controller board into the appropriate expansion slot alignment guides.

5. Insert the controller board until it's resting on the top of the slot connector.

6. Secure the board by pushing the ejector levers downward.

7. Close the expansion slot release lever from the rear of the unit to secure the board. Make sure the lever latches into the closed position.

8. Close and lock the server access panels.

9. Power up the server.

10. Run the server's configuration utility and the RAID controller's configuration utility as required to set up the RAID card.

Configuring the RAID Controller

Once you've configured the new RAID controller in the server's system configuration utility, you'll need to run the RAID controller's configuration utility in order to set up the controller card itself. The configuration utility allows a wide range of disk array management controls such as adding more disk drives, selecting RAID levels, creating new arrays, expanding and extending capacity, changing stripe sizes, and the ability to modify other key RAID features.

Travel Advisory

Depending on the network operating system in use, you may need to take the network offline before using the configuration utility. For example, the configuration utility with the Compaq SmartArray 4250ES is an online utility in servers running Windows NT and later versions of Novell NetWare, but it is an offline utility for the other operating systems.

Starting the Configuration Utility Online

If you're using a network operating system that supports the RAID controller's configuration utility online (i.e., Windows NT), you can install and run the utility while the network is running. When you install the Software Support Diskette for Windows NT (NT SSD), the diskette prompts you to insert the configuration utility diskette to install the utility. A program icon is created automatically. Simply select the icon to run the configuration utility. To run the configuration utility from the RAID controller's support CD, insert the CD in the CD-ROM drive and power up the server. When you see the menu, select the Configuration Utility option. After completing the configuration, remove the CD and restart the server.

Manual Configuration

Rather than using the Configuration Wizards to enable your drive array, you can use the RAID controller's configuration utility to manually configure the controller and your drive array. The procedures below outline the techniques used with a SmartArray 4250ES RAID controller to create a new array, expand an array, extend a logical drive, alter the stripe size, and alter the RAID level.

Creating a New Array

To create a new drive array, you'll need to choose a RAID controller to manage the array, group selected drives (of the same size) into the array, then create logical drives from the physical array. Suppose that you have four 4.3GB drives and two 9.1GB drives connected to your SCSI RAID controller. You'd probably create two arrays. Array A would consist of three 4.3GB drives (with the fourth 4.3GB drive used as a spare), and array B would be the two 9.1GB drives. The fault-tolerance method for all logical drives in array A might be RAID 5 (distributed data guarding), and the fault-tolerance method for all logical drives in array B may be RAID 1 (drive mirroring). Let's review the steps to set up this type of example manually:

1. Start the RAID controller's configuration utility. In the Main Configuration screen, select the Controller Selection box.
2. Select one of the listed controllers. If there is only one RAID controller in the server, only one controller should be listed.
3. Click the Controller Settings button, and the Controller Setting screen appears.
4. Select the correct operating system (see Figure 8-1).
5. Click the Create Array button, and the Create Drive Array screen appears (see Figure 8-2).
6. Select the three drives you want to make up array A from the drives listed (for example, SCSI IDs 0, 1, and 2). Remember to always group physical drives of the *same* size—if you mix drive sizes, the capacity of the larger drives is wasted.
7. Click the Assign Drive(s) to Array button.

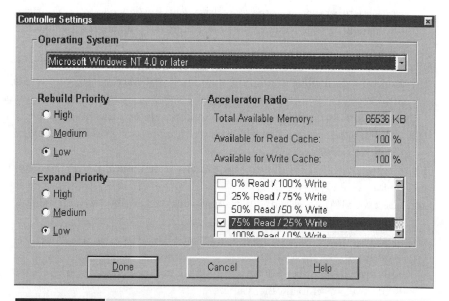

FIGURE 8-1   A basic RAID Controller Settings dialog box

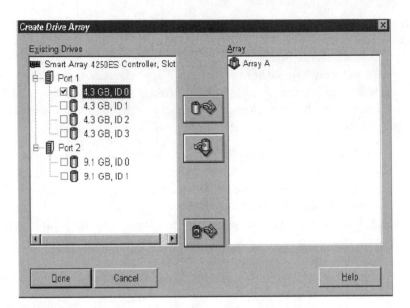

FIGURE 8-2 Creating a RAID drive array

8. Select the last 4.3GB drive (ID 3) and click the Assign Spare to Array button. Remember that the same spare drive may be assigned to multiple arrays, but spare drives should have the same (or greater) capacity as the drives in the array.

9. Click Done to return to the Main Configuration screen.

10. Select the controller again, then click the Create Array button to create array B.

11. Assign both 9.1GB drives to the array and click the Done button.

12. Select array A (or the Unused Space icon under array A) in the Logical Configuration View.

13. Click the Create Logical Drive button. A Create Logical Drive dialog box appears (see Figure 8-3).

14. Select your RAID level. For our example, click the Distributed Data Guarding (RAID 5) option button.

15. Click the Array Accelerator Enable button (if your controller provides array acceleration).

16. Select your stripe size. Stripe size can be left at the default for the selected RAID level, or set to another value.

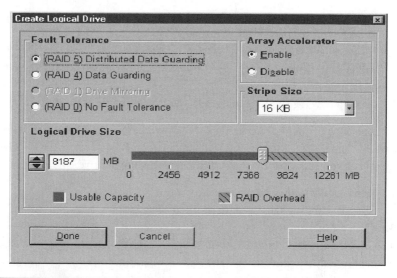

FIGURE 8-3   Creating a logical RAID drive

17. Size your logical drive. The Logical Drive Size area includes a graphical representation of the storage capacity available. To create a single logical drive across this array, accept the default values.
18. Click the Done button.
19. Click array B (or the Unused Space icon under array B) in the Logical Configuration View.
20. Repeat the preceding steps to create a single logical drive on array B, this time selecting RAID 1 fault tolerance.
21. This should complete the basic configuration of your drive array(s).

Expanding Capacity

Capacity expansion involves adding storage capacity (drives) to an array that has already been configured. If an existing array is nearly full of data, you can expand the capacity *without* disturbing the existing data. When you run the RAID controller's configuration utility, the program checks the drive hardware and configuration. If the configuration utility discovers a physical drive that is not being used, the Configuration Wizard leads you through the steps for adding the drive, or you can expand the capacity manually.

1. Install the new physical drive(s). Always group physical drives of the same size—if you mix drive sizes, the capacity of the larger drives is wasted.
2. Assign the new physical drive(s) to an existing array. Existing logical drive(s) will automatically expand across the physical drives (including the newly added ones).
3. Create a new logical drive to use the extra space on the expanded array.

Consider a configuration similar to the previous example: three 4.3GB drives in array A (no spare), and two 9.1GB drives in array B. If a fourth 4.3GB drive is added later, you can expand array A to include the fourth drive:

1. Select array A and click the Expand button.
2. Select the unassigned 4.3GB drive, then click Assign Drive(s) to Array.
3. Click the Next button at the bottom of the screen.
4. Click the Create Logical Drive button (see Figure 8-4).
5. Set the fault tolerance, enable the array accelerator, set the stripe size, and set the size for logical drive 2.
6. Click the Done button.

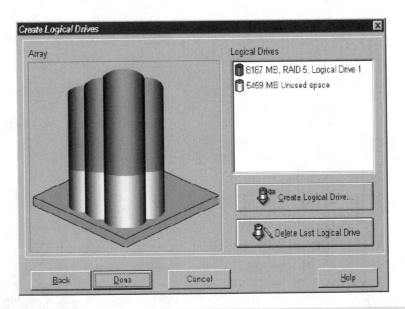

FIGURE 8-4   Expanding capacity

7. Back at the main screen, select Controller and Save Configuration from the menu bar. This saves the new settings for logical drive 2 and starts the capacity expansion process.

> ### Travel Advisory
>
> In the event of power loss, capacity expansion information is temporarily stored in the array accelerator's memory. To prevent the loss of data in the expanding logical drive, do not interchange RAID controllers or array accelerator boards during a capacity expansion process.

Extending Capacity

Logical drive extension allows you to increase the size of existing logical drives without disturbing the data on those logical drives. Keep in mind that logical drive extension is *not* supported by all operating systems. If an existing logical drive is full of data, you can extend the logical drive when there is free space in the array. If there is no free space available, you can add drives to the array and proceed to extend the logical drive:

1. Click the logical drive that you want to extend.
2. Click the Drive menu.
3. Select Extend Logical Drive.
4. The Extend Logical Drive screen displays the current capacity and RAID overhead of the selected logical drive (see Figure 8-5).
5. Click the slider control to change (increase) the size of the logical drive. You cannot reduce the size of the logical drive from this screen.
6. Click Done.
7. Save the logical drive by opening the Controller menu and selecting the Save Configuration option.
8. The logical drive will be restructured so that its data will be preserved.
9. Make the extended space of the logical drive available for use by creating a new partition in the extended space of the logical drive, or by increasing the size of existing partition(s) in the extended logical drive.

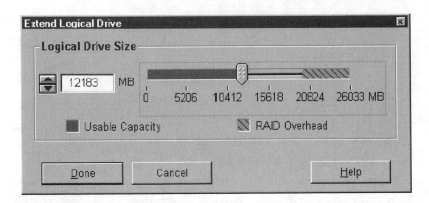

FIGURE 8-5 Extending capacity

Changing RAID Level and Stripe Size

Use the RAID Level dialog box to reconfigure a currently configured logical drive to a new fault-tolerance (RAID) level, or use the Stripe Size Migration dialog box to change an existing logical drive's stripe size to a new stripe size. Both processes can be accomplished online without causing any data loss:

1. Select a logical drive from the Logical Configuration View.
2. Select the Drive menu.
3. Click the Migrate RAID/Stripe Size option button.
4. Select a new RAID level (i.e., click the RAID 5 Distributed Data Guarding button).
5. The stripe size can be left at the default for the selected RAID level, or set to another value. For example, you can set the stripe size to 16KB.
6. Click Done.

Objective 8.03

Installing Operating System Drivers

Once the physical RAID controller is installed and configured, you'll need to install the drivers for the particular operating system. This part of the chapter covers the installation guidelines for controllers (such as the Compaq SmartArray 4250ES) under Windows NT 4.0 (refer to the controller's installation instructions for OS-specific installation procedures). Before installing the operating system drivers, you should update your server BIOS (if necessary) and configure your drive array(s) with the RAID controller's configuration utility.

> **Travel Assistance**
>
> You can learn more about the SmartArray 4250ES and obtain documents/drivers from www.compaq.com/products/storageworks/array_scsi_controllers.html.

Windows NT 4.0

To install a RAID controller's Windows NT driver on your server, you will need the controller's driver/support CD, blank diskettes, and access to a server or workstation with a bootable CD-ROM drive (in most cases, this may be the system where you install the RAID controller. To access the driver on your support CD, you'll first need to create the Windows NT SSD diskettes. These diskettes will contain the latest operating system software, drivers, and support documentation for the controller. To create the diskettes, follow these steps:

1. Boot the server from the controller CD.
2. From the System Utilities screen, select Create Support Software.
3. From the Diskette Builder screen, select Create Support Server Diskettes from CD.
4. Scroll down the list and select Support Software for Windows NT.
5. Follow the instructions on the screen to create the Windows NT SSD diskettes.

Installing the RAID Controller with Windows NT

You can install the RAID controller's driver during the initial installation of Windows NT 4.0 using the files on the Windows NT SSD diskettes:

1. Begin the Windows NT 4.0 installation process.
2. Setup automatically detects mass storage devices. Press S when prompted to specify additional mass storage devices.
3. From the list, highlight Other (Requires Disk Provided by Manufacturer) and press ENTER.
4. Insert Windows NT 4.0 SSD diskette #1 and press ENTER.

5. Select the RAID controller (i.e., Compaq Integrated Smart Array 42XX Controllers for Windows NT 4.0) from the list of displayed controllers and press ENTER.

6. Press ENTER again and continue installation of Windows NT 4.0.

7. Reinsert the Windows NT 4.0 SSD diskette when prompted—Setup copies the drivers to your system.

Installing the RAID Controller after Windows NT

If you must install the RAID controller after Windows NT is installed, you can use the Setup utility located on the Windows NT SSD diskettes. Setup identifies hardware components that are physically installed in the system, and recommends the device drivers that you should install or update:

1. Start Windows NT on the system where you're installing the drivers, and log on to an account with administrative privileges.

2. Insert the Windows NT SSD diskette #1 into the floppy drive.

3. From the Program Manager, select File, and then select Run.

4. Type in **A:\SETUP** and press ENTER.

5. Select Custom.

6. Select the RAID controller (i.e., Compaq Integrated Smart Array 42XX Controllers). If you have previously installed this driver on your system, Setup indicates if the driver can be updated. If it can, click Update. If you have not installed the driver, click Install and insert the correct diskettes as prompted during the installation.

7. You can install other components through Setup, or click Close if you're done. Setup prompts you to reboot the system to enable the newly installed/updated driver.

Removing the Driver

It might be necessary to remove the RAID controller's driver prior to upgrading the controller or resolving device conflicts. Device drivers can only be done through the Control Panel:

1. Start Windows NT and log in to an account with administrative privileges.

2. From the Control Panel, launch the SCSI Adapter utility.

3. Select the Drivers tab.

4. Select the controller (i.e., Compaq Integrated Smart Array 42XX Controllers); then click Remove.

5. After the driver has been removed, click OK. You must reboot the system for the removal to take effect.

> ### Travel Advisory
>
> Do *not* remove this driver if the system is booting from a device attached to the RAID controller. You'll get a dialog box reporting that the selected controller is used as a boot device — removing it may cause the system not to boot.

Installing Redundancy Software

If your operating system supports redundancy software, you can install the software following these steps:

1. Start Windows NT on the system where you're installing the redundancy software, and log on to an account with administrative privileges.
2. Insert the Windows NT SSD diskette (usually diskette #7) into the floppy drive.
3. From the Program Manager, select File, and then select Run.
4. Type **A:\setup** and press ENTER.
5. Select the RAID controller's redundancy software component. If you've previously installed this software on your system, Setup indicates whether it can be updated. If so, click Update. If you have not installed the software, click Install.
6. You can install other components through Setup, or click Close if you're done. Setup will prompt you to reboot the system and load the newly installed software.

Objective 8.04 ## Altering the Controller Setup

Once a RAID controller is installed and operational, you may need to adjust the setup and make changes to the controller's installation. Before attempting to make any changes to an existing RAID setup, you should carefully review the precautions and requirements for your particular RAID controller and server chassis. Here are some points to check before proceeding:

- Each RAID channel may support a large number of drives (i.e., up to 14 drives), but the controller will be limited by the number of physical drives supported by your server.

- Check for acceptable drive combinations. Some RAID controllers allow the use of Wide Ultra2 SCSI, Wide Ultra SCSI-3, or a mixture of the two in servers and storage systems supporting hot-pluggable drives. However, that may not be true for all controller/server combinations.
- Drives may not require termination. For example, Compaq servers and internal cabling provide the required termination of the SCSI bus.
- Check the acceptable drive sizes. Your RAID controller may be limited in the sizes and interfaces that can be supported.
- Drives should be of the same capacity to provide the greatest storage space efficiency when grouped in the same drive array.
- Check for *reserved ID*s. For example, external (or non-hot-pluggable) drives that are attached to some RAID controllers (i.e., a Compaq SmartArray 4250ES) must not be installed as SCSI ID6—SCSI IDs 6 and 7 are reserved for redundant controller operation.

Tweaking the Fault Tolerance

You may find it necessary to alter the fault tolerance (RAID level) used in an array. This may be necessary when drives are added or removed from the server, or when the network's needs change. For example, early implementations of a network may emphasize data storage performance over fault tolerance, but the need to protect valuable data may require you to update the RAID fault-tolerance selection. Here are the general steps:

- **Pick the New RAID Level**   The first task is to decide which level you'll need to use (see the "Disk Array Types" section earlier in this chapter).
- **Back Up the Disk Array**   A RAID level can typically be migrated without data loss using the RAID controller's configuration utility. If this is not possible (the configuration utility should inform you when this is not possible), you'll need to back up your data first and then change the RAID level.
- **Configure the Array**   Run the RAID controller's configuration utility in order to reconfigure your drive array with the new fault-tolerance method. If an error message states that the number of sectors needs to be increased, you must delete the old volume and reconfigure it as a new volume with the different fault-tolerance method you've selected.
- **Restore the Data**   Copy your protected data back into the same logical drives (if necessary). Your system automatically redistributes the data according to the new fault-tolerance scheme.

Tweaking the Stripe Size

You might find it necessary to alter the stripe size used in an array. This may be necessary when drives are added or removed from the server, or when the network's needs change. The typical guidelines are listed here:

- **Pick the New Stripe Size**   Select the desired stripe size for your array and RAID level (see the "Distributing Data and Striping" section earlier in this chapter).
- **Back Up the Disk Array**   Stripe size can typically be migrated without data loss using the RAID controller's configuration utility. If this is not possible (the configuration utility should inform you when this is not possible), you'll need to back up your data first and then change the stripe size.
- **Configure the Stripe Size**   Run the RAID controller's configuration utility in order to reconfigure your drive array with the new stripe size. If an error message states that the number of sectors needs to be increased, you must delete the old volume and reconfigure it as a new volume with the different stripe size that you've selected.
- **Restore the Data**   Copy your protected data back into the same logical drives (if necessary). Your system automatically redistributes the data according to the striping scheme.

Restoring an Array

In addition to moving an array, you can also restore an array to its original controller. This may be necessary if you encounter server problems with an array or controller, or if the network's needs change. The actual physical process of restoring an array is straightforward, but the logical sequence of events required to restore an array to its original controller (or to a new controller in the event of RAID controller failure) is a bit more convoluted. To restore an array, the server

---

Travel Advisory

These steps are intended to provide general guidelines only. Always refer to your specific server platform and RAID controller documentation for specific instructions. Any deviation from the manufacturer's instructions can result in the loss of all data across all moved arrays.

power must be off (including all system components), the move must not result in more than 32 logical drives (volumes) connected to a single controller, and the array should be in its original configuration with no active spare drives. It is also helpful to be using the latest RAID controller firmware. When the required conditions are met, follow these steps:

1. Power off the system.
2. Move your array back to the original controller (include all drives in the array), but retain its drive position from the consolidated configuration.
3. Restore system power.
4. Each of the controllers will indicate a "missing drives" error (i.e., a 1789 POST message). Press the appropriate key (i.e., F2) to fail the missing drives.
5. Run the RAID controller's configuration utility to remove the appropriate failed arrays.
6. Reboot the server.

Consider a SCSI RAID controller with an A array of four disks (IDs 0, 1, 2, and 3) and a B array of two disks (IDs 4 and 5). Moving the B array back to controller 2 creates an interim four-array state—array B on controller 1 and array A on controller 2 appear to the server as failed. You'll need to run the RAID controller's configuration utility to remove the failed arrays and restore the original two-array configuration.

Objective 8.05 RAID Troubleshooting

R AID controllers and servers are generally regarded as some of the most reliable PC hardware available today, and the fault-tolerance features of most modern RAID controllers allow defective hard drives to be replaced without losing any data (often without even taking the server offline). However, disk arrays and controllers are not problem-free, and the steps taken immediately after a fault can have a profound impact on the integrity of your valuable data. This part of the chapter shows you how to recognize and deal with drive failures, then highlights the numerous problems that can occur with the RAID controller itself. The first step in recovering from a drive problem is to identify a drive problem in the first place. In most installations, a drive failure can be detected in several ways:

- The operating system (or network console) indicates a logical drive failure.
- An LED illuminates on failed drives in a hot-pluggable drive tray.

- An LED illuminates on the front of a server (such as a Compaq ProLiant server) if failed drives are inside (though other problems such as fan failure or overtemperature conditions will also cause this LED to illuminate).
- The server's power on self test (POST) message lists failed drives whenever the system is restarted.
- The RAID controller's diagnostic utility (i.e., an array diagnostics utility, or ADU) lists all failed drives.

> **Travel Advisory**
>
> Problems such as reduced system performance or general disk errors reported by the operating system do not necessarily indicate that a drive has or has not been failed. If drive failures or repeated errors are suspected, run the array diagnostics.

Handling Drive Faults

The server informs you that a drive has failed. Depending on your level of fault tolerance, the network may (or may not) still be functioning. Still, you will have to take immediate corrective action to repair the fault and prevent further data loss. If your RAID controller is configured to support hardware fault tolerance, use these general steps to correct the trouble:

- **Find the Faulty Drive**   While the operating system will typically report the logical drive failure, you will still need to determine which *physical* drive failed. With hot-pluggable drives in a server (such as a Compaq ProLiant system) or storage system, faults are indicated by an LED (i.e., an amber "Drive Failure LED" on each drive tray).
- **Evaluate a Server Shutdown**   If the server containing the failed drive does not support hot-pluggable drives, perform a normal system shutdown of the server. If hot-pluggable drives are supported, you may not need to shut down the server.
- **Replace the Faulty Drive**   Remove the failed drive and replace it with a drive that is of the same capacity. For hot-pluggable drives, the LEDs on the drive each light once in an alternating pattern to indicate that the connection was successful (after you secure the drive in the bay). The online LED blinks (if the server is so equipped) indicating that

the controller recognized the drive replacement and began the recovery process.

- **Restart the Server**   Power up the server (if necessary).
- **Allow the Recovery to Finish**   The RAID controller's firmware reconstructs the information on the new drive based on information from the remaining physical drives in the logical drive array. While reconstructing the data on hot-pluggable drives, the online LED blinks. When drive rebuild is complete, the online LED is illuminated.

In the event of a drive failure, the condition of the corresponding logical drive varies depending upon the fault-tolerance level used. Since a single array of physical drives can contain multiple logical drives with different fault-tolerance methods, the condition of each logical drive on the same array is not necessarily the same. If more drives are failed at any one time than the fault-tolerance level allows, fault tolerance is considered to be compromised and the condition of that logical drive can be referred to as "failed". If a logical volume is failed, all requests from the operating system to access that logical drive will be rejected with "unrecoverable" data errors. The system will respond to faults based on the RAID level that you have selected, as shown here:

- **RAID 0 (striping)**   Under RAID level 0, there is no fault tolerance, and your disk array cannot sustain any drive failures. If any physical drive in the array is failed, the condition of *all* non-fault-tolerant logical drives in the same array will also be failed. This is because data is striped across all drives in the array.
- **RAID 1 (mirroring)**   This type of fault tolerance replaces the failed drive with the mirrored copy. Mirroring can sustain multiple drive failures (as long as failed drives are not mirrored to one another), so a RAID 1 drive will only be failed if the two failed drives are mirrored to one another. RAID 1 will attempt to rebuild data if a failed drive has been replaced, or if a spare drive kicks in to take the place of the defective drive.
- **Spare Drives**   In the event of a drive failure, the spare drive acts as an immediate replacement for the failed drive (if a spare drive is assigned and available). Data is reconstructed automatically from the remaining drive(s) in the volume, and written to the spare drive using the automatic data recovery process. Once the spare drive is completely built, the logical drive again runs at full fault tolerance, and is able to sustain another subsequent drive failure. However, if another drive fails before the spare drive is completely built, the spare drive cannot

prevent failure of the entire logical drive. Also note that it is possible for noncorrectable disk errors to prevent completion of the automatic data recovery process.

Drive Replacement Notes

As a rule, failed drives in hot-pluggable trays can be removed and replaced while host system and storage system power are both *on* (hot-pluggable drives can also be replaced when the power is *off*). However, *never* turn off an external storage system while the host system (server) power is on. This results in the failure of all drives in the storage system, which would likely compromise your fault tolerance. When a hot-pluggable drive is inserted, all disk activity on the controller is temporarily paused while the drive is spinning up (usually 20 seconds or so). If the drive is inserted into a fault-tolerant configuration while system power is on, the recovery of data on the replacement drive begins automatically (normally indicated by a blinking LED). Non-hot-pluggable drives should be replaced only while the system power is off.

Be sure to check the SCSI ID jumpers on all non-hot-pluggable drives to make sure that the correct drive is being replaced. Also verify that the SCSI ID jumpers are set to the same SCSI ID on the replacement drive. The SCSI ID jumpers may be located at different places on different drive models, but it is necessary that the SCSI ID on the replacement drive *always* be set to the same value as the original failed drive to prevent SCSI ID conflicts that could compromise the fault tolerance.

The capacity of replacement drives must be at least as large as the capacity of the other drives in the array—drives of insufficient capacity will be failed immediately by the controller without starting the automatic data recovery process.

Travel Advisory

Always replace a failed drive with a new or known-good replacement drive. In some cases, a drive that previously been marked as failed by the controller may appear to be operational after the system is power-cycled, or after removal and reinsertion of a hot-pluggable drive. This practice is highly discouraged because the use of such marginal drives may eventually result in data loss.

Removing a Reserved Sector

When any array is created using a RAID controller, a *reserved sector* is placed on each drive that belongs to the newly created array. This reserved sector allows the RAID controller to identify which drives belong to which array. The reserved sector also contains file allocation information that is needed for reading and writing to any array. The reserved sector can become corrupt or bad from time to time, causing any number of issues to arise such as

- An inability to partition or format a drive successfully.
- The volume name is unreadable when attempting to remove a partition with FDISK—making it impossible to complete the removal.
- Problems with reading/writing to the drives or array (such as fatal errors or data corruption).
- The array constantly goes into critical or offline mode during a reboot.
- Problems with rebuilding mirrored (RAID 1) and mirrored/striped (RAID 0+1) drives.

Exam Tip

Always perform a complete backup of the array before attempting to remove the reserved sector on a drive. When removing the reserved sector on drives that belong to any mirror, you should remove the sector from the mirrored drive first—remove the sector on the master drive only as a last resort. Finally, removing the sector from any striped drive will cause a non-functional array.

Removing the reserved sector will remedy most issues related directly to a "Bad Reserve Sector" error. These steps outline the process for an IDE RAID controller such as a FastTrak 66/100:

1. When the controller's BIOS banner comes up, press the required key combination to enter the controller's Setup utility (i.e., CTRL-F).
2. Select View Drive Assignments and highlight the suspect drive.
3. Opt to delete the reserved sector. A message will appear indicating that the reserved sector on the disk will be wiped. Press Y to confirm the deletion.
4. Repeat this for each member of the particular array that is having a problem.
5. When finished, reboot the system.

Now re-create the drive array, then partition and format it. You should be using FDISK and FORMAT to set up the array. Reload your data from a current backup.

Controller POST Errors

The firmware incorporated into most RAID controllers will execute an onboard POST process when the server initializes. If an error is encountered with the controller, the system will generate a corresponding POST code on the display, and you can use the code to quickly cross-reference the error. Refer to the controller's documentation for specific POST errors and corrective actions.

CHECKPOINT

✔ **Objective 8.01: RAID Primer** A redundant array of independent disks (RAID) allows you to use multiple physical drives to create a variety of logical volumes that can mirror drives or share data across several physical drives. The advantage of an array is to provide better performance and data fault tolerance. The individual disk drives in an array are called *members*. A *logical drive* is storage space that is distributed across multiple physical drives in an array (except for online spares).

✔ **Objective 8.02: Installing and Configuring a RAID Controller** RAID controllers are normally installed as expansion cards in the server. The server and RAID card are then reconfigured to accommodate the RAID controller as needed. Finally, the RAID controller's drivers are installed under Windows NT or other network OS.

✔ **Objective 8.03: Installing Operating System Drivers** Given the many features and high reliability required by a RAID controller, RAID drivers are operating system specific, and you'll need to install (and periodically update) the RAID drivers depending on the network OS in use. If the OS is updated or changed, you will need to reinstall the appropriate drivers for the RAID controller.

✔ **Objective 8.04: Altering the Controller Setup** To create a new drive array, you'll need to choose a RAID controller to manage the array, group selected drives (of the same size) into the array, then create logical drives from the physical array. *Capacity expansion* involves adding storage capacity (drives) to an array that has already been configured. If an existing array is nearly full of data, you can expand the capacity *without* disturbing the existing data. Logical *drive extension* allows you to increase the size of existing logical drives without disturbing the data on those logical drives.

✔ **Objective 8.05: RAID Troubleshooting**   Failed drives in hot-pluggable trays can be removed and replaced while host system and storage system power are both *on* (hot-pluggable drives can also be replaced when the power is *off*). If a drive in a fault-tolerant configuration is replaced while the system power is *off*, the replacement drive is detected, and automatic data recovery (ADR) may need to be started. Removing the reserved sector will remedy most issues related directly to a "Bad Reserve Sector" error.

REVIEW QUESTIONS

1. A group of two or more physical disk drives that appear to the system as a *single* drive is known as a...

   A. Disk array
   B. Logical drive
   C. Drive interface
   D. Disk errors

2. Which RAID feature distributes data across the drives, and is automatically handled on a RAID controller in order to store data?

   A. Data mirroring
   B. Data striping
   C. Data backup
   D. Data calibration

3. RAID 1 is known as...

   A. Data mirroring
   B. Data striping
   C. Data backup
   D. Data calibration

4. Disk striping with parity is known as...

   A. RAID 0
   B. RAID 1

C. RAID 2

D. RAID 3

5. The means of increasing the size of an array by adding physical drives and creating additional logical drives is known as...

   A. Capacity extension

   B. Capacity conversion

   C. Capacity override

   D. Capacity expansion

6. Distributed data guarding is known as...

   A. RAID 1

   B. RAID 2

   C. RAID 4

   D. RAID 5

7. The RAID device used to cache system data is called...

   A. CMOS RAM

   B. Array accelerator

   C. Spare sectors

   D. Drive compression

8. The means increasing the size of an array by adding physical drives and growing your existing logical drive(s) without adding more logical drives is known as...

   A. Capacity extension

   B. Capacity conversion

   C. Capacity override

   D. Capacity expansion

9. What part of the disk allows the RAID controller to identify which drives belong to which array?

   A. Sparred sector

   B. Spared sector

   C. Reserved sector

   D. Regular sector

10. RAID POST message "1724" means...

   A. Slot 1 Drive Array Not Configured
   B. Slot "x" Drive Array - Array Accelerator Battery Depleted
   C. Slot "x" Drive Array - Array Accelerator Configuration Error
   D. Slot "x" Drive Array - Physical Drive Position Changes(s) Detected

REVIEW ANSWERS

1. **A** Disk array: A group of two or more physical disk drives that appear to the system as a single drive is known as a disk array.

2. **B** Data striping: Data striping distributes data across the drives, and is automatically handled on a RAID controller in order to store data. A stripe is a collection of contiguous data that is distributed evenly across all the physical drives of a logical drive.

3. **A** Data mirroring: RAID 1 is known as data mirroring.

4. **D** RAID 3: Disk striping with parity is known as RAID 3.

5. **D** Capacity expansion: Capacity expansion means increasing the size of an array by adding physical drives and creating additional logical drives.

6. **D** RAID 5: Distributed data guarding is known as RAID 5.

7. **B** Array accelerator: The RAID device used to cache system data is called an array accelerator.

8. **A** Capacity extension: Capacity extension means increasing the size of an array by adding physical drives and "growing" your existing logical drive(s) without adding more logical drives.

9. **C** Reserved sector: Vital information is saved in a special location, called the reserved sector, on each disk member. This area contains array configuration data about the drive and other members in the disk array. If reserved data on any member of the array becomes corrupted or lost, the redundant configuration data on the other members can be used for automatic rebuilds.

10. **D** Slot "x" Drive Array - Physical Drive Position Changes(s) Detected: An error message (i.e., a 1724 POST message) should indicate that logical drives were added to the configuration, and the configuration was updated.

Core
Processing
Technologies

	NEWBIE	SOME EXPERIENCE	EXPERT
ETA	6 hours	4 hours	2 hours

305

The *motherboard* (or main board) is at the heart of every server, workstation, or ordinary desktop system that you'll ever work on. The motherboard provides all of the system resources (i.e., IRQs, DMA channels, and I/O locations), and supports the "core processing" devices needed by the system: the CPU, memory, real-time clock, BIOS, and expansion slots. A server's motherboard supports even more resources that are critical to a network: additional CPUs, a video controller, an on-board SCSI host adapter, an on-board IDE controller, and other network-related tools (which you'll see later). This chapter explains the features and layout of a typical server motherboard, highlights the CPUs, memory, and other devices that you'll find there, and explain the essentials of troubleshooting so that you can fix serious server problems as effectively as possible.

Objective 9.01   Understanding a Server Motherboard

B efore you can install, upgrade, or troubleshoot a server's motherboard effectively, it is vital that you know your way around and be able to identify every critical device on-sight. While each motherboard is certainly designed a bit differently, the devices are surprisingly simple to sort out. For the purposes of this book, we'll look closely at an Intel L440GX+ server board, shown in Figure 9-1, and talk a bit about the Intel SKA4 server chassis.

Processor

You must install at least one processor (i.e., items B and D). A server motherboard will typically support more than one 242-pin cartridge-style processor (i.e., two, four, or eight processors) such as the Pentium II or Pentium III—often Pentium II/III Xeon variations. The L440GX+ processor interface is MP (multiprocessor) ready, and operates at 100MHz. A local APIC (advanced programmable interrupt controller) is included for interrupt handling in both single- and multiprocessor environments. The cartridge assembly includes the processor core with an integrated 16KB primary (L1) cache and a 512KB secondary (L2) cache. The Pentium II/III L2 cache includes burst pipelined synchronous static RAM (BSRAM), and error-correcting code (ECC) performance operates at half the core clock rate. The processor's numeric coprocessor (the floating-point unit, or FPU) significantly increases the speed of floating-point operations. Cartridge processors are secured by a retention mechanism attached to the server board. The CPU cooling fan for

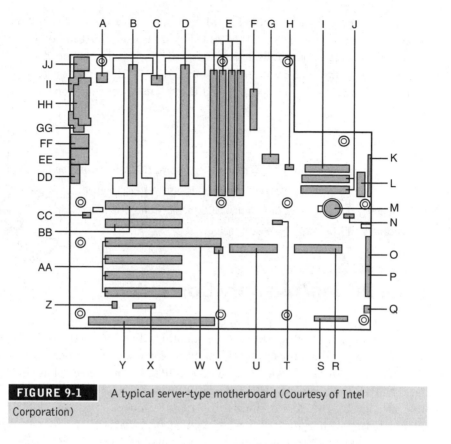

FIGURE 9-1   A typical server-type motherboard (Courtesy of Intel Corporation)

each processor is attached to a local fan power/tachometer connection (items A and C in Figure 9-1, respectively).

Memory

Servers require memory—*lots* of memory—in order to contend with the network operating system, applications, and network traffic. For best performance, you should fill the system with the best-performing memory for your particular motherboard. For the L440GX+, only 100MHz PC100 ECC (or non-ECC) SDRAM is supported by the server board. Your own motherboard may be quite different, so be sure to double-check the motherboard's specifications. For example, your server may use PC133 SDRAM or Rambus DRAM (RDRAM). The L440GX+ partitions memory as four banks of SDRAM DIMMs (item E), each providing 72-bits of noninterleaved memory (i.e., 64-bit main memory plus ECC). You may install

64MB to 2GB of *registered* memory DIMMs, or install 32MB to 1GB of *unbuffered* memory DIMMs. Memory should be added in order from slot 1 to slot 4. The memory controller automatically detects, sizes, and initializes the memory depending on the type, size, and speed of the installed DIMMs/RIMMs. The controller then reports memory size and allocation to the server using configuration registers.

Exam Tip

Never mix registered and unbuffered memory. Non-ECC memory may be installed, but ECC memory is recommended in a server environment for superior data integrity. Mixing non-ECC memory and ECC memory causes all ECC features to be disabled.

Host Bridge/Memory Controller

Server motherboards are designed around a central chipset, and most of the features supported by your motherboard are handled by the chipset. The L440GX+ is designed around the Intel 82440GX AGPSet (440GX). The chipset provides 100MHz processor host bus interface support, DRAM controller, PCI bus interface, AGP interface, and power management functions. The host bus/memory interface in the 440GX is optimized for 100MHz operation using 100MHz SDRAM main memory. It also supports a PCI interface that is PCI 2.1 compliant. The 440GX memory controller supports up to 2GB of ECC (or non-ECC) memory using PC100 SDRAM SIMMs. ECC can detect and correct single-bit errors, and detect multiple-bit errors for outstanding data integrity.

Peripheral Device Support

The server needs a means of communicating with the real world through ports and expansion slots, so you should be familiar with the varied devices and ports incorporated into your motherboard. A super I/O chip controls many of the system's I/O ports. Controllers (such as the National 87309) support two serial ports, one parallel port, the diskette drive, a PS/2-compatible keyboard, and a mouse. The server board provides a connector for each port, as shown in Figure 9-2.

- **Serial Ports** Items GG and II in Figure 9-1, or item D in Figure 9-2.
- **Parallel Port** Item HH in Figure 9-1, or item C in Figure 9-2.

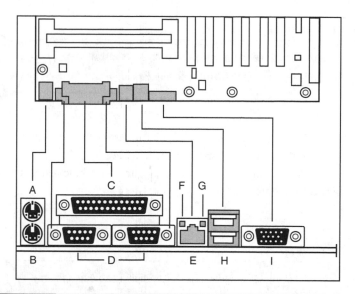

FIGURE 9-2   I/O connections on a server-type motherboard (Courtesy of Intel Corporation)

- **USB Ports**   Item EE in Figure 9-1, or item H in Figure 9-2.
- **Chassis Intrusion Switch**   Item Z in Figure 9-1.
- **Backup Battery**   Item M in Figure 9-1.
- **Expansion Slots**   Item Y and items AA and BB in Figure 9-1.
- **Video Port**   Item DD in Figure 9-1, or item I in Figure 9-2.
- **SCSI Controller**   Items U and R in Figure 9-1, and item W in Figure 9-1.
- **IDE and Floppy Controller**   Item J and item V in Figure 9-1 respectively.
- **Network Controller (NIC)**   Item FF in Figure 9-1, or item E in Figure 9-2.
- **Keyboard and Mouse**   Item JJ in Figure 9-1, or items B and A in Figure 9-2, respectively.

Travel Advisory

The SCSI bus is terminated on the server board with active terminators that *cannot* be disabled, so the on-board SCSI controller must always be at one end of the bus. The SCSI device at the end of the cable must also be terminated.

Travel Advisory

The components on some full-length expansion cards installed in slot 6 may interfere with the DIMM connector latches.

- **Power Management (ACPI)**   Item T in Figure 9-1.
- **Power and Cooling**   Items F and G in Figure 9-1.
- **Front Panel Connector**   Item K in Figure 9-1. These connections are detailed in Figure 9-3.

Exam Tip

The maximum IDE cable length is 18 in. Additional cable length may result in poor data transfer rates or data loss.

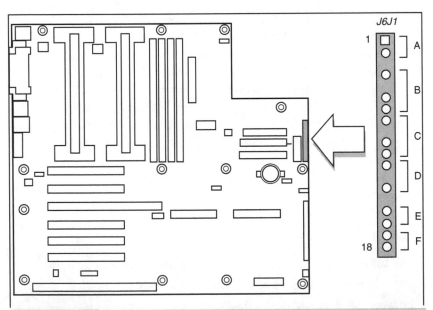

FIGURE 9-3   Close-up of a front panel connector (Courtesy of Intel Corporation)

Objective 9.02   Server Management and Security Features

N etwork administrators and technicians will need to access the server for test-ing and configuration changes. Consequently, you should be familiar with the various management tools supported by the server, and understand the secu-rity features that are available. This discussion will cover the features found in the Intel L440GX+ server motherboard.

Server Management

Server management is handled through a microcontroller on the motherboard. Intel refers to this as the *Baseboard Management Controller* (BMC). The BMC is basically an autonomous motherboard subsystem that monitors system events and logs their occurrence in nonvolatile memory called the *system event log* (SEL) and the *sensor data record* (SDR). Typical events include overtemperature and overvoltage conditions, fan failure, or chassis intrusion. The BMC provides access to the SEL information so that software running on the server can poll and retrieve the server's current status.

The BMC and associated circuitry are powered from the ATX +5V standby supply, which remains active even when server power is switched off (the server must still be plugged into ac power). SEL contents can be retrieved after system failure, and used for analysis by field service personnel. Server management soft-ware tools (such as Intel Server Control software on the CD included with the L440GX+ server board) can be used to retrieve the SEL. You can generally update the software tools directly from the manufacturer's Web site.

Depending on the design of your motherboard, SEL and SDR information may also be available. The L440GX+ makes that data available through Intel's *Intelligent Management Bus* (IMB, shown as item N in Figure 9-1). An emergency server management card such as the Intel LANDesk Server Monitor Module card (SMM) can be inserted into the motherboard (item S in Figure 9-1), obtain the

---

Travel Assistance

For the L440GX+, you'd download the software from support.intel.com/support/motherboards/server/l440gx.

SEL data, and make it remotely accessible using a LAN or telephone line connection. The SMM is available with the LANDesk Server Manager Pro package.

Emergency Management and Event Paging

Every minute offline can affect the productivity and sales of even a small company, so the purpose of server management tools and data logs is to allow fast, decisive system recovery when trouble strikes. The L440GX+ motherboard includes *Emergency Management Port* (EMP) software that allows remote server management through a modem or direct (serial port-to-serial port) connection. A technician can access and check the server from a remote location (i.e., an offsite support office). The EMP software allows you to connect to a server remotely, power the server on or off, and reset the server. You can also examine the contents of your SEL and SDR in order to check any events that may have precipitated the problem. Obtaining this information from a remote location can allow a technician to select replacement parts and have them on hand before physically reaching the server.

Event paging enables the server to dial out and generate a page when an issue arises. Your server can be configured to automatically dial up a paging service and page you when a platform event occurs (events include out-of-range temperatures, out-of-range voltages, chassis intrusion, fan failure, and so on). This gives technicians and administrators almost immediate warning when server trouble strikes. Because paging is also part of the autonomous BMC, a page can be generated even if the server's processors are down, or system software is unavailable. Paging requires an external modem connected to the server's EMP serial connection (typically the COM2 serial port).

Security

Security is a vital concern for network administrators. Unauthorized users must be prevented from accessing the network, and the physical server must be secured to protect the hardware from accidental (or even intentional) damage. The server typically offers both hardware and software security features.

Mechanical Interlocks

If the server supports mechanical interlocks, you can use the chassis intrusion alarm switch. When the server's outer cover is opened, the switch transmits an alarm signal to the server board, where BMC firmware and server management software handles the signal. The server can be programmed to respond to an intrusion by powering down or by locking the keyboard.

Software Locks

The CMOS Setup and the *System Setup Utility* (SSU) provide password security features to prevent unauthorized or accidental access to the system. Once security is enabled, you can only access the system after you enter the correct password(s). For example, software security will

- Enable the keyboard lockout timer—the server requires a password to reactivate the keyboard and mouse after a specified timeout period.
- Set and enable an administrative password.
- Set and enable a user password.
- Set a secure mode to prevent keyboard or mouse input, and prevent use of the front panel reset and power switches.
- Activate a hot-key combination to start the secure mode.
- Disable writing to the floppy drive when the secure mode is set.
- Disable access to the boot sector of the primary hard disk drive.

The software security features allow both a user password and an administrator password. Both passwords give you different privileges in the server.

Objective 9.03

Installing a Server Motherboard

Whether you're replacing a failed motherboard or upgrading an existing server, chances are that you'll need to install a motherboard at some point. Motherboard installation is a highly intrusive procedure, so great care is required to properly reinstall all of your existing devices. This part of the chapter highlights the motherboard installation process, and covers installation of the processor and memory. We'll assume the use of an ATX motherboard such as the Intel L440GX+, as shown in Figure 9-4. Always refer to the documentation accompanying your particular motherboard for specific instructions and cautions.

Standard Precautions

Before you get started, there are several warnings and cautions that you must understand thoroughly. Take a moment to review this section of the chapter before attempting any work on the network server.

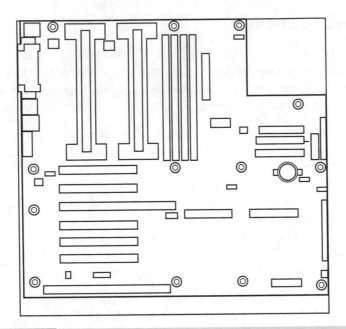

FIGURE 9-4   Mounting locations on a typical ATX server motherboard (Courtesy of Intel Corporation)

- **Shut Down and Unplug the Server**   Remember that it's not enough to simply shut down the server through Windows. Standby power is always fed to the system as long as the power supply is connected to ac power. You *must* unplug the ac cord from the wall outlet before opening the chassis or beginning your work. Also, remember to shut off the monitor.
- **Disconnect Peripheral Cables**   Power is also present on most peripheral cables attached to the server. Once the system is shut down and the ac power cord is unplugged, be sure to disconnect the network cable, the telephone (modem) cable, and other local peripheral devices (such as a parallel port printer) still under power (or shut those local devices off).
- **Manage Your ESD**   The motherboard—and most other devices in the server—are *extremely* sensitive to damage from accidental electrostatic discharge (ESD). Before opening the server, you must ground yourself using a properly grounded antistatic wrist strap. You should also work on a properly grounded antistatic mat on your work surface. Hold all electronic boards only by their edges. After removing a board from its protective wrapper (or from the server), place the board component side up on a grounded, static-free surface.

Removing the Board

Let's start with a review of motherboard removal. This can be particularly important during server upgrades where you'll need to remove the existing motherboard first. Be sure to power down the server and disconnect the ac cord before proceeding.

| Travel Advisory |

> As with all major computer upgrades, you may want to perform a complete server backup to tape before proceeding. Changes to the drive controller hardware and other main components of the motherboard may sometimes cause unexpected operation of the system—and this may result in accidental data loss.

To remove a motherboard, follow these steps:

1. Open the server and remove all peripherals and components blocking access to the server board. In most cases, this will involve the removal of all expansion cards and cables attached to the motherboard, but you may also need to remove one or more drives. It will really depend on the design of your particular chassis (your server chassis manual will probably offer detailed information on this issue).
2. Label and disconnect all internal and external cables connected to expansion boards.
3. Remove all expansion boards. Remember to store the boards on an antistatic mat, or place them in antistatic bags to prevent accidental ESD damage.
4. Label and disconnect all internal and external cables connected to the server board (including the ATX power cable).
5. If you'll be transferring the memory and processor(s) to the new motherboard, remove the memory and processor(s) from the motherboard now. Place these sensitive devices in an appropriate antistatic container until you're ready to reinstall them.
6. Remove the server board retaining screws and set them aside.
7. Remove the server board and place it (component side up) on an antistatic mat, or place it in an antistatic bag to prevent accidental ESD damage.
8. If you're going to be storing the old server board for an extended period of time, remove the backup battery, place the battery into a heavy plastic bag, then tape the bag to the motherboard's antistatic bag.

9. You may also need to remove and save the EMI gasket that covers the I/O connectors on the board (the new motherboard may provide an appropriate new shield).

Installing the Board

Now it's time to install the new motherboard. Use extreme caution when positioning the new board so that standoffs do not scrape the printed circuit runs on the board. At high signal speeds, even minor scratches can impair signal reliability. Serious scratches can even damage the new motherboard. You should generally install the new motherboard first, then install the memory and processor before powering up and configuring the system:

1. You might need to install an EMI gasket to accommodate the I/O port layout of your new motherboard.
2. Seat the new motherboard in the chassis, and verify that all of the mounting holes align properly. Do *not* proceed with the installation unless all of the mounting points are clear.
3. Insert screws through the mounting holes and into the threaded standoffs. Make sure the board is properly seated, and then tighten all the screws firmly (do not overtighten the screws).
4. Connect the 20-pin ATX power cable to the corresponding power connector on the motherboard.
5. Connect all internal and external cables to the server board, and install a fresh battery to preserve the motherboard's configuration data. When connecting cables, be sure to check the alignment of pin 1 with each cable and header (the red or blue stripe down one side of the cable always represents pin 1).
6. Reinstall all expansion boards and bolt them into place on the chassis.
7. Connect all internal and external cables to the expansion boards.

Travel Advisory

Double-check that all screws securing the motherboard are snugged into place. Loose screws may work out and drop onto live circuitry or into a fan and result in serious system problems.

Installing/Replacing Peripherals

Network servers typically rely on fast processors and a great deal of memory. Once the new motherboard is installed, you'll need to install memory devices and at least one processor before powering up and configuring the server. Be sure to keep the server powered off and unplugged while working inside of it.

Memory

Memory is often installed in the form of DIMMs (Dual Inline Memory Modules), and a typical server motherboard will support 1GB or more of synchronous DRAM (SDRAM) memory across up to four DIMM slots (i.e., four 256MB DIMMs), such as in Figure 9-5. Some servers will employ Rambus memory (RDRAM) fitted into RIMM (Rambus Inline Memory Module) slots. This part of the chapter focuses on the more popular DIMM architecture, so RIMM users should refer to the specific instructions and cautions accompanying the motherboard. Since you may need to upgrade memory in an existing configuration, let's look at DIMM removal first:

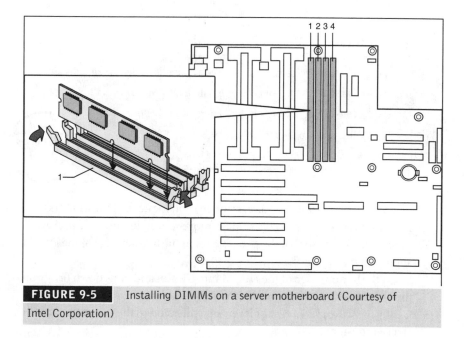

FIGURE 9-5   Installing DIMMs on a server motherboard (Courtesy of Intel Corporation)

Travel Advisory

Memory is extremely sensitive to accidental damage from
ESD. Use all antistatic precautions when handling a DIMM.

1. Open the server (if it's not already open) and locate the DIMM slot(s).
2. Gently push the plastic ejector levers out and down to eject the selected
    DIMM from its slot.
3. Hold the DIMM only by its edges (careful not to touch its components or
    gold edge connectors) and carefully lift it away from the socket. Store the old
    DIMM in an antistatic package.
4. Repeat to remove other DIMMs as necessary.

Refer to the motherboard's documentation and select one or more DIMMs to
provide an adequate amount of memory for the server. DIMMs must be selected
based on capacity (i.e., 128MB), memory type (i.e., SDRAM), speed (i.e., 8ns cycle
time), and error checking (i.e., parity, nonparity, ECC, or non-ECC). Let's review
the process for DIMM installation:

Exam Tip

DIMMs and sockets may use tin or gold in the connectors, but mixing dissimilar metals (i.e., a DIMM with gold contacts into a DIMM slot with tin
contacts) may cause later memory failures—resulting in data corruption. Only install DIMMs with gold-plated edge connectors in gold-
plated sockets.

1. Open your server (if it's not already open) and locate the DIMM slot(s).
2. Hold a DIMM only by its edges, and remove it from its antistatic package.
3. Orient the DIMM so that the two notches in the bottom edge of the DIMM
    align with the keys in the slot.
4. Insert the bottom edge of the DIMM into the slot and press down firmly on
    the DIMM until it seats correctly and fully in the slot.
5. Gently push the plastic ejector levers on either end of the slot to the upright
    (locked) position.
6. Repeat to install other DIMMs as necessary.

Travel Advisory

Use extreme care when removing or installing a DIMM—too much pressure can damage the slot (and ruin the motherboard). Apply only enough pressure on the plastic ejector levers to release or secure the DIMM. DIMMs are keyed to allow insertion in only one way.

Processor(s)

A server motherboard will normally accommodate two or four (or more) processors. You'll need to attach an appropriate heat sink/fan unit to each processor being installed now, and have a termination card available for other processor slot(s). Refer to the documentation that accompanied the server motherboard and verify the type and speed of compatible processors (i.e., one or two 1GHz Pentium III processors). If you're adding a second processor, be sure that the new processor matches the existing one (including the processor's manufacturing revision if necessary), or is otherwise suitable for use with the original CPU. Let's review correct processor removal first:

Travel Advisory

Processors are extremely sensitive to accidental damage from ESD. Use all antistatic precautions when handling a processor.

1. Open your server (if it's not already open) and locate the processor slot(s).
2. If the selected processor has a heat sink/fan unit, disconnect the power wire from its connector on the server motherboard:
   - For cartridge-type processors, carefully pull back the tab of the retention mechanism with your left hand until the processor can be rotated out of the slot. With your right hand, grasp the processor on the side closest to the retention mechanism tab you're pulling and rotate the one side of the processor out of the slot. Once that side is free, you can pull the other side out of the slot. This can be a difficult process. Pull the retention mechanism tab just far enough for the retention lock to free the processor.

- For socket-type processors, locate and disengage the ZIF lever, then raise the lever to the full upright position. You may need to gently rock the processor back and forth to remove it from the socket. Do *not* pry the processor from one side only—this can cause pins to bend and damage the processor.

Travel Advisory

If the server has been running, any installed processor and heat sink motherboard will be *hot*. To avoid possible burn injury, allow the system to remain off for at least 15 minutes before servicing the processors.

3. Remove the processor and place it in an antistatic bag or box.
4. Select one or more suitable processors for the motherboard, and verify that their heat sink/fan units are properly attached.
5. Locate the corresponding CPU slots (or sockets) on the motherboard, and also locate the small fan connectors near each slot (or socket). Virtually all modern server motherboards will autodetect the processor, and configure the bus speed, multiplier, and CPU voltage automatically. This means you rarely need to set jumpers to prepare a motherboard for new CPUs.

Exam Tip

You generally must install a termination card into any vacant processor slot to ensure reliable system operation. A termination card contains AGTL+ termination circuitry and clock termination. The server may not boot unless all vacant processor slots contain a termination card.

Let's cover the essentials of processor installation now:

1. Open your server (if it's not already open) and locate the processor slot(s):
   - If your server has one processor and you're adding a second, you must remove the termination card from the secondary processor slot. Carefully pull back the tab of the retention mechanism until the termination card can be rotated out of the slot. Grasp the card on the side closest to the retention mechanism tab and rotate the one side of the card out of the slot. Once that side is free, you can pull the other side out of the slot.

- If your server has one processor and you're replacing it, leave the termination card in place in the empty secondary slot. Remove the processor you want to replace.
- If your server has two processors and you are replacing one or both, remove the appropriate one(s).

Exam Tip

The grounded retention mechanisms (GRMs) are not compatible with SECC-type processor packaging—the new GRMs only support SECC2-type (i.e., Pentium II/III Xeon) processors. If you plan on using SECC-type (i.e., ordinary Pentium II/III) processors, you must use a universal retention mechanism (URM).

---

2. Remove the new processor from its antistatic package and orient the processor in its slot (or socket), using special care to align pin 1 properly.
3. For cartridge-type processors, slide the processor into the retention mechanism. Push down firmly, with even pressure on both sides of the top, until the processor is seated. It should click into place.
4. For socket-type processors, seat the processor fully into the socket, then close and lock the ZIF lever.
5. Attach the fan power cable to the three-pin connector on the server board.
6. Close the server and secure the outer cover (make sure that any intrusion switch is closed).
7. Connect any remaining external cables and attach the ac power cord.
8. Turn on the monitor and then power up the server. Start the server's setup routine to configure the new server motherboard, memory, and CPU(s).

Objective 9.04

Configuring the Motherboard

After the motherboard is secured in a server, and the memory and processor(s) have been installed, it's time to configure the motherboard in its new hardware setup. Server configuration usually involves setting the motherboard's jumpers, running the CMOS Setup, and executing other utilities needed to settle the server into its network environment.

Setting the Jumpers

Modern motherboards use relatively few jumpers—the vast majority of the server's configuration is set through the CMOS Setup and other software tools. However, the few jumpers present on your motherboard will affect major security issues (i.e., clearing a password, chassis intrusion, and so on). The documentation accompanying your server motherboard will detail the location and use of each jumper. For the Intel L440GX+ motherboard (see Figure 9-6), you'll need to recognize nine critical jumpers:

- **BIOS WR EN**   BIOS Write Enable
- **BMC FRC UP**   Baseboard Management Controller Firmware Upgrade
- **BMC WR EN**   Baseboard Management Controller Write Enable
- **CMOS CLR**   Clear the CMOS
- **FRB**   Fault Resilient Booting
- **INT DET**   Intrusion Detection
- **PSWD CLR**   Clear the Password
- **RCVRY BOOT**   Recovery Boot
- **WOL EN**   Wake On LAN Enable

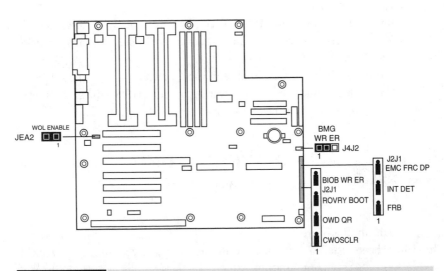

FIGURE 9-6   Jumper locations for a server motherboard (Courtesy of Intel Corporation)

Travel Advisory

In virtually all cases, the server should be powered off and unplugged before changing a jumper position. Most jumpers will need to be returned to their original (default) positions after the respective feature has been used (i.e., after the system password has been cleared).

POST

Each time you start (or restart) the server, a power on self test (POST) program is executed from the motherboard's BIOS. A typical POST checks the server board, the installed processor(s), the installed memory, the keyboard, and most installed peripheral devices. During the memory test, POST displays the amount of memory that it is able to access and test (the length of time needed to test memory depends on the amount of memory installed in the system). If an error is detected in the motherboard, processors, memory, or other installed devices, the POST will generate an error (more about this in the "Troubleshooting" section later in this chapter). A normal POST process will proceed similar to the steps shown next.

Local Lingo

POST (power on self test)   The process of initialization and self diagnosis that starts up a PC at boot time and leads to the loading of an operating system.

---

1. Turn on the video monitor and power up the server. After a moment, the POST will run and the memory count will start.
2. After the memory count, you'll see messages and screen prompts such as

```
Press F2 key if you want to run SETUP
Keyboard...Detected
Mouse...Detected
```

3. In this example, you'd press F2 to start the system's CMOS Setup routine. Other motherboard and BIOS versions may use different keys, but you'll see the key(s) called out in the message.
4. If you do *not* press the key(s) to start your CMOS Setup, the POST will end and transfer control to the operating system. If you do not have a device (a

drive) with an operating system loaded, the previous message remains for a few seconds while the boot process continues, and the system beeps once. Then you'll see a message such as

```
Operating system not found
```

5. When the operating system is found, the boot process continues. If your motherboard includes an on-board SCSI host adapter, you may see other BIOS messages such as

```
Press <Ctrl><A> to enter SCSI Utility
```

6. In this example, you'd press CTRL-A to start the SCSI controller's setup utility. Other motherboard and BIOS versions may use different keys, but you'll see the key(s) called out in the message. Start the SCSI utility if there are SCSI devices installed on the server. When the utility opens, follow the onscreen instructions to configure the on-board SCSI host adapter and devices. If you do not enter the SCSI utility, the boot process continues normally.

7. Press ESC during POST to open a boot menu when POST finishes—from this menu, you can choose the boot device (i.e., the C: drive or D: drive) or enter the CMOS Setup.

8. After the POST cycle is complete, the system beeps once.

9. Now you'll see the operating system logo, and the actual operating system will begin to load.

Travel Advisory

If the system halts before the POST finishes, the system speaker emits a beep code indicating a fatal system error that requires immediate attention. If the POST has initialized the video system, you may see a message on the video display (and the system may beep twice).
Record any beep or text error messages.

CMOS Setup

The CMOS Setup routine is part of the motherboard BIOS, and the many variables that define the system's configuration are stored in battery-supported CMOS RAM or flash memory. You may elect to enter the CMOS Setup (sometimes referred to as the BIOS Setup or simply Setup) when the server motherboard is upgraded, the backup battery is replaced, or other hardware changes are made to the system that must be identified at the system hardware level. The mother-board's documentation lists a selection of common settings (settings in bold are default values).

Exam Tip

If the values stored in CMOS RAM do not agree with the hardware detected by the POST (i.e., after the CMOS RAM is cleared), an error message is generated. In many cases, you can reenter the CMOS Setup to correct the error, or use the Clear CMOS jumper to reset factory default values.

System Setup Utility (SSU)

While the motherboard's CMOS Setup routine is vital to the configuration of low-level server hardware, there are several critical issues that are not addressed by Setup. Motherboards (such as the L440GX+) include a System Setup Utility (SSU) on the driver/resource CD. The SSU allows a higher-level configuration of the server. For example, an SSU assigns resources to baseboard devices and add-in cards *prior* to loading the operating system. It allows you to specify boot device order and system security options outside of the CMOS Setup. The SSU permits viewing (and clearing) the system's critical event log, and provides a system-level view of the server's I/O devices. The SSU also allows you to perform basic server troubleshooting when the OS is not operational.

Legacy and PnP Devices

The SSU is "PCI aware," and it should comply with ISA Plug-and-Play specifications—the SSU works with any compliant configuration (.CFG) files supplied by individual peripheral device manufacturers. As a rule, you do *not* need to run the SSU when adding or removing PnP ISA/PCI devices, but you *must* run the SSU to reconfigure the server when installing or removing a legacy ISA device.

POST checks the system configuration data against the actual hardware configuration. If the two do not agree, POST generates an error message. You must then run the SSU to specify the correct configuration before the server boots. An SSU allows you to specify a system configuration using the information provided by .CFG files, configuration registers, flash memory, and any information that you enter manually. The SSU writes this configuration information to flash memory. Changes to the configuration will take effect when you boot the server. The SSU always includes a checksum with the configuration data so the BIOS can detect any potential data corruption before the actual hardware configuration takes place.

Managing BIOS

BIOS is frequently referred to as *firmware*—software that has been permanently recorded onto one or more memory devices. When bugs are corrected, compatibility issues are resolved, and performance is tweaked in the BIOS code, it may be necessary for you to update the BIOS in your own server to the latest version available. Traditional BIOS was recorded on ROM chips that had to be physically replaced when the BIOS was updated. Today, virtually all PCs use flash memory (or flash BIOS), which allows the BIOS to be reprogrammed on the chip right in the system. In virtually all cases, you can download the updated BIOS file and flash loader utility from the motherboard maker's Web site. You'll need to set at least one motherboard jumper in order to permit the BIOS to be reprogrammed.

Travel Advisory

Please review the specific instructions distributed with the upgrade utility before attempting a BIOS upgrade.

Objective 9.05

Understanding the Processor

The processor (also known as the microprocessor, CPU, or central processing unit) is the single most important component in the PC. This powerful programmable logic device handles all of the program instructions (and much of the data) on the system—including Windows modules, applications, and data files. As a technician, it's important that you understand some of the important issues involved in processor technology and its implications on the desktop or server.

Knowing the Chip

It's usually helpful to understand some key physical characteristics of a processor chip. Issues related to the design and manufacture of the physical chip itself will have a direct impact on the chips' size, performance, power consumption, and heat generation. This will consequently have an influence on how the processor is employed in the system.

Circuit Size and Die Size

The *circuit size* (or feature size) relates to the level of miniaturization in a processor. To make more powerful processors, more transistors are needed. This means the transistors must continually be made smaller. Technology advancements in integrated circuit fabrication allow circuit sizes to shrink. It was once considered impossible to shrink the circuit size below 1 micron, but most recent processors use a 0.35-micron process, 0.25-micron processors are commonplace, and newer chips employ a 0.18-micron process. It is now thought that fabrication technology can eventually be shrunk to as low as 0.08 microns. The issue of *heat* is important here. Packing more transistors onto a chip causes additional heat generation, so each transistor must be made smaller. The size and layout of transistors will also have an effect on die size.

The *die size* of the processor refers to its physical surface area—the area of the chip—and it is typically measured in square millimeters (mm^2). Smaller die sizes allow designers to get more chips from a single wafer, so manufacturing costs are lower (and the resulting processor tends to be less expensive). Smaller die sizes also consume less power.

Processor Speed

The processor's speed is a function of several critical factors. Speed is largely related to design of the processor circuit itself. This dictates the internal timing requirements that limit the maximum speed the processor can handle. Speed is also influenced by manufacturing factors such as the circuit size and die size. In general, smaller chips can run faster because of smaller signal runs and lower power consumption. Finally, process quality (how well the manufacturer uses their equipment to make wafers) can vary, and this allows some chips to run faster than others even though they were produced with the same process (and even with the same wafer). Processors are tested and rated for their speed during the testing phase of the manufacturing process.

Processor Power and Management

Processors consume a relatively large amount of power. In order to reduce the PC's power demands and improve performance, the traditional +5-volt operating voltages of years past have given way to processors, support chips, and expansion devices that operate at far lower voltages. The first step in this evolution was to reduce the operating voltage level to +3.3 volts. This was apparent in early Pentium processors. Newer processors (such as the Pentium MMX and Pentium II/III) reduce voltage levels even more using a *dual voltage* (or *split rail*) design. A split rail processor uses two different voltages. The external (or I/O voltage) is usually +3.3 volts, and this ensures compatibility with the other chips on the motherboard. The internal (or core voltage) is somewhat lower (usually +2.5 to +2.9 volts, though +1.8 to +2.4 volt operation is appearing in the latest processors). The I/O voltage lets the processor "talk" to the motherboard, while the core voltage allows the processor to run cooler internally.

Because the power consumption of a CPU is related to its processing speed and internal activity, Intel eventually developed power management circuitry that enables processors to conserve power (and lengthen battery life in laptop systems). Power management was originally introduced with the Intel 486SL processor (an enhanced version of the 486DX processor), but power management features were soon standardized and incorporated into all Pentium and later processors. These power management features are referred to as *System Management Mode* (SMM). SMM circuitry is integrated into the physical processor chip, but operates independently to control the processor's power use based on its activity level. SMM allows the system to specify time intervals after which the CPU will be powered down partially or fully (aka throttled back), and also enables the suspend/resume feature that supports today's system *standby* and *hibernate* modes. SMM settings are normally controlled through the CMOS Setup.

Processor Cooling

The millions of transistors operating inside a processor all liberate a small amount of heat each time they switch on or off. When this switching action takes place hundreds of millions or times each second, heat (and its management) becomes a serious concern. Processors have a specified safe temperature range that represents their limits for normal operation. If the processor overheats, serious system problems will usually result. These will usually take the form of system reboots, lockups, or crashes. An overheated processor can also manifest itself through memory errors, application errors, disk problems, or a host of other things. A severely (or repeatedly) overheated processor can also be permanently damaged, though this rarely happens. These problems can be extremely difficult to diagnose because they often appear to implicate other parts of the system. For example, a system crash or lockup is often associated with a software bug or hardware conflict rather than an overheated CPU.

Processors are cooled by active heat sinks—that is, a fast fan mounted to a large metal heat sink with numerous fins. The heat sink pulls heat away from the processor, and the fan in turn cools the heat sink. Air warmed by the heat sink is vented from the case (this is the warm air you feel exhausting from the back of the case). The problem with active heat sinks is that they rely on the fan. If the fan fails, the processor can overheat in a very short time. To protect the processor from an accidental fan failure, many motherboards integrate tachometers that check the fan's rotational speed, and thermostats that measure the processor's case temperature. If the fan stops turning—or the processor's temperature climbs over a preset limit—a warning will indicate the fault and allow you to address the trouble before a crash or other system problem occurs.

Processor Packages

Raw chips (the small "dies") are not used directly—they are far too fragile and sensitive. Instead, the die is placed in a *package* that will protect the die and help it to dissipate heat. The form of that standardized package normally takes the form of a slotted or socketed device. Slot-type processors are normally classified as slot 1, slot 2, or slot A. Socket-type processors are usually denoted as socket 370 or socket A. You can see four slot 1 connectors (marked "H") for the SKA4 quad processor server motherboard in Figure 9-7.

Typical processor classifications are highlighted here:

- **Slot 1**   These single edge contact (SEC) packages are normally associated with Intel Pentium II and Pentium III processors.
- **Slot 2**   These are slightly larger SEC packages that are intended for Intel Pentium II/III Xeon processors, and are commonly found in server and multiprocessor platforms.
- **Slot A**   These are SEC packages (almost identical to slot 1) that are found with AMD Athlon processors.
- **Socket 370**   These are 370-pin processor packages that are used with many Intel Celeron processors.
- **Socket A**   These are 460-pin processor packages (sometimes called socket 460) that are used with late-model AMD Athlon (Thunderbird), and Duron processors.
- **Socket 423**   These are 423-pin processor packages used for Intel Pentium 4 devices.

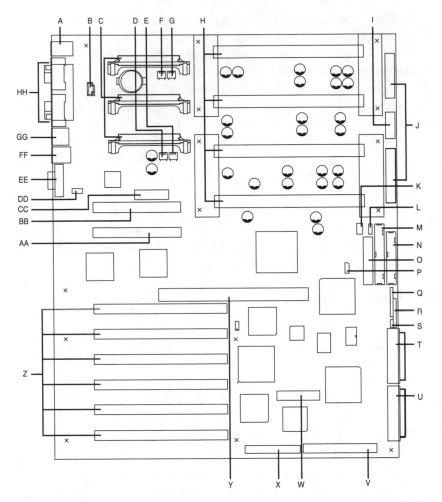

FIGURE 9-7   CPU locations on an Intel SKA4 quad server motherboard (Courtesy of Intel Corporation)

Bus Architecture and Notes

A processor executes program instructions (a.k.a. software) that allow your computer to perform useful functions for you. The effectiveness and efficiency with which a processor does this is a function of its *architecture*—a word used to describe the processor's internal design. Architecture describes the internal way that data is processed—one of the most important factors in determining overall performance.

The processor's external interface describes the way it communicates information with the memory, chipset, and other devices in the PC. The processor controls the entire PC, and uses dedicated control pathways (buses) to transfer information between itself and the system cache, memory, and other devices. These are referred to as the processor's *external interfaces*. The way that the processor "talks" to other parts of the system is an important factor in system performance.

Cache Bus (Backside Bus)

Conventional processors use the level 2 (or L2) cache on the motherboard, and connect it using the standard memory bus arrangement. To achieve better performance, many newer processors use a dedicated high-speed bus to connect the processor to the L2 cache. For example, the Pentium 200 runs on a 66MHz system bus, and the system cache runs at this speed as well, but the PentiumPro 200 has an integrated L2 cache that runs at full processor speed—200MHz. A special *backside* bus manages this high-speed data link between the processor and the L2 cache (entirely within the PentiumPro package because it contains both the processor and L2 cache). The Pentium II/III processor has a similar arrangement—it runs at half the processor speed, so a 266MHz Pentium II runs its cache bus at 133MHz (slower than the PentiumPro but much faster than the classic Pentium). Both of these buses are transactional (nonblocking), so they allow for concurrent requests to the system cache, and this greatly improves performance. Another advantage of this design is that having separate caches (and buses to run them) is a real plus for multiprocessing. Not only does each processor have its own cache, but each cache has an independent, noninterfering bus to service it.

Travel Advisory

Intel terms the use of a separate bus for the cache and memory "dual independent bus" (DIB) architecture.

Data Bus

The data bus is what most people refer to when talking about a bus—these are the signals that actually carry the data being transferred. The more data signals that are available, the more information that can be transferred simultaneously. Wider data buses generally result in higher performance, and the speed of the bus is dictated by the system clock speed. The bandwidth of the data bus is a function of the bus width (in bits) and its speed (in MHz). With processors today running so much faster than other parts of the system, increasing the speed at which data can be fed to the processor from the system usually has more of an impact on overall performance than speeding up the processor itself. For example, a Pentium 150 is not much faster than a Pentium 133—the P150 runs on a 60MHz bus, and the P133 runs on a 66MHz bus. Ten percent more clock speed on the system bus improves overall performance much more than a 10-percent faster processor.

Address Bus

The address bus is the set of signals that detail just where in memory the data is to be transferred to (or from). No actual data is carried on this bus. Instead, memory addresses control locations. The speed of the address bus is the same as the data bus. The width of the address bus controls the *addressability* of the processor (how much system memory the processor can read or write to). The wider the address bus, the more addresses can be accessed. Newer processors have both wider data and address buses. Processors usually can address far more physical memory than most people will ever use, and the system chipset or motherboard usually places much tighter restrictions on maximum system memory than the processor does. For example, a Pentium III can theoretically address 4GB of system memory, but most normal motherboards won't take even one quarter that amount.

Multiprocessing

Multiprocessing is the technique of running a system with more than one processor. The idea is that you can double system performance using two processors instead of one, quadruple performance with four processors instead of one, and so on. This doesn't always work that well in actual practice, but multiprocessing can result in improved performance under certain conditions. In order to employ multiprocessing effectively, the host computer must have all of the following elements in place:

- **Motherboard Support** You'll need a motherboard capable of handling multiple processors. This means additional sockets or slots for the extra CPUs, and a chipset capable of handling the multiprocessor configuration.
- **Processor Support** You'll need processors that are suitable for use in a multiprocessing system. Not all processors are suitable, and only some versions of the same processor are suitable. Be sure to check the motherboard's documentation for processor recommendations.

- **Operating System Support**   You'll also need an operating system that supports multiprocessing such as Windows NT/2000 or UNIX. Other operating systems such as Windows 98 do not support multiprocessing.

Multiprocessing is most effective when used with application software designed specifically for it. Multiprocessing is managed by the operating system, which allocates different tasks to be performed by the various processors in the system. Applications designed for multiprocessing use are said to be "threaded"— they are broken into smaller routines that can be run independently. This allows the operating system to let threads run on more than one processor simultaneously, and that is how multiprocessing results in improved performance. If the application isn't designed this way, it can't take advantage of multiple processors (though the operating system can still make use of the additional processors if you use more than one application at a time).

Multiprocessing can be said to be either asymmetric or symmetric. These terms indicate how the operating system divides tasks between the processors in the system. *Asymmetric* multiprocessing designates some processors to perform system tasks only, and others to run applications only. This rigid design results in poor performance during times when the computer needs to run more system tasks than user tasks (or vice versa). *Symmetric* multiprocessing (SMP) allows *either* system or user tasks to run on any processor. It's a more flexible approach, and therefore offers better performance. SMP is what most multiprocessing PC motherboards use.

For a processor to support multiprocessing, it must support a multiprocessing protocol that dictates the way that the processors and chipset talk to each other in order to implement SMP. Intel processors typically use an SMP protocol called APIC, and Intel chipsets that support multiprocessing are designed to work with these chips. APIC is a proprietary Intel standard, so even though AMD and Cyrix can make Intel-compatible processors, they cannot make them work in SMP configurations. AMD and Cyrix implement their own SMP standard called OpenPIC.

Processor Modes

Processors are capable of operating in several different modes. The term *mode* refers to the way(s) in which a processor creates (and supports) an operating environment for itself. The processor mode controls how the processor sees and manages the system memory and the tasks that use it. Three different modes of operation have evolved for the PC: the real mode, the protected mode, and the virtual real mode. You should have a basic understanding of these three modes.

Real Mode

The original IBM PC could only address 1MB of RAM. The decisions made in those early days have carried forward, and in each new processor, the processor had to support a mode that would be compatible with the original Intel 8088 chip—this is called *real mode*. When a processor is running in real mode, it has the advantage of speed, but it otherwise accesses memory with the same restrictions of the original 8088: an addressable RAM limit of 1MB and memory access that doesn't take advantage of the 32-bit processing found in modern CPUs. All processors can support the real mode—in fact, the computer normally starts up in real (DOS) mode. Real mode is used by DOS and standard DOS applications.

Protected Mode

Starting with the IBM AT, a new processor *protected mode* was introduced. This is a much more powerful mode of operation than real mode, and is used in all modern multitasking operating systems. The protected mode has numerous advantages:

- The protected mode offers full access to all of the system's memory (there is no 1MB limit in protected mode).
- The protected mode has the ability to multitask, meaning that the operating system can manage the execution of multiple programs simultaneously.
- The protected mode offers support for virtual memory, which allows the system to use the hard disk to emulate additional system RAM when needed.
- The protected mode also offers faster (32-bit) access to memory, and faster 32-bit drivers to handle I/O transfers.

Each running program has its own assigned memory locations, which are protected from conflicting with other programs. If a program tries to use a memory address that it isn't allowed to, a protection fault is generated. All of the major operating systems today use protected mode, including Windows 9x/ME, Windows NT/2000, OS/2, and Linux. Even DOS (which normally runs in real mode) can access protected mode memory using DPMI (DOS Protected Mode Interface), used by DOS games to break the 640KB DOS conventional memory barrier. The 386 (and later) processors can switch on the fly from real to protected mode, and vice versa. Protected mode is also sometimes called 386 enhanced mode, since it became mainstream with that family of processors.

Virtual Real Mode

The third mode of processor operation is actually an enhancement of the protected mode. Protected mode is normally used to run graphical multitasking operating systems such as the various types of Windows. There is sometimes a need to run DOS programs under Windows, but DOS programs need to be run in real mode—not protected mode. *Virtual real mode* was created to solve this problem. It emulates the real mode from within the protected mode and allows DOS programs to run. A protected mode operating system such as Windows can actually create multiple virtual real mode machines, each of which appear to the software running them as if they are the only software running on the machine. Each virtual machine gets its own 1MB address space, an image of the real hardware BIOS routines, and so on. Virtual real mode is what is used when you use a DOS window or run a DOS game in Windows 95/98. When you start a DOS application, Windows creates a virtual DOS machine for it to run under.

Architectural Performance Features

The past several years have seen an explosion of technologies and techniques intended to wring more performance out of a processor. Designers have invested tremendous effort to develop the improvements that we take for granted each time we boot the system. This part of the chapter describes some of the performance-enhancing features found in a modern microprocessor:

- **Superscalar Architecture**   Program instructions are processed through circuits called *execution units*. Superscalar architecture refers to the use of multiple execution units to allow the CPU to process more than one instruction simultaneously. This is a form of multiprocessing within the CPU itself, since multiple processing chores are taking place at the same time. Most modern processors are superscalar at one level or another.
- **Superpipelining**   Instructions are processed in a pipeline, with each step in the pipeline performing a certain amount of work on the instruction. By making the pipeline longer (with more stages), each stage performs less work, and the processor can be scaled to a higher clock frequency. This is known as *superpipelining*, and is generally regarded as an improvement over regular pipelining.

- **Speculative Execution**   Some CPUs have the ability to execute multiple instructions at once. In some cases, not all of the results of the execution will be used because changes in the program flow may mean that the given instruction should never have been executed in the first place. This often occurs in the vicinity of program branches—where a condition is tested and the program path is altered depending on the results. Branches represent a real problem for pipelining, because you can't always be sure that instructions will go in a linear sequence. A less sophisticated processor may stall the pipeline until the results are known, and this can hurt performance. More advanced processors will *speculatively execute* the next instruction anyway. The hope is that the CPU will be able to use the results if the branch goes the way it thinks it will.

- **Branch Prediction**   Even more advanced processors combine this with *branch prediction*, where the processor can actually predict (with fairly good accuracy) which way the branch will go based on past history. Branch prediction improves the handling of branches by making use of a special small cache called the *branch target buffer* or *BTB*. Whenever the processor executes a branch, it stores information about it in this area. When the processor next encounters the same branch, it is able to make an informed guess about which way the branch is likely to result. This helps keep the pipeline flowing and improves performance.

- **Out-of-Order Execution**   Processors that use multiple execution units can actually complete the processing of program instructions in the wrong order. For example, instruction 2 can be executed before instruction 1 has finished. This versatility improves performance since it allows execution with less waiting time. The results of the execution are reassembled in the correct order to ensure that the program runs correctly. This is normally done by the retirement unit on translating processors.

- **Register Renaming and Write Buffers**   *Register renaming* is a technique used to support multiple execution paths without conflicts between different execution units trying to use the same registers. Instead of just one set of registers being used, multiple sets are put into the processor. This allows different execution units to work simultaneously without unnecessary stalls in the pipeline. Write buffers are used to hold the results of instruction execution until they can be written back to registers or memory locations. More write buffers allow more instructions to be executed without stalling the pipelines.

Understanding Bus Architectures

Objective 9.06

Inside the PC, data is passed from device to device over groups of related signal paths, called a *bus*. CPUs, memory, chipsets, drive interfaces, and expansion cards are just some of the important devices that use buses. There are numerous levels of buses within the PC—a hierarchy where each higher level is further removed from the processor, but each are connected to integrate various parts of the PC. Each higher level is also generally slower than the one below it. The four general bus levels are shown here:

- **Processor Bus**   This is the fastest, lowest-level bus that the motherboard uses to manage the processor-to-memory interface (i.e. operating at 100MHz, 133MHz, or 150MHz). Some motherboard block diagrams may illustrate this as the "memory bus."
- **Cache Bus**   Many more advanced PCs (such as Pentium Pro, and Pentium II/III systems) employ a dedicated bus for accessing the system cache. This is sometimes called a "backside bus." Some current motherboards and chipsets integrate the cache bus with the standard memory bus.
- **Local I/O Bus**   This is a medium-speed I/O bus used for connecting performance-critical peripheral devices to the system memory, chipset, and processor. For example, video cards, disk controllers, and NIC adapters generally use a bus of this sort. The two most common local I/O buses are the 66MHz AGP bus and the 33MHz PCI bus.
- **Standard I/O Bus**   The slowest bus architectures are 8.3MHz ISA and 10MHz EISA buses, and these are ideal for interfacing slower peripheral devices (i.e., mice, modems, regular sound cards, or low-speed network cards) to the PC.

Expansion cards use standardized I/O bus slots (i.e., local or standard) that allow you to plug a wide variety of devices (i.e., video cards or NIC adapters) into the system or server. This part of the chapter outlines the concepts of expansion buses, and focuses on the two most popular bus architectures: PCI and AGP.

Bus Signals

Every bus is comprised of two distinct parts: the data bus and the address bus. The *data bus* is the set of signal lines that actually carry the data being transferred between the expansion device and system—the data bus is what most people refer to when talking about a bus. The *address bus* is the set of signal lines that indicate where (in memory) the data is to be transferred to or from. There are also a number of control lines (a.k.a. the control bus) that control how the bus functions, and allow devices to signal the system when data is available.

Bus width is another important consideration. Remember that a bus is a channel over which information flows—the wider the bus, the more information that can flow across the channel. The ISA bus used today is 16 bits wide. The other I/O buses (such as PCI and AGP) are 32 bits wide. By comparison, the memory and processor buses on Pentium PCs (and later) are 64 bits wide.

> ### Exam Tip
>
> The address bus width can be specified independently of the data bus width. The width of the address bus indicates the number of different memory locations that can be accessed.

Bus Speed and Bandwidth

The *speed* of the bus indicates how many bits of information can be sent across each wire each second. Most traditional buses transmit one bit of data per data line every clock cycle. However, newer high-performance buses like AGP may actually move two or four bits of data per clock cycle—doubling (even quadrupling) performance. On the other hand, older buses like ISA may take two clock cycles to move one bit—halving the effective performance. By comparison, *bandwidth* (also called throughput) refers to the total amount of data that can theoretically be transferred on the bus in a given unit of time (i.e., MB/s).

Bus Bridges

When a system has multiple buses, circuitry must be provided on the motherboard to connect the buses and allow devices on one bus to talk to devices on the other. This device is called a *bridge*. The most commonly found bridge is the PCI-ISA bridge—part of the motherboard's chipset. The PCI bus also has a bridge to the processor bus. You can see these devices under System Devices in the Device Manager in Windows 98/SE (see Figure 9-8).

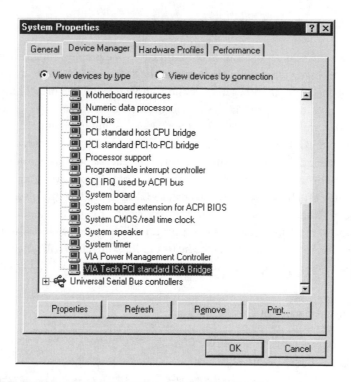

FIGURE 9-8   Checking the PCI-ISA bridge in Windows

Bus Mastering

One of the problems with traditional PC architectures is that the processor was forced to manage all of the data transfers taking place in the system. As device bandwidth increased, the processor was forced to devote a greater portion of its time to routine data transfer tasks. With the introduction of IBM's PS/2 system (and its MicroChannel bus), it became possible for individual devices to take control of the bus and transfer data themselves. This is called *bus mastering* (or first-party DMA), and devices that can do this are called *bus masters*. Ideally, bus mastering leaves the processor free to do other work simultaneously. The motherboard's chipset arbitrates all requests to assume control of the bus. Most current bus mastering in the PC takes place across devices on the PCI bus.

PCI Bus Basics

By the late 1980s, the proliferation of 32-bit CPUs and graphics-intensive operating systems made it painfully obvious that the 8.33MHz ISA bus was becoming obsolete. The PC industry began to develop alternative architectures for improved performance. In mid-1992, Intel Corporation and a comprehensive consortium of manufacturers introduced the Peripheral Component Interconnect (PCI) bus. The 188-pin PCI bus looked to the future of CPUs (and PCs in general) by providing a bus architecture that also supports peripherals such as hard drive controllers, network adapters, and so on. PCI is a 33MHz fixed-frequency bus architecture capable of transferring data at 132MB/s—a great improvement over the anemic transfer rates of a 16-bit ISA bus. Another key advantage of the PCI bus is that it has automatic configuration capabilities for switchless/jumperless peripherals. Autoconfiguration (the heart of Plug-and-Play) will take care of all addresses, interrupt requests, and DMA assignments used by a PCI peripheral.

Travel Advisory

While the 32-bit implementation of PCI is the most common, a 64-bit version of PCI is available. Both 32- and 64-bit cards can be installed in either a 64- or 32-bit slot. When a 64-bit card is installed in a 32-bit slot, the extra pins just overhang without plugging into anything.

The PCI bus supports *linear bursts*, which is a method of transferring data that ensures the bus is continually filled with data. The peripheral devices expect to receive data from the system main memory in a linear address order. This means that large amounts of data are read from or written to a single address, which is then incremented for the next byte in the stream. The linear burst is one of the unique aspects of the PCI bus since it will perform both burst reads and burst writes. In short, it will transfer data on the bus *every* clock cycle. This doubles the PCI throughput compared to buses without linear burst capabilities.

Exam Tip

While the 33MHz implementation of PCI is the most common, a 66MHz version of PCI is available.

The devices designed to support PCI have low *access latency*, reducing the time required for a peripheral to be granted control of the bus after requesting access. For example, an Ethernet controller card connected to a LAN has large data files from the network coming into its buffer. Waiting for access to the bus, the Ethernet is unable to transfer the data to the CPU quickly enough to avoid a buffer overflow—forcing it to temporarily store the file's contents in extra RAM. Because PCI-compliant devices support faster access times, the Ethernet card can promptly send data to the CPU.

The PCI bus supports bus mastering, which allows one of a number of intelligent peripherals to take control of the bus in order to accelerate a high-throughput, high-priority task. PCI architecture also supports *concurrency*—a technique that ensures the microprocessor operates simultaneously with these masters, instead of waiting for them. As one example, concurrency allows the CPU to perform floating-point calculations on a spreadsheet while an Ethernet card and the LAN have control of the bus. Finally, PCI was developed as a dual-voltage architecture. Normally, the bus is a +5Vdc system like other buses. However, the bus can also operate in a +3.3Vdc (low-voltage) mode.

PCI Interrupts and Bus Mastering

The PCI bus uses its own internal interrupt system for dealing with requests from the cards on the bus. These interrupts are denoted #A, #B, #C, and #D (though they are sometimes numbered #1 through #4) to avoid confusion with the normal numbered system IRQs. These interrupt levels are not generally seen by the user except in the PCI Configuration menu of your CMOS Setup where they can be used to control how PCI cards operate. These PCI interrupts are then mapped to regular interrupts (normally IRQ9 through IRQ12). The PCI slots in most systems can be mapped to four regular IRQs at the most. In systems that have more than four PCI slots (or that have four slots and a USB controller), two or more of the PCI devices share an IRQ.

If you're using Windows 98 or later, you may see additional entries for your PCI devices in the Device Manager—each device may have an additional entry labeled "IRQ Holder for PCI IRQ Steering" (see Figure 9-9). PCI steering is actually a feature that is part of the Plug-and-Play system, and enables the IRQ used for PCI devices to be controlled by the operating system in order to avoid resource problems. Having an IRQ holder listed in addition to another device in the IRQ list does *not* mean you have a resource conflict.

The PCI bus supports bus mastering, so devices on the PCI bus can take control of the bus and perform data transfers directly without the direct intervention

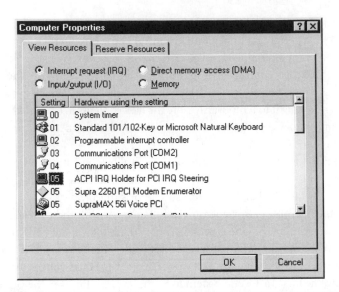

FIGURE 9-9　　IRQ holders for PCI interrupt steering

of the system processor. The PCI bus is the first bus to make bus mastering commonplace—probably because for the first time there are operating systems and chipsets that are really capable of taking advantage of it. PCI allows bus mastering of multiple devices on the bus simultaneously, with the motherboard's chipset arbitration circuitry working to ensure that no device on the bus (including the processor) locks out any other device. At the same time, it allows any given device to use the full bus throughput if no other device needs to transfer data.

The PCI bus also allows you to set up compatible IDE/ATA hard disk drives to be bus masters. With all of the necessary elements in place, PCI IDE bus mastering can increase performance over the use of traditional PIO (programmed I/O) data transfer modes (which are the default means used by IDE/ATA hard disks to transfer data). When PCI IDE bus mastering is enabled, IDE/ATA devices use DMA modes to transfer data instead of PIO. PCI IDE bus mastering requires all of the following in order to function:

- **Bus-Mastering–Capable System Hardware**　This includes the motherboard, chipset, bus, and BIOS. Virtually all current motherboards using a Pentium II/III or AMD Athlon chipset will support bus-mastering IDE.
- **Bus-Mastering Hard Disk**　This means that the drive must be capable of at least multiword DMA mode 2 data transfers. Essentially, all Ultra

ATA hard disks (i.e., UDMA/33, UDMA/66, and UDMA/100) support bus mastering.

- **32-bit Multitasking Operating System**   This means usually Windows NT/2000, Windows 95/98/ME, or Linux.
- **Bus-Mastering Drivers**   A special driver must be provided to the operating system to enable the system's bus-mastering support.

Exam Tip

It's important to remember that bus mastering will not be a significant performance benefit under DOS and nonmultitasking operating systems (such as Windows 95/98).

AGP Bus Basics

The PC's video system continues to improve in color depth and resolutions. Today's video information generates a tremendous amount of data. Not only does this data require memory, but it also needs a lot of bandwidth to pass that data to the video card. The *Accelerated Graphics Port* (AGP) bus opens a freeway for graphics information that is especially well suited for 3D and visualization applications. For example, the fast floating-point performance of today's CPUs can smooth the drawing of 3D meshes and animation effects, and adds depth to a 3D scene. The next step is to add lifelike realism. To do this, the PC must render a 3D image by adding textures, alpha-blended transparencies, texture mapping, lighting, and other effects. AGP technology accelerates graphics performance by providing a dedicated high-speed bus for the movement of large blocks of 3D texture data between the PC's graphics controller and system memory. In practice, AGP enables a hardware-accelerated graphics controller to execute texture maps directly from system RAM (instead of caching them in the relatively limited local video memory). It also helps speed the flow of decoded video from the CPU to the graphics controller. In addition, off-loading this tremendous data overhead from the PCI bus leaves PCI free to handle drive data transfers and other controllers.

High bandwidth is the key to AGP's power. The 32-bit 66MHz AGP interface is positioned between the PC's chipset and graphics controller. This architecture significantly increases the bandwidth available to a graphics accelerator. In its basic form, AGP offers a bandwidth of 266MB/s (twice the bandwidth of PCI). This is referred to as AGP 1X. With advanced data-handling techniques, 2 bytes can be passed on every AGP clock for a bandwidth of 532MB/s (known as AGP 2X). Further refinements to AGP data handling and the introduction of new chipsets allow 4 bytes to be passed on every AGP clock for a bandwidth of more than 1GB/s (called AGP 4X). The 32-bit AGP bus gets its roots in the PCI local bus specification, but makes some significant improvements and additions intended to optimize AGP for high-performance 3D graphics. The most notable difference is the clock speed. PCI uses a fixed 33MHz bus, but AGP ups the clock speed to 66MHz. There are other major differences, including

- Deeply pipelined memory read and write operations—this hides memory access latency.
- Demultiplexing of address and data on the bus, allowing almost 100-percent bus efficiency.
- New ac timing for the 3.3V electrical specification that provides for one (AGP 1X) or two (AGP 2X) data transfers per 66MHz clock cycle, allowing for real data throughput in excess of 500MB/s.
- A new low-voltage electrical specification that allows four (AGP 4X) data transfers per 66MHz clock cycle, providing real data throughput of over 1GB/s.
- The bus slot defined for AGP uses a new connector body (for electrical signaling reasons) that is *not* compatible with the PCI connector, so PCI and AGP boards are *not* mechanically interchangeable.

There are a number of different requirements in order to allow a system to take advantage of AGP:

- **AGP Video Card**   You'll need a suitable video adapter for the AGP slot.
- **Motherboard with AGP Chipset**   The motherboard must be fully compliant with AGP including a chipset, bus slot, and BIOS.
- **Operating System Support**   Plan on using Windows 98 or later for full AGP support.
- **AGP Driver Support**   You'll need drivers to enable the AGP features of the motherboard chipset, as well as video drivers for the AGP card.

I²O Basics

Every aspect of computer technology is feeling the demand for more processing power and higher I/O bandwidth. Unfortunately, I/O technology has not kept pace with processor speed, and a bottleneck inevitably occurs—restricting the flow of data. As attempts are made to increase the I/O bandwidth, we increase the number of interrupts sent to the host processor. An interrupt occurs whenever a disk subsystem, a network interface card, or any other real-world I/O device needs attention. In any given operation, an I/O device may interrupt the processor many times. While the processors are startlingly fast at straight computational functions, they were not designed to handle interrupt duties. The answer is to allow the processor to do what it does best—manage the applications, and offload the I/O functions by implementing *Intelligent I/O* (known as I^2O) processing.

Intelligent I/O most commonly refers to any server system that uses a processing element as part of the I/O subsystem. The I/O processor performs tasks that would normally be executed by the system processor, reducing the host processor overhead. By giving the processor some relief, overall system response time and I/O throughput are increased. I^2O allows a specialized I/O processor to offload the tasks from the system processor. I^2O allows requests to come in from one PCI device, destined for another PCI device, and the request never has to go through the system processor. The I^2O processor recognizes these requests and handles them locally. It also allows requests to queue up at the I^2O processor while the system processor is working on other important tasks.

Since the initial implementation of intelligent subsystems, vendors have built servers with increasingly high bandwidth I/O. But as demand has increased, software developers have struggled to keep up with the multiple hardware drivers that interface to the various operating systems. The need arose for a hardware standard that would work across diverse operating systems and revisions. In 1996, Intel and other industry leaders formed a special interest group to address the need for a standard interface for intelligent I/O systems. The resulting standard was dubbed I^2O. Peripheral vendors are then spared the task of writing drivers for multiple operating systems. Peripheral vendors only need to write one driver to the I^2O architecture, and the operating system will work with the I^2O subsystem. The I^2O architecture also eases the task of building peripherals by simplifying the demands on the I/O cards—much of the processing that was previously done on the card can now be done by the I^2O processor.

I^2O drivers are divided into two modules: the OS services module (OSM), and the hardware device module (HDM). The OSM interfaces with the operating system, and the HDM interfaces with the hardware device. The two modules exchange information through a two-layer communication system in which a message layer sets up a communication session while a transport layer defines how information will be shared. The modules communicate without knowledge of underlying bus architectures or topologies.

Objective 9.07

Understanding Server Memory

System memory (called RAM) holds the program code and data that is processed by the server's CPU(s)—and it is this intimate relationship between memory and the CPU that forms the basis of computer performance. Larger and faster CPUs are constantly being introduced, and more complex software is regularly developed to take advantage of that processing power. In turn, the more complex software demands larger amounts of faster memory. Networks and network servers must provide files and applications to a number of simultaneous users (often a *large* number of users), so servers are particularly memory hungry. These demands have resulted in a proliferation of memory types that go far beyond the simple, traditional DRAM. Pipeline-burst cache, fast synchronous DRAM (SDRAM), and other exotic memory types such as Rambus DRAM (RDRAM) now compete for the attention of PC technicians. These new forms of memory also present some new problems.

Memory Speed

In terms of memory, cost cutting typically involves using cheaper (slower) memory devices. Unfortunately, when slower memory is used, the CPU must be made to wait until memory can catch up. All memory is rated in terms of speed—specifically, *access time*. Access time is the delay between the time data in memory is successfully addressed, to the point at which the data has been successfully delivered to the data bus. For traditional PC memory, access time is measured in nanoseconds (ns), and current memory offers access times of 50–60ns—70ns memory is extremely common in older i486 systems. SDRAM is an exception to this rule, and is typically rated in terms of *cycle time* rather than access time. Cycle time is the minimum amount of time needed between accesses. Cycle time for SDRAM averages around 12ns (nanoseconds), with 10ns, 8ns (and faster) SDRAM devices available.

It is almost always possible to use *faster* memory than the manufacturer recommends. The system should continue to operate normally, but there's rarely ever a performance benefit. As you'll see in the following sections, memory and architectures are typically tailored for specific performance. Using memory that is faster should not hurt the memory, or impair system performance, but it costs more and will not produce a noticeable performance improvement—simply because the system is not equipped to employ the faster memory to its best advantage. The only time such a tactic would be advised is when your current system is almost obsolete, and you would want the new memory to be usable on a new, faster motherboard if you choose to upgrade the motherboard later on.

Megabytes and Memory Layout

Now is a good time to explain the idea of bytes and megabytes. Very simply, a *byte* is 8 bits (binary 1s and 0s), and a *megabyte* is one million of those bytes (1,048,576 bytes to be exact, but manufacturers often round down to the nearest million or so). The idea of megabytes (MB) is important when measuring memory in your PC. For example, if a SIMM is laid out as 1M by 8 bits, it has 1MB. If the SIMM is laid out as 4M by 8 bits, it has 4MB. Unfortunately, memory has not been laid out as 8 bits since the IBM XT. More practical memory layouts involve 32-bit memory (for 486 and OverDrive processors), or 64-bit memory (for Pentium II/III processors). When memory is "wider" than 1 byte, it is still measured in MB. For example, a 1M × 32-bit (4 bytes) SIMM would be 4MB (that is, the *capacity* of the device is 4MB), while a 4M × 32-bit SIMM would be 16MB. So when you go shopping for an 8MB 72-pin SIMM, chances are you're getting a 2M × 32-bit memory module.

Presence Detect

Another feature of modern memory devices is a series of physical signals known as the *Presence Detect* (PD) lines. By setting the appropriate conditions of the PD signals, it is possible for a computer to immediately recognize the characteristics of the installed memory devices and configure itself accordingly. Presence Detect lines typically specify three operating characteristics of memory: size, device layout, and speed. Many memory devices today use serial EEPROM chips to pass *Serial Presence Detect* (SPD) data to the motherboard at start time.

Memory Refresh

The electrical signals placed in each RAM storage cell must be replenished (or refreshed) periodically every few milliseconds. Without refresh, RAM data will be lost (this is why RAM is referred to as "volatile" memory). In principle, refresh requires that each storage cell be read and rewritten to the memory array. This is typically accomplished by reading and rewriting an entire row of the array at one time. Each row of bits is sequentially read into a sense/refresh amplifier (part of the memory chip), which basically recharges the appropriate storage capacitors, then rewrites each row bit to the array. In actual operation, a row of bits is automatically refreshed whenever an array row is selected—the entire memory array can be refreshed by reading each row in the array every few milliseconds.

The key to refresh is in the *way* RAM is addressed. Unlike other memory chips that supply all address signals to a chip simultaneously, RAM is addressed in a two-step sequence. The overall address is separated into a row (low) address and a column (high) address. Row address bits are placed on the DRAM address bus first, and the *-Row Address Select* (-RAS) line is pulsed logic 0 to multiplex the bits into the chip's address decoding circuitry. The low portion of the address activates an entire array row and causes each bit in the row to be sensed and refreshed. Logic 0s remain logic 0s, and logic 1s are recharged to their full value.

Column address bits are then placed on the DRAM address bus, and the *-Column Address Select* (-CAS) is pulsed to logic 0. The column portion of the address selects the appropriate bits within the chosen row. If a read operation is taking place, the selected bits pass through the data buffer to the data bus. During a write operation, the read/write line must be logic 0, and valid data must be available to the chip before -CAS is strobed. New data bits are then placed in their corresponding locations in the memory array.

Even if the chip is not being accessed for reading or writing, the memory must *still* be refreshed to ensure data integrity. Fortunately, refresh can be accomplished by interrupting the microprocessor to run a refresh routine that simply steps through every row address in sequence (column addresses need not be selected for simple refresh). This *row-only* (or RAS only) refresh technique speeds the refresh process. Although refreshing the RAM every few milliseconds may seem like a constant aggravation, the computer can execute quite a few instructions before being interrupted for refresh. Refresh operations are generally handled by the chipset on your motherboard. Often, memory problems (especially parity errors) that cannot be resolved by replacing a memory module can be traced to a refresh fault on the motherboard.

Memory Types

In order for a computer to work, the CPU must take program instructions and exchange data directly with memory. As a consequence, memory must keep pace with the CPU (or make the CPU wait for it to catch up). Now that processors are so incredibly fast—and getting faster every few months—traditional memory architectures are being replaced by specialized memory devices that have been tailored to serve specific functions in the PC. As you upgrade and repair various systems, you will undoubtedly encounter some of the memory designations explained below (listed alphabetically).

DDR SDRAM

One limitation of SDRAM is that the theoretical limitation of the design is 125MHz (though technology advances may allow up to 133MHz and 150MHz operation), but bus speeds will need to increase well beyond that in order for memory bandwidth to keep up with future processors. There are several competing standards on the horizon, but most of them require special pinouts, smaller bus widths, or other design considerations. First introduced in 2000, Double Data Rate SDRAM (DDR SDRAM) allows output operations to occur on both the rising and falling edge of the system clock. Currently, only the rising edge signals an event to occur, so the DDR SDRAM design can effectively double the speed of operation up to at least 200MHz or 266MHz (a prime candidate for AMD Athlon motherboards). There are already numerous AMD-based chipsets that support DDR SDRAM, and even Intel Pentium 4 chipsets will be supporting DDR SDRAM in the future.

PC100/PC133 SDRAM

When Intel decided to officially implement a 100MHz system bus speed, they understood that most of the early SDRAM modules available at that time would not operate properly above 83MHz. In order to support 100MHz bus speeds, Intel introduced the PC100 specification as a guideline to manufacturers for building modules that would function properly on their 100MHz chipsets (i.e., the 440BX). With the PC100 specification, Intel laid out a number of guidelines for trace lengths, trace widths and spacing, the number of printed circuit layers, EEPROM programming specs, and so on.

There is still quite a bit of confusion regarding what a "true" PC100 module actually consists of. While the chip speed rating is used most often to determine the overall performance of the chip, a number of other timings are very important: *tRCD* (RAS to CAS delay), *tRP* (RAS precharge time), and *CAS latency* all play a role in determining the fastest bus speed the module will operate on to still achieve a 4-1-1-1 timing. PC100 SDRAM on a 100MHz (or faster) system bus will provide a performance boost for Socket 7 systems of between 10 percent and 15 percent, since the L2 cache is running at system bus speed. Pentium II/III systems will not see as big a boost because the L2 cache is running at half the processor speed (with the exception of the cacheless Celeron chips, of course). Pentium 4 and Athlon processors require the faster PC133 SDRAM for a 133MHz mother-board, or 200/266MHz DDR SDRAM.

RDRAM (Rambus DRAM)

Most of the memory alternatives so far have been variations of the same basic DRAM architecture. Rambus, Inc. (joint developers of EDRAM) has developed a relatively new memory architecture called the Rambus channel. A CPU or specialized controller chip is used as the "master" device, and the RDRAMs are used as "slave" devices. Blocks of data are then sent back and forth across the Rambus channel. With a 400MHz clock, the Rambus channel can transfer data on both edges of the clock—this results in 16-bit data transfer rates approaching 800MHz (called PC800 RDRAM), and offers 1.6GB/s of data bandwidth. Earlier implementations of RDRAM used a 300MHz clock, resulting in PC600 RDRAM. By late 2000, Intel had embraced Rambus completely, and the current generation of 850 chipset (for the Pentium 4 processor) supports Rambus exclusively.

SDRAM (Synchronous or Synchronized DRAM)

Typical memory can only transfer data during certain portions of a clock cycle. Introduced in late 1996, the SDRAM modifies memory operation so that outputs can be valid at *any* point in the clock cycle. By itself, this is not really significant, but SDRAM also provides a "pipeline burst" mode that allows a second access to begin before the current access is complete. This "continuous" memory access offers effective access speeds as fast as 10ns, and can transfer data at up to 100MB/s. SDRAM is now quite popular on current motherboard designs and is supported by the Intel VX (and later) chipsets, as well as VIA 580VP, 590VP, and 680VP (and later) chipsets. Like BEDO, SDRAM can transfer data in a 5-1-1-1 pattern, but it can support motherboard speeds up to 100MHz and 133MHz that are so vital for Pentium II/III systems (see "PC100/PC133 SDRAM" earlier in this chapter).

Synchronous Graphics RAM (SGRAM)

SGRAM is a video-specific extension of SDRAM that includes graphics-optimized read/write features. SGRAM also allows data to be retrieved and modified in blocks instead of individually—this reduces the number of reads and writes that memory must perform, and increases the performance of the graphics controller by making the read/write process more efficient.

SRAM (Static Random Access Memory)

The SRAM is also a classical memory design that is even older than DRAM. SRAM does not require regular refresh operations, and can be made to operate at access speeds that are much faster than DRAM. However, SRAM uses six transistors or more to hold a single bit. This reduces the density of SRAM and increases its power demands (which is why SRAM was never adopted for general PC use in the first place). Still, the high speed of SRAM has earned it a place as the PC's L2 (or external) cache. You'll probably encounter three types of SRAM cache schemes: Asynchronous, Synchronous Burst, and Pipeline Burst.

Asynchronous Static RAM (Async SRAM or ASRAM) is the "traditional" form of L2 cache introduced with i386 systems. There's really nothing too special about ASRAM except that its contents can be accessed much faster (20ns, 15ns, or 12ns) than DRAM. ASRAM does not have enough performance to be accessed synchronously, and has long since been replaced by better types of cache. *Synchronous Burst Static RAM* (Sync SRAM or SBSRAM) is largely regarded as the best type of L2 cache for intermediate speed motherboards (~ 60–66MHz). With access times of 8.5ns and 12ns, the SBSRAM can provide synchronous bursts of cache information in 2-1-1-1 cycles (i.e., two clock cycles for the first access, then one cycle per access—in time with the CPU clock). However, as motherboards pass 66MHz (i.e., 75MHz and 83MHz designs), SBSRAM loses its advantage to Pipelined Burst SRAM. *Pipelined Burst Static RAM* (PB SRAM) is the fastest form of high-performance cache now available for 75MHz+ motherboards (with speeds of about 4.5ns to 8ns). PBSRAM requires an extra clock cycle for "lead off," but then can sync with the motherboard clock (with timing such as 3-1-1-1) across a wide range of motherboard frequencies.

Memory Modules

Memory has always pushed the envelope of integrated circuit design. This trend has given us tremendous amounts of memory in very small chips, but it also has kept memory relatively expensive. Traditional PCs often included a small amount of RAM on the motherboard, and provided slots for additional RAM modules. Today, virtually every motherboard relies on standardized memory modules for all system memory. You'll find three essential types of memory modules—SIMMs, DIMMs, and RIMMs—as detailed here.

SIMMs and DIMMs

By the time 386 systems took hold in the PC industry, proprietary memory modules had been largely abandoned in favor of the standard 30-pin memory module. A SIMM (single inline memory module) is light, small, and contains a relatively large block of memory, but perhaps the greatest advantage of a SIMM is *standardization*—using a standard pin layout, a SIMM from one PC could be physically installed into almost any other PC. The 30-pin SIMM provides eight data bits, and generally holds up to 4MB of RAM. The 30-pin SIMM proved its worth in 386 and early 486 systems, but fell short when providing more memory to later-model PCs. The slightly larger 72-pin SIMM replaced the 30-pin SIMM version by providing 32 data bits, and may hold up to 32MB (or more).

You'll also find such structures referred to as DIMMs (or dual inline memory modules). DIMMs appear virtually identical to SIMMs (see Figure 9-10), but they are physically *larger*. And where each electrical contact on the SIMM is tied together between the front and back, the DIMM keeps front and back contacts

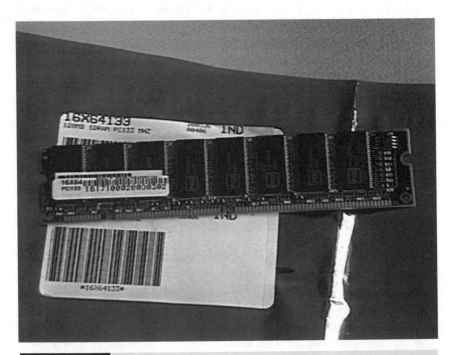

FIGURE 9-10   A basic DIMM

separate—effectively doubling the number of contacts available on the device. For example, if you look at a 72-pin SIMM, you will see 72 electrical contacts on both sides of the device (144 contacts total), but these are tied together, so there are only 72 signals (even with 144 contacts). On the other hand, a DIMM keeps the front and back contacts electrically *separate* (and usually adds some additional pins to keep SIMMs and DIMMs from accidentally being mixed). Today, virtually all DIMM versions provide 168 pins (84 pins on each side). DIMMs first appeared in high-end 64-bit data bus PCs (such as Pentium, PentiumPro, and PowerPC RISC workstations). As PCs have continued to advance, DIMMs have completely replaced SIMMs as the preferred memory expansion device, and the typical DIMM today can provide 128MB or 256MB of very fast memory (such as PC133 SDRAM). As a result, a server can be populated with 512MB of RAM or more with just a *few* memory modules.

Finally, you may see SIMMs and DIMMs referred to as "composite" or "non-composite" modules. These terms are used infrequently to describe the technology level of the memory module. For example, a *composite* module uses older, lower-density memory, so more chips are required to achieve the required storage capacity. Conversely, a *noncomposite* module uses newer memory technology, so fewer chips are needed to reach the same storage capacity. In other words, if you encounter a high-density SIMM with only a few memory chips on it, chances are that the SIMM is noncomposite.

RIMMs

RDRAM is used on RIMMs (Rambus inline memory modules). RIMMs appear almost identical to DIMMs, but are slightly bigger (with several keys between the metal contact fingers). Early RIMM implementations used 168 pins, but the 600MHz, 711MHz, and 800MHz (PC800) RIMMs available today use 184 pins. Figure 9-11 shows a typical RIMM and also illustrates the heat sink (or heat spreader) used to manage the elevated operating temperatures encountered with RDRAM chips.

Unbuffered, Buffered, and Registered

Memory modules may be unbuffered, buffered, or registered. This distinction is defined by the way in which electrical signals are handled by the memory module, and your choice of module will affect the maximum amount of RAM that can be installed on the server motherboard. An *unbuffered* memory module contains

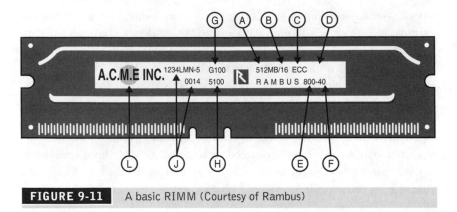

FIGURE 9-11 A basic RIMM (Courtesy of Rambus)

only memory devices, and the raw data is not boosted by buffers on the module itself. Unbuffered modules are fast because there is no buffering circuitry to slow the signals, and their slightly lower cost makes them ideal for use in everyday PCs. Unfortunately, unbuffered electrical signals are prone to attenuation, so only a few unbuffered modules (usually one or two) can be used at a time.

By adding *buffers* or *registers* to the memory module, the electrical signals entering and leaving the memory module are strengthened. This slows the module's performance by a few nanoseconds, but allows the use of additional memory modules—thus the motherboard can support much *more* memory (this is particularly important for memory-hungry systems such as network servers). For EDO and FPM memory modules, the process of redriving memory signals is called *buffering*. For SDRAM memory modules, the process of redriving memory signals is called *registering*. Registering is similar to buffering, but registering clocks data into and out of the module using the system's clock. The motherboard's memory controller chip determines the type of memory modules required, so you cannot use unbuffered and buffered (or registered) modules together on the same system (they're also keyed differently so that you cannot use them on an incompatible motherboard).

Parity and ECC

As you might imagine, it is *vital* that data and program instructions remain error free. Even one incorrect bit due to electrical noise or a component failure can crash the PC, corrupt drive information, cause video problems, or result in a myriad of other faults. PC designers approached the issue of memory integrity by employing a technique known as *parity* (the same technique used to check serial data integrity). More recently, PCs (especially mission-critical PCs such as servers) employ a more robust and versatile error scheme called error correction code (ECC).

The Parity Principle

The basic idea behind parity is simple: each byte written to memory is checked, and a ninth bit is added to the byte as a checking (or parity) bit. When a memory address is later read by the CPU, memory-checking circuitry on the motherboard will calculate the *expected* parity bit, and compare it to the bit actually *read* from memory. In this fashion, the PC can continuously diagnose system memory by checking the integrity of its data. If the read parity bit *matches* the expected parity bit, the data (and indirectly the RAM) is assumed to be valid, and the CPU can go on its way. If the read and expected parity bits *do not* match, the system registers an error and halts. Every byte is given a parity bit, so for a 32-bit PC, there will be four parity bits for every address. For a 64-bit PC, there are 8 parity bits, and so on.

While parity has proven to be a simple and cost-effective means of continuously checking memory, there are two significant limitations. First, though parity can detect an error, it cannot correct the error because there is no way to tell *which* bit has gone bad. This is why a system simply halts when a parity error is detected. Second, parity is unable to detect multibit errors. For example, if a 1 accidentally becomes a 0 and a 0 accidentally becomes a 1 within the same byte, parity conditions will still be satisfied. Fortunately, the probability of a multibit error in the same byte is extremely remote. You are not required to employ parity checking, and nonparity RAM is quite common in desktop systems. However, the critical nature of servers demands that some form of error checking be implemented to prevent the server from suffering major (and costly) data errors.

ECC and EOS

In the world of personal computing, parity is an ancient technique. Frankly, it could easily be replaced by more sophisticated techniques such as error correction code (ECC) or ECC on SIMM (EOS). ECC (which is a popular technique used on today's high-end PCs and file servers) uses a mathematical process in conjunction with the motherboard's memory controller, and appends a number of ECC bits to the data bits. When data is read back from memory, the ECC memory controller checks the ECC data read back as well. ECC has two important advantages over parity. It can actually *correct* single-bit errors on the fly without the user ever knowing there's been a problem. In addition, ECC can successfully detect 2-bit, 3-bit, and 4-bit errors, which makes it an incredibly powerful error-detection tool. If a rare multibit error is detected, ECC is unable to correct it, but it will be reported and the system will halt.

It takes 7 or 7 bits at each address to successfully implement ECC. For a 32-bit system, you'll need to use x39 or x40 SIMMs (i.e., 8M x 39 or 8M x 40). These are relatively new designations, so you should at least recognize them as ECC SIMMs if you encounter them. As an alternative, some 64-bit systems use two 36-bit SIMMs for a total of 72 bits—64 bits for data and 8 bits (which would otherwise be for parity) for ECC information.

EOS is a relatively new (and rather expensive) technology that places ECC functions on the memory module itself, but provides ECC results as parity—so while the memory module runs ECC, the motherboard continues to see parity. This is an interesting experiment, but it is unlikely that EOS will gain significant market share. Systems that use parity can be fitted with parity memory much more cheaply than EOS memory.

Objective 9.08   General Troubleshooting

While most server motherboards should provide years of reliable operation, there are certainly many problems that can arise with the motherboard and peripheral devices. Servers present a special challenge for technicians, because server problems affect the entire network, and a down server can cost a busy company thousands of dollars in lost sales and productivity for every hour that it's offline. As a technician, it's vital that you recognize server problems and be equipped to correct them promptly.

Initial System Startup Problems

A server must boot, pass the POST, and load the operating system properly before it can service the network. If the server fails to boot properly, the network will remain offline until you can identify and correct the problem. Fortunately, initial system startup problems are usually caused by incorrect device installation (or configuration). The following checklist will help you isolate potential problems:

- See that the system power cords are properly connected to the system.
- Press the system power button on the front panel and verify that the power LED is on. Cooling fans should also be running properly.
- Check to see that all internal and external cables are correctly connected and secured.
- Check to see that the processors are fully seated in their slots on the baseboard. CPU slots without a processor should have a terminator card.
- Verify that all PCI boards are fully seated in their expansion slots and secured to the chassis.
- Verify that all switch and jumper settings on the motherboard are correct.
- Verify that all the jumper and switch settings on expansion boards and peripheral devices are correct.
- Check that all DIMMs are installed correctly and securely. The DIMMs should be the correct type and speed and error-correction scheme for the motherboard. On some server motherboards, the system will not start unless all DIMM slots are filled.
- Check that all peripheral devices are installed correctly.
- If the system has a hard disk drive, verify that it is properly partitioned, formatted, and configured in the CMOS Setup.
- Verify that all device drivers are properly installed. You may need to load updated versions of critical device drivers for best operation (i.e., SCSI host adapter drivers or NIC drivers).
- Verify that all configuration settings made with the SSU are correct.
- Check that the operating system has properly loaded.

Software Issues

In addition to hardware issues, software problems (namely software bugs and incompatibilities) can also interfere with normal server operations. Problems that occur when you run new application software are usually related to the software:

- Verify that the PC meets the minimum hardware requirements for all installed software.
- Verify that you're using an authorized copy of the software (rather than a modified or OEM version).
- Verify that your original installation media is good (try a known-good installation CD).

- Verify that the CD is not damaged or scratched.
- Verify that the software is installed correctly (recheck the installation).
- Check that the correct device drivers are installed.
- Check that the software is correctly configured for your particular system.
- Check the software user manual and see that you're using the software correctly.

When Problems Occur

Even when the system hardware and software are proven out, problems can occur after the server has been in operation for a period of time. Issues that occur *after* the system hardware and software have been running correctly often indicate hardware failure (i.e., a drive or controller failure). System upgrades and alterations may also cause hardware problems. In most situations, server hardware problems are not difficult to identify and correct, but the following checklist may help isolate the more obvious trouble:

- If you're running software from a diskette, try a new copy of the software on a fresh diskette, or clean the floppy drive and try the diskette again.
- If you're running software from a CD-ROM, try a different CD to see if the problem occurs on all discs, try the CD in another drive, clean the suspect disc or drive, or replace the suspect CD-ROM drive.
- If you're running software from a hard drive, try running it from a diskette or CD. If the software runs correctly, there may be a problem with the copy on your hard drive. Reinstall the software on the hard disk and try running it again. Make sure all necessary files are installed.
- If the system problems are intermittent, there may be a loose cable or expansion card, a marginal power supply, or other component failure(s) in the system. Run diagnostics or look for specific error messages to help isolate the exact problem.
- Keyboard and mouse input problems are usually caused by accumulations of dirt or debris, and can almost always be corrected by cleaning the keyboard or mouse.
- If you suspect that a transient voltage spike, power outage, or brownout might have occurred, reload the software (or reboot the system) and try running the system again. Symptoms of voltage spikes include a flickering video display, unexpected system reboots, and the system failing to respond to user commands.

Travel Advisory

If you're getting random errors in your data, the files may be corrupted by voltage spikes on the ac power line. You may want to install a new surge suppressor between the power outlet and the system power cords.

Understanding SEL Messages

The *system event log* (SEL) viewer is the user interface that allows users or technicians to access the SEL. This interface can be accessed both from the *Emergency Management Port* (EMP) and the *System Setup Utility* (SSU). The viewer extracts information from the SEL and presents it to the user in either a "hex" or "verbose" format. Users can also save the current SEL data to a file (for later analysis) or clear the current SEL records at the server. This part of the chapter highlights the typical codes found in the SEL for server motherboards such as the L440GX+. An administrator or technician can use this SEL information to monitor the server for warnings (i.e., the chassis door has been opened), or potentially critical problems (i.e., a processor has failed or a temperature threshold has been exceeded). For current server systems, events can be generated from the *Baseboard Management Controller* (BMC), *Hot Swap Controller* (HSC), and BIOS.

POST Codes and Messages

When serious system problems arise, the motherboard probably will not boot completely—this may make it impossible to load the operating system or run diagnostic software. Fortunately, the BIOS places two-digit hexadecimal codes (called POST codes) on I/O port 80h during the boot process. If you install an ISA POST reader card, you can see these codes as they flash by. If the system halts or freezes on a particular code, you can cross-reference the code with the POST status and determine the last step to be successfully completed. Motherboard documentation normally lists a set of POST codes for a current server-type BIOS. If the system boots to a point that initializes the video system, errors may be displayed as four-digit codes. You'll need the documentation that accompanies your particular server motherboard in order to decode the exact meaning of each code.

Parity Errors

Parity errors constitute many of the memory faults that you will see as a technician. As you saw earlier in this chapter, parity is an important part of a computer's self-checking capability. Errors in memory will cause the system to halt, rather than continue blindly along with a potentially catastrophic error. But it is not just faulty memory that causes parity errors. Parity can also be influenced by your system's configuration. Here are the major causes of parity problems:

- One or more memory bits is intermittent or has failed entirely
- Poor connections between the SIMM/DIMM and socket
- Too few wait states entered in BIOS (memory is too slow for the CPU)
- An intermittent failure or other fault has occurred in the power supply
- A bug, computer virus, or other rogue software is operating
- A fault has occurred in the memory controller IC or BIOS

When you're faced with a parity error after a memory upgrade, you should suspect a problem with wait states or memory type settings in the CMOS Setup routine, so check them first. If the wait states or other memory settings are correct, systematically remove each SIMM/DIMM, clean the contacts, and reseat each SIMM/DIMM. If the errors continue, try removing one bank of memory modules at a time (chances are that the memory is bad). You may have to relocate memory so that bank 0 remains filled. When the error disappears, the memory you removed is likely to be defective.

When parity errors occur spontaneously (with no apparent cause), you should clean and reinstall each SIMM/DIMM first to eliminate the possibility of bad contacts. Next, check the power supply outputs—low or electrically noisy outputs may allow random bit errors. You may have to upgrade the supply if it is overloaded. Try booting the system clean from a write-protected floppy disk to eliminate the possibility of buggy software or computer viruses. If the problem persists, suspect a memory defect in the memory module.

✔ **Objective 9.01: Understanding a Server Motherboard**   The motherboard is the heart of every server, workstation, or ordinary desktop system. It provides all of the system resources, and supports the "core processing" devices needed by the system such as the CPU, memory, real-time clock, BIOS, and expansion slots. Server motherboards support even more resources that are critical to a network.

✔ **Objective 9.02: Server Management and Security Features**   Server management is handled through a microcontroller on the motherboard. Intel refers to this as the Baseboard Management Controller (BMC). The BMC is basically an autonomous motherboard subsystem that monitors system events and logs their occurrence in nonvolatile memory called the system event log (SEL) and the sensor data record (SDR).

✔ **Objective 9.03: Installing a Server Motherboard**   Motherboard installation is a highly intrusive procedure, so great care is required to properly reinstall all of your existing devices. It is very important to perform a full system backup before replacing a motherboard. All memory, processors, cables, and expansion devices must be removed from the old motherboard, which is then replaced with the new model, and all original devices are reinstalled.

✔ **Objective 9.04: Configuring the Motherboard**   Jumpers are used to configure key motherboard operating parameters—though most device-related settings are made through the CMOS Setup. The SSU allows a higher-level configuration of the server. A lithium battery powers the system clock/calendar and maintains the CMOS RAM for as long as 10 years while system power is off.

✔ **Objective 9.05: Understanding the Processor**   Processors are capable of operating in several different "modes"—the ways in which a processor creates and supports an operating environment. The *real mode* stays within the first 1MB of RAM, which is compatible with the original Intel 8088 chip. The *protected mode* is a much more powerful mode of operation used in all modern multitasking operating systems. The protected mode offers full access to all of the system's memory, it has the ability to multitask, it offers support for virtual memory, it offers faster (32-bit) access to memory, and it offers faster 32-bit drivers to handle I/O transfers. The *virtual real mode* emulates the real mode from within the protected mode and allows DOS programs to run.

✔ **Objective 9.06: Understanding Bus Architectures**   Motherboards incorporate numerous buses to carry data around the system. There are data, address, and control buses that are internal to the motherboard itself. There are also expansion bus connections for add-on devices. Today, PCI and AGP are the most popular expansion bus architectures.

✔ **Objective 9.07: Understanding Server Memory**   DIMMs appear virtually identical to SIMMs, but they are physically *larger*. Where each electrical contact on the SIMM is tied together between the front and back, the DIMM keeps front and back contacts separate—effectively doubling the number of contacts. RDRAM is used on RIMMs (Rambus inline memory modules). RIMMs appear almost identical to DIMMs, but are slightly bigger (with several keys between the metal contact fingers). Memory modules may be *unbuffered*, *buffered*, or *registered*. PC designers approached the issue of memory integrity by employing a technique known as *parity*. More recent PCs (especially servers) employ a versatile scheme called error correction code (ECC).

✔ **Objective 9.08: General Troubleshooting**   Most problems with new motherboards are caused by improper installation or configuration. Stability or random errors are often caused by memory, processor, or cabling issues. Outright motherboard faults are best dealt with by replacing the motherboard entirely.

REVIEW QUESTIONS

1. The processor's numeric coprocessor is also referred to as…

    A. A floating-point unit or FPU
    B. A superscaler architecture or SSA
    C. A write-back cache buffer
    D. A superpipeline architecture or SPA

2. The term ECC stands for…

    A. Error Checking and Calibration
    B. Error Checking and Correction
    C. Error Confirmation and Correction
    D. None of the above

3. The standard ATX power connection to the motherboard uses…

    A. 4 pins
    B. 6pins
    C. 20 pins
    D. 34 pins

4. The autonomous control system used to monitor a motherboard's operation is known as…

    A. The BIOS (basic input/output system)
    B. The BMC (Baseboard Management Controller)

    C. The CMOS (Complementary Metal Oxide Semiconductor)

    D. The RTC (Real-time clock)

5. BIOS is normally protected from accidental corruption through the use of a...

    A. Key switch

    B. Jumper

    C. Software utility

    D. Master password

6. A memory module using Rambus memory is referred to as...

    A. DIMM

    B. SDRAM

    C. SIMM

    D. RIMM

7. A cache bus is sometimes referred to as a...

    A. Backside bus

    B. Write through bus

    C. Asymmetrical bus

    D. Dedicated bus

8. A heat sink with a built-in fan is said to be...

    A. A passive heat sink

    B. An active heat sink

    C. A Peltier heat sink

    D. An overclocking heat sink

9. The most common form of multiprocessing used today is...

    A. Symmetric multiprocessing

    B. Asymmetric multiprocessing

    C. PIP multiprocessing

    D. CIP multiprocessing

10. The AGP bus operates at...

    A. 8.3MHz

    B. 16MHz

    C. 33MHz

    D. 66MHz

REVIEW ANSWERS

1. **A** A floating-point unit or FPU: The processor's numeric coprocessor is also referred to as a *floating-point unit* or *FPU*.

2. **C** Error Checking and Correction: The term ECC stands for Error Checking and Correction.

3. **C** Twenty pins: The standard ATX power connection to the motherboard uses 20 pins.

4. **B** The BMC (Baseboard Management Controller): Server management is handled through a microcontroller on the motherboard. Intel refers to this as the Baseboard Management Controller (BMC). The BMC is basically an autonomous motherboard subsystem that monitors system events and logs their occurrence in nonvolatile memory called the system event log (SEL) and the sensor data record (SDR).

5. **B** Jumper: BIOS is normally protected from accidental corruption through the use of a jumper.

6. **D** A RIMM: A memory module using Rambus memory is referred to as a RIMM.

7. **A** Backside bus: A cache bus is sometimes referred to as a backside bus.

8. **B** An active heat sink: A heat sink with a built-in fan is said to be an active heat sink.

9. **A** Symmetric multiprocessing: Symmetric multiprocessing (SMP) allows either system or user tasks to run on any processor. It's a more flexible approach, and therefore offers better performance. SMP is what most multi-processing PC motherboards use.

10. **D** 66MHz: The AGP bus operates at 66MHz.

NIC Adapters and Troubleshooting

	NEWBIE	SOME EXPERIENCE	EXPERT
ETA	4 hours	1 hours	0.5 hour

Networks allow computers to share files, applications, Internet access, and other resources. However, computers must be connected in order to operate on the network. Computers are interfaced to a network using a *network interface card* (NIC), as shown in Figure 10-1. Servers typically use one or more multiport NICs, and workstation/desktop systems need only a single-port NIC. If you spend any time working with networks, chances are that you'll need to work with network cards. This chapter explains the characteristics of a typical NIC, reviews an installation process, and outlines a series of handy troubleshooting guidelines.

Objective 10.01   NIC Basics

Simply stated, an NIC is an expansion board device that fits into a computer and provides that computer with a connection to a network. You may use a different type of NIC depending on whether you're working with a workstation/desktop or server system—there is a difference. A desktop NIC is installed in a desktop PC or workstation and only supports a single user (i.e., a single-port NIC). A server NIC is used in a server system intended to connect many users, and this supports important business and mission-critical network situations. Consequently, a server NIC is usually a multiport NIC, and it must provide greater functionality (such as increased reliability and throughput), reduced CPU overhead, and better overall communications performance. If a server NIC is inadequate for the network (or fails), it can affect the productivity and profitability of an entire workgroup, department, or company.

Network cards act as the physical interface between the computer (server or workstation) and the network cable. A NIC converts the parallel data of the PC's internal

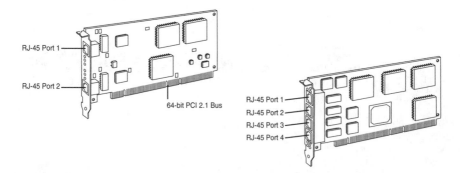

RJ-45 Port 1
RJ-45 Port 2
64-bit PCI 2.1 Bus

RJ-45 Port 1
RJ-45 Port 2
RJ-45 Port 3
RJ-45 Port 4

FIGURE 10-1   Two typical multiport NIC adapters (Courtesy of Adaptec)

> ### Local Lingo
>
> **NIC (network interface card)**   A hardware device that interfaces a
> PC (server or client) to the network.

bus into serial signals for transfer over coaxial, twisted-pair, or fiber-optic cables (and back again). Before you can install and configure a NIC, you'll need to understand the ideas of network addressing and system resource assignments (i.e., interrupts, I/O, and memory). You'll also need to understand the factors that influence NIC performance on the network. In general, a NIC performs four essential tasks:

- It prepares the parallel data from the host computer's (server or workstation) bus into serial data suitable for the network cable.
- It transmits that serial data to another computer on the network.
- It controls the flow of data between a computer and the network cabling.
- It receives incoming serial data from the network cable and translates it into parallel data that can be passed to the computer's bus and processed by the system's CPU.

> ### Exam Tip
>
> In strict networking circles, a NIC implements the logical link
> control and Media Access Control functions in the data link layer
> of an OSI model.

NIC Network Addressing

The NIC also has to advertise its own location (or address) to the rest of the network in order to distinguish it from all the other NICs on the network. The Institute of Electrical and Electronics Engineers (IEEE) has assigned blocks of addresses to each NIC manufacturer, and each manufacturer hardwires these addresses onto their cards—this essentially "burns" the address into the card. Each NIC (and therefore each computer) has a unique address on a network. The NIC also performs several other functions as it takes data from the computer and prepares it for the network cable:

- The computer and NIC must communicate in order to move data from the computer to the card. If your NIC card can utilize direct memory access (or DMA) data transfers, the computer will assign some of its memory space to the NIC.

- The NIC then signals the computer and requests the computer's data.
- The computer's bus then moves the data from system memory (RAM) to the NIC.

Because data can often move faster on the PC bus or the network cable than the NIC can handle, the data is sent to an on-board buffer (a reserved portion of RAM on the NIC). The data is held in that buffer temporarily during both the transmission and reception of network data.

Negotiating Data

Before the sending NIC actually sends data over the network, it carries on a complex electronic dialog with the receiving NIC (called "negotiation") so that both cards agree on the following:

- The maximum size of the data chunks to be sent
- The amount of data to be sent before confirmation of receipt is issued
- The time intervals between sending data chunks
- The amount of time to wait before confirmation is sent
- How much data each card can hold before its buffer overflows
- The speed of data transmission

For example, if a newer, faster, more sophisticated NIC needs to communicate with an older, slower NIC, both devices need to negotiate a common transmission speed and other parameters that each can accommodate. Many newer NICs incorporate circuitry that allows the faster card to adjust to the rate of the slower card. Each NIC signals to the other, indicating its own parameters and accepting or adjusting to the other card's parameters until a "lowest common denominator" is found. After all the communication details have been worked out, the two cards begin to exchange data.

Port Failover

Failover is a method of redundancy that provides protection from system failures on servers running mission-critical applications. During a port failure, failover keeps the connection to the server established by moving all traffic on the affected segment to a standby NIC (or NIC port). When a failure is detected on the primary port, that port is disabled and a secondary port takes over to carry the load—and keeps the network running without interruption. Failover operation occurs when there is a network (i.e., Ethernet) link loss, a watchdog timer expires, an abnormal hardware interrupt occurs, or abnormal send/receive counts occur on the segment (such as too many collisions or errors).

Port Aggregation

Port aggregation is a software-supported NIC feature that provides network path redundancy and increased bandwidth for network (i.e., Fast Ethernet) servers running mission-critical applications. Port aggregation works by load balancing the data throughput over multiple ports. With port aggregation, you can create a virtual port by grouping multiple ports together. This grouping distributes the network load by sharing the resources of all ports in a group. In the port aggregation group, one port becomes the primary port and its Media Access Control (MAC) address is given to the protocol. The entire group behaves as a single interface, allowing the software to manage the combined resources of the group efficiently. In the event of a port failure, the remaining ports carry the load and keep the network running and uninterrupted.

Not all NICs and network operating systems support port aggregation. For example, Adaptec Duralink64 Port Aggregation software is compatible with Adaptec ANA-69011/TX and ANA-62011/TX single-port NICs, ANA-62022 dual-port NICs, and ANA-62044 quad-port NICs. Duralink64 Port Aggregation software supports Windows NT 4.0 and 3.51, as well as Novell NetWare 4.x– and 5.0–based servers (Windows 95/98/SE doesn't support port aggregation). A server with Duralink64 Port Aggregation can use up to 12 Adaptec PCI Fast Ethernet ports in one aggregated group (at 1.2Gbps per group). If any of the supporting members of a specific aggregated group should fail, that member is excluded from the group, and the remaining ports balance the existing load. The combination of failover and port aggregation technologies can help you to create a network that is both fast and fault tolerant.

FEC (Fast EtherChannel)

Fast EtherChannel (FEC) is a technology developed by Cisco Systems (based on standard Fast Ethernet) to provide the additional bandwidth that network backbones need today. FEC combines two or four Fast Ethernet links to a single logical connection capable of carrying 800Mbps of aggregate full-duplex data throughput. In addition to scalable bandwidth, the technology also provides fault tolerance and resiliency—protecting the network from outages due to failed links. Fast EtherChannel allows grouping of ports or NICs, enabling full utilization of available bandwidth (up to 800Mbps). Up to four single-port NICs, two two-port NICs, or one four-port NIC can be grouped. This technology also provides load balancing and management of each link by distributing traffic across multiple links in the channel. As an example, Adaptec Duralink64 v4.2 software and all of the Adaptec DuraLAN NICs support Fast EtherChannel technology, allowing redundancy and high-speed aggregation between switches and servers.

Travel Assistance

Fast EtherChannel is available on select Cisco Catalyst switches and Cisco routers. For additional information on Cisco's Fast EtherChannel technology, visit the Cisco Systems Web site: www.cisco.com/warp/public/729/fec.

Full Duplex

Full-duplex support allows a NIC to send and receive data at the same time—effectively doubling your available network bandwidth. To implement full-duplex operation on your network, you'll need both a NIC and a switch that supports full duplex. Full duplex can also be enabled point to point with a crossover cable instead of a switch.

Travel Advisory

BNC connections do not support full-duplex operation.

Objective 10.02 NIC Configuration Issues

Because a NIC is an internal device, it must be configured to use the computer's hardware resources (typically interrupts, I/O addresses, memory range, and transceiver type). With the explosive growth of Plug-and-Play (PnP) BIOS and operating systems, many network cards can automatically configure themselves to the computer's available resources. However, older cards (or cards used with older computer platforms) may need to be configured manually through the use of jumpers or DIP switches.

Exam Tip

It is important that each device in the computer uses a different interrupt line or other resource. If more than one device uses the same IRQ, a hardware conflict will result, and that can cause the NIC (or other system devices) to behave unexpectedly.

Resource Assignments

Interrupt request lines (IRQs) are hardware signal lines over which devices such as I/O ports, keyboards, disk drive controllers, and NICs can demand the attention of the computer's CPU. Interrupt lines are accessible from the bus, and each IRQ is assigned different levels of priority so that the CPU can determine the relative importance of incoming service requests. Lower IRQ levels represent a *higher* priority. For example, the system processor will service IRQ3 before IRQ12—even if the signals are asserted together. Given the importance of NIC performance, you should try to use the *lowest* available IRQ for your NIC. In most cases, IRQ3 or IRQ5 can be used for the NIC. IRQ5 is typically the recommended setting (if it is available), and it is the default setting for most systems.

Although an interrupt can get the processor's attention, there must still be a means of passing commands and data between the NIC and host PC. By assigning a base *I/O port*, the NIC establishes a channel for communication with the system.

Direct memory access (or DMA) is a technique that allows data to be moved from place to place inside the computer (i.e., between system RAM and the NIC buffer) without the direct control of your computer's CPU. Otherwise, the CPU would need to manage every data transfer (known as *programmed I/O* or PIO). Not all network cards support DMA data transfers, but those that do—especially newer NICs—will usually provide better performance.

Many NICs utilize a certain amount of memory (RAM) space that serves as a buffer—a temporary storage area that can handle incoming and outgoing *data frames* (a packet of information transmitted as a unit on the network). By setting a *base RAM address* (sometimes called a RAM start address), you can control the memory range occupied by the NIC. Often, the base RAM address for a NIC is D0000h, though there is typically a selection of possible addresses that can be selected (i.e., D8000h).

The same situation is true for ROM address space. Most NICs incorporate their on-board instructions (or firmware) on a BIOS ROM chip located on the network card itself. Remember that the motherboard has a BIOS, and other devices in the system often use a BIOS (i.e., video BIOS or SCSI controller BIOS). This means you must set the *base ROM address* (or ROM start address) so that the NIC will occupy a ROM memory range not used by other devices in the system. Often, the base ROM address for a NIC is D0000h, though there is typically a selection of possible addresses that can be selected (i.e., D8000h).

Travel Advisory

A NIC that does not use system RAM will not have a setting for the base memory address. However, some NICs offer a setting that allows you to specify memory blocks to be set aside for storing data frames. For example, some cards let you specify either 16KB or 32KB of memory. Configuring more memory provides better network performance, but leaves less memory available for other uses.

Typical NIC Settings

Now that you've reviewed the elements involved in NIC configuration, you can see the default settings for typical NIC shown next. Keep in mind that these are usually default settings, and can be adjusted manually (through the use of jumpers and DIP switches) or automatically (through the use of PnP).

- **Interrupt** IRQ5 (with a second choice of IRQ2)
- **DMA** DMA1 or DMA3 (when using 16-bit network adapters, try DMA5)
- **I/O Port** 300h usually will work fine
- **Base Address** D0000h or above
- **ROM Address** D0000h or above

Remember that the card's real-mode (DOS) drivers *must* match the card's physical configuration. Network operating systems create these drivers in different ways. For example, 3Com (and many other manufacturers) adjusts the software driver in the CONFIG.SYS using some optional command-line switches. By comparison, Novell creates the driver with either SHGEN (NetWare 2.1x) or GENSH (NetWare 2.0a). In either case, your driver parameters must match the card.

Selecting a Transceiver

Finally, some network cards come with one external and one on-board *transceiver* (the circuit that drives the network cable). When you connect a cable directly to the

NIC, you're using the card's *internal* transceiver. When you must connect a transceiver module to the NIC first (then connect the cable to the module), you're using an *external* transceiver. If your NIC offers this selection, you would have to decide which transceiver to use, and then make the appropriate choice on your card using a jumper or DIP switch (though some NIC models may autoselect the transceiver).

Cabling and Connectors

To select the appropriate NIC for your network, you must also determine the type of network cabling and cable connectors to be used. Remember that each type of network cable has different physical characteristics that the NIC must accommodate. Each card is built to accept at least one type of cable—the most common cable types are *coaxial* (usually thinnet), twisted pair, and fiber optic. Some NICs have more than one network cable connector. For example, it is not uncommon for a NIC to have a thinnet, thicknet, and twisted-pair connector. If a card has more than one network connector and does not have built-in interface detection, you should make a selection manually by setting jumpers on the card itself (or by using a software-selectable option).

Use particular caution when working with thicknet connections. A thicknet network connection uses a 15-pin attachment unit interface (AUI) cable to connect the 15-pin (DB-15) connector on the back of the NIC to an external transceiver. The external transceiver uses a "vampire tap" to connect to the thicknet cable. Do not confuse a 15-pin joystick port with an AUI external transceiver port. They may look alike, but some joystick pins carry +5 volts dc, which can be harmful to network hardware as well as to the computer.

There are other potential connection problems to be aware of. Do not to confuse 25-pin SCSI ports with parallel printer ports. Some older SCSI devices communicated through the same kind of DB-25 connector as these parallel ports, but neither device will function when plugged into the wrong connector. Finally, an unshielded twisted-pair connection uses an RJ-45 connector. The RJ-45 connector is similar to a RJ-11 telephone connector, but the RJ-45 is larger in size and has eight conductors—an RJ-11 only has four conductors.

NICs and Network Performance

Since the NIC has a direct relationship to data transmission across a network, your choice of NIC will have a profound impact on the performance of that network. If the NIC is slow, data will not pass to and from the network as quickly—on a bus network where no one can use the network until the cable is clear, a slow NIC can increase wait times for all users. After identifying the physical requirements of a NIC (i.e., the bus type, the type of network connector, and the type of network in which the NIC will operate), it's necessary to consider several other factors that will affect the capabilities of the card. While all NICs conform to certain minimum standards and specifications, some cards feature the following enhancements that greatly improve server, client, and overall network performance:

- Select a NIC that supports *direct memory access* (DMA). DMA allows a computer to move data directly from the NIC's buffer to the computer's memory (RAM) without the direct intervention of the system processor. This frees the CPU for other tasks and improves relative computer performance.

- Select a NIC that supports *shared adapter memory*. The NIC supplies a buffer (RAM) that it shares with the computer, and the computer identifies this buffer RAM as if it were actually part of the computer's system RAM.

- As an alternative to shared adapter memory, you can try a NIC with *shared system memory*. With this technique, the NIC's on-board controller selects a section of the system's memory (RAM) and uses it to process data.

- If you're using a NIC intended for a PCI slot, select a *bus-mastering* NIC. With bus mastering, the NIC takes temporary control of the computer's PCI bus, bypasses the computer's CPU, and moves data directly to the computer's system memory. This speeds up computer operations by freeing the system processor to deal with other tasks, and that can improve network performance.

- Employ *RAM buffers* wherever possible. Network traffic often travels too fast for most NICs to handle, so RAM chips on the NIC serve as a buffer. When the card receives more data than it can process immediately, the RAM buffer holds some of the data until the NIC can process it. This speeds up the card's apparent performance to the network and helps keep the card from becoming a bottleneck.

- Employ *NIC processors* wherever possible. With an on-board processor (also referred to as a microcontroller), the NIC has much lower reliance on the system processor for handling data. This offloads more tasks from the system processor and can improve network performance.

As a rule, you should select the best possible NIC for your server since a server generally handles the majority of network traffic. High-performance multiport NICs are frequently employed in servers. By comparison, workstation/desktop network users can often work adequately with less expensive single-port

NICs. Older NICs will work when their activities are limited to low-traffic applications (such as word processing). Keep in mind that bus networks can be impaired by a single slow NIC. There are also specialized NIC types that you should be familiar with.

Objective 10.03   Installing the NIC Hardware

The first step is to install the network card itself. For this discussion, we'll consider a recent PCI-based card such as an Adaptec NIC. This installation process is virtually identical to the installation of any other PnP PCI expansion device. There are three basic steps involved in NIC installation: installing the card, connecting the network cable, and configuring the card. Experienced readers can skip this section, but novices may find this part of the chapter to be helpful.

Starting the Installation

Turn off the power to your PC and disconnect the power cord from the wall outlet. During the installation, you should ground yourself by touching any unpainted surface of the PC case. Then, follow these steps:

1. Remove the outer cover from your computer according to the manufacturer's instructions.
2. Carefully remove the NIC from its antistatic container. Verify the model by looking at the model name on the NIC itself (keep the antistatic container for future use).
3. Check the NIC for any visible signs of damage that may have occurred during shipping or handling. If you find a problem, immediately notify your network supplier and the shipping service that delivered your NIC—you'll need to arrange for a replacement NIC.

Exam Tip

PCI slots and NICs come in two varieties: 3.3 volt, and the more common 5 volt. PCI NICs generally support 5-volt slots. Some models also support 3.3-volt slots. To improve performance with multiport NICs, install these NICs in PCI bus slot 0.

4. Once the PC is opened, locate an unused expansion slot (a PCI slot in this case). Remove the bracket screw and remove the expansion slot bracket that covers the card slot's opening.
5. Insert the NIC into the PCI expansion slot, pressing down firmly and evenly until the bus contacts are seated in the slot.
6. Secure the NIC in the expansion slot with the bracket screw you removed earlier.
7. Replace the computer's outer cover on the computer.
8. Reconnect any other devices and cables that you might have removed during the installation. Do not reapply power to the computer yet.

Attach the Cables

For a thinnet cable, connect the T connector to the card's BNC connector. Align the T connector's slots with the pegs on the card's BNC connector. Push the T connector in and twist it clockwise until it stops. Attach the cable from the network to one side of the T, and place a terminator on the other side (or the cable to the next workstation). For thicknet cable (when a 15-pin attachment unit interface, or AUI, is needed), locate the card's AUI connector and move the slide latch to the open position. Connect the AUI cable or transceiver to the AUI connector on the NIC. Move the slide latch to the closed position to lock the cable into place. Connect the other end of the AUI cable to the external transceiver.

For a twisted-pair cable, make sure that the RJ-45 connector on your cable is wired appropriately for a standard 10Base-T adapter (you'd be surprised at how often these connectors are wired wrong). Align the RJ-45 plug on the end of the twisted-pair cable with the notch on the adapter's connector, and insert the cable into the card's RJ-45 socket. See that the other end of the cable is attached to the network.

The card's selection of cabling should normally be automatic. When the appropriate driver is installed for a particular operating system, the driver automatically selects the media type based on the type of cable connection. If you change the cable type later, you must reinstall the driver for it to automatically detect the cable type. If the driver *cannot* detect which cable is connected (or whether a cable is connected), the Auto Select Media Type function defaults to the

Travel Advisory

If you install a quad- or dual-port NIC, and a port does not have a cable attached, you may receive a startup error message on your server. This is normal and does not affect performance.

type of connector stored in the card's firmware. For example, the default is AUI for a 3Com 3C900-COMBO NIC. You can change this default by selecting another media type from the list of options.

Configuring the NIC

Because most NICs are now PnP compliant, your computer's BIOS *may* determine the available NIC resources and configure the PCI NIC automatically. However, depending on your particular system, you may need to configure the card yourself (or verify that the settings are correct). To do this, enter your computer's CMOS Setup and select Advanced Settings from the Main menu. Make sure the following settings are enabled (your BIOS may not match the following options exactly):

- **PCI Slot Enabled**   Enable all of the PCI slots in your system.
- **Bus Mastering**   Enable PCI bus mastering for the slot(s) being used by the NICs.
- **PCI INTA**   Assign an ISA interrupt (10, 11, 12, etc.) to PCI interrupt vector A.
- **PCI INT Vector**   Assign PCI interrupt vector A to the PCI slot(s) used by the NIC.
- **PCI Bus Latency**   Set to a value between 40 and 80.
- **Triggering**   Set the slot to level triggering rather than edge triggering.

Travel Advisory

Quad and dual NICs typically employ the motherboard's PCI-to-PCI bridge chip. If your system's BIOS does not support the PCI-to-PCI bridge chip, such NICs will not be configured properly. Contact your computer manufacturer to obtain a new BIOS version that supports the PCI-to-PCI bridge chip.

Objective 10.04 **Installing the NIC Drivers**

After installing the NIC itself, you must install the appropriate NIC driver. Depending on your particular NIC device and your network operating system, you may install one of three drivers: a standard driver, a failover driver, or a port aggregation driver. Please note that you may install one type only. As an example, the Adaptec Duralink64 diskettes provide the following drivers:

- The standard driver (i.e., a DuraLAN Standard Driver) uses each port independently.
- The failover driver (i.e., a Duralink64 Failover Driver) groups two NIC ports as a set—one as the primary port and the other as the backup port. The ports may be connected to a hub or switch.
- The port aggregation or Fast EtherChannel driver (i.e., a Duralink64 Port Aggregation Driver) groups up to 12 ports together, and must be used with a switch. By comparison, Fast EtherChannel (FEC) can be arranged in groups of two or four, though this type of setup requires a switch that supports Fast EtherChannel.

Travel Advisory

Windows 95, Windows 98, and Novell Client32 do not support Adaptec's Duralink64 failover. Install the standard driver for these operating systems.

Installing the New Driver(s)

Once you've cleared old drivers from the system (if necessary), you can install the current NIC drivers for your particular network operating system. Before proceeding, it's usually a good idea to check for driver updates and patches with the NIC manufacturer. This section of the chapter illustrates the installation process for Adaptec DuraLAN drivers under Windows NT/2000. The NIC's user guide will generally provide detailed installation instructions for numerous other NOS environments.

Windows NT 4.0

If you are installing Windows NT at this time, start with step 6 when prompted for the DuraLAN NIC. To install the DuraLAN driver on a Windows NT 4.0 platform, follow these steps:

1. Start the system to Windows NT.
2. From the Start menu, choose Settings | Control Panel.
3. In the Control Panel, double-click the Network icon.
4. In the Network window, click the Adapters tab.

5. In the Adapters tab, click Add.

6. In the Select Network Adapter window, click Have Disk.

7. At the Insert Disk window, insert the driver diskette (i.e., Duralink64 for Windows NT diskette), and then click OK.

8. In the Select OEM Option window, click the NIC model that's installed (i.e., DuraLAN NIC), and then click OK.

9. In the installation window that appears (i.e., Adaptec DuraLAN NIC Driver Installation window), select the desired driver and then click OK.

10. Continue on to install the standard driver, the failover driver, or the port aggregation driver.

Windows 2000

Use the following procedure to install the driver and diagnostics on a computer that is running Windows 2000:

1. Reboot the computer and then start Windows 2000.

2. Log on to a suitable Windows 2000 administrator account. The Windows 2000 Found New Hardware Wizard detects the new NIC(s) and begins the driver installation.

3. Insert the NIC driver CD (i.e., a 3Com EtherLink Server CD) in the CD-ROM drive.

4. Select NIC Software from the Main menu.

5. Click NIC Drivers and Diagnostics from the list that appears.

6. Follow the wizard's prompts.

7. Choose Typical or Custom installation. The Please Wait screen appears. After the installation is completed, an Update dialog box appears.

8. Click OK, and a Setup Complete screen appears.

9. Click Finish to complete the installation.

10. Click Exit. You may need to reboot the system so that your new drivers take effect.

Verify the Windows Driver(s)

You can use the following steps to verify that the standard Windows driver is installed properly:

1. From the Start menu, point to Settings and then click Control Panel.

2. In the Control Panel, double-click the System icon.

3. In the Device Manager tab, look under Network Adapters. Your NIC should appear under Network Adapters. Click OK. If the NIC does not appear, it has

not been installed properly. If a yellow exclamation mark appears beside your NIC entry, the drivers may be incorrect. Remove the NIC driver and reinstall it (check for driver updates, if possible).

4. If the Network window lists both old and new NICs, you should remove the old NIC entry from the Device Manager.

Configuring the Standard Driver(s)

If you select the standard NIC driver, you'll need to configure that driver now. The actual setup will depend on whether you use Windows NT, Windows 2000, or Novell NetWare. The following section shows you a configuration example using Windows NT:

1. In the New Hardware Found window, each NIC port is assigned to auto-detect and use a default connection type that will always detect the port connection and negotiate a compatible speed and transmission mode.
2. In the New Hardware Found window, make sure that all the NIC ports appear.
3. In the New NIC Port(s) Available window, click the appropriate port.
4. In the Connection Types list, click the connection type for your network, or use Autodetect Default Connection.
5. Click Apply.
6. Repeat the first four steps for each existing port.
7. When you're done, click OK.
8. When you're done, click Close in the Network window.
9. Restart the system.

Travel Advisory

If you're required to insert the Windows NT CD, you must reinstall the latest version of the Windows NT Service Pack and then restart the system.

Objective 10.05   **Basic NIC Troubleshooting**

Although the vast majority of NIC devices should install and operate without errors, there are certainly many situations when a server or workstation system may encounter problems. Trouble can surface in the hardware setup, network cabling, driver installation, or the system configuration. As a technician, you should be able to quickly identify and correct NIC problems. This part of the chapter outlines some of the more common symptoms and solutions for a typical NIC, and explains some common diagnostic commands for an Adaptec DuraLAN NIC.

General Troubleshooting Tips

Before you jump right into a series of specific symptoms, you should always start a troubleshooting effort by reviewing the basic installation and setup of a NIC. If your NIC is not functioning properly, verify that it was installed and set up according to instructions in its manual. These tips offer some general troubleshooting guidelines:

- Verify that your NIC is installed properly and configured correctly in the host computer according to the manufacturer's recommendations.
- When using a PCI NIC, make sure the PCI slots are bus-master enabled.
- Make sure the network cable is securely attached to both the adapter and the rest of the network (i.e., the network hub). Try another cable, if necessary.
- Make sure the hub port is configured for the same duplex mode as the adapter (i.e., full duplex or half duplex).
- Verify that the NIC driver (i.e., Adaptec DuraLAN driver) is installed correctly.
- Make sure that you're using the specific drivers that come with this adapter (rather than generic or default drivers). You may also wish to check with the NIC manufacturer and obtain the latest NIC drivers.
- Verify that you are using the latest BIOS for your computer.
- Verify that your cable, terminators, and connectors are functioning properly, or install the NIC in a different PCI bus slot.
- If you're replacing an existing adapter under NetWare, make sure the link statements in your NET.CFG are correct for the new adapter. For example, the link statement for a NetWare client should be link driver e100bodi.
- Under NetWare, verify that the FRAME type in your NET.CFG file matches your server.
- If setting up a server under NetWare, check your load and bind statements.
- Under Windows NT, make sure the driver is loaded and the protocols are bound. See the Network Bindings dialog box in Windows NT to make sure. If the problem persists, try the following:

1. Replace the NIC with the same type of NIC that is known to work. If the new NIC functions properly, the problem is related to the original NIC (which is probably defective and should be replaced).
2. Install the NIC in another functioning computer and run the tests again. If the NIC works in another machine, the problem is related to one of three areas: the original computer is faulty, there is a hardware conflict in the original computer, or there are problems with the cables or connectors in the original computer.

NIC Troubleshooting Guide

Installing and configuring a NIC is normally a quick and painless effort, but there are cases when a hardware or software issue prevents the NIC from being identified or used properly. This part of the chapter examines the typical "punch list" for troubleshooting a NIC under Windows. This may be particularly handy when dealing with client PCs. Advanced technicians may skip this section, but novices may find these steps handy.

Change the IRQ Setting

The PCI BIOS controls all resource assignments, so the system BIOS allocates resources to all PCI devices (whether they are on the motherboard or in card slots). As the computer boots up, the BIOS determines what type of resources each PCI device needs (i.e., I/O, memory, IRQs, and so on). The BIOS then allocates those system resources as it sees fit. The PCI devices themselves cannot request specific or control the resources allocated by the BIOS.

In many PCI systems, the CMOS Setup program offers user-configurable PCI device settings. This allows you to override the BIOS assignments or reserve resources for certain devices. You'll need your system documentation to learn how to access the CMOS Setup and determine which (if any) resource controls are available. Some systems (especially older systems) have no user-configurable PCI settings. In these systems, try moving the PCI card to a different slot—this often causes the system to allocate a different IRQ to the card. Regardless of how you set resources for a NIC, you should avoid using IRQ9, avoid using shared IRQs, and avoid using IRQs used by ISA or EISA (a.k.a. legacy) cards.

Check Resources with the Device Manager

The Windows Device Manager reports the status and settings for all the recognized devices in your system. Use the following steps to determine which resources are already in use, and which are (or can be made) available for your network adapter:

1. Start Windows normally.
2. Click Start, select Settings, and then select Control Panel.
3. Double-click the System icon.
4. Select the Device Manager tab.
5. Select Computer at the top of the list of devices and then click Properties (see Figure 10-2).

Travel Advisory

If all available IRQs are already in use, you may have to reconfigure, disable, or remove a device from your computer to make an IRQ available for the NIC. Some users change their sound card to IRQ 9 and use IRQ 5 for the NIC. Other users disable the COM2 port and use IRQ3 for the NIC. Since each system is unique, you will have to decide which devices are most important to you and how you want to configure them.

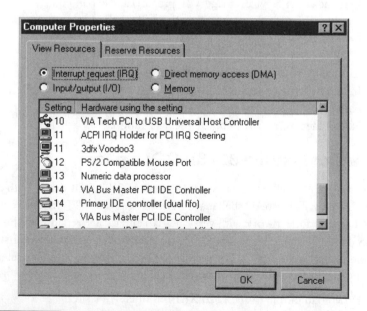

FIGURE 10-2   Reviewing IRQ assignments

6. Examine the list of IRQs to see which IRQ the BIOS has assigned to the NIC. If there is a conflict (that is, more than one device is attempting to use the same resource), try changing the IRQ.
7. Click OK in the System Properties dialog box when you have finished viewing system resources.

Use Device Manager to Add Missing Drivers

Occasionally Windows may fail to recognize the NIC properly. When this happens, the Device Manager displays a device category called Other Devices, and in this category you'll see a NIC device (i.e., Other PCI Ethernet Controller). Use this unidentified device to load the drivers for your particular NIC:

1. Start Windows normally.
2. Click Start, select Settings, and then select Control Panel.
3. Double-click the System icon.
4. Click the Device Manager tab.
5. Find the Network Adapter category (if present) and expand it by clicking the plus (+) sign next to it.
6. Remove the driver (if present) from the Network Adapter category (i.e., highlight the Intel EtherExpress PRO/10 PCI driver and click Remove).
7. Find the Other Devices category (if present) and expand it.
8. Double-click the other device (i.e., Other PCI Ethernet device) to display its properties.
9. Click the Drivers tab and click the Change Drivers button.
10. Choose Network Adapter and click Have Disk.
11. Insert the driver diskette (i.e., EtherExpress PRO/10 PCI diskette), enter a path to the drivers, and then click OK.
12. Follow the prompts to complete the installation.

Try a Compatible 32-Bit ODI Driver

If you're using Novell, you may want to use the 32-bit ODI driver with Novell Client 32. Novell's Client 32 shell may not work with your NIC drivers. For example, Client 32 doesn't work with versions 1.10 and earlier versions of the 32-bit NDIS driver for the EtherExpress Pro/10 PCI adapter. Download and install the updated files for your NIC. For the Pro/10 NIC example, Intel has released a 32-bit ODI driver that does work with the Client 32 shell:

1. Download the file E10PCL32.EXE from Intel's Web site.
2. Execute the archive to extract the files.
3. Follow the instructions in the E10PCL32.TXT file.

Check the Path to Your .CAB Files

If Windows has trouble finding the NETAPI.DLL or other .VXD or .DLL files, you'll need to enter the path to your Windows cabinet (.CAB) files. Check your documentation to determine the exact path(s) for your required .CAB file(s).

Use Network Icon to Remove and Reinstall the NIC Driver

If the NIC does not work properly, you can often correct the problem by simply removing the driver, restarting Windows, and reinstalling the driver:

1. Start Windows normally.
2. Click Start, select Settings, and then select Control Panel.
3. Double-click the Network icon.
4. Select your NIC from the list of installed network devices (see Figure 10-3), and then click Remove.

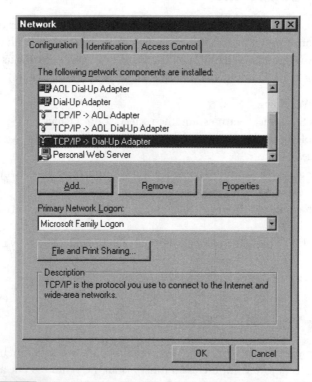

FIGURE 10-3   Selecting a network device to remove

5. Click OK and then restart the system when prompted.
6. Return to the Network dialog box in the Control Panel.
7. Click Add and then select Adapter.
8. Click Have Disk.
9. Insert the driver diskette, enter the path to the drivers, and then click OK in the Install from Disk dialog box.
10. Click OK in the Select Network Adapters dialog box to select your NIC driver.
11. Add or remove any additional clients, protocols, and/or services you need (if any).
12. Click OK in the Network dialog box and allow Windows to copy the required files.
13. Restart your computer when prompted.

Use Network Icon to Check the Workgroup Name

Users in the same workgroup are generally able to see each other quite easily (though sometimes it takes several minutes). It can be more difficult to see users in other workgroups. Make sure all the people on your network use the same workgroup name (unless you have a specific reason to do otherwise):

1. Start Windows.
2. Click Start, select Settings, and then select Control Panel.
3. Double-click the Network icon, then select the Identification tab (see Figure 10-4).
4. Enter a unique computer name for each computer on the network.
5. Enter the same workgroup for all computers on the network.
6. Enter a unique computer description for each computer, or you can leave the field blank.
7. Click OK in the Network dialog box and allow Windows to copy the required files.
8. Restart your computer when prompted.

Check Your File Sharing

Verify that your file sharing is enabled on at least one workstation. In order for others to access your computer, you must install the Windows File and Printer Sharing service. You must also select the directories or printers you want to share,

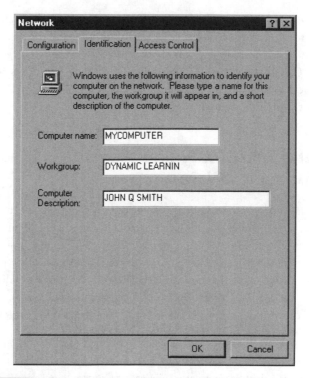

FIGURE 10-4   Adjusting the system identification

and configure them using the sharing option in the My Computer or Printers dialog boxes. Follow these steps to install the File and Printer Sharing service.

1. Click Start, select Settings, and then choose Control Panel.
2. Double-click the Network icon.
3. Scroll the list of network components and look for the File and Printer Sharing service.

Exam Tip

Only workstations with the File and Printer Sharing service installed will appear in the Network Neighborhood dialog box. There is no reason to list workstations that have no resources to share with the workgroup. As long as a workstation can see all the stations with shared resources, the station is working properly.

4. If the entry is not listed, click on File and Print Sharing, select the desired boxes to allow access to your files, printers, or both, and then click OK in the File and Print Sharing dialog box.
5. Click OK in the Network dialog box and allow Windows to copy the required files.
6. Restart your computer when prompted.

Force the IPX/SPX Frame Type when Using NetWare

Windows attempts to automatically determine the frame type used by your NetWare server(s). Usually Windows succeeds, but occasionally it fails. By forcing the IPX frame type, you can improve your chances of connecting to NetWare servers. Determine the frame type(s) used on your NetWare servers (consult your network administrator). Keep in mind that NetWare 3.11 servers default to the 802.3 frame type, and NetWare 3.12 and 4.x servers default to the 802.2 frame type. If you can access the console of the NetWare server, use the protocols or config commands to determine which frame types are in use:

1. Start Windows.
2. Click Start, select Settings, and then select Control Panel.
3. Double-click the Network icon.
4. Select the IPX/SPX-compatible protocol and then click Properties.
5. Select the Advanced tab and then select the Frame Type entry in the Property list.
6. Change the Value to the frame type your server uses.
7. Click OK in the Protocol Properties dialog box.
8. Click OK in the Network dialog box and allow Windows to copy the required files.
9. Restart your computer when prompted.

Run the NIC Diagnostics

If you're still having trouble detecting, configuring, or using a NIC, restart the PC in the DOS mode and run the diagnostics that accompanied the NIC. If the NIC passes its internal diagnostics, chances are that you're still dealing with a conflict or NIC setup problem. If the NIC fails its internal diagnostics, the NIC itself may be faulty or incompatible with the host PC (try another NIC).

Remove and Reinstall the Dial-Up Adapter

If you install the Dial-Up adapter *before* the network adapter, Windows may bind the network protocols to the Dial-Up adapter instead of the NIC. Removing the Dial-Up adapter causes Windows to bind the protocols to the network adapter. If you need the Dial-Up adapter, you can reinstall it after you get the network card working:

1. Start Windows normally.
2. Choose Start | Settings | Control Panel.
3. Double-click the Add/Remove Programs icon and then select the Windows Setup tab.
4. Select Communications | Details.
5. Uncheck the check box for Dial-up Networking; then click OK in the Communications dialog box.
6. Click OK in the Add/Remove Programs dialog box.

After you have NIC installed and working properly, you can restore dial-up support if you need to access remote host systems. Repeat the above procedure, but simply check the check box for Dial-up Networking, then click OK in the Communications dialog box.

Check and Correct the Registry

The Windows Registry is a database of all the hardware and software in your system recognized by Windows. Using the REGEDIT program, you can verify that your network adapter settings are correct:

1. Start Windows.
2. Choose Start | Run.
3. Enter **regedit** and then press ENTER.
4. In the left-hand side of the REGEDIT dialog box, open each of the following folders:
   - HKEY_LOCAL_MACHINE
   - System
   - CurrentControlSet
   - Services
   - Class
   - Net

Under the Net folder, you should see one or more subfolders named with four-digit numbers. The total of numbered subfolders should match the number of adapters shown in the Network dialog box. For example, if you only saw an Intel

Travel Advisory

Incorrectly editing the Registry may cause severe system problems, and may prevent the system from booting. Always make a complete backup of the Registry file and REGEDIT utility to a startup disk *before* attempting any kind of editing.

EtherExpress PRO/10 PCI adapter in the Network dialog box, you should have only one numbered subfolder. If you saw the Intel EtherExpress PRO/10 PCI adapter and the Dial-Up adapter in the Network dialog box, you should see two numbered subfolders, and so on. If you have too many subfolders, follow these steps:

1. Close the REGEDIT window.
2. Open the Network icon found in the Control Panel.
3. Remove all adapter drivers—this will also remove all clients, protocols, and services.
4. Go back to REGEDIT and make sure the Net, NetClient, NetServices, and NetTrans folders are completely empty (no plus symbol to the left of the folders).
5. Exit REGEDIT and restart Windows.
6. Reinstall the driver for your NIC.

If your NIC still does not work correctly after reinstalling, select the four-digit folder number and find DriverDesc in the Name column on the right-hand side of the REGEDIT dialog box. Just to the right of DriverDesc, you should see the NIC (i.e., Intel EtherExpress PRO/10 PCI). If not, select the next numbered folder. After finding the folder for the NIC, locate DeviceVxDs in the Name column on the right-hand side of the REGEDIT dialog box. Just to the right of DeviceVxDs, you should see the driver filename (i.e., e10p.sys). If the filename is missing or incorrect, double-click the entry, type the correct filename, then press ENTER (or click OK). Close the REGEDIT utility and restart your computer.

CHECKPOINT

✔ **Objective 10.01: NIC Basics**   Computers are interfaced to a network using a network interface card (NIC). Servers typically use one or more multiport NICs, and workstation/desktop systems need only a single-port NIC.

Network cards act as the physical interface between the computer (server or workstation) and the network cable. A NIC converts the parallel data of the PC's internal bus into serial signals for transfer over coaxial, twisted-pair, or fiber-optic cables (and back again). The NIC also has to advertise its own location (or address) to the rest of the network in order to distinguish it from all the other NICs on the network. Each NIC (and therefore each computer) has a unique address on a network.

✔ **Objective 10.02: NIC Configuration Issues**   Since a NIC is an internal device, it must be configured to use the computer's hardware resources. *Interrupt request lines* (or IRQs) are hardware signal lines over which devices such as I/O ports, keyboards, disk drive controllers, and NICs can demand the attention of the computer's CPU. A base *I/O port* establishes a channel for communication with the system and allows passing commands and data between the NIC and host PC. Direct memory access (or DMA) is a technique that allows data to be moved from place to place inside the computer (i.e., between system RAM and the NIC buffer) without the direct control of your computer's CPU. By setting a *base RAM address* (sometimes called a RAM start address), you can control the memory range occupied by the NIC.

✔ **Objective 10.03: Installing the NIC Hardware**   NIC hardware installation generally involves removing any old NIC drivers and hardware, then installing the new NIC into an suitable expansion slot (usually a PCI slot). Network cabling can then be attached to the NIC.

✔ **Objective 10.04: Installing the NIC Drivers**   After the network hardware is installed and connected, you will need to install the basic NIC drivers, along with advanced drivers such as failover or port aggregation drivers. Drivers should be verified after installation.

✔ **Objective 10.05: Basic NIC Troubleshooting**   NIC problems generally focus on network cabling/connection problems, NIC configuration issues, NIC faults, or NIC drivers that are damaged, buggy, or improperly installed.

REVIEW QUESTIONS

1. A server normally uses a...

    A. Single-port NIC
    B. Multiport NIC
    C. Delta-port NIC
    D. ISA NIC

2. Each NIC (and therefore each computer) has a unique _____ on a network.

   A. Address

   B. Interlock

   C. Encoding scheme

   D. Driver

3. Before the sending NIC actually sends data over the network, it carries on a complex electronic dialog with the receiving NIC called…

   A. Regression

   B. Quartering

   C. Negotiation

   D. Cabling

4. _____ keeps the connection to the server established by moving all traffic on the affected segment to a standby NIC.

   A. Aggregation

   B. Failover

   C. Interfacing

   D. Cabling

5. _____ is a software-supported NIC feature that provides network path redundancy and increased bandwidth for a network.

   A. Aggregation

   B. Failover

   C. Interfacing

   D. Cabling

6. The on-board _____ is the circuit that drives the network cable.

   A. Communicator

   B. Impeller

   C. Receiver

   D. Transceiver

7. The default ROM base address for a NIC is _____ or above.

   A. D0000h

   B. C0000h

   C. B0000h

   D. A0000h

8. When you connect a cable directly to the NIC, you're using the card's _____ transceiver.

   A. Quad
   B. Internal
   C. External
   D. Backup

9. The term "FEC" means…

   A. Follow Each Connector
   B. Fast EtherChannel
   C. Functional Ethernet Connector
   D. Forward Enabled Connector

10. Current NIC adapters are typically designed for a _____ slot.

   A. MCA
   B. ISA
   C. AGP
   D. PCI

REVIEW ANSWERS

1. **B** Multiport NIC: A server normally uses a multiport NIC. A client (workstation) generally uses a single-port NIC.

2. **A** Address: Each NIC (and therefore each computer) has a unique address on a network.

3. **C** Negotiation: Before the sending NIC actually sends data over the network, it carries on an a complex electronic dialog with the receiving NIC, called negotiation.

4. **B** Failover: Failover keeps the connection to the server established by moving all traffic on the affected segment to a standby NIC.

5. **A** Aggregation: Port aggregation is a software-supported NIC feature that provides network path redundancy and increased bandwidth for a network.

6. **D** Transceiver: The on-board transceiver is the circuit that drives the network cable.

7. **A** D0000h: The default ROM base address for a NIC is D0000h or above.

8. **B** Internal: When you connect a cable directly to the NIC, you're using the card's internal transceiver.

9. **B** Fast EtherChannel: The term *FEC* means *Fast EtherChannel*.

10. **D** PCI: Current NIC adapters are typically designed for a PCI expansion slot.

Understanding Server+

The "Server Hardware Specialist" (or Server+) exam is a new CompTIA certification intended to deal with advanced PC hardware issues such as RAID, SCSI, multiple CPUs, and so on. The Server Hardware Specialist focuses on the activities and complex problems involved in server configuration, maintenance, and repair. A Server+ specialist is expected to have an in-depth understanding of the planning, installation, and maintenance of servers—including knowledge of server-level hardware, data storage, data recovery, and I/O subsystems. A server technician should know the behavior of all parts of the server system, and understand the ramifications of their actions. The Server+ specialist usually works independently, solves complex problems, and may seek assistance from systems support for particularly challenging issues. The recommended experience for this certification includes

- Approximately 18–24 months of experience in the server technologies (networking) industry.
- Direct experience installing, configuring, diagnosing, and troubleshooting server hardware and NOS issues.
- At least one other IT certification such as CompTIA A+, Compaq ACT, Novell CNA, Microsoft MCP, HP STAR, SCO, or Banyan.
- An ability to communicate and document effectively.

The Server+ Exam

For the initial release of the Server+ exam, candidates are expected to know the following topic areas, and each area is detailed next.

- Installation   17%
- Configuration   18%
- Upgrading   12%
- Preventive Maintenance   9%
- Environmental Issues   5%
- Troubleshooting   27%
- Disaster Recovery   12%

Installation

- Conduct preinstallation planning activities:
  1. Plan the installation.
  2. Verify the installation plan.
  3. Verify hardware compatibility with operating system.
  4. Verify power sources, space, UPS, and network availability.
  5. Verify that all correct components and cables have been delivered.
- Install hardware (i.e., boards, drives, processors, memory, internal cable, etc.):
  1. Mount a rack installation.
  2. Cut and crimp network cabling.
  3. Install a UPS.
  4. Verify SCSI ID configuration and termination.
  5. Install external devices (i.e., keyboards, monitors, subsystems, modem rack, etc.).
  6. Verify the power-on via power-on sequence.

Configuration

- Check and upgrade BIOS/firmware levels (i.e. system board, RAID, controller, hard drive, etc.).
- Configure RAID.
- Install an NOS:
  1. Configure network and verify network connectivity.
  2. Verify network connectivity.
- Configure external peripherals (i.e., UPS, external drive subsystems, etc.).
- Install NOS updates.
- Update manufacturer's drivers.
- Install service tools (i.e., backup software, system monitoring agents, event logs, etc.).

- Perform a server baseline.
- Document the configuration.

Upgrading

- Perform backup/restore operations:
  1. Verify backup.
- Add processors:
  1. On single processor upgrade, verify compatibility.
  2. Verify N 1 stepping.
  3. Verify speed and cache matching.
  4. Perform BIOS upgrade.
  5. Perform OS upgrade to support multiprocessors.
  6. Locate/obtain latest test drivers, OS updates, software.
- Add hard drives:
  1. Verify that drives are the appropriate type.
  2. Confirm termination and cabling.
  3. For ATA/IDE drives, confirm cabling, master/slave and potential cross-brand compatibility.
  4. Upgrade mass storage devices.
  5. Add drives to a RAID array.
  6. Replace existing drives.
  7. Integrate drives into a storage solution and make it available to the operating system.
- Increase memory:
  1. Verify hardware and OS support for capacity increase.
  2. Verify memory is on hardware/vendor compatibility list.
  3. Verify memory compatibility.
  4. Verify that the server and OS recognize the added memory.
  5. Perform server optimization to make use of additional RAM.
- Upgrade BIOS/firmware.
- Upgrade important adapters (i.e. NICs, SCSI cards, RAID, etc.).
- Upgrade internal and external peripheral devices:
  1. Verify appropriate system resources (i.e. expansion slots, IRQ, DMA, etc.).
- Upgrade system monitoring agents.
- Upgrade service tools (i.e. diagnostic tools, diagnostic partition, SSU, etc.).
- Upgrade UPS.

Preventive Maintenance

- Perform regular backup.
- Create baseline and compare performance.
- Set SNMP thresholds.
- Perform physical housekeeping.
- Perform hardware verification.
- Establish remote notification.

Environmental Issues

- Recognize and report on physical security issues:
    1. Limit access to server room and backup tapes.
    2. Ensure physical locks exist on doors.
    3. Establish antitheft devices for hardware (lock server racks).
- Recognize and report on server room environmental issues.

Troubleshooting

- Perform problem determination:
    1. Learn how to handle problem determination.
    2. Identify contact(s) responsible for problem resolution.
    3. Use senses to observe problem.
- Use diagnostic hardware and software tools and utilities:
    1. Identify common diagnostic tools.
    2. Perform OS shutdowns.
    3. Select the appropriate tool.
    4. Use the selected tool effectively.
    5. Replace defective hardware components as appropriate.
    6. Identify defective devices and replace with correct part.
    7. Interpret error logs, operating system errors, health logs, and critical events.
    8. Use documentation from a previous technician successfully.
    9. Gather resources to get problem solved.
    10. Describe how to perform remote troubleshooting for a wake-on-LAN.
    11. Describe how to perform remote troubleshooting for a remote alert.
- Identify bottlenecks (i.e., processor, bus transfer, I/O, disk I/O, network I/O, memory).

- Identify and correct configuration problems and/or upgrades.
- Determine if problem is hardware, software, or virus related.

Disaster Recovery

- Plan for disaster recovery:
  1. Plan for redundancy (i.e., hard drives, power supplies, fans, NICs, processors, UPS).
  2. Use the techniques of hot swap, warm swap, and hot spare to ensure availability.
  3. Use the concepts of fault tolerance/fault recovery to create a disaster recovery plan.
  4. Develop disaster recovery plan.
  5. Identify types of backup hardware.
  6. Identify types of backup and restoration schemes.
  7. Confirm and use offsite storage for backup.
  8. Document and test the disaster recovery plan regularly, and update as needed.
- Restoring:
  1. Identify hardware replacements.
  2. Identify hot and cold sites.
  3. Implement disaster recovery plan.

About the CD-ROM

Mike Meyers' Certification Passport
CD-ROM Instructions

To install the *Passport* Practice Exam software, perform these steps:

1. Insert the CD-ROM into your CD-ROM drive. An auto-run program will initiate, and a dialog box will appear indicating that you are installing the Passport setup program. If the auto-run program does not launch on your system, select Run from the Start menu and type **d:\setup.exe** (where **d** is the "name" of your CD-ROM drive).
2. Follow the installation wizard's instructions to complete the installation of the software.
3. You can start the program by going to your desktop and double-clicking the *Passport* Exam Review icon or by going to Start | Program Files | ExamWeb | Server+.

System Requirements

- **Operating Systems Supported**   Windows 98, Windows NT 4.0, Windows 2000, and Windows Me
- **CPU**   400 MHz or faster recommended
- **Memory** 64MB of RAM
- **CD-ROM**   4X or greater
- **Internet Connection**   Required for optional exam upgrade

Technical Support

For basic *Passport* CD-ROM technical support, contact Hudson Technical Support:

- Phone: 800-217-0059
- E-mail: mcgraw-hill@hudsonsoft.com

For content/subject matter questions concerning the book or the CD-ROM, contact MH Customer Service:

- Phone: 800-722-4726
- E-mail: customer.service@mcgraw-hill.com

For inquiries about the available upgrade, CD-ROM, or online technology, or for in-depth technical support, contact ExamWeb Technical Support:

- Phone: 949-566-9375
- E-mail: support@examweb.com

Career Flight Path

The Server+ certification enjoys a unique position in your career flight path in that it makes the perfect launch point to several of different certifications. From the Server+, you have a number of certification options. Take a look at these four in particular:

- CompTIA Network+
- Microsoft Networking Certification
- Novell Netware Certification
- Cisco

CompTIA Network+

If haven't already taken the Network+, make it your next certification! CompTIA's Network+ is a natural fit for continuing toward your Microsoft, Novell, or Cisco certifications.

Microsoft Networking Certification

Microsoft's ever-popular Microsoft Certified systems Engineer (MCSE) holds a lot of clout for those looking to work in the networking field. Microsoft's NT, 2000, and XP operating systems' control a huge portion of all the installed networks—and those networks need qualified support people to make them run. The MCSE consists of seven exams: four core and three electives. Check out Microsoft's training Web site at http://www.microsoft.com/trainingandservices for details. Most techs will find the Windows 2000 track the most obvious choice and almost everyone takes the Microsoft 70-210 – Installing, Configuring, and Administering Microsoft Windows 2000 Professional followed by the 70-215 – Installing, Configuring, and Administering Microsoft Windows 2000 Server as the first two exams toward MCSE.

Novell Netware Certification

Novell's Netware may not be the powerhouse it once was, but there's still a huge installed base of Netware networks out there! The surge of techs toward Microsoft certifications actually created a bit of a shortage of good Netware certified techs. The Certified Netware Engineer (CNE) is the certification to go for if you want to get into Novell networks. Novell has a number of tracks, but most techs will go for the 50-653 – Netware 5.1 Admin and the 50-632 – Networking Technologies exam. Check out Novell's certification Web site http://www.novell.com/education/ certinfo/cne/ for more details.

Cisco

Let's face it, Cisco routers pretty much run the Internet and most intranets in the world and Cisco provides three levels of certification for folks who want to show their skills at handling Cisco products. Most everyone interested in Cisco certification starts with the Certified Cisco Network Associate (CCNA). The CCNA is only one exam (640-507) and a darn easy way to slap the word Cisco on your resume! After your CCNA, you should consider the CCNP (Certified Cisco Networking Professional) certification. See the Cisco certification Web site (http://www.novell.com/education/certinfo/cne/) for more details.

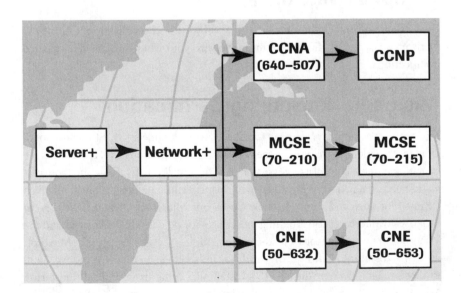

Index

ExamWeb is a leader in assessment technology. We use this technology to deliver customized online testing programs, corporate training, pre packaged exam preparation courses, and licensed technology. ExamWeb has partnered with Osborne McGraw Hill to develop the CD contained in this book and its corresponding online exam simulators. Please read about our services below and contact us to see how we can help you with your own assessment needs.

www.examweb.com

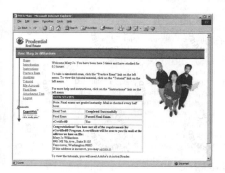

Technology Licenses and Partnerships

Publishers, exam preparation companies and schools use ExamWeb technology to offer online testing or exam preparation branded in their own style and delivered via their websites. Improve your assessment offerings by using our technology!

Check www.examweb.com for an updated list of course offerings.

Corporate Assessment

ExamWeb can customize its course and testing engines to meet your training and assessment needs as a trainer. We can provide you with stand alone assessments and courses or can easily integrate our assessment engines with your existing courses or learning management system. Features may include:

- ✓ Corporate level access and reporting

- ✓ Multiple question types

- ✓ Detailed strength and weakness reports by key subject area and topic

- ✓ Performance comparisons amongst groups

click. study. pass.™

Coming soon:

CCNA™ Passport / A+™ Passport / Server+™ Passport / Network+™ Passport / Java™ 2 Passp
MCSE Windows 2000™ Professional Passport / MCSE Windows 2000™ Server Passport
MCSE Windows 2000™ Directory Services Passport
MCSE Windows 2000™ Network Infrastructure Passport

For more infomation, please contact corpsales@examweb.com or call 949.566.9

LICENSE AGREEMENT

THIS PRODUCT (THE "PRODUCT") CONTAINS PROPRIETARY SOFTWARE, DATA AND INFORMATION (INCLUDING DOCUMENTATION) OWNED BY THE McGRAW-HILL COMPANIES, INC. ("McGRAW-HILL") AND ITS LICENSORS. YOUR RIGHT TO USE THE PRODUCT IS GOVERNED BY THE TERMS AND CONDITIONS OF THIS AGREEMENT.

LICENSE: Throughout this License Agreement, "you" shall mean either the individual or the entity whose agent opens this package. You are granted a non-exclusive and non-transferable license to use the Product subject to the following terms:
(i) If you have licensed a single user version of the Product, the Product may only be used on a single computer (i.e., a single CPU). If you licensed and paid the fee applicable to a local area network or wide area network version of the Product, you are subject to the terms of the following subparagraph (ii).
(ii) If you have licensed a local area network version, you may use the Product on unlimited workstations located in one single building selected by you that is served by such local area network. If you have licensed a wide area network version, you may use the Product on unlimited workstations located in multiple buildings on the same site selected by you that is served by such wide area network; provided, however, that any building will not be considered located in the same site if it is more than five (5) miles away from any building included in such site. In addition, you may only use a local area or wide area network version of the Product on one single server. If you wish to use the Product on more than one server, you must obtain written authorization from McGraw-Hill and pay additional fees.
(iii) You may make one copy of the Product for back-up purposes only and you must maintain an accurate record as to the location of the back-up at all times.

COPYRIGHT; RESTRICTIONS ON USE AND TRANSFER: All rights (including copyright) in and to the Product are owned by McGraw-Hill and its licensors. You are the owner of the enclosed disc on which the Product is recorded. You may not use, copy, decompile, disassemble, reverse engineer, modify, reproduce, create derivative works, transmit, distribute, sublicense, store in a database or retrieval system of any kind, rent or transfer the Product, or any portion thereof, in any form or by any means (including electronically or otherwise) except as expressly provided for in this License Agreement. You must reproduce the copyright notices, trademark notices, legends and logos of McGraw-Hill and its licensors that appear on the Product on the back-up copy of the Product which you are permitted to make hereunder. All rights in the Product not expressly granted herein are reserved by McGraw-Hill and its licensors.

TERM: This License Agreement is effective until terminated. It will terminate if you fail to comply with any term or condition of this License Agreement. Upon termination, you are obligated to return to McGraw-Hill the Product together with all copies thereof and to purge all copies of the Product included in any and all servers and computer facilities.

DISCLAIMER OF WARRANTY: THE PRODUCT AND THE BACK-UP COPY ARE LICENSED "AS IS." McGRAW-HILL, ITS LICENSORS AND THE AUTHORS MAKE NO WARRANTIES, EXPRESS OR IMPLIED, AS TO THE RESULTS TO BE OBTAINED BY ANY PERSON OR ENTITY FROM USE OF THE PRODUCT, ANY INFORMATION OR DATA INCLUDED THEREIN AND/OR ANY TECHNICAL SUPPORT SERVICES PROVIDED HEREUNDER, IF ANY ("TECHNICAL SUPPORT SERVICES"). McGRAW-HILL, ITS LICENSORS AND THE AUTHORS MAKE NO EXPRESS OR IMPLIED WARRANTIES OF MERCHANTABILITY OR FITNESS FOR A PARTICULAR PURPOSE OR USE WITH RESPECT TO THE PRODUCT. McGRAW-HILL, ITS LICENSORS, AND THE AUTHORS MAKE NO GUARANTEE THAT YOU WILL PASS ANY CERTIFICATION EXAM WHATSOEVER BY USING THIS PRODUCT. NEITHER McGRAW-HILL, ANY OF ITS LICENSORS NOR THE AUTHORS WARRANT THAT THE FUNCTIONS CONTAINED IN THE PRODUCT WILL MEET YOUR REQUIREMENTS OR THAT THE OPERATION OF THE PRODUCT WILL BE UNINTERRUPTED OR ERROR FREE. YOU ASSUME THE ENTIRE RISK WITH RESPECT TO THE QUALITY AND PERFORMANCE OF THE PRODUCT.

LIMITED WARRANTY FOR DISC: To the original licensee only, McGraw-Hill warrants that the enclosed disc on which the Product is recorded is free from defects in materials and workmanship under normal use and service for a period of ninety (90) days from the date of purchase. In the event of a defect in the disc covered by the foregoing warranty, McGraw-Hill will replace the disc.

LIMITATION OF LIABILITY: NEITHER McGRAW-HILL, ITS LICENSORS NOR THE AUTHORS SHALL BE LIABLE FOR ANY INDIRECT, SPECIAL OR CONSEQUENTIAL DAMAGES, SUCH AS BUT NOT LIMITED TO, LOSS OF ANTICIPATED PROFITS OR BENEFITS, RESULTING FROM THE USE OR INABILITY TO USE THE PRODUCT EVEN IF ANY OF THEM HAS BEEN ADVISED OF THE POSSIBILITY OF SUCH DAMAGES. THIS LIMITATION OF LIABILITY SHALL APPLY TO ANY CLAIM OR CAUSE WHATSOEVER WHETHER SUCH CLAIM OR CAUSE ARISES IN CONTRACT, TORT, OR OTHERWISE. Some states do not allow the exclusion or limitation of indirect, special or consequential damages, so the above limitation may not apply to you.

U.S. GOVERNMENT RESTRICTED RIGHTS: Any software included in the Product is provided with restricted rights subject to subparagraphs (c), (1) and (2) of the Commercial Computer Software-Restricted Rights clause at 48 C.F.R. 52.227-19. The terms of this Agreement applicable to the use of the data in the Product are those under which the data are generally made available to the general public by McGraw-Hill. Except as provided herein, no reproduction, use, or disclosure rights are granted with respect to the data included in the Product and no right to modify or create derivative works from any such data is hereby granted.

GENERAL: This License Agreement constitutes the entire agreement between the parties relating to the Product. The terms of any Purchase Order shall have no effect on the terms of this License Agreement. Failure of McGraw-Hill to insist at any time on strict compliance with License Agreement shall not constitute a waiver of any rights under this License Agreement. This License Agreement shall be construed governed in accordance with the laws of the State of New York. If any provision of this License Agreement is held to be contrary to law, ovision will be enforced to the maximum extent permissible and the remaining provisions will remain in full force and effect.